MARVEL MASTERWORKS

PRESENTS

HERE COMES... DAREDEVIL THE MAN WITHOUT FEAR!

VOLUME 1

COLLECTING

DAREDEVIL Nos.1-11

STAN LEE • WALLACE WOOD

WITH JOE ORLANDO & BILL EVERETT

MARVEL ENTERPRISES, INC.

MARVEL MASTERWORKS
CREDITS

DAREDEVIL
Nos. 1-11

Writers: **Stan Lee**
Wallace Wood (No. 10)

Pencilers: **Wallace Wood** (Nos. 5-8, 9, 10)
Bill Everett (No. 1)
Joe Orlando (Nos. 2-4)
Bob Powell (Nos. 9-11)

Inkers: Wallace Wood (Nos. 5-11)
Bill Everett (No. 1)
Vince Colletta (Nos. 2-4)

Letterers: Sam Rosen (Nos. 1-6, 8, 9, 11)
Art Simek (Nos. 7, 10)

Color Reconstruction: Richard Howell

Art Reconstruction: Don Hudson (Nos. 1, 2, 5-10)
Joe Rosas (Nos. 3, 11)
Mickey Ritter (No. 4)

Special Thanks: Tom Brevoort, Ralph Macchio
& Pond Scum

MARVEL MASTERWORKS: DAREDEVIL VOL. 1. Contains material originally published in magazine form as DAREDEVIL (Vol. 1) #1-11. Second edition. First printing 2003. ISBN# 0-7851-1257-X. Published by MARVEL COMICS, a division of MARVEL ENTERTAINMENT GROUP, INC. OFFICE OF PUBLICATION: 10 East 40th Street, New York, NY 10016. Copyright © 1964, 1965 and 1991 Marvel Characters, Inc. All rights reserved. $49.99 per copy in the U.S. and $80.00 in Canada (GST #R127032852); Canadian Agreement #40668537. All characters featured in this issue and the distinctive names and likenesses thereof, and all related indicia are trademarks of Marvel Characters, Inc. No similarity between any of the names, characters, persons, and/or institutions in this magazine with those of any living or dead person or institution is intended, and any such similarity which may exist is purely coincidental. **Printed in Italy.** STAN LEE, Chairman Emeritus. For information regarding advertising in Marvel Comics or on Marvel.com, please contact Russell Brown, Executive Vice President, Consumer Products, Promotions and Media Sales at 212-576-8561 or rbrown@marvel.com

10 9 8 7 6 5 4 3 2 1

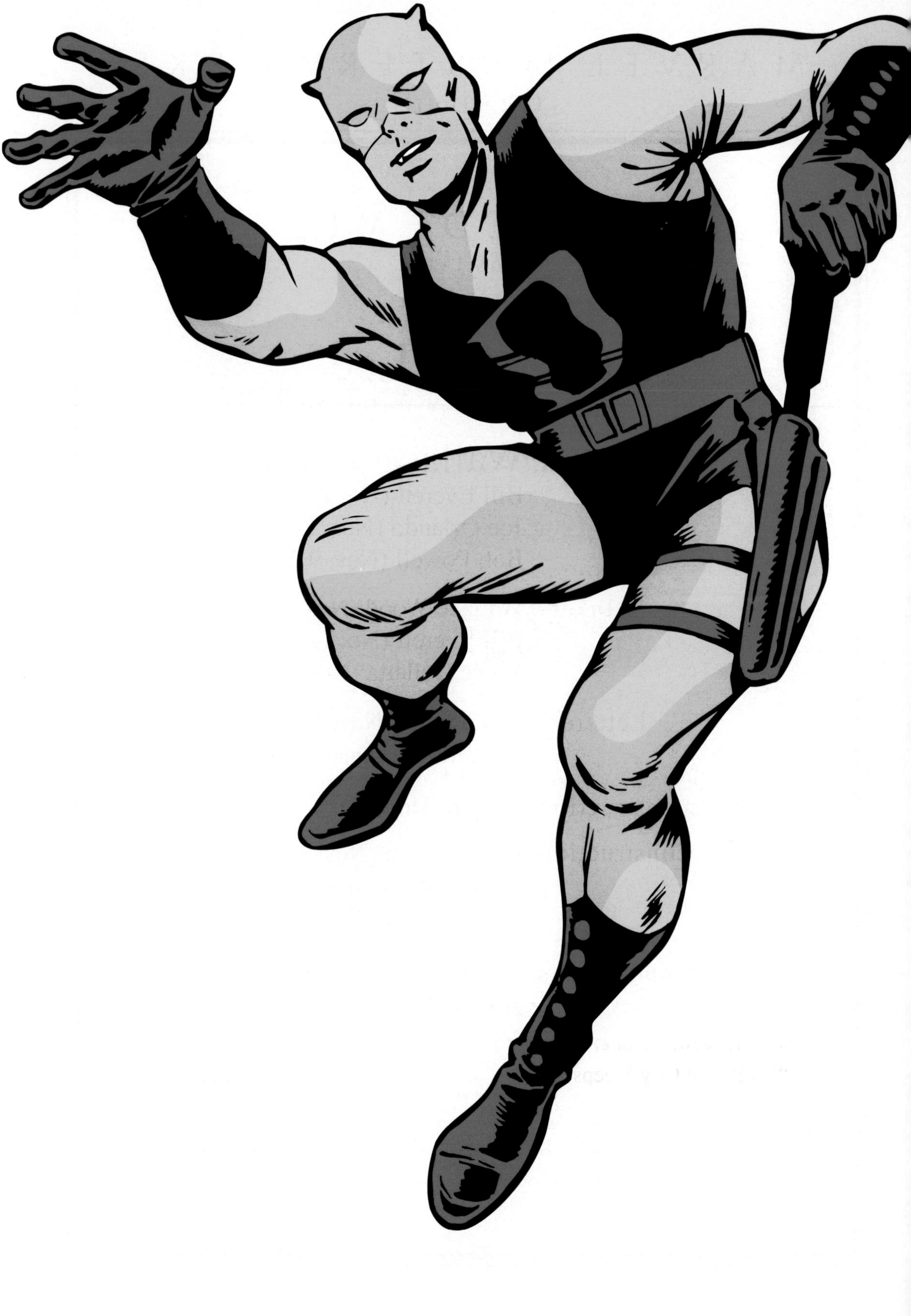

MARVEL MASTERWORKS
CONTENTS

INTRODUCTION
BY STAN LEE

Of all the colorful super heroes who make up the mighty Marvel Universe, I've always relished the fact that there was something particularly special about our dazzling, high-steppin' Man Without Fear.

Anyone who's been following Daredevil's adventures will instantly know the special quality to which I'm alluding. Ol' Hornhead was the very first and, as far as we know, is still the only blind hero in the annals of comicdom. What's more, he's not only sightless, but he's probably the most daring and acrobatic crimefighter of all!

Among my most treasured memories in connection with *Daredevil* are the many letters we've received over the past years, letters from people associated with organizations which aid the handicapped, and particularly the blind. These letters have told of the warm reception given to Daredevil's adventures by handicapped readers, readers who feel they have finally found a hero with whom they can empathize, a hero whose fantastic exploits help to strengthen their own sense of pride and self-esteem. There are so many intriguing aspects to the legend of Daredevil that I hardly know where to begin. We heralded him in his origin issue as a hero in the tradition of Spider-Man and a worthy companion to the Fantastic Four. That was a might big boast for a brand-new character who had yet to prove his worth. But prove it he did, in a spectacular fashion, as you're about to see!

The toughest thing about doing any super-hero series is producing the very first issue. If the introductory story doesn't grab the readers the chances are they won't come back for the subsequent issues. Well, in the case of *Daredevil* luck was with us. I had just run into the legendary Bill Everett, creator of Prince Namor the Sub-Mariner, after having lost track of him for a number of years. Bill told me he'd like to try his hand at a new super hero. That was all I had to hear.

Within minutes I had chewed Bill's ear off about our newest concept, a blind lawyer named Matt Murdock who was the world's greatest and most agile crime-fighting gymnast. I told him about Karen Page and Foggy Nelson and about the weird and wild super-villains we were planning to unleash upon the happy hordes of Marveldom. Even before I stopped talking he had whipped out a pencil and was making preliminary sketches on some scrap paper. I knew he was hooked! It was a red-letter day for all of fandom!

A short time later, the first issue of *Daredevil* hit the stands and the rest is history. The fans gobbled it up and panted for more. But, by now we were involved in a number of other comic-book productions, and after helping to launch *Daredevil* so successfully, Bill asked if he could transfer to some of our other projects, which he did with equal brilliance.

Luck was with us once again. I was able to track down Joe Orlando, who had long been one of EC Comics' most acclaimed artists, and he agreed to help out with a few issues until we could find a permanent Daredevil penciler. Joe was matched with Vince Colletta, one of our bullpen's most consistently dependable star inkers. Together they were able to continue the momentum that Bill Everett had started until issue number five when another of comicdom's greats entered the picture.

His name—Wally Wood. Anyone who had ever been involved with comics knew him as one of the giants of our field. Wally both penciled and inked issues number five, six, seven, and eight. With issue number nine, he was joined by another famous name in comics, the talented Bob Powell who collaborated with Wally on the artwork until issue number eleven, which wraps up the stories in this particular volume.

In a sense, the first eleven issues of *Daredevil* are a virtual microcosm of comic-book history. Almost everything that can happen to a fledgling series happened to the Man Without Fear. We had changes in artists, changes in inkers, and changes in costume (by issue number seven, Wally and I decided to redesign Daredevil's outfit. We felt it would be more dramatic if it was just one color). As for Daredevil's villains, I always felt that his early adventures pitted him against the most colorful assortment of foes to be found everywhere. Here's a serendipitous sampling of some you're about to meet…

In his origin issue, ol' Hornhead tackles the merciless gangsters who caused his father's death. Then, the following issues pit him against Electro, the Owl, the Purple Man, the Mysterious Masked Matador, the Fellowship of Fear, the Sub-Mariner, Stiltman, the Killer's Castle, and the ever-deadly Organizer and his bestial henchmen—Ape-Man, Cat Man, Bird Man, and Frog Man.

Incidentally, I just have to tell you that "In Mortal Battle With Sub-Mariner" is one of my all-time favorite stories. The reason is, when two super heroes battle each other, the toughest task for any writer is to figure out how to have one combatant win without demoralizing the other by having him lose. I mean readers hate to see their favorite costumed character lose, no matter who he's fighting. Yet, we can't have every battle between two heroes end in a tie. Well, I think you'll agree that Prince Namor has never been nobler and Daredevil never more heroic than in this truly monumental tale—and the battle's conclusion is, to me, the most satisfying ending of all.

Well, I could go on like this for hours, but it isn't fair to keep you from the fun and excitement waiting on the pages ahead. So, I'll reluctantly leave you with this one final thought—if you enjoy the stories you're about to read half as much as we enjoyed doing them, I envy you. You're in for a Marvel-ous good time!

EXCELSIOR!

Stan Lee

1991

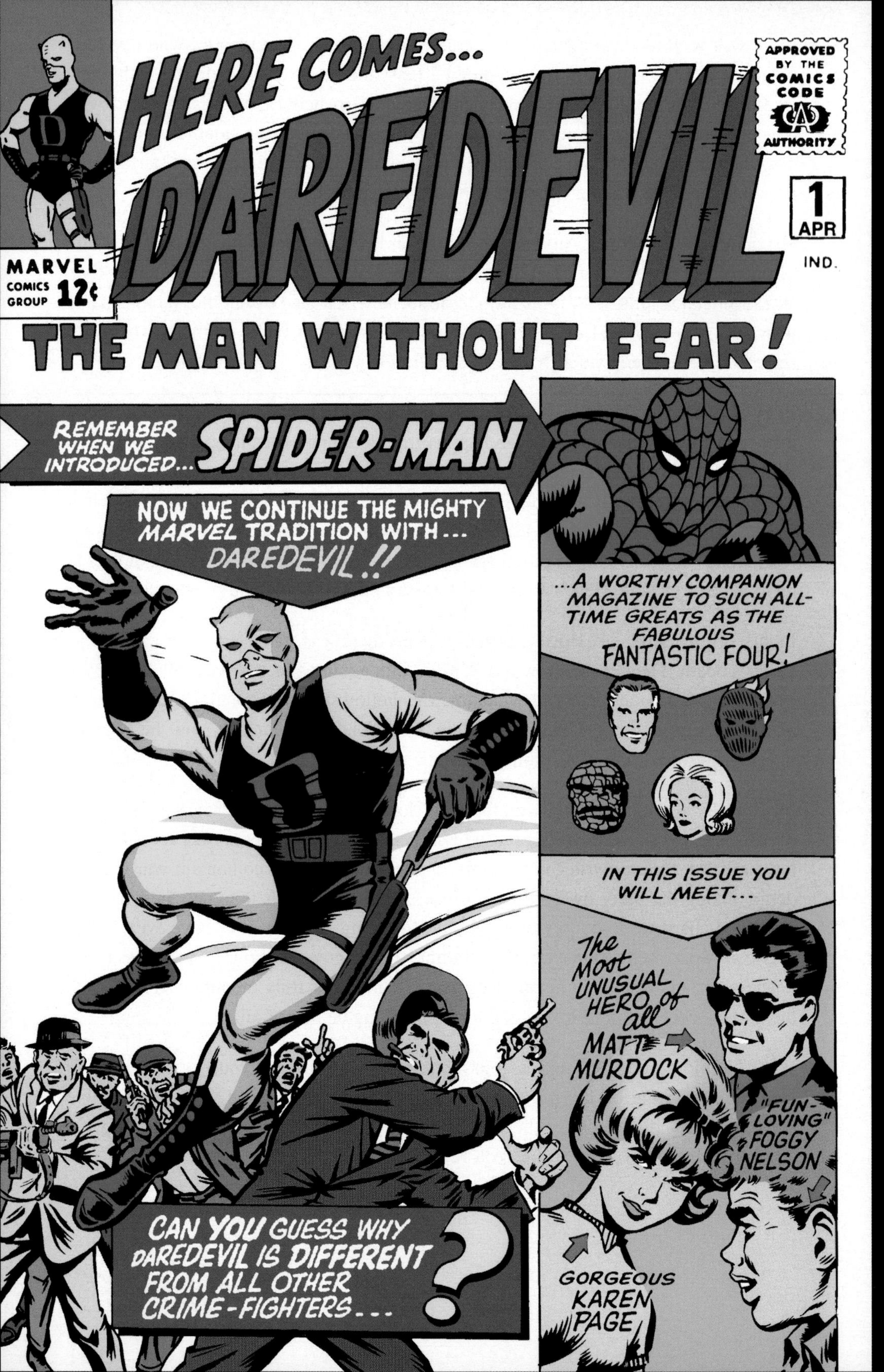
MARVEL COMICS GROUP 12¢
HERE COMES...
DAREDEVIL
APPROVED BY THE COMICS CODE AUTHORITY
1 APR
IND.
THE MAN WITHOUT FEAR!
REMEMBER WHEN WE INTRODUCED... SPIDER-MAN
NOW WE CONTINUE THE MIGHTY MARVEL TRADITION WITH... DAREDEVIL!!
...A WORTHY COMPANION MAGAZINE TO SUCH ALL-TIME GREATS AS THE FABULOUS FANTASTIC FOUR!
IN THIS ISSUE YOU WILL MEET...
The Most UNUSUAL HERO of all MATT MURDOCK
"FUN-LOVING" FOGGY NELSON
GORGEOUS KAREN PAGE
CAN YOU GUESS WHY DAREDEVIL IS DIFFERENT FROM ALL OTHER CRIME-FIGHTERS...?

THE ORIGIN OF DAREDEVIL

REMEMBER THIS COVER? IF YOU ARE ONE OF THE FORTUNATE FEW WHO BOUGHT THIS FIRST COPY-- YOU PROBABLY WOULDN'T PART WITH IT FOR ANYTHING!

NOW WE CONGRATULATE YOU FOR HAVING BOUGHT ANOTHER PRIZED FIRST-EDITION! THIS MAGAZINE IS CERTAIN TO BE ONE OF YOUR MOST VALUED COMIC MAG POSSESSIONS IN THE MONTHS TO COME!

WRITTEN BY.......STAN LEE
ILLUSTRATED BY...BILL EVERETT
LETTERED BY......SAM ROSEN

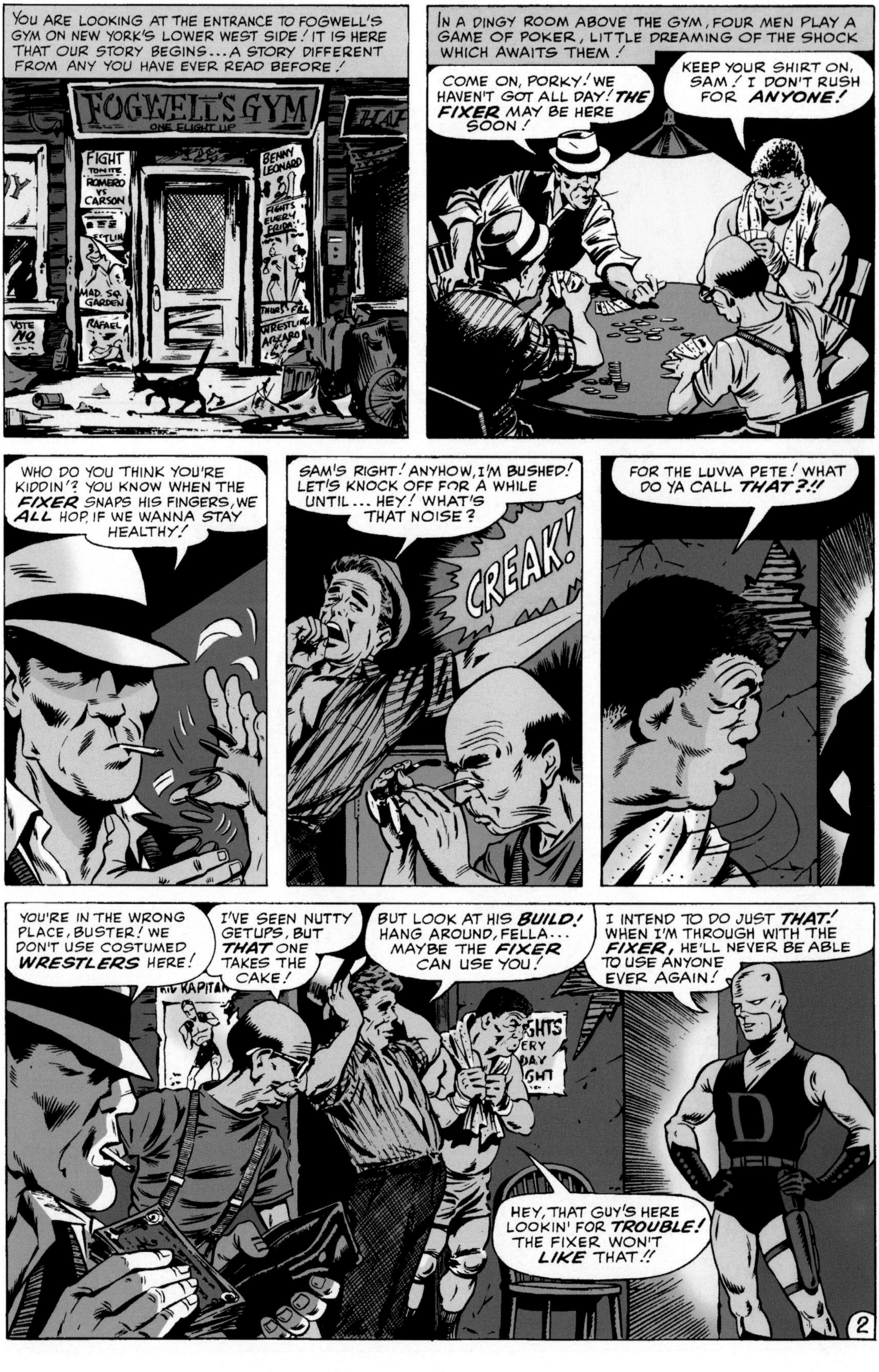
YOU ARE LOOKING AT THE ENTRANCE TO FOGWELL'S GYM ON NEW YORK'S LOWER WEST SIDE! IT IS HERE THAT OUR STORY BEGINS... A STORY DIFFERENT FROM ANY YOU HAVE EVER READ BEFORE!
FOGWELL'S GYM
ONE FLIGHT UP
FIGHT TONITE ROMERO VS CARSON
BENNY LEONARD
FIGHTS EVERY FRIDA
MAD. SQ. GARDEN
RAFAEL
VOTE NO
THURS. FEL
WRESTLING
IN A DINGY ROOM ABOVE THE GYM, FOUR MEN PLAY A GAME OF POKER, LITTLE DREAMING OF THE SHOCK WHICH AWAITS THEM!
COME ON, PORKY! WE HAVEN'T GOT ALL DAY! THE FIXER MAY BE HERE SOON!
KEEP YOUR SHIRT ON, SAM! I DON'T RUSH FOR ANYONE!
WHO DO YOU THINK YOU'RE KIDDIN'? YOU KNOW WHEN THE FIXER SNAPS HIS FINGERS, WE ALL HOP, IF WE WANNA STAY HEALTHY!
SAM'S RIGHT! ANYHOW, I'M BUSHED! LET'S KNOCK OFF FOR A WHILE UNTIL... HEY! WHAT'S THAT NOISE?
CREAK!
FOR THE LUVVA PETE! WHAT DO YA CALL THAT?!!
YOU'RE IN THE WRONG PLACE, BUSTER! WE DON'T USE COSTUMED WRESTLERS HERE!
I'VE SEEN NUTTY GETUPS, BUT THAT ONE TAKES THE CAKE!
BUT LOOK AT HIS BUILD! HANG AROUND, FELLA... MAYBE THE FIXER CAN USE YOU!
I INTEND TO DO JUST THAT! WHEN I'M THROUGH WITH THE FIXER, HE'LL NEVER BE ABLE TO USE ANYONE EVER AGAIN!
HEY, THAT GUY'S HERE LOOKIN' FOR TROUBLE! THE FIXER WON'T LIKE THAT!!
2

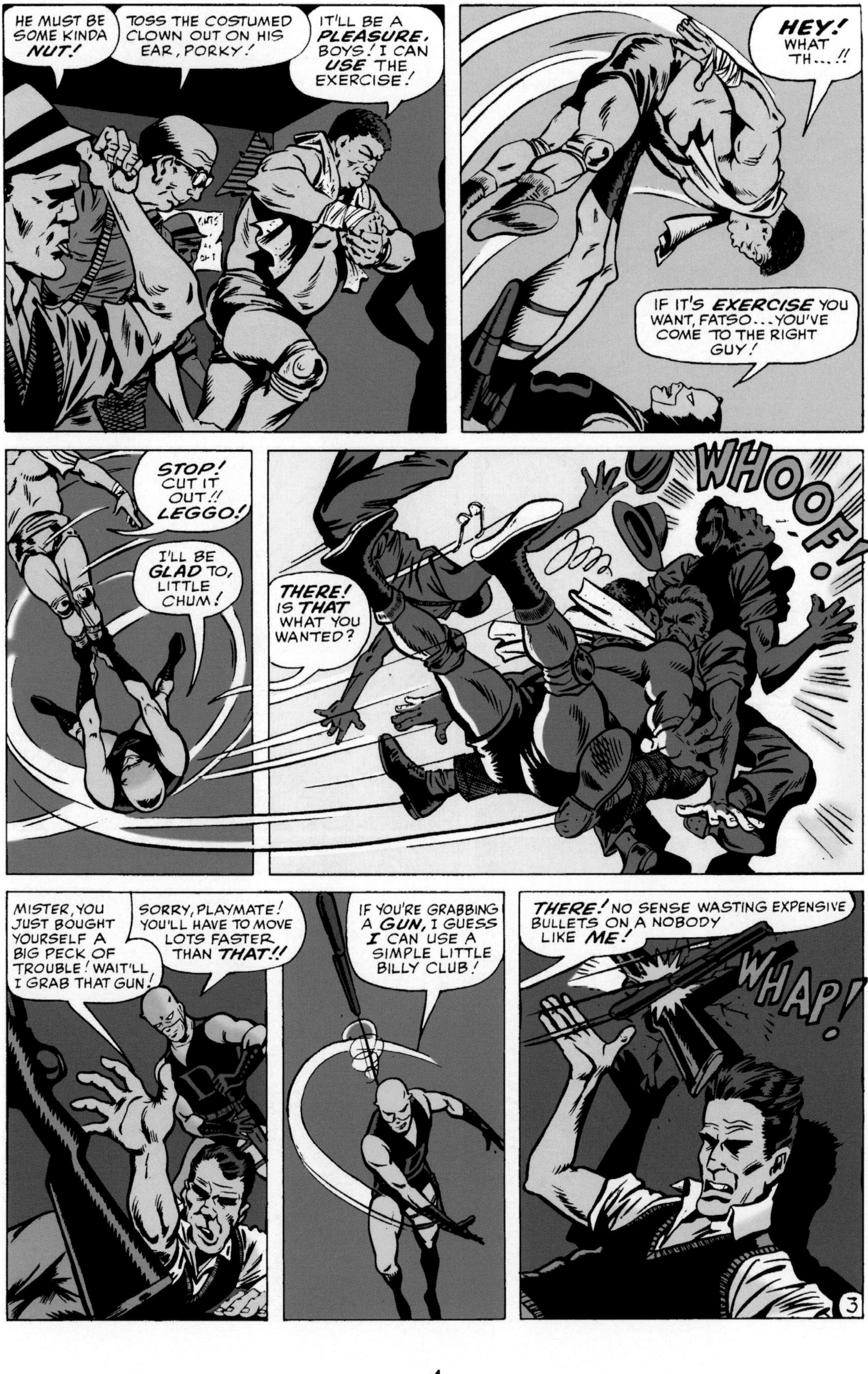
HE MUST BE SOME KINDA NUT!
TOSS THE COSTUMED CLOWN OUT ON HIS EAR, PORKY!
IT'LL BE A PLEASURE, BOYS! I CAN USE THE EXERCISE!
HEY! WHAT TH...!!
IF IT'S EXERCISE YOU WANT, FATSO...YOU'VE COME TO THE RIGHT GUY!
STOP! CUT IT OUT!! LEGGO!
I'LL BE GLAD TO, LITTLE CHUM!
THERE! IS THAT WHAT YOU WANTED?
WHOOF!
MISTER, YOU JUST BOUGHT YOURSELF A BIG PECK OF TROUBLE! WAIT'LL I GRAB THAT GUN!
SORRY, PLAYMATE! YOU'LL HAVE TO MOVE LOTS FASTER THAN THAT!!
IF YOU'RE GRABBING A GUN, I GUESS I CAN USE A SIMPLE LITTLE BILLY CLUB!
THERE! NO SENSE WASTING EXPENSIVE BULLETS ON A NOBODY LIKE ME!
WHAP!
3

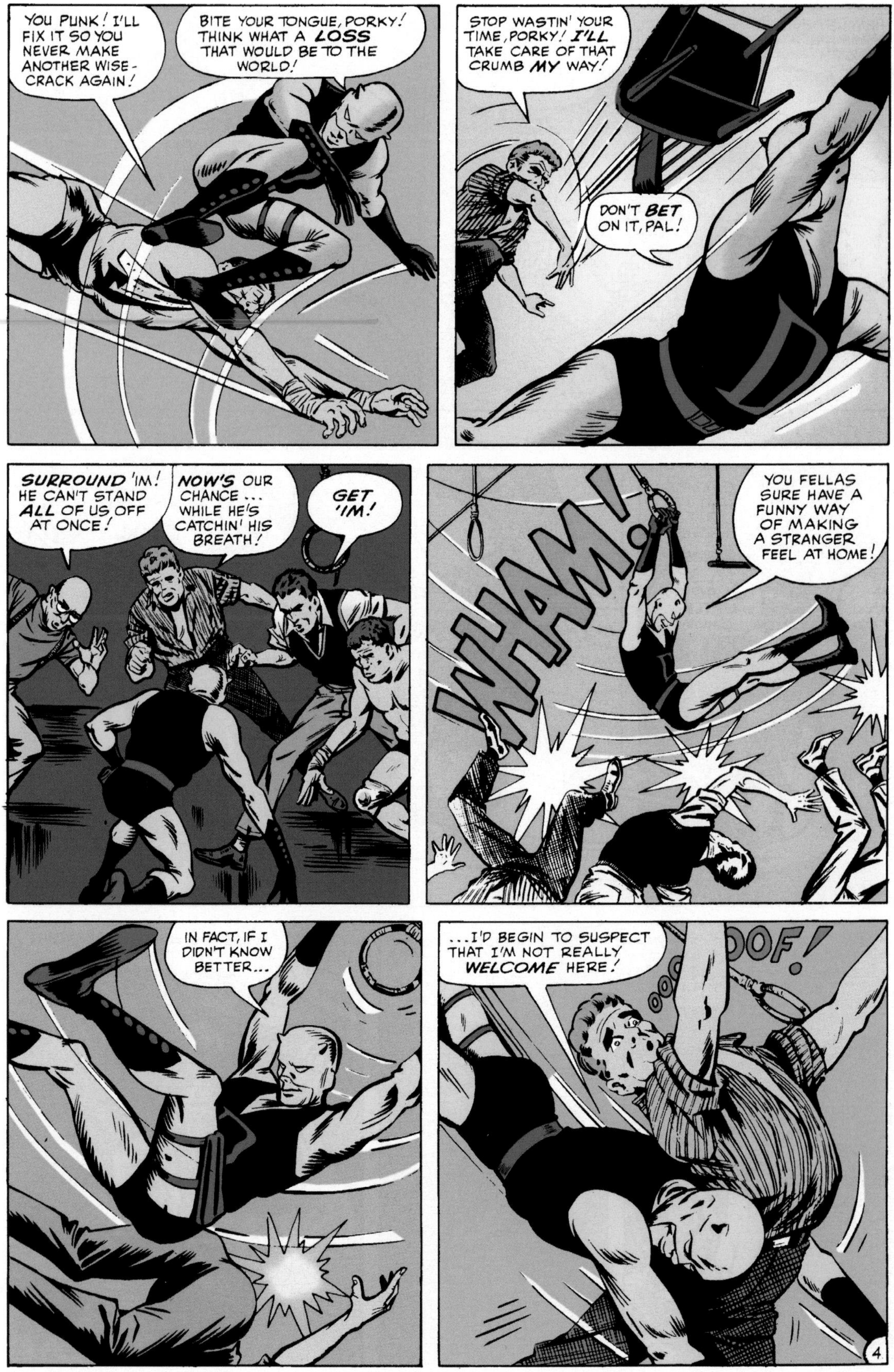
YOU PUNK! I'LL FIX IT SO YOU NEVER MAKE ANOTHER WISE-CRACK AGAIN!
BITE YOUR TONGUE, PORKY! THINK WHAT A LOSS THAT WOULD BE TO THE WORLD!
STOP WASTIN' YOUR TIME, PORKY! I'LL TAKE CARE OF THAT CRUMB MY WAY!
DON'T BET ON IT, PAL!
SURROUND 'IM! HE CAN'T STAND ALL OF US OFF AT ONCE!
NOW'S OUR CHANCE... WHILE HE'S CATCHIN' HIS BREATH!
GET 'IM!
WHAM!
YOU FELLAS SURE HAVE A FUNNY WAY OF MAKING A STRANGER FEEL AT HOME!
IN FACT, IF I DIDN'T KNOW BETTER...
...I'D BEGIN TO SUSPECT THAT I'M NOT REALLY WELCOME HERE!
OOOOOF!
4

OKAY, MISTER... WE'VE *HAD* IT! NOW WHO *ARE* YOU, AND WHAT DO YOU *WANT*?

IT AIN'T *POSSIBLE!* NOBODY CAN FIGHT LIKE THAT! HE MUST DO IT WITH *MIRRORS!!*

NOW THAT PLAY TIME'S OVER, I'LL HANG AROUND UNTIL I FIND THE *FIXER!* AS FOR WHO I *AM*, YOU CAN JUST CALL ME... *DAREDEVIL!!*

"DAREDEVIL"! A BRAND NEW NAME IN THE WORLD OF SUPER HEROES! BUT ONE WHICH IS DESTINED TO REACH THE VERY HEIGHTS OF GLORY! FOR *DAREDEVIL* HAS A *SPECIAL* TYPE OF POWER... SUCH AS NO ADVENTURER HAS EVER HAD BEFORE! TO LEARN WHAT IT IS, LET US GO BACK A FEW YEARS... BACK TO THE *ORIGIN* OF THE MAN CALLED

DAREDEVIL!

THE YEAR IS 1950, AS THE PRIZEFIGHTER KNOWN AS *BATTLING MURDOCK* TALKS TO HIS EIGHT-YEAR OLD SON MATTHEW...

BUT I DON'T *WANT* TO STUDY NOW, DAD! WHY CAN'T I GO OUT AND PLAY BALL WITH THE KIDS? I CAN STUDY LATER ON!

NO, MATT! YOU'LL DO IT *NOW!* YOU'LL STUDY EVERY CHANCE YOU GET, HEAR?

I PROMISED YOUR MOTHER, BEFORE SHE DIED, THAT I WOULDN'T LET YOU GROW UP TO BE AN UNEDUCATED PUG LIKE ME! *YOU'RE* GOING TO AMOUNT TO SOMETHING, MATT!

BUT I *WANT* TO BE LIKE YOU, DAD! I'M *PROUD* OF YOU! YOU'RE THE GREATEST...

DON'T SAY IT, BOY! I'M PAST MY PRIME! I'VE NO FUTURE... NOTHING I CAN DO BUT BECOME A PUNCHING BAG FOR YOUNGER MEN!

BUT I WON'T LET THAT HAPPEN TO *YOU!* YOU'RE GONNA *STUDY*... BECOME A LAWYER, OR A DOCTOR ... YOU'LL *BE* SOMEBODY... THE SOMEBODY THAT I CAN NEVER BE!

NOW GO BACK TO YOUR ROOM, SON... AND GET BUSY WITH YOUR BOOKS!

OKAY, DAD!

As the years roll by, Matt Murdock does his best to live up to his father's dream! He becomes top student in his class, forsaking all sports, all athletic activities, although his heart aches for the thrills of the baseball diamond and the gridiron!

If only dad would let me try out for the team! I'd be as good as ANY of them... I just KNOW I would!

But I can't go against his wishes! I can't defy dad, after all he's done for me...after all his sacrifices!...I've GOT to be the son he WANTS me to be!

And so, young Matt Murdock goes his lonely way, spending every minute he can spare with his books, never sharing in the games of the other teen-agers!

The kids are Indian rassling! If only I could go down and join them!

No one can be as cruel as an unthinking youth! It is only a matter of time before the neighborhood kids make up a nickname for Matt...a name he will long remember...

Well, well! If it ain't ol' DAREDEVIL himself!

Hi, Daredevil! Be sure you don't tire yourself out turning all those heavy pages in your school books!

They're LAUGHING at me! They think I'm a sissy!

Then, when he reaches his room...

Someday I'll SHOW them! I'll make them EAT those words!

I'm as strong as any of them...as rugged as any of them! And I'll PROVE it! Someday I'll prove it!!

His anger boiling within him, the resentful youth strikes out at his dad's punching bag, with the pent-up fury of a thunderclap...

The day will come when no one will ever laugh at me again! When... HEY! I..I knocked the bag clean OFF!

6.

THEN, AFTER REPAIRING THE CLASP...

WHAT A *NUMBSKULL* I AM! WHY DON'T I DO THIS *EVERY DAY!?* JUST TO KEEP IN SHAPE!

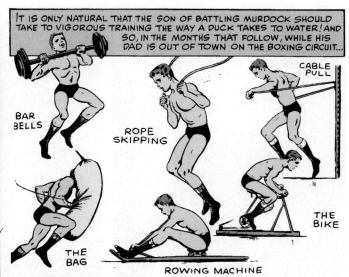

IT IS ONLY NATURAL THAT THE SON OF BATTLING MURDOCK SHOULD TAKE TO VIGOROUS TRAINING THE WAY A DUCK TAKES TO WATER! AND SO, IN THE MONTHS THAT FOLLOW, WHILE HIS DAD IS OUT OF TOWN ON THE BOXING CIRCUIT...

BAR BELLS

ROPE SKIPPING

CABLE PULL

THE BAG

ROWING MACHINE

THE BIKE

BUT, NO MATTER HOW HARD HE TRAINS, THE DETERMINED TEEN-AGER NEVER FORGETS THE GOAL HE HAS SET FOR HIMSELF...

HOW WERE THINGS AT SCHOOL WHILE I WAS AWAY, MATT? EVERYTHING ALL RIGHT, SON?

GUESS SO, DAD... IF YOU CALL STRAIGHT "A'S" ALL RIGHT!

MATT, I KNOW HOW TOUGH IT'S BEEN FOR YOU WHILE THE OTHER KIDS WERE OUT PLAYIN' AND HAVIN' GOOD TIMES! BUT THE DAY WILL COME WHEN YOU'LL *THANK* ME, BOY! YOU'RE GONNA AMOUNT TO SOMETHING... JUST THE WAY YOUR MOTHER WOULD'VE *WANTED* YOU TO!

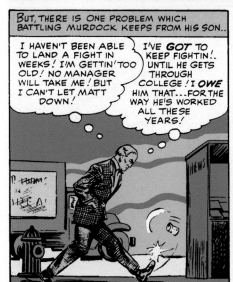

BUT, THERE IS ONE PROBLEM WHICH BATTLING MURDOCK KEEPS FROM HIS SON...

I HAVEN'T BEEN ABLE TO LAND A FIGHT IN WEEKS! I'M GETTIN' TOO OLD! NO MANAGER WILL TAKE ME! BUT I CAN'T LET MATT DOWN!

I'VE *GOT* TO KEEP FIGHTIN'!.. UNTIL HE GETS THROUGH COLLEGE! I *OWE* HIM THAT... FOR THE WAY HE'S WORKED ALL THESE YEARS!

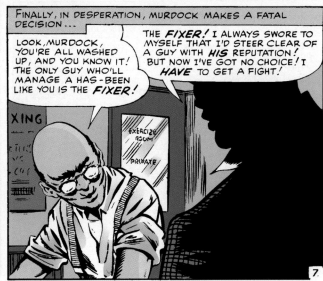

FINALLY, IN DESPERATION, MURDOCK MAKES A FATAL DECISION...

LOOK, MURDOCK, YOU'RE ALL WASHED UP, AND YOU KNOW IT! THE ONLY GUY WHO'LL MANAGE A HAS-BEEN LIKE YOU IS THE *FIXER!*

THE *FIXER!* I ALWAYS SWORE TO MYSELF THAT I'D STEER CLEAR OF A GUY WITH *HIS* REPUTATION! BUT NOW I'VE GOT NO CHOICE! I *HAVE* TO GET A FIGHT!

EXERCISE ROOM PRIVATE

7

AND SO...

WELL, WELL, IF IT AIN'T BATTLING MURDOCK! TEN YEARS AGO YOU KICKED ME OUT OF YOUR DRESSING ROOM WHEN I OFFERED YOU A DEAL! BUT I KNEW YOU'D COME AROUND, SOONER OR LATER!

SURE, I'LL GET YA SOME FIGHTS! AND YOU WON'T HAVE TO TAKE A DIVE, EITHER! JUST BECAUSE I'M REALLY A SOFT-HEARTED FOOL! HERE, SIGN THIS CONTRACT!

WITH TREMBLING FINGERS, THE MIDDLE-AGED FIGHTER GRASPS THE PEN, AS A DROWNING MAN WOULD CLUTCH AT A STRAW! AND THEN...

THIS IS THE LUCKIEST DAY OF MY LIFE! NOW I'LL BE ABLE TO SEND MATT TO COLLEGE! I DON'T HAVE A THING TO WORRY ABOUT!

EXCITEDLY, THE JOYFUL PRIZE-FIGHTER RUSHES TO HIS APARTMENT, ONLY TO FIND...

MATT! WAIT'LL I TELL YOU THE NEWS! MATT... HE'S NOT HERE!

AS FATE WOULD HAVE IT, MATHEW MURDOCK, AT THAT VERY MOMENT, IS RETURNING FROM THE LIBRARY...TAKING THE MOST IMPORTANT FEW STEPS OF HIS ENTIRE LIFE!

GEE, YOU'D THINK SOMEONE WOULD HELP THAT BLIND MAN ACROSS THE STREET!

SAY, MISTER... CAN I GIVE YOU A HAND?

COZY CLEANERS

HE DIDN'T SEEM TO HEAR ME! HE MIGHT BE DEAF, TOO! SAY...THERE'S A TRUCK TURNING THE CORNER... COMING TOWARDS HIM!

8.

HANK... SLAM ON THE BRAKES! SOMEONE'S CROSSIN' IN FRONT OF US!

I CAN'T! SOMETHING'S WRONG! SHE WON'T STOP!

SCR/REECH!

AJAX ATOMIC LABS RADIO-ACTIVE MATERIALS DANGER

WITHOUT A MOMENT'S HESITATION... HIS SUPPLE MUSCLES RESPONDING TO THE EMERGENCY WITH THE SPEED OF THOUGHT... MATT MURDOCK HURTLES TOWARD THE SCENE OF IMPENDING DISASTER...

HE WON'T HAVE A CHANCE... UNLESS I CAN REACH HIM IN TIME!

THE SWIFT-MOVING TEEN-AGER HURLS THE UNSUSPECTING BLIND MAN OUT OF THE TRUCK'S PATH... BUT HE HIMSELF IS NOT SO FORTUNATE...

OHHH...

HE SAVED THAT MAN'S LIFE!

MOST HEROIC ACT I'VE EVER SEEN!

BUT A CYLINDER FELL FROM THE TRUCK... IT STRUCK HIS FACE! IS... IS IT SOMETHING RADIOACTIVE??

DON'T JUST STAND THERE! SOMEONE CALL AN AMBULANCE!

ATOMIC LABS INC. TIVE MATERIALS ANGER

LATER, AT MUNICIPAL HOSPITAL...

YOUR SON IS A VERY BRAVE LAD, MR. MURDOCK! YOU MUST TRY TO BE EQUALLY AS BRAVE IN THE DAYS AHEAD!

IF... IF ONLY IT HAD HAPPENED TO ME INSTEAD OF HIM! IF ONLY I HAD BEEN THERE!

DON'T, DAD! IT COULD BE WORSE! EVEN IF I DO LOSE MY SIGHT... AT LEAST I'M ALIVE!

AND, DAYS LATER, AFTER THE INJURED BOY RETURNS HOME...

- GOOD NEWS, MATT! THE DOCTOR'S REPORT SAYS THAT AN OPERATION MAY RESTORE YOUR SIGHT IN A FEW YEARS, AFTER THE TISSUES HAVE HEALED!

THAT'S GREAT, DAD! AND TILL THEN, DON'T WORRY! I'LL STILL KEEP UP MY STUDIES, USING BOOKS WRITTEN IN BRAILLE! I'LL GET MY DIPLOMA YET! YOU'LL SEE!!

9

BUT, IN THE DAYS THAT FOLLOW, MATT MURDOCK STUDIES *MORE* THAN THE WRITTEN WORD! HE BEGINS A STILL MORE INTENSIVE PROGRAM OF PHYSICAL EXERCISES...

I DON'T GET IT! EVER SINCE MY ACCIDENT, I SEEM ABLE TO DO EVERY-THING LOTS BETTER THAN BEFORE... EVEN WITHOUT MY SIGHT!

BONG!!

IT'S AS THOUGH NATURE MADE ALL MY SENSES FAR MORE POWER-FUL, TO COMPENSATE FOR MY BLINDNESS!

I WONDER... COULD THE *RADIO-ACTIVE ELEMENTS* WHICH STRUCK MY EYES HAVE ANYTHING TO DO WITH MY INCREASED POWERS?? STRANGER THINGS HAVE BEEN KNOWN TO HAPPEN!

BUT, WHATEVER THE EXPLANATION, IT IS A SUPREMELY CONFIDENT, SELF-ASSURED MATT MURDOCK WHO FINALLY GRADUATES FROM HIGH SCHOOL AND IS EAGERLY ACCEPTED BY THE DIRECTOR OF ADMISSIONS OF STATE COLLEGE, WHERE WE FIND HIM SHARING A DORMITORY ROOM WITH HIS NEW BUDDY, FRANKLIN "FOGGY" NELSON...

D

MATT, YOU OL' HOUND DOG! HOW DO YOU DO IT? I STUDY LIKE A DEMON BUT *YOU* JUST BREEZE THROUGH THE COURSES WITH ALL THE TOP GRADES!

I GUESS MY DAD DESERVES THE CREDIT, FOGGY! HE HAD ME STUDY SO HARD WHEN I WAS YOUNGER, THAT IT ALL SEEMS TO COME EASY TO ME NOW!

AND, I WOULDN'T BE SURPRISED IF THAT RADIATION I ABSORBED IN THE ACCIDENT DOESN'T HAVE SOMETHING TO DO WITH IT, TOO! *EVERYTHING* SEEMS EASY FOR ME NOW! ALL MY SENSES ARE RAZOR SHARP!

"MY *HEARING* IS SO ACUTE, THAT I CAN TELL IF SOMEONE IS IN A ROOM WITH ME JUST BY HEARING THE *HEARTBEAT!*"

"AND I NEVER FORGET AN ODOR ONCE I *SMELL* IT! I COULD RECOGNIZE ANY GIRL BY HER PERFUME... OR ANY MAN BY HIS HAIR TONIC..."

"EVEN MY *FINGERS* HAVE BECOME INCREDIBLY SENSITIVE! I CAN TELL HOW MANY BULLETS ARE IN A GUN JUST BY THE WEIGHT OF THE BARREL!"

"WHILE MY SENSE OF *TASTE* HAS BECOME SO HIGHLY DEVELOPED THAT I CAN TELL EXACTLY HOW MANY GRAINS OF SALT ARE ON A PIECE OF PRETZEL..."

10.

"BUT MY MOST *IMPORTANT* NEW ABILITY IS IN THE FORM OF A BUILT-IN *RADAR* THAT I SEEM TO HAVE DEVELOPED! IT ENABLES ME TO WALK ANYWHERE SAFELY, WITHOUT BUMPING INTO ANYTHING!"

I FEEL A STRANGE TINGLING SENSATION WHEN I APPROACH ANY SOLID OBSTACLE, WARNING ME WHICH WAY TO TURN!

PING!

PING!

PING!

SAY, SON... WANT ANY HELP CROSSIN' THE STREET?

NO THANKS! I CAN MAKE IT!

LITTLE DOES HE SUSPECT I CAN CROSS MORE SAFELY THAN *HE* CAN.. FOR I HAVE EVERY ONE OF MY REMAINING SENSES WORKING AT ABSOLUTE PEAK CAPACITY!

PING!

MEANWHILE, THE CAREER OF BATTLING MURDOCK TAKES A SURPRISING TURN...

MADISON SQU
KID MURDOCK VS. PEDRO GARI
THURS. OCT. 10:00 P.M.

KID MUR FAVORITE
CENTRAL AR

MURDOCK K.O.S SIMS IN 9TH

MURDOCK 12TH KNOC

HERE'S YOUR DOUGH, MURDOCK! KEEP IT UP AND YOU MAY BE CHAMP SOME - DAY!

I CAN'T BELIEVE IT, FIXER! IT ALL SEEMS LIKE SOME KINDA *MIRACLE!*

THEN, AFTER MURDOCK LEAVES...

WAIT'LL THE OLD FOOL FINDS OUT THAT ALL HIS FIGHTS WERE *SETUPS!* YOU PAID HIS OPPONENTS TO TAKE A DIVE!

SURE! I DID IT TO GIVE MURDOCK A BUILD-UP...TO DRAW THE CROWDS! BUT, HE'LL LEARN THE FACTS OF LIFE IN HIS *NEXT* FIGHT! THAT'S WHERE I GET *HIM* TO TAKE THE COUNT!

AND, A FEW DAYS BEFORE BATTLING MURDOCK'S LATEST FIGHT...

FOOTSTEPS! I CAN TELL BY THE WEIGHT... THE DISTANCE BETWEEN EACH... IT'S FOGGY NELSON!

HEY, MATT! WAIT UP! I WANNA READ YOU THE SPORTS HEADLINE! IT'S ABOUT YOUR *DAD!*

HE'S FIGHTING DYNAMITE DAVIS TOMORROW NIGHT IN NEW YORK! HOW *ABOUT* THAT? WANNA GO ??

I'VE ALREADY GOT THE TICKETS, FOGGY...ONE FOR EACH OF US!

I "READ" THE HEADLINE BEFORE ---JUST BY RUNNING MY FINGER OVER THE PAGE AND FEELING THE IMPRESSION OF THE INK!

DAILY CHRONICLE
"KID" MURDOCK TO FACE DAVIS, NO.2 CONTENDER!

SEMI-TIT
AT GARDE
PROMISE
THRILLS

11.

AND SO THE NEXT NIGHT...

THE FIXER SAID I HAVE TO TAKE A DIVE IN THE FIRST ROUND TONIGHT!

...AND IN THIS CORNER, THE MIDDLE-AGED SENSATION... BATTLING MURDOCK!

BUT MY BOY'S HERE TONIGHT, TO ROOT FOR HIS DAD! I'VE ALWAYS TRAINED HIM TO DO HIS BEST... I CAN'T DISAPPOINT HIM NOW!

MURDOCK! YOU FOOL! TAKE IT EASY! WHAT ARE YOU DOIN'?!

IF YOU'RE TRYIN' TO DOUBLE-CROSS ME, YOU'LL LIVE TO REGRET IT! YOU'RE SUPPOSED TO DIVE NOW.. HEAR? DIVE!

HE'S WINNIN', MATT! YOUR DAD'S PULVERIZING HIM!

I KNOW IT! I CAN FOLLOW THE FIGHT PERFECTLY, BY HEARING THE SOUND OF EACH BLOW, EACH FOOT-STEP!

IT'S MY ONE CHANCE! ...MAYBE MY LAST CHANCE... TO DO SOMETHING TO MAKE MY SON PROUD OF ME! I'M NOT GONNA FAIL HIM! I'M GONNA WIN...DO YA HEAR... I'M GONNA WIN!

WHAM!

WHOP!

CALL IT A MIRACLE! CALL IT PURE WILL POWER... SHEER DETERMINATION! CALL IT WHAT YOU WILL, BUT A FEW SECONDS LATER...

THE WINNAH... BATTLING MURDOCK!!

AND THEN, IN THE DRESSING ROOM...

YOU DID IT, DAD! YOU PROVED THAT NOTHING'S IMPOSSIBLE IF A MAN HAS THE COURAGE! IF A MAN'S NOT AFRAID!!

I WANTED YOU TO BE PROUD OF ME, MATT... MY SON!

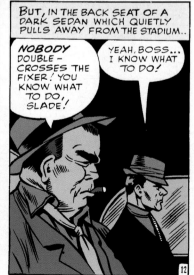

BUT, IN THE BACK SEAT OF A DARK SEDAN WHICH QUIETLY PULLS AWAY FROM THE STADIUM..

NOBODY DOUBLE-CROSSES THE FIXER! YOU KNOW WHAT TO DO, SLADE!

YEAH, BOSS... I KNOW WHAT TO DO!

12

A FEW MINUTES LATER, AS MATT'S HAPPY FATHER LEAVES THE GYM...

NO MATTER WHAT THE FIXER DOES, I WON'T CARE! MY SON IS *PROUD* OF ME! NOTHING CAN EVER CHANGE THAT NOW!

SUDDENLY, THE SHARP, EXPLOSIVE SOUND OF A GUN SHOT DESTROYS THE SILENCE OF NIGHT, AND ENDS ONE MAN'S REVERIE, FOREVER!

CRACK!

WITHIN SECONDS...

IT'S *BATTLING MURDOCK!* HE WON THE BIG FIGHT TONIGHT!

SOMEBODY MUST HAVE BEEN AWFULLY SORE ABOUT HIS VICTORY! AND WE'RE NOT GOING TO REST UNTIL WE FIND OUT *WHO!!*

NOTHING I CAN DO FOR HIM... IT'S TOO LATE!

LATER, AFTER A GRIEVING MATT MURDOCK HAS HEARD THE TRAGIC NEWS...

YOU'VE GOTTA SNAP OUT OF IT, MATT! PULL YOURSELF TOGETHER, FELLA! THAT'S WHAT YOUR DAD WOULD HAVE WANTED!

WE'LL BE GRADUATING SOON, AND MY DAD'S SETTING ME UP IN A LAW OFFICE! I WANT YOU TO JOIN ME, MATT...AS MY PARTNER!

FINALLY...THE BIG DAY ARRIVES... GRADUATION...

MATTHEW MURDOCK, I AM ESPECIALLY PROUD TO CONGRATULATE YOU FOR BEING CHOSEN CLASS VALEDICTORIAN! YOU HAVE PROVEN THAT AN ALERT MIND AND A STRONG WILL CAN CONQUER ANY OBSTACLES!

THANK YOU, SIR!

AND HE'S GONNA BE MY PARTNER! BOY! CAN I PICK 'EM!

THE NEXT DAY, IN NEW YORK...

WE'RE IN *BUSINESS,* MATT! WITH YOUR BRAINS AND MY DAD'S MONEY, *NOTHING'LL* STOP US!

C'MON IN AND MEET THE SECRETARY I HIRED!

NELSON AND MURDOCK
·
ATTORNEYS AT LAW

ENTER

MY NAME IS KAREN PAGE, MR. MURDOCK! I HOPE YOU'LL BE PLEASED WITH ME!

HER VOICE IS LIKE MUSIC! FROM THE SOUND, SHE'S FIVE-FEET-FOUR, YOUNG, AND I *KNOW* SHE'S LOVELY!

LATER THAT NIGHT, IN THE FURNISHED ROOM MATT HAS RENTED NEAR THE OFFICE...

I'LL *NEVER* BE ABLE TO CONCENTRATE ON MY LAW WORK UNTIL DAD'S MURDERER IS FINALLY BROUGHT TO JUSTICE! BUT YEARS AGO I PROMISED DAD THAT MATT MURDOCK WOULD USE HIS *HEAD*... NEVER BECOME A FIGHTER.. NEVER DEPEND ON MY STRENGTH, THE WAY *DAD* DID!

13.

I CAN'T BREAK THAT PROMISE I MADE! AND YET, WITH MY AGILITY, MY EXTRA-SHARP SENSES, THERE IS SO MUCH I COULD DO! I CAN'T LET ALL MY POWERS GO TO WASTE!

WAIT! I HAVE IT!

SNAP!

I'LL SEE TO IT THAT MATT MURDOCK NEVER DOES RESORT TO FORCE... BUT SOMEBODY ELSE WILL...! SOMEBODY TOTALLY DIFFERENT FROM MATT MURDOCK... ALL I NEED ARE SOME OLD SHIRTS WHICH I CAN STITCH TOGETHER!

I'M NO BETSY ROSS, BUT I SHOULD BE ABLE TO HANDLE THIS! LUCKY MY TOUCH IS SO SENSITIVE!

I CAN EVEN BLEND THE COLORS, FOR EACH COLORED FABRIC HAS A DIFFERENT FEEL TO ME!

A FEW HOURS LATER...

THERE! WHENEVER I DON THIS COSTUME, I'LL NO LONGER BE MATT MURDOCK! BUT I'LL NEED A NEW NAME! WHAT IF THE KIDS IN THE OLD NEIGHBORHOOD COULD SEE ME NOW!! THE KIDS WHO TAUNTED ME...CALLED ME "DAREDEVIL"! WAIT! THAT'S IT!!

"DAREDEVIL" THEY CALLED ME... BUT THEY MEANT IT AS AN INSULT! WELL, THAT'S WHO I'LL BE... THE NAME IS PERFECT!

THE COSTUME IS TIGHT ENOUGH TO WEAR UNDER MY CLOTHES IF NEED BE! I'LL JUST MAKE A FEW FINISHING TOUCHES ON THE HEADPIECE! WHEN I'M THROUGH, DAREDEVIL WILL BE RECOGNIZED ANYWHERE!!

EVEN THOUGH I DON'T NEED IT, I'LL CONTINUE TO CARRY A CANE AS MATT MURDOCK! MMM...THAT GIVES ME ANOTHER IDEA! THAT CANE WOULD MAKE A GREAT WEAPON FOR DAREDEVIL!

THROUGH THE LONG NIGHT, THE UNSEEING MAN WORKS ...HIS SUPER-SENSITIVE FINGERS MOLDING AND MANIPULATING HIS CANE FAR MORE PRECISELY THAN ANY NORMAL CRAFTSMAN MIGHT DO IT!

FLEXIBLE HANDLE

I'LL HINGE IT IN THE MIDDLE... DESIGN A SHEATH FOR IT...IT'LL BE THE PERFECT ALL-PURPOSE WEAPON!

HINGE

14

IT'S *PERFECT!*

I CAN USE IT IN A HUNDRED WAYS!

BONG.

AND NOW FOR THE JOB AT HAND! I'VE GOT TO BRING MY FATHER'S MURDERER TO JUSTICE! TOMORROW'S SATURDAY! THE OFFICE WILL BE CLOSED... SO I'LL START IN THE MORNING!

AND I KNOW JUST WHERE TO BEGIN!

AND SO:... DAD'S MANAGER WAS A MAN CALLED THE *FIXER!* I HAVE A HUNCH HE *DESERVES* THAT NICKNAME!

HOW *CONFIDENTLY* THAT BLIND YOUNG MAN WALKS THROUGH THE STREET!

UNERRINGLY GUIDED BY HIS ATOM-INDUCED RADAR-SENSE, MATT MURDOCK REACHES HIS DESTINATION...

THIS WILL BE *DAREDEVIL'S* FIRST TEST! NOW TO CHANGE CLOTHES IN AN ALLEY AND SEE IF I'M AS GOOD AS I THINK!

AND SO WE RETURN TO THE PRESENT, AS OUR DAREDEVIL SAGA CONTINUES...

NOW, DO YOU TAKE ME TO THE *FIXER,* OR...?

OR, *NOTHING!* WE'VE *HAD* IT, FELLA! JUST HANG AROUND...HE'LL BE HERE ANY MINUTE!

SOMEBODY *ASKIN'* FOR ME? WHAT DO YA WANT?

HEY, BOSS, DIG THE GETUP ON THAT CLOWN!

HE LOOKS LIKE *TROUBLE* TO ME, FIXER! WANT WE SHOULD LEAN ON 'IM A LITTLE?

MY "ASSOCIATES" DON'T SEEM TO LIKE YOUR LOOKS, MISTER! YOU BETTER TALK FAST!

FROM THE HEAVY TONE OF HIS VOICE HE'S BEEFY, ROUGH! I HEAR BREATHING ON EACH SIDE OF HIM... SO THE OTHER TWO MUST BE FLANKING HIM!

CORRECTION, FIXER! *YOU'RE* THE ONE WHO'S GOING TO TALK!!

15.

16

I WANT TO KNOW WHAT ARRANGEMENT YOU HAD WITH BATTLING MURDOCK!

BATTLING MURDOCK!! WHAT'S THAT TO YOU??! IT AIN'T HEALTHY TO MENTION HIM AROUND HERE!

HE MUST KNOW SOMETHING, BOSS! I'LL TAKE CARE OF HIM!

THE SOUND OF A SUIT JACKET BEING DRAWN ASIDE! FINGERS TOUCHING A METAL OBJECT! MUST BE A GUN BUTT---IN A SHOULDER HOLSTER!

THE SOUND OF HIS BREATHING... THE TELLTALE CLICK OF THE PISTOL'S SAFETY RELEASE... ARE ALL I NEED HEAR TO PINPOINT MY TARGET!

...AND THE ALMOST INAUDIBLE SOUND OF MY CANE CUTTING THROUGH THE AIR IS LIKE A LOUD RADAR BEEP TO MY SUPER-SENSITIVE EARS!

I WAS RIGHT ALL THE TIME! MY SENSES ARE SO ULTRA-KEEN THAT I CAN DO ANY-THING A MAN WITH EYESIGHT CAN...AND DO IT BETTER!!

I'LL SNEAK UP ON HIM FROM BEHIND AND...HEY! HE SWUNG AROUND JUST IN TIME!

HOW'D YOU KNOW I WAS BEHIND YOU?!

THAT'S MY SECRET, PAL!

NO MATTER HOW SOFTLY HE CREPT UP BEHIND ME, HIS MUFFLED FOOT-STEPS SOUNDED LIKE HEAVY DRUM BEATS TO ME!!

RAPID FOOTSTEPS HURRYING AWAY FROM ME! HE'S TRYING TO ESCAPE!

HOLD IT, SPEEDY! I HAVEN'T DISMISSED THE CLASS YET!!

HOW DOES HE DO IT? HE DOESN'T MISS A TRICK!!

16.

NOW LET'S ALL SETTLE DOWN FOR A NICE TALK... UNLESS YOU'D LIKE ANOTHER SESSION WITH ME!
SLAM!
LOOK, YOU...
QUIET! I'LL HANDLE THIS! I'M STILL THE BOSS!
MISTER, WHOEVER YOU ARE... YOU'RE IN A MESS OF TROUBLE! YOU'RE NOT GETTIN' AWAY WITH COMIN' HERE AND ROUGHING US UP! WE GOT LAWS TO PROTECT INNOCENT PEOPLE! SAM, CALL THE COPS!!
THE SOUND OF A HAND PICKING UP A RECEIVER! THIS IS ALMOST TOO EASY!
YEOWP!
CLANK!
FIXER, I SUSPECT YOU WERE RESPONSIBLE FOR THE DEATH OF BATTLING MURDOCK! WHY DON'T YOU CONFESS NOW AND SAVE US ALL A LOT OF TROUBLE!?
YOU'RE NUTS! I HAD NOTHIN' TO DO WITH IT! I GOT A PERFECT ALIBI!
I HAVE ANOTHER POWER I WASN'T EVEN AWARE OF! I CAN HEAR HIS PULSE RATE! IT'S SPEEDING UP, INDICATING HE'S LYING! MY SUPER-SENSE OF HEARING IS LIKE A BUILT-IN LIE DETECTOR!
MAYBE YOU DO HAVE AN ALIBI! MAYBE YOURS WASN'T THE FINGER THAT SQUEEZED THE TRIGGER! BUT YOU GAVE THE ORDER... DIDN'T YOU??
NO! NO! STAY BACK!! STOP HIM, YOU GUYS... DON'T LET 'IM GET ME!
17.

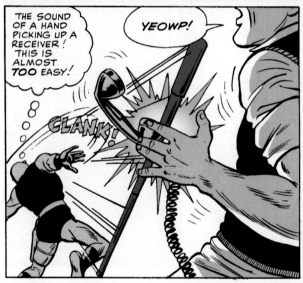

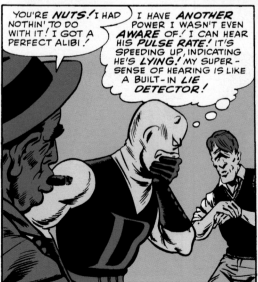

HE KNOWS TOO MUCH!! HE MIGHT EVEN KNOW *I'M* THE MURDERER! CAN'T TAKE ANY CHANCES!

SO INTENT IS DAREDEVIL UPON LISTENING TO THE FIXER'S PULSE RATE, TO DETERMINE IF HE IS THE GUILTY MAN, THAT HIS ULTRA-SHARP HEARING SENSE REACTS A FRACTION OF A SECOND TOO SLOW, AND...

IT WAS *ME*... BUT YOU'LL NEVER BE ABLE TO *DO* ANYTHING ABOUT IT!

BEHIND ME!! SOMEONE... OHHH!

A NORMAL MAN, WITH ALL HIS SENSES, MIGHT BE DOOMED IN SUCH A SITUATION! BUT, THE MOMENT THE FEARLESS *DAREDEVIL* FEELS HIMSELF HURTLING INTO SPACE, HIS SUPER-KEEN EARS CATCH THE RUSTLING OF A FLAG, AS HIS LIGHTNING-FAST REFLEXES GO INTO ACTION...

A FLAGPOLE ALONGSIDE ME... ONLY ONE CHANCE!!

PRESSING THE HIDDEN STUD WHICH RELEASES HIS CANE HANDLE AT THE SAME SPLIT SECOND AS HE LUNGES OUT, HE STOPS HIS FALL IN MIDAIR!!

GOT IT!!

FROM HERE ON IN, IT'S ALL A BREEZE!

NOW THEN, GENTS... WHERE *WERE* WE??

HE'S *BACK*!!

WHUMP!

MEANWHILE, AT THE OTHER SIDE OF TOWN...

FUNNY, MATT DOESN'T ANSWER! MAYBE HE'S STILL ASLEEP! OH... THE DOOR'S OPEN!

HEY, LAZYBONES! I THOUGHT I'D SEE IF YOU *NEED* ANYTHING, AND... MATT?? HE'S *GONE!*

GOSH, I WISH HE'D *CALLED* ME! I HATE TO THINK OF POOR MATT WALKING AROUND TOWN ALL ALONE, WITH ALL THE TRAFFIC IN NEW YORK!

18.

I'LL GO UP TO THE OFFICE...MAYBE HE DECIDED TO COME HERE AND GET FAMILIAR WITH THE PLACE BEFORE STARTING WORK ON MONDAY!

BUT, ENTERING THE NEW OFFICE, FOGGY FINDS IT UNOCCUPIED, EXCEPT FOR THE MOST DECORATIVE ACCESSORY...

KAREN! TODAY'S YOUR DAY OFF!

I KNOW, MR. NELSON! BUT I'M A STRANGER IN NEW YORK, AND HAD NO ONE TO VISIT, SO I THOUGHT I'D TIDY UP THE OFFICE WHILE I HAD A CHANCE! IS MR. MURDOCK WITH YOU?

NO! MATTER OF FACT, I HOPED HE'D BE HERE! I DON'T LIKE HIM WANDERING AROUND TOWN ALONE!

I UNDERSTAND! WHAT A PITY SUCH A WONDERFUL, HANDSOME MAN IS SO HANDICAPPED!

WOW! I'D SURE LIKE TO HEAR HER TALK ABOUT ME IN THAT ADORING TONE OF VOICE!

DON'T LET HIS BLINDNESS FOOL YOU, KAREN! HE'S STILL THE SMARTEST, MOST CAPABLE, MOST COURAGEOUS FELLA I KNOW! HE DOESN'T EVEN SEEM TO MIND NOT SEEING!

THERE'S SOMETHING ABOUT HIM THAT MAKES A GIRL WANT TO TAKE HIM IN HER ARMS AND... OH, I'M SORRY, MR. NELSON! I HAD NO RIGHT TO SPEAK THAT WAY! IT'S JUST THAT HE SEEMS TO NEED SOMEONE TO LOOK AFTER HIM!

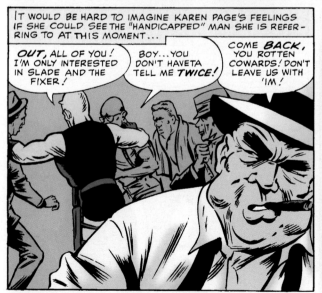

IT WOULD BE HARD TO IMAGINE KAREN PAGE'S FEELINGS IF SHE COULD SEE THE "HANDICAPPED" MAN SHE IS REFERRING TO AT THIS MOMENT...

OUT, ALL OF YOU! I'M ONLY INTERESTED IN SLADE AND THE FIXER!

BOY...YOU DON'T HAVETA TELL ME TWICE!

COME BACK, YOU ROTTEN COWARDS! DON'T LEAVE US WITH 'IM!

NOW, YOU TWO, I'VE LEARNED WHAT I WANTED! SLADE ACTUALLY DID THE SHOOTING, BUT YOU GAVE THE ORDER!

WHAT GOOD'LL IT DO YOU?? YOU CAN'T PROVE IT!

YEAH! WHERE'S YOUR EVIDENCE??

19.

NOW FOR MY FINAL BLUFF! THEY'RE SO WORRIED NOW, THEY'LL BELIEVE *ANYTHING!*

RIGHT *HERE!* I HAVE A MINIATURE TAPE RECORDER CONCEALED IN MY BILLY CLUB! IT'LL TELL THE POLICE ALL THEY NEED TO KNOW!

HE'S *GOT* US!

THEN, BEFORE DAREDEVIL CAN MAKE A MOVE, THE FIXER TRIES ONE LAST, DESPERATE MANEUVER...

QUICK, SLADE... *RUN!* BEFORE HE CAN GET HIS BALANCE!

OHHH...

MY ARM! I WRENCHED IT! I WAS A FOOL FOR BEING SO OVERCONFIDENT! I SHOULD HAVE *KNOWN* THEY'D MAKE ONE FINAL TRY TO ESCAPE!

THEY CAN'T HAVE GOTTEN FAR! I'LL GET THEM *YET!*

BUT, RACING AROUND THE CORNER, SLADE AND THE FIXER QUICKLY MINGLE WITH THE SATURDAY AFTERNOON SHOPPING CROWD...

HE'LL NEVER FIND US NOW, IN THE MIDDLE OF THIS CROWD!

JUST THE SAME, KEEP MOVING! THERE'S NO TELLIN' *WHAT* THAT GUY CAN DO!

MEANWHILE...

I CAN STILL SMELL THE TRACES OF THE FIXER'S CIGAR SMOKE! I CAN FOLLOW THE SCENT LIKE A BLOODHOUND... BUT I'LL BE ABLE TO GET AROUND EASIER IN THE CROWD *WITHOUT* A COSTUME!!

AND SO BEGINS ONE OF THE STRANGEST PURSUITS ON RECORD, AS A MAN WITHOUT SIGHT UNERRINGLY MAKES HIS WAY THROUGH A CROWDED AVENUE, ON THE TRAIL OF TWO KILLERS!

I'M GLAD HIS CIGAR IS A STRONG ONE! HE MIGHT AS WELL BE *TELLING* ME WHERE HE IS... BUT HE DOESN'T *KNOW* IT!!

20.

WITHIN MINUTES, THE GRACEFUL, SUPPLE FIGURE OF MATT MURDOCK HAS KNIFED THROUGH THE UNSUSPECTING CROWD LIKE A SHADOWY WRAITH, AND THEN...

I HOPE THEY'RE STAYING TOGETHER! I WANT TO BRING THEM *BOTH* TO JUSTICE! THE CIGAR SCENT IS STRONGER NOW... I'M ALMOST UP TO THEM!

SLOW DOWN, SLADE! WE'RE SAFE NOW! HE'S NOWHERE IN SIGHT!

GUESS YOU'RE RIGHT! NO ONE NEAR US NOW BUT THAT BLIND GUY! WE'VE LOST 'IM FOR SURE!

C'MON, WE'LL DUCK INTO THAT SUBWAY STATION ACROSS THE STREET AND GET OFF AT PENN STATION! WE'LL BE OUTTA TOWN IN AN HOUR!

THAT'S WHAT *THEY* THINK!

HEY! DIDJA SEE HOW FAST THAT BLIND GUY PUSHED PAST US?

WHO CARES? WE GOT OUR *OWN* PROBLEMS!

BUT UNKNOWN TO THE FLEEING DUO, THEIR PROBLEMS ARE JUST *BEGINNING!* FOR, DIRECTLY *AHEAD* OF THEM...

THEIR FOOTSTEPS ARE GETTING CLOSER! I'LL JUST MAKE IT!!

GOING SOMEWHERE, BOYS?!

IT'S *HIM!!*

IT... IT AIN'T *POSSIBLE!*

SEPARATE! HE CAN'T GET US *BOTH!!*

I WAS *AFRAID* THEY'D TRY THAT!

I CAN TELL BY THE UNBROKEN SOUND OF SLADE'S FOOTSTEPS, THERE'S NO ONE BETWEEN US! ... SO IT'S SAFE TO THROW MY CANE!

GOOD! HE'S TACKLING *SLADE!* THAT MEANS *I'LL* ESCAPE!

21.

22

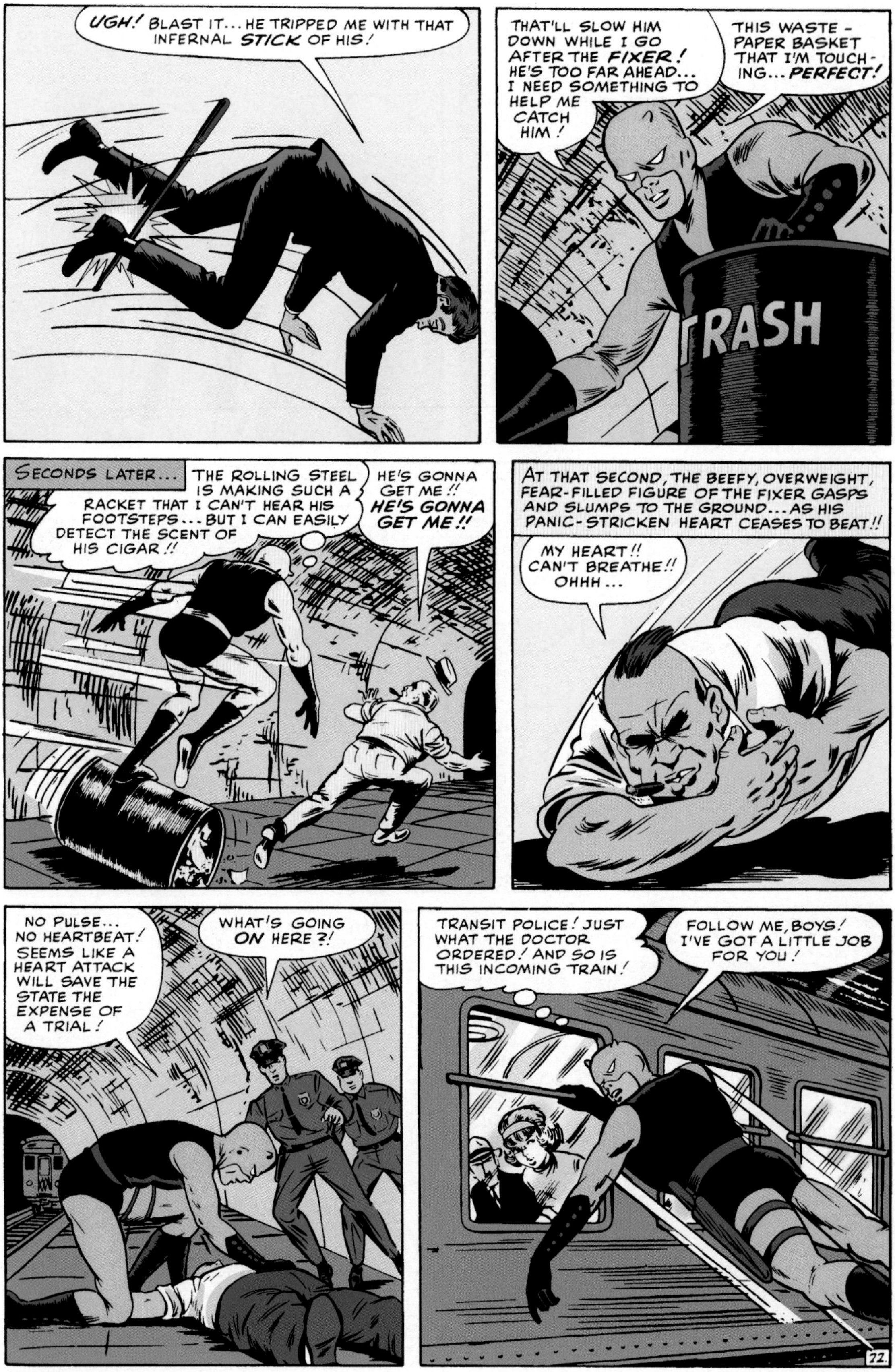
UGH! BLAST IT... HE TRIPPED ME WITH THAT INFERNAL STICK OF HIS!
THAT'LL SLOW HIM DOWN WHILE I GO AFTER THE FIXER! HE'S TOO FAR AHEAD... I NEED SOMETHING TO HELP ME CATCH HIM!
THIS WASTE-PAPER BASKET THAT I'M TOUCHING... PERFECT!
TRASH
SECONDS LATER...
THE ROLLING STEEL IS MAKING SUCH A RACKET THAT I CAN'T HEAR HIS FOOTSTEPS... BUT I CAN EASILY DETECT THE SCENT OF HIS CIGAR!!
HE'S GONNA GET ME!! HE'S GONNA GET ME!!
AT THAT SECOND, THE BEEFY, OVERWEIGHT, FEAR-FILLED FIGURE OF THE FIXER GASPS AND SLUMPS TO THE GROUND... AS HIS PANIC-STRICKEN HEART CEASES TO BEAT!!
MY HEART!! CAN'T BREATHE!! OHHH...
NO PULSE... NO HEARTBEAT! SEEMS LIKE A HEART ATTACK WILL SAVE THE STATE THE EXPENSE OF A TRIAL!
WHAT'S GOING ON HERE?!
TRANSIT POLICE! JUST WHAT THE DOCTOR ORDERED! AND SO IS THIS INCOMING TRAIN!
FOLLOW ME, BOYS! I'VE GOT A LITTLE JOB FOR YOU!
22.

DON'T YOU KNOW ENOUGH TO STAY WHERE I LEFT YOU??

UHH!!

NOW FOR MY LAST BLUFF!

THE FIXER JUST TOLD US EVERYTHING, SLADE! HE'S INNOCENT! YOU ARE MURDOCK'S MURDERER!

THE DIRTY CRUMB! HE'S NOT GONNA WIGGLE OUT OF THIS! HE'S AS GUILTY AS I AM! I ONLY PULLED THE TRIGGER.. BUT HE GAVE THE ORDERS!

HEAR ENOUGH, BOYS??

WE SURE DID! BUT...

WAIT! WHO ARE YOU?

THE NAME'S DAREDEVIL ... REMEMBER IT! YOU'LL BE HEARING IT AGAIN... I PROMISE!!

NOT LONG AFTERWARDS...

MATT! SAY, I WAS WORRIED ABOUT YOU, FELLA! WHERE'VE YOU BEEN?

JUST OUT FOR A WALK, FOGGY! I'D HAVE BEEN HERE SOONER, BUT AS YOU KNOW.. I CAN'T GET AROUND TOO FAST!

WE JUST HAD A CALL, MR. MURDOCK! AN ACCUSED MURDERER, NAMED SLADE... HE WANTED TO KNOW IF WE'D DEFEND HIM!

BUT I TURNED HIM DOWN! FROM THE POLICE REPORT, I WAS CONVINCED HE'S GUILTY! HOPE YOU DON'T MIND, MATT!

MIND??

NO! I DON'T MIND AT ALL! NOT A BIT! NOT ONE SINGLE BIT!

DAD, WHEREVER YOU ARE... I KINDA HOPE YOU'RE RESTING EASIER NOW!

DON'T WASTE A MINUTE!! WE CAN'T WAIT TO HEAR WHAT YOU THINK OF DAREDEVIL!! SEND YOUR LETTERS TO DAREDEVIL, c/o STAN LEE, 3RD FLOOR, 655 MADISON AVE, N.Y.C. 21 AND IN THE MEANTIME, REMEMBER.. THIS IS JUST THE BEGINNING! WE'VE ONLY SCRATCHED THE SURFACE!! DAREDEVIL REALLY HITS HIS STRIDE IN ISH #2, WHEN HE FACES HIS FIRST SUPER-VILLAIN! DON'T MISS IT!!

D

23.

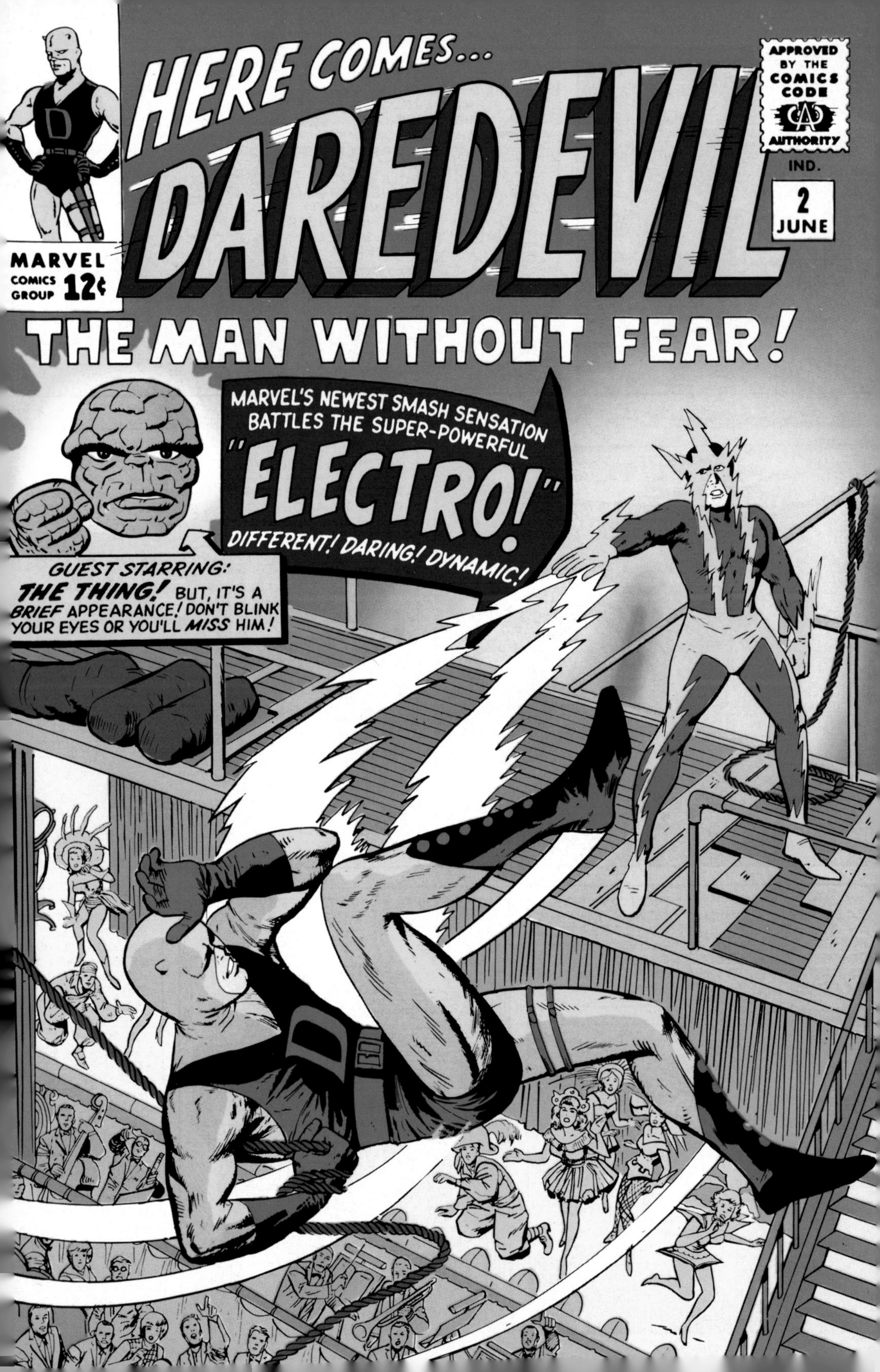

HERE COMES...
DAREDEVIL
APPROVED BY THE COMICS CODE AUTHORITY
IND.
2
JUNE
MARVEL COMICS GROUP 12¢
THE MAN WITHOUT FEAR!
MARVEL'S NEWEST SMASH SENSATION BATTLES THE SUPER-POWERFUL "ELECTRO!"
DIFFERENT! DARING! DYNAMIC!
GUEST STARRING: THE THING! BUT, IT'S A BRIEF APPEARANCE! DON'T BLINK YOUR EYES OR YOU'LL MISS HIM!

DAREDEVIL "The EVIL MENACE of ELECTRO!"

STORY:
STAN LEE
ART:
JOE ORLANDO
INKING:
VINCE COLLETTA
LETTERING:
S. ROSEN

WHAT CHANCE DOES A BLIND MAN HAVE OF DEFEATING ONE OF THE MOST DANGEROUS ARCH-VILLAINS OF ALL TIME? MORE CHANCE THAN YOU THINK...IF HIS NAME HAPPENS TO BE... DAREDEVIL!!

ELECTRO! THIS SENSATIONAL SUPER-POWERED CRIMINAL BECAME AN INSTANT SENSATION WHEN HE FIRST APPEARED IN *THE AMAZING SPIDER-MAN #9!* AND NOW HE RETURNS, MORE SINISTER THAN EVER, TO FACE ANOTHER MIGHTY *MARVEL* SUPER HERO...AND THIS, THE THRILLING ACCOUNT OF THEIR EPIC BATTLE, MAY WELL BE REMEMBERED AS LONG AS LITERATURE ENDURES!!

X-691

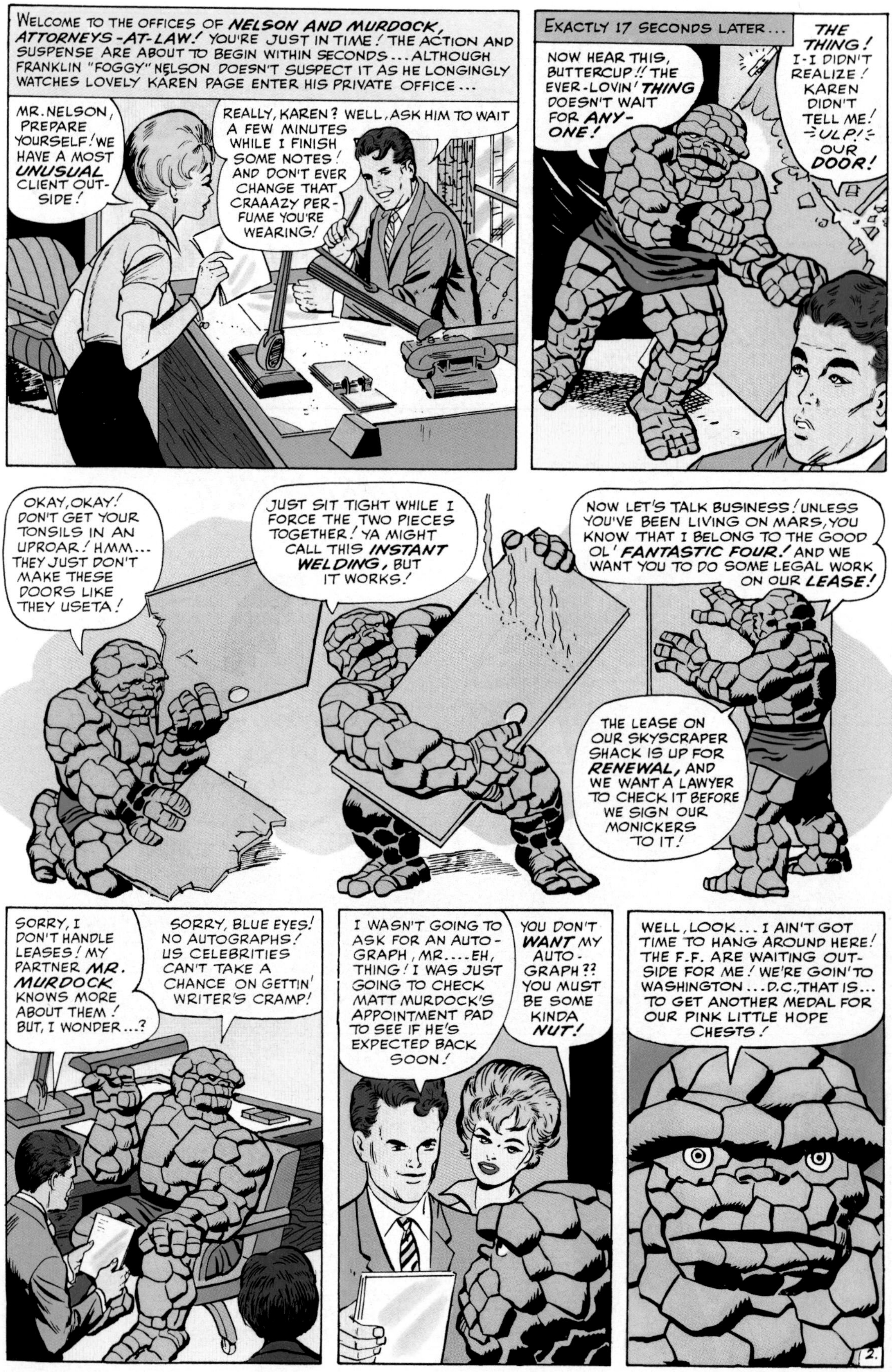
WELCOME TO THE OFFICES OF NELSON AND MURDOCK, ATTORNEYS-AT-LAW! YOU'RE JUST IN TIME! THE ACTION AND SUSPENSE ARE ABOUT TO BEGIN WITHIN SECONDS... ALTHOUGH FRANKLIN "FOGGY" NELSON DOESN'T SUSPECT IT AS HE LONGINGLY WATCHES LOVELY KAREN PAGE ENTER HIS PRIVATE OFFICE...
MR. NELSON, PREPARE YOURSELF! WE HAVE A MOST UNUSUAL CLIENT OUTSIDE!
REALLY, KAREN? WELL, ASK HIM TO WAIT A FEW MINUTES WHILE I FINISH SOME NOTES! AND DON'T EVER CHANGE THAT CRAAAZY PERFUME YOU'RE WEARING!
EXACTLY 17 SECONDS LATER...
NOW HEAR THIS, BUTTERCUP!! THE EVER-LOVIN' THING DOESN'T WAIT FOR ANY-ONE!
THE THING! I-I DIDN'T REALIZE! KAREN DIDN'T TELL ME! ULP! OUR DOOR!
OKAY, OKAY! DON'T GET YOUR TONSILS IN AN UPROAR! HMM... THEY JUST DON'T MAKE THESE DOORS LIKE THEY USETA!
JUST SIT TIGHT WHILE I FORCE THE TWO PIECES TOGETHER! YA MIGHT CALL THIS INSTANT WELDING, BUT IT WORKS!
NOW LET'S TALK BUSINESS! UNLESS YOU'VE BEEN LIVING ON MARS, YOU KNOW THAT I BELONG TO THE GOOD OL' FANTASTIC FOUR! AND WE WANT YOU TO DO SOME LEGAL WORK ON OUR LEASE!
THE LEASE ON OUR SKYSCRAPER SHACK IS UP FOR RENEWAL, AND WE WANT A LAWYER TO CHECK IT BEFORE WE SIGN OUR MONICKERS TO IT!
SORRY, I DON'T HANDLE LEASES! MY PARTNER MR. MURDOCK KNOWS MORE ABOUT THEM! BUT, I WONDER...?
SORRY, BLUE EYES! NO AUTOGRAPHS! US CELEBRITIES CAN'T TAKE A CHANCE ON GETTIN' WRITER'S CRAMP!
I WASN'T GOING TO ASK FOR AN AUTO-GRAPH, MR.... EH, THING! I WAS JUST GOING TO CHECK MATT MURDOCK'S APPOINTMENT PAD TO SEE IF HE'S EXPECTED BACK SOON!
YOU DON'T WANT MY AUTO-GRAPH?? YOU MUST BE SOME KINDA NUT!
WELL, LOOK... I AIN'T GOT TIME TO HANG AROUND HERE! THE F.F. ARE WAITING OUT-SIDE FOR ME! WE'RE GOIN' TO WASHINGTON... D.C., THAT IS... TO GET ANOTHER MEDAL FOR OUR PINK LITTLE HOPE CHESTS!
2.

SO WHEN MURDOCK GETS HERE, TELL HIM HE'LL HAVE TO GO TO OUR HEADQUARTERS AND EXAMINE THE PLACE TO MAKE SURE THAT IT'S EVERYTHING THE LEASE *SAYS* IT IS!

BUT HOW WILL HE GET *IN*?

OL' BIGBRAIN RICHARDS THOUGHT OF THAT! JUST GIMME A *PHOTO* OF HIM, AND I'LL FEED IT TO OUR ELECTRIC-EYE WATCHDOG GIZMO! THEN, WHEN MURDOCK ARRIVES IN THE FLESH, THE DOOR'LL *OPEN* FOR HIM!

HMM! I MIGHT HAVE KNOWN!

I HAVE A PICTURE OF MR. MURDOCK... IN MY DESK DRAWER!

HE AIN'T GONNA WIN ANY *BEAUTY CONTESTS*, BUT WE CAN'T *ALL* LOOK LIKE *ME*! OKAY, THIS IS GOOD ENOUGH!

TELL HIM TO FINISH THE JOB BEFORE WE GET BACK FROM WASHINGTON!

SAY! I DIDN'T REALIZE YOUR FANTASTI-CAR WAS HOVERING RIGHT OUT-SIDE!

'NATCH! THEY DON'T LET ME OUTTA THEIR SIGHT! THEY'RE LOST WITHOUT OL' BASHFUL BENJAMIN!

JUST YOU BE SURE I GET MY *PHOTO* BACK!! IT'S MY ONLY ONE!!

LET'S *GO*, BIG FELLA! IT'S GETTING LATE!

MY! WHAT AN ATTRACTIVE *HAIRDO*! I'LL HAVE TO *TRY* THAT SOME-TIME!

C'MON, REED... WHY WON'T YOU LET *ME* DRIVE THIS BUGGY??!

NUTS! IT'S NO FUN BEIN' A *PASSENGER!* I THINK I'LL *FLAME ON* AND FLY THE REST OF THE WAY!

STAY WHERE YOU ARE AND WAVE TO THE CROWDS, JOHNNY!

LOOK AT *REED!* THAT CORN-BALL IS GONNA START THROWIN' *KISSES* NEXT!

MEANTIME, WHERE *IS* MATT MURDOCK?? CAN THERE BE ANY CONNECTION BETWEEN THE BLIND, SOFT-SPOKEN YOUNG LAWYER AND *THIS* MAN??

THIS MAN, WHO UNHESITATINGLY APPROACHES A DINGY GARAGE WITH FIRM STEP AND SURE TREAD! THIS MAN WITH MUSCLES LIKE STEEL BANDS!

THIS MAN, WHOSE GLOVED HAND HOLDS A HEAVY CANE, KNOCKING COMMANDINGLY ON THE BOLTED DOOR OF THE LONELY GARAGE!

TAP!

TAP!

3.

SLOWLY, THE BOLT IS WITHDRAWN, AS A GRUFF, BEEFY FIGURE PEERS CAUTIOUSLY OUT, AND THEN...

NOBODY HERE! WHAT IS THIS? A GAG?!

GUESS I WAS JUST *HEARING* THINGS! WELL, AT LEAST IT AIN'T THE *COPS!*

HEY!! AWWKK...

THANKS FOR UNBOLTING THE DOOR FOR ME, BUSTER! NOW JUST STAY THERE NICE AND QUIET UNTIL THE POLICE COME AND UNTIE YOU!

AS FOR ME, I'LL GO VISIT THE *REST* OF YOU NAUGHTY LITTLE CAR THIEVES!

HEY! WHO OPENED THAT BLASTED *DOOR??* WANNA LAND US ALL IN *JAIL?!*

THAT'S JUST WHERE YOU'RE *GOING,* BOYS! IN CASE YOU DIDN'T *KNOW* IT, THERE ARE A FEW LITTLE *LAWS* AGAINST STEALING CARS AND REPAINTING THEM IN A CAMOUFLAGED GARAGE!

HOLY COW!! IT'S THE GUY WHO CALLS HIMSELF *DAREDEVIL!!* WE GOTTA MAKE SURE HE DOESN'T GET *OUT* OF HERE TO PUT THE FINGER ON US!!

WE'LL HANDLE 'IM!! HE MUSTA BEEN *BATTY* TO COME HERE ALONE!!

4.

I CAN TELL BY THEIR *BREATHING*... THERE ARE *SIX* OF THEM! IT SHOULDN'T BE TOO DIFFICULT FOR ME TO OUTMANEUVER THEM IF I DON'T GET CARELESS!! HMM... MY TOE IS TOUCHING A SMALL, FOUR-WHEELED *DOLLY*... JUST WHAT I NEED!

I HEAR SOMETHING FLYING THROUGH THE AIR AT ME! EASY ENOUGH TO DUCK IT WHILE I HOOK MY CANE HANDLE ONTO THE DOLLY!

YOU CLUMSY MEAT-HEAD...YOU *MISSED* 'IM! C'MON, LET'S *RUSH* HIM BEFORE HE CAN ESCAPE!

NO NEED TO HURRY, LITTLE FRIENDS! *I'M* NOT GOING ANYPLACE... *YOU* ARE!!

PRETTY TRICKY, AREN'T YA?? WELL, YOU'LL BE LAUGHIN' OUTTA THE *OTHER* SIDE OF YOUR MOUTH WHEN *I* GET THROUGH WITH YA!!

THAT CONCENTRATED HEAT IN FRONT OF ME! IT MUST BE AN ACETYLENE TORCH!!

NOT MUCH YOU CAN *DO* WITH THAT GADGET ONCE A PAIL OF PAINT! HAS BEEN THROWN OVER IT!! WHY DON'T YOU BUNGLERS GIVE UP BEFORE I REALLY GET MAD??!

NOW'S OUR CHANCE! *GET* 'IM!

SSSSS!

FOOTSTEPS ON ALL SIDES! STARTING TO *RUSH* ME! BUT I HEAR A SMALL *CRANE* SWAYING ABOVE ME! I'LL JUST HOOK ONTO IT AND TAKE TO THE *AIR*!!

STOP 'IM, YOU GUYS!

SURE! TELL US *HOW*!!

5.

30

NIMBLY LANDING NEAR A PILE OF TIRES, THE MAN WITHOUT FEAR USES THEM AS WHIRLING WEAPONS!!

WITH THE SOUND OF THEIR FOOT-STEPS, AND THEIR BREATHING TO GUIDE ME, I CAN'T MISS!

BUT SUDDENLY, THE MASKED ADVENTURER HALTS IN HIS TRACKS, HIS SUPER-SHARP SENSES ANALYZING A NEW, MENACING SOUND!

THE SOUND OF A TRUCK STARTING! COMING TOWARDS ME! I HAVEN'T ENOUGH ROOM TO DODGE! ONLY ONE THING TO DO...!!

I'LL USE A TIRE AS A SLINGSHOT, AND THIS ENGINE AS A MISSILE! THE SOUND IS GETTING CLOSER... JUST ONE MORE SECOND, AND NOW...

THIS'LL FINISH HIM AND... HEY! LOOK WHAT HE'S DOING! CAN'T STOP IN TIME!

WHOOM!!

A FEW SECONDS LATER, AFTER THE SMOKE HAS CLEARED...

THAT'S RIGHT, LIEUTENANT! YOU'LL FIND THE ENTIRE GANG OF CAR THIEVES HERE, ALL GIFT-WRAPPED FOR YOU! ALTHOUGH I'M SORRY THEIR BOSS WASN'T HERE!

I WOULDN'T WANNA BE IN DAREDEVIL'S SHOES WHEN THE BOSS FINDS OUT ABOUT THIS!

YEAH! ELECTRO WILL MAKE MINCE-MEAT OUTTA HIM!

ELECTRO!! THE MASTER OF ELECTRICITY! THE ARCH-VILLAIN WHO ALMOST DEFEATED THE AMAZING SPIDER-MAN HIMSELF NOT LONG AGO!!* THE SUPER-MENACE WHO IS WATCHING THE ENTIRE SCENE RIGHT NOW!!

BAH! I WAS BORED WITH STEALING CARS, ANY-WAY!

* SPIDER-MAN #9...EDITOR

WHO IS ELECTRO?? HOW DID HE BECOME THE EVIL MONARCH OF ELECTRIC-ITY HE IS? FOR THOSE OF YOU LUCKLESS ENOUGH TO HAVE MISSED SPIDER-MAN #9, WE'LL REVEAL THAT HE ONCE HAD BEEN AN ELECTRIC LINEMAN NAMED MAX DILLON! ONE DAY, WHILE ON A HIGH-TENSION REPAIR JOB...LIGHTNING STRUCK HIM...

I SHOULD HAVE BEEN KILLED... BUT I'M NOT!

MY ENTIRE BODY IS ELECTRICALLY CHARGED!

THEN, DILLON DESIGNED A COSTUME FOR HIM-SELF...

I'LL USE MY GREAT NEW POWER TO PREY ON HELP-LESS HUMANITY!

I'LL CALL MYSELF ELECTRO, AND NOBODY HUMAN CAN STOP ME!

AND THUS WAS BORN ONE OF THE MOST DANGEROUS VILLAINS OF ALL TIME!

6.

LATER...IN A HIDDEN HIDEOUT...

...AND THE FAMOUS *FANTASTIC FOUR* ARE EN ROUTE TO THE NATION'S CAPITAL, WHERE THEY ARE TO RECEIVE A PRESIDENTIAL MEDAL! THAT WINDS UP OUR SIX O'CLOCK NEWS...

HMM! VERY INTERESTING!

I'VE THOUGHT OF A CRIME *WORTHY* OF MY GREAT POWERS!!

WHILE THE F.F. ARE OUT OF TOWN, I'LL BREAK INTO THEIR HEADQUARTERS! I'LL STEAL THEIR SCIENTIFIC SECRETS AND SELL THEM TO A HOSTILE NATION FOR A *FORTUNE!!*

MEANWHILE, LITTLE DREAMING OF THE DEADLY BATTLE FATE IS PREPARING FOR HIM, THE MAN CALLED *DAREDEVIL* CHANGES BACK TO NORMAL IDENTITY... BECOMING THE HANDSOME BLIND LAWYER, *MATT MURDOCK!*

BREAKING UP STOLEN-CAR GANGS IS TOO SIMPLE FOR SOMEONE WITH MY POWERS! I ALMOST WISH I HAD A MORE DIFFICULT CHALLENGE TO FACE! OH, WELL, MAYBE SOMEDAY...

A SHORT TIME LATER, AT THE LAW OFFICES OF NELSON AND MURDOCK...

HELLO, MATT! WISH YOU'D BEEN HERE SOONER!

WHY, FOGGY? DID I MISS A CLIENT?

YOU SURE *DID*, MR. MURDOCK! IT WAS THE *THING* HIMSELF!

HE WANTS YOU TO INSPECT THE F.F. HEADQUARTERS AND MAKE SURE THE NEW LEASE THEY'RE ABOUT TO SIGN IS ALL IN ORDER!

I'LL BE GLAD TO, KAREN! I'LL LEAVE IN A FEW MINUTES!

KAREN HAS *ANOTHER* PIECE OF NEWS FOR YOU, MATT! TELL HIM ABOUT IT...

I WROTE TO AN EYE SPECIALIST IN MY HOME TOWN! I DESCRIBED YOUR FORM OF BLINDNESS, AND HE HAS OPERATED ON CASES LIKE YOURS BEFORE! HE THINKS HE CAN *CURE* YOU! YOU'LL BE ABLE TO *SEE* AGAIN!

I'LL READ HIS LETTER TO YOU...

A FEW SECONDS LATER...

IT'S VERY INTERESTING, KAREN! I'LL THINK ABOUT IT A WHILE...

YOU DON'T SOUND VERY PLEASED...

FORGIVE ME, KAREN! IT'S JUST THAT I...EH..DON'T WANT TO BE DISAPPOINTED!

7.

POOR MATT MURDOCK! HE'S SO HANDSOME...SO INTELLIGENT... SO DOGGONE **WONDERFUL!** I'D MARRY HIM IN A MINUTE, EVEN THOUGH HE'S BLIND...IF ONLY HE'D ASK ME! BUT, FOR **HIS** SAKE, I PRAY HE'LL REGAIN HIS SIGHT SOMEDAY!

BUT MATT MURDOCK'S THOUGHTS ARE EXACTLY THE **OPPOSITE** OF HIS LOVELY SECRETARY'S...

I **KNOW** THERE'S A CHANCE OF GETTING MY EYESIGHT BACK BY AN OPERATION... BUT I'M AFRAID TO RISK IT! I'M AFRAID I MIGHT LOSE MY **OTHER** POWERS IF MY SIGHT RETURNS! I STILL REMEMBER THE ACCIDENT IN WHICH I LOST MY SIGHT...

I HAD SAVED AN OLD MAN FROM BEING HIT BY A SPEEDING TRUCK, AND THE TRUCK STRUCK **ME** INSTEAD! THEN, IN THE HOSPITAL, I LEARNED MY FATE!

BUT THE TRUCK HAD CARRIED **RADIO- ACTIVE** MATERIALS WHICH HAD HIT MY EYES! ...AND THEY SHARPENED MY REMAINING SENSES MANY TIMES MORE THAN NORMAL!

I DARE NOT DO ANYTHING WHICH MAY **LOSE** ME MY SUPER- SHARP SENSES... THE SENSES THAT MAKE ME... **DAREDEVIL!**

SO, I MUST CONTINUE TO REFUSE THE OPERATION, FOR I'D RATHER BE BLIND AND BE **DAREDEVIL,** THAN BE AN AVERAGE NORMAL MAN!

I'LL BE BACK AFTER I'VE CHECKED THE F.F. HEAD- QUARTERS! TAKE ANY MESSAGES FOR ME!

MEANWHILE, AS MATT LEAVES HIS OFFICE, TAPPING THE CANE WHICH HE REALLY DOESN'T NEED, DUE TO HIS BUILT-IN **RADAR-SENSE...**

IT'S A SIMPLE MATTER FOR ME TO RAISE MYSELF TO THE TOP FLOORS OF THE BAXTER BUILDING BY USING THE POWER OF THE ELECTRIC CABLES WHICH RUN UP THE INSIDE OF THE WALLS!

AND, BEING MASTER OF ELECTRICITY, I CAN DE- ACTIVATE ALL OF **MR. FANTASTIC'S** ELECTRONIC ALARMS, THEREBY ENTERING THROUGH THE WINDOW WITH EASE!

AND, IN THE STREET BELOW, NOT SUSPECTING THE DREAD DANGER WHICH AWAITS HIM ABOVE...

I CAN VISUALIZE THE SHAPE OF THE BAXTER BUILDING BY THE SOUND OF THE AIR CURRENTS HITTING IT...JUST AS EASILY AS IF I COULD **SEE** IT!

THEN, MATT MURDOCK REACHES THE TOWER FLOOR OF THE BAXTER BUILDING, ADMITTED INTO THE GUARDED AREA BECAUSE THE ELECTRONIC ALARM DEVICES MATCH HIS FACE WITH THE PHOTOGRAPH THEY HAVE BEEN "FED"! BUT, SUDDENLY HIS SUPER-SHARP SENSES REACT TO A FEELING OF DANGER, AND HE INSTANTLY CHANGES INTO... *DAREDEVIL*, SECONDS BEFORE ELECTRO TOUCHES A VISOR-SWITCH...

THE AUTOMATIC RECEPTIONIST IS *BUZZING!* SOMEONE IS ENTERING! I'LL SEE WHO IT IS!

SLOWLY, AN IMAGE BEGINS TO FORM ON THE GLEAMING SCREEN...

AN IMAGE WHICH REVEALS...

DAREDEVIL! THE ONE WHO SMASHED MY AUTO THEFT GANG! WHAT A LUCKY BREAK FOR ME!

I DON'T KNOW WHY HE'S HERE... BUT HE'S GIVING ME A CHANCE TO GET MY *REVENGE* ON HIM FOR SPOILING MY LITTLE SIDE-LINE!

HE MOVES CAUTIOUSLY... AS THOUGH HE'S EXPECTING DANGER! BUT HE CAN'T *POSSIBLY* EXPECT WHAT'S GOING TO HAPPEN NEXT!

THE ELECTRICAL MACHINES OF MR. FANTASTIC ARE AMONG THE MOST POWERFUL IN THE WORLD... AND ALL THE CONTROLS ARE AT *MY* FINGERTIPS!

AND WHAT'S MORE ...*ELECTRO* IS THE MASTER OF ELECTRICITY! *MY* POWER... PLUS THESE MACHINES, CAN ACCOMPLISH *ANYTHING*... AS DAREDEVIL WILL NOW LEARN!

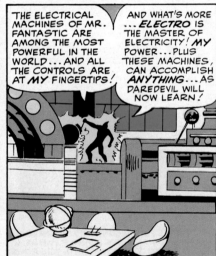

AT THAT INSTANT, THE MASKED CRIME-FIGHTER'S UNCANNY HEARING DETECTS THE SOUND OF AN ELECTRICAL CHARGE BEING ACTIVATED... BUT, BEFORE HE CAN ACT...

I HEAR A MIGHTY *DYNAMO* BEING CHARGED! IT MEANS THAT SOMEONE IS ---≷ UHH!! ≶

I'M SURROUNDED BY A VIBRATING WALL OF ELECTRICAL ENERGY!! IT'S CLOSING IN ON ME... ABOUT TO ELECTROCUTE ME!!

9.

BUT THE MAN WITHOUT FEAR IS NOT TO BE DEFEATED SO EASILY!!

MY CANE IS A NON-CONDUCTOR! I'LL HURL IT AT THE SOURCE!

GOOD! GOOD! HE IS A FOE WORTHY OF MY METTLE! HE SHORT-CIRCUITED THE CURRENT JUST IN TIME! BUT HE IS MERELY PROLONGING MY PLEASURE!

THEN, LIKE A CAT PLAYING WITH A MOUSE, ELECTRO HURLS BOLT AFTER BOLT OF LIVE CURRENT AT DAREDEVIL, CAUSING THE MASKED WONDER MAN TO EMPLOY HIS RAZOR SHARP SENSES TO THE FULLEST EXTENT!

CRACK!

CRASH!

CAN'T DODGE THESE BLASTS MUCH LONGER! I'VE GOT TO FIND THE LIGHT SWITCH!

THEN, AS THE SINISTER ARCH-VILLAIN PAUSES TO PREPARE FOR A NEW ATTACK, DAREDEVIL'S INCREDIBLE SENSE OF TOUCH FINDS WHAT HE'S AFTER!

I'VE GOT IT! JUST IN TIME!!

THERE! I'VE PLUNGED THE ROOM INTO DARKNESS! NOW THE ODDS ARE ON MY SIDE! WAIT... WHAT'S THIS I FEEL??

IT'S A DUMB-BELL OF SOME SORT! IT WILL MAKE A PERFECT WEAPON TO HURL AT MY UNSEEN ENEMY!

BUT, THEN DAREDEVIL MAKES HIS FIRST SERIOUS BLUNDER! THE WEIGHT HE HOLDS BELONGS TO THE THING, BOLTED TO A SPRING CABLE BENEATH THE FLOOR WHICH EVEN DAREDEVIL'S MIGHTY MUSCLES CANNOT BUDGE!

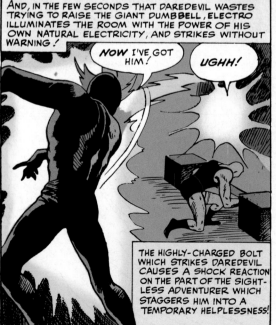

AND, IN THE FEW SECONDS THAT DAREDEVIL WASTES TRYING TO RAISE THE GIANT DUMBBELL, ELECTRO ILLUMINATES THE ROOM WITH THE POWER OF HIS OWN NATURAL ELECTRICITY, AND STRIKES WITHOUT WARNING!

NOW I'VE GOT HIM!

UGHH!

THE HIGHLY-CHARGED BOLT WHICH STRIKES DAREDEVIL CAUSES A SHOCK REACTION ON THE PART OF THE SIGHT-LESS ADVENTURER WHICH STAGGERS HIM INTO A TEMPORARY HELPLESSNESS!

AND, BEFORE THE MASKED CRIME-FIGHTER CAN RECOVER HIMSELF, ELECTRO LASHES OUT IN A MERCILESS ATTACK!

SURELY YOU DON'T THINK YOU HAVE A CHANCE AGAINST THE ONE WHO ALMOST DEFEATED SPIDER-MAN HIMSELF!?

I WAS A FOOL TO RELAX MY GUARD... I...OHHH!

CRACK!

HE STRUCK HIS HEAD AGAINST THE GIANT DUMBBELL! HE'LL BE UNCONSCIOUS LONG ENOUGH FOR ME TO MAKE SURE HE CAN NEVER INTERFERE WITH ELECTRO AGAIN!

I MUST FIND A FITTING FATE FOR HIM...ONE WORTHY OF THE INGENUITY OF THE MASTER OF ELECTRICITY! HERE, AMONG THE MARVELOUS POSSESSIONS OF THE FANTASTIC FOUR, I'M SURE TO FIND WHAT I WANT!

OF COURSE! HERE IT IS!! HOW PERFECT! HOW SIMPLE... AND HOW FOOLPROOF! HERE IS THE WORLD-FAMOUS SKY-SCRAPER ROCKET LAUNCHER OF THE FF!!

ALL I NEED DO IS PUT THE HELPLESS BODY OF DAREDEVIL ABOARD THE SHIP AND SEND IT FAR OUT INTO SPACE...ON AN ETERNAL ONE-WAY JOURNEY!! WHEN THE BEWILDERED FANTASTIC FOUR RETURN, THEY'LL THINK DAREDEVIL HAD STOLEN THEIR ROCKET!

THIS WILL ONLY BE THE FIRST OF MANY TRIUMPHS FOR ME! NOTHING THAT LIVES CAN DEFEAT A MAN WHO IS MASTER OF ELECTRICITY!

NOW THAT HE'S SAFELY ABOARD, I NEED ONLY SEAL THE HATCH AND SET THE MISSILE FOR ITS LAUNCHING! THANKS TO THE UNWITTING GENIUS OF REED RICHARDS, THE WORLD WILL NEVER AGAIN SET EYES ON THE ONE CALLED DAREDEVIL!

WHIRRR!

CLANK!

11.

36

BUT THEN...

WHAT'S *WRONG??!* I'VE WORKED THE CONTROLS *PERFECTLY*, BUT NOTHING IS HAPPENING!! PERHAPS RICHARDS *ISN'T* THE GENIUS I THOUGHT HE WAS!

AND, A SPLIT-SECOND LATER...

EVEN THE SHREWD, SLY ELECTRO DOES NOT SUSPECT THAT MR. FANTASTIC IS *MORE* BRILLIANT THAN HE THOUGHT! FOR, TO GUARD AGAINST THE VERY ACT ELECTRO IS TRYING TO COMMIT, REED RICHARDS' LAUNCHING DEVICE WILL ONLY RESPOND TO A HUMAN BEING HAVING THE SAME MOLECULAR BODY STRUCTURE AS ONE OF THE FANTASTIC FOUR!!

IT'S *HOPELESS!* I CAN'T GET IT TO RESPOND!

ANY *OTHER* ARCH-FOE WOULD HAVE BEEN HELPLESS TO ACTIVATE THE MIGHTY MISSILE, BUT *ELECTRO* IS DIFFERENT! FOR WITHIN HIS OWN BODY HE POSSESSES ENOUGH ELECTRICAL ENERGY TO *FORCE* THE LAUNCHING DEVICE TO OPERATE... USING HIS OWN SUPERNATURAL POWER AS THE CATALYST!

BAH! I DON'T *NEED* HIS LAUNCHER! I *MYSELF* CAN GENERATE ENOUGH POWER TO HURL THE MISSILE INTO SPACE!

CRACK!

TICK-TICK-TICK-

ROAR-RRR!

FARE-WELL, FOREVER, DARE-DEVIL!!

37

SO QUICKLY IS THE ROCKET LAUNCHED...SO POWERFUL ARE THE MIGHTY JETS DESIGNED BY REED RICHARDS, THAT THE GLEAMING SLEEK SPACECRAFT REACHES THE EDGE OF EARTH'S ATMOSPHERE IN A MATTER OF SHEER SECONDS !!!

WHILE WITHIN ITS AIRTIGHT HULL, THE MAGNIFICENTLY MUSCLED BODY OF DARE-DEVIL BEGINS TO STIR, AS CONSCIOUSNESS SLOWLY RETURNS...

UNTIL... ELECTRO KNOCKED ME OUT! MY HANDS ARE TIED! I'VE GOT TO THINK...FIND A WAY TO ESCAPE! WHEREVER I AM, I'M ALONE! I HEAR NO OTHER HEARTBEATS...NO SOUND OF BREATHING!

FIRST, I MUST UNTIE MY HANDS! IT'S AN *EASY* MATTER FOR ONE WHOSE SENSE OF TOUCH IS SO KEEN THAT HE CAN FEEL EACH AND EVERY STRESS POINT OF THE KNOTTED CORD, AND LOOSEN THEM BY TENSING AND UN-TENSING THE PROPER MUSCLES TO THE NECESSARY DEGREE! *

*NOTE: IT IS BELIEVED THAT THE GREAT MAGICIAN HARRY HOUDINI MAY HAVE USED THIS METHOD FOR HIS FAMOUS ESCAPE ACT... EDITOR.

ONCE FREE OF HIS BONDS, THE MAN WITHOUT FEAR SOON REALIZES HIS DESPERATE PERIL!

THOSE HUMMING ROCKET ENGINES...THIS SENSATION OF LESSENING GRAVITY... MEAN ONLY ONE THING!!

ELECTRO HAS SHUT ME IN THE F.F.'S SPACE MISSILE AND LAUNCHED IT TOWARD THE STARS !!

BUT MR. FANTASTIC ORIGINALLY DESIGNED THIS AS A *MANNED* ROCKET... SO IT MUST HAVE A CONTROL ROOM, WITH OPERATION-AL CONTROLS! IF I CAN WORK THEM IN TIME...!

IMAGINE A BLIND MAN OPERATING A SPACE SHIP!! NOT AS IMPOSSIBLE AS IT SEEMS IF THAT MAN CAN HEAR THE LEVERS MOVE, *FEEL* THE POWER NEEDED, *SENSE* THE DIRECTION OF FLIGHT!!

I'VE *DONE* IT! I'VE REVERSED THE MISSILE'S COURSE !!

CLICK! CLICK!

AND THEN, THE MOST INCREDIBLE TASK OF ALL BEGINS...THE TASK OF *LANDING* THE POWERFUL SPACESHIP BACK ON EARTH WITHOUT INJURING ANY HAPLESS HUMANS!

BY HEARING THE SLIGHT MOVE-MENT OF THE ASTRO-COMPASS, I CAN GAUGE MY DIRECTION PERFECTLY! AND BY *FEELING* THE ACTION OF THE RADARSCOPE I CAN PINPOINT MY LANDING! I'LL BRING THE SHIP DOWN IN THE MIDDLE OF *CENTRAL PARK* IN NEW YORK, FINDING AN OPEN SPOT WHERE I HEAR NO HUMAN HEARTBEATS!

13.

Only a man with super-senses could have done it! But, such a man is *DAREDEVIL*!! Then, moments later...

VOICES GATHERING! HEARTBEATS INCREASING! A *CROWD* IS FORMING!

DON'T MOVE, MISTER! WE'VE GOT *LAWS* AGAINST ENDANGERING PEOPLE AND PROPERTY THAT WAY!

I'VE GOT TO MOVE FAST! CAN'T LET THEM BOOK ME! THEY'LL TRY TO LEARN MY REAL IDENTITY!

HEARING THE SOFT WHINNY OF A HORSE NEARBY, THE COSTUMED CHAMPION MOVES LIKE A FLASHING STREAK, LEAPING UPON ITS BACK WITH PERFECT COORDINATION!

IF I CAN LOOSE THIS HORSE FROM THE HANSOM CAB BEHIND IT, IT'LL BE MY BEST METHOD OF ESCAPE!

STOP!!

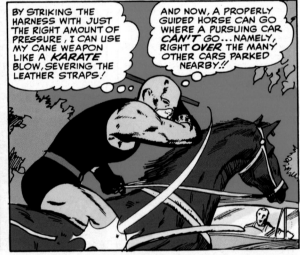

BY STRIKING THE HARNESS WITH JUST THE RIGHT AMOUNT OF PRESSURE, I CAN USE MY CANE WEAPON LIKE A *KARATE* BLOW, SEVERING THE LEATHER STRAPS!

AND NOW, A PROPERLY GUIDED HORSE CAN GO WHERE A PURSUING CAR *CAN'T* GO...NAMELY, RIGHT *OVER* THE MANY OTHER CARS PARKED NEARBY!!

IT'S EASY FOR ME TO DIRECT MY MOUNT OVER THE TRAFFIC, FOR THE SOUND OF EACH CAR'S ENGINE IS LIKE A BEACON TO ME...AND THE ODOR OF THE GASOLINE, MAGNIFIED MANY TIMES BY MY SUPER SENSE OF SMELL, IS UNMISTAKABLE!

BUT, AS THE GALLOPING BEAST TURNS THE CORNER BELOW THE SOARING BAXTER BUILDING...

I HEAR A FLAG RUSTLING IN THE BREEZE ABOVE ME! I'LL SWING TO THE SECOND FLOOR AND REGAIN MY MATT MURDOCK CLOTHES WHERE I LEFT THEM BEFORE ANYONE CAN PICK UP MY TRAIL!

14

MINUTES LATER, THE HANDSOME FIGURE OF MATT MURDOCK SEEMS TO BLEND IN WITH THE PASSING CROWD, UNTIL A LOVELY VOICE, BELONGING TO AN EQUALLY LOVELY GIRL, CRIES OUT...

MR. MURDOCK! IT'S KAREN! MR. MURDOCK... DON'T YOU *HEAR* ME ??

KAREN PAGE! MY SECRETARY! CAN'T STOP NOW.. MUSTN'T GIVE ELECTRO A CHANCE TO ESCAPE!

* I *KNOW* HE HEARD ME, BUT HE DELIBERATELY IGNORED ME! COULD I HAVE OFFENDED HIM WHEN I MENTIONED THAT OPERATION BEFORE ??

HOW STARTLED KAREN PAGE WOULD BE IF SHE KNEW THE *REAL* REASON THAT MATT MURDOCK RUSHED PAST HER !!

THERE IS NO WAY I CAN RETURN TO THE F.F. HEADQUARTERS WITHOUT ELECTRO BEING WARNED BY MR. FANTASTIC'S MANY SECRET ALARMS! OR, *IS* THERE ??

TAKING THE ELEVATOR TO THE ROOF OF THE *HELIPORT* BUILDING, MATT QUICKLY CHANGES TO *DAREDEVIL* ONCE AGAIN, AND THEN...

THE ONLY WAY TO ATTACK ELECTRO SUDDENLY, WITHOUT WARNING, IS TO DROP DOWN ON HIM FROM ABOVE! IT'S ONE CHANCE IN A MILLION, BUT I'VE *GOT* TO TAKE IT!!

FROM THE SOUND OF THE MOTOR, I CAN TELL THAT THE SIGHTSEEING HELICOPTER IS ABOUT TO TAKE OFF! IT'S DIRECTLY AHEAD! I'VE GOT TO REACH IT IN TIME!

CAN'T AFFORD TO WAIT FOR THE NEXT ONE! ELECTRO WON'T REMAIN ATOP THE BAXTER BUILDING FOREVER! IN FACT, I HOPE I'M NOT TOO LATE EVEN NOW!

AND THEN, ONE OF THE MOST DARING FEATS EVER RECORDED IS WITNESSED BY THE FEW STARTLED ONLOOKERS ATOP THE N.Y. HELIPORT! BEFORE THEIR EYES THEY SEE A COLORFUL, WELL-MUSCLED FIGURE IN A DRAMATIC COSTUME LEAP INTO THE AIR, CATCHING ONTO THE UNDERSIDE OF THE DEPARTING HELICOPTER BY A CANE HANDLE!

MADE IT !!

BUT, HOW MUCH *GREATER* WOULD THEIR SHOCK AND SUR-PRISE BE, IF THEY COULD BUT SUSPECT THAT THE INCREDIBLE FEAT THEY ARE WITNESSING IS PERFORMED BY...A *BLIND MAN* !!

15

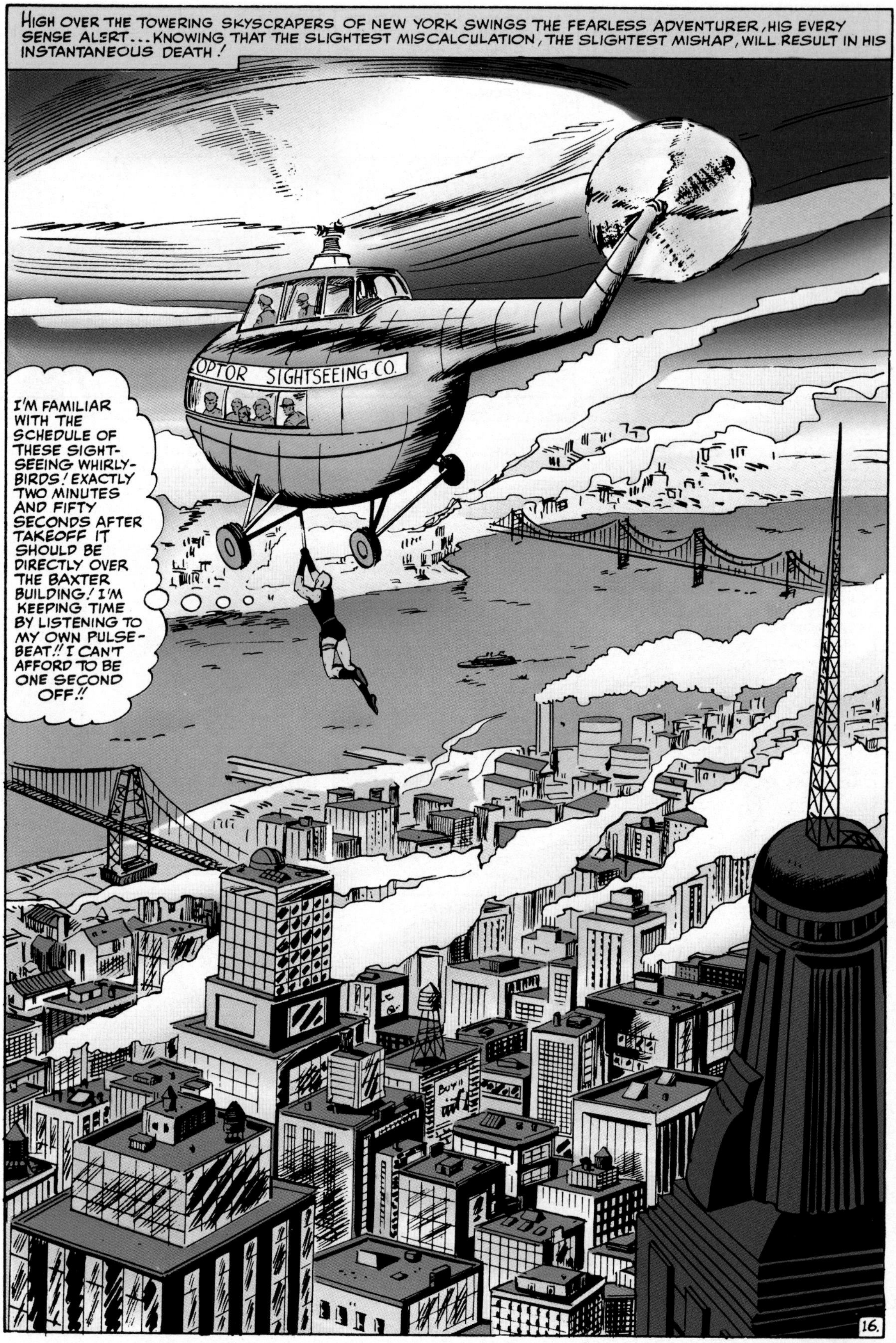
HIGH OVER THE TOWERING SKYSCRAPERS OF NEW YORK SWINGS THE FEARLESS ADVENTURER, HIS EVERY SENSE ALERT... KNOWING THAT THE SLIGHTEST MISCALCULATION, THE SLIGHTEST MISHAP, WILL RESULT IN HIS INSTANTANEOUS DEATH!
OPTOR SIGHTSEEING CO.
I'M FAMILIAR WITH THE SCHEDULE OF THESE SIGHT-SEEING WHIRLY-BIRDS! EXACTLY TWO MINUTES AND FIFTY SECONDS AFTER TAKEOFF IT SHOULD BE DIRECTLY OVER THE BAXTER BUILDING! I'M KEEPING TIME BY LISTENING TO MY OWN PULSE-BEAT!! I CAN'T AFFORD TO BE ONE SECOND OFF!!
BUY!!
16.

MEANTIME, WE FIND ELECTRO STILL WITHIN THE F.F. HEADQUARTERS, APPLYING HIS AWESOME POWERS TO REED RICHARDS' PRIVATE VAULT...

THE ELECTRICAL ENERGY I CAN GENERATE IS MORE THAN ENOUGH TO CUT THROUGH ANY STEEL VAULT DOOR EVER BUILT!!

I *DID* IT! AND NOW, ALL THE SECRETS OF MR. FANTASTIC SHALL BE *MINE!*

THUD!

JUST AS I EXPECTED! ALL SORTS OF MATHEMATICAL EQUATIONS AND NOTES!! *I* CAN'T UNDERSTAND THEM, BUT THEY'LL BE WORTH A *FORTUNE* TO ANY FOREIGN POWER I CONTACT!

AND, DIRECTLY ABOVE...

EXACTLY TWO MINUTES AND FIFTY SECONDS.. AND I CAN SENSE A GREAT SURGE OF ELECTRICAL POWER DIRECTLY BENEATH ME!

A PAIR OF EYES CAN BE DECEIVED...BUT ALL MY SENSES TOGETHER CAN NEVER BE MISTAKEN! *THIS* IS THE SPLIT SECOND! THE SKYLIGHT MUST BE RIGHT BELOW ME!

AND THEN...

MADE IT! IN EXACTLY ONE HALF SECOND, I'LL DO A COMPLETE SOMER-SAULT, BREAKING MY FALL, AND ENABLING ME TO LAND GENTLY ON MY FEET!

DAREDEVIL!!!

17.

IT'S *IMPOSSIBLE!!* NOBODY COULD HAVE ESCAPED FROM THAT MISSILE!! I SAW IT HEAD FOR SPACE *MYSELF!!*

NOBODY *COULD* HAVE ESCAPED...EXCEPT *DAREDEVIL!!*

THERE'S NO NEED FOR ME TO FIGHT YOU NOW! I'VE *GOT* WHAT I WANT!

ONCE I BURN THROUGH THE ELEVATOR DOOR AND REACH THE ELECTRIC CABLE, EVEN DAREDEVIL WILL NEVER BE ABLE TO CATCH ME!!

I THINK I KNOW WHAT HE'S PLANNING...BUT I CAN'T LET HIM GET AWAY WITH IT!!

I *THOUGHT* SO! I CAN TELL BY THE SOUND! HE'S SLIDING DOWN THE ELECTRIC CABLES BY MEANS OF HIS OWN ELECTRICAL POWER! HE'LL REACH THE STREET IN SECONDS!

FAREWELL, DAREDEVIL!! IF YOU SHOULD SEE THE FANTASTIC FOUR, THANK THEM FOR THEIR SECRET FORMULAE! I'M SURE AN ENEMY NATION WILL PAY ME A *FORTUNE* FOR THEM!

SO! HE'S ESCAPING WITH THE F.F.'S SCIENTIFIC SECRETS!! NOW I *DARE* NOT LET HIM ESCAPE! OUR ENTIRE NATION'S SECURITY MAY BE AT STAKE!! WELL, WHERE ELECTRO CAN GO, DAREDEVIL CAN FOLLOW!

WITHOUT A SECOND THOUGHT, THE MAN WITHOUT FEAR HURLS HIMSELF INTO THE ELEVATOR SHAFT, THIRTY-FIVE STORIES ABOVE STREET LEVEL!! THEN, WAVING HIS CANE FRANTICALLY, UNTIL THE CURVED HANDLE CATCHES ONTO THE ELEVATOR CABLE, HE SWINGS HIMSELF AROUND THE MOMENTUM OF HIS LUNGE CARRYING HIM 'ROUND AND 'ROUND THE CABLE LIKE A PIN-WHEEL, BREAKING HIS FALL AND ENABLING HIM TO MAKE HIS DESCENT SMOOTHLY AND SWIFTLY!!

THIS IS ONE OF THE TIMES I'M *LUCKY* TO BE BLIND! IF I COULD *SEE* WHAT I'M DOING, I MIGHT BE SCARED STIFF!!

18.

SECONDS LATER, AFTER THE TWO ANTAGONISTS HAVE REACHED THE STREET...

NO MATTER WHERE HE RUNS, THE SOUND OF HIS RACING FEET IS LIKE DRUMBEATS TO MY EARS!

IT'S INCREDIBLE!! I HAVE ALL THE POWERS OF ELECTRICITY AT MY COMMAND, AND YET DAREDEVIL, WITH NOTHING BUT HIS OWN SKILL AND STRENGTH, MANAGES TO THWART ME AT EVERY TURN!

I'LL USE MY ELECTRIC MAGNETISM TO HITCH A RIDE ATOP THIS CAR! THIS IS ONE FEAT THAT DAREDEVIL WON'T BE ABLE TO DUPLICATE!!

THE FOOTSTEPS HAVE STOPPED! IT CAN MEAN ONLY ONE THING! HE'S HOPPED ONTO A CAR!!

LUCKILY I CAN STILL SENSE ELECTRICAL VIBRATIONS! THEY'RE STRONG ENOUGH TO GUIDE ME IN THE RIGHT DIRECTION! I HAVEN'T LOST HIM YET!

A CAR WON'T HELP ELECTRO IN THIS MIDTOWN NEW YORK TRAFFIC! I CAN MAKE FASTER TIME BY RUNNING FROM ROOF TO ROOF WHILE THEY ALL STOP FOR THE TRAFFIC LIGHTS!

GUIDED BY THE POWERFUL ELECTRIC EMANATIONS FROM HIS BODY, I CAN'T MISS HIM!

TAXI

FINALLY, REALIZING HE CANNOT HOPE TO OUTDISTANCE HIS RELENTLESS PURSUER IN THE STREETS, ELECTRO USES HIS AMAZING POWER TO DRAW HIM UNDER A THEATER MARQUEE AS HE HEADS FOR THE INTERIOR OF ONE OF THE LARGEST AND MOST LUXURIOUS MOVIE HOUSES IN THE CITY...

THE SOUNDS OF MANY VOICES...FLICKERING BULBS...TICKETS BEING TORN AND CHANGING HANDS...IT CAN MEAN ONLY ONE THING! ELECTRO IS RACING INTO A MOVIE THEATER!

IF HE FOLLOWS ME IN HERE, IT'LL BE HIS UNDOING! THERE ARE COUNTLESS FORMS OF ELECTRICITY INSIDE, WHICH I'LL BE ABLE TO USE AGAINST HIM!

FIRST RUN NEW YORK

19.

44

THEN, INSIDE THE PALATIAL SHOWPLACE, WHERE A STAGE REVUE IS IN PROGRESS...

I CAN SMELL BURNING IONS! IT'S INCREDIBLE! ELECTRO IS PROPELLING HIMSELF TOWARDS THE STAGE BY THE ELECTRICAL ATTRACTION OF THE METAL SEAT PLATES IN THE **THEATER AISLE!**

THE ELECTRIC CHARGE OF HIS BODY IS SO POWERFUL THAT I CAN ESTIMATE HIS EXACT SPEED... AND THE SOUND OF HIS OVER-ACTIVE PULSE RATE IS ENOUGH TO LEAD ME UNERRINGLY AFTER HIM!

MAY I SEE YOUR TICKET, PLEASE? I SAID...I..I.. ~ULP!~

EACH ELECTRIC BULB I PASS...EACH LIVE WIRE...EACH CIRCUIT AND SWITCH INCREASES MY POWER AS MY BODY **ABSORBS** THEIR ENERGY

THE TEMPERATURE HAS RISEN 27 DEGREES! IT CAN ONLY MEAN ARC LIGHTS, INDICATING A STAGE SHOW! AND THE SCENT OF PERFUME AND THEATRI-CAL MAKE-UP...SHOW-GIRLS!! THEY'RE SCREAMING! THEY MUST SEE **ELECTRO!**

FROM THE SOUND OF THE GIRLS' CRIES, THEIR HEADS ARE TILTED BACK! THEY'RE LOOKING UP!! I HEAR A RUSTLING IN THE CURTAINS ABOVE ME! ELECTRO MUST BE ON THE CATWALK OVERHEAD!

WITH ALL THE GUIDE ROPES AND CABLES HANGING IN THE WINGS, EVEN A MAN WITHOUT SIGHT CAN MAKE HIS WAY ABOVE EASILY ENOUGH!

I DIDN'T THINK YOU'D BE STUPID ENOUGH TO FOLLOW ME UP HERE, DAREDEVIL! EVEN YOUR STRENGTH AND AGILITY WON'T PROTECT YOU AGAINST MY ELECTRIC BOLTS!

OHHH! THAT FELT LIKE THE KICK OF A MULE!! THE PEOPLE BELOW WERE SCREAMING SO LOUD THAT I COULDN'T HEAR ELECTRO'S BOLT FLASHING TOWARD ME...WASN'T ABLE TO DODGE!

20.

45

I'M *FALLING!* HAVE TO REACH OUT WITH MY CANE HANDLE... FAST!!

I'M IN LUCK!! CAUGHT ON TO SOMETHING!

LOOKS LIKE MY *FINISH!* HE'S TOSSING MORE *BOLTS!* HE'S JUST *TOYING* WITH ME NOW!

HE'LL KNOCK ME OFF AGAIN, WHENEVER HE'S READY, UNLESS... *WAIT!* MY FINGER TIPS FEEL LINES OF ELECTRIC ENERGY BENEATH THEM! IT MEANS WIRES.. LEADING TO A CENTRAL CONTROL BOX!!

IT MUST BE THE CONTROL PANEL FOR THE MOVING CURTAINS!! I'LL REACH IN THE DIRECTION OF THE CURRENT'S FLOW, AND IF I'M LUCKY...

WHERE IS YOUR FOOLISH CONFIDENCE *NOW,* DAREDEVIL?? OR, HAS IT *DESERTED* YOU, BECAUSE YOUR TIME IS UP?!!

AND NOW, I'VE *TIRED* OF THIS *GAME!* AND SO, I'LL FINISH YOU OFF, AND... *WHA...??* WHAT'S *THAT??* OH... NO!

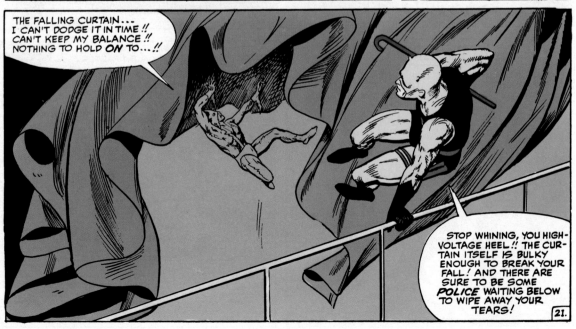

THE FALLING CURTAIN... I CAN'T DODGE IT IN TIME!! CAN'T KEEP MY BALANCE!! NOTHING TO HOLD *ON* TO....!!

STOP WHINING, YOU HIGH-VOLTAGE HEEL!! THE CURTAIN ITSELF IS BULKY ENOUGH TO BREAK YOUR FALL! AND THERE ARE SURE TO BE SOME *POLICE* WAITING BELOW TO WIPE AWAY YOUR TEARS!

21.

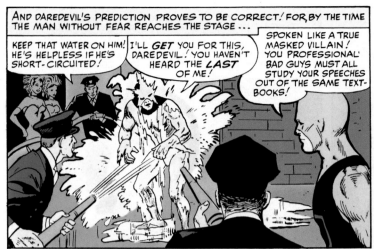

AND DAREDEVIL'S PREDICTION PROVES TO BE CORRECT! FOR BY THE TIME THE MAN WITHOUT FEAR REACHES THE STAGE...

KEEP THAT WATER ON HIM! HE'S HELPLESS IF HE'S SHORT-CIRCUITED!

I'LL *GET* YOU FOR THIS, DAREDEVIL! YOU HAVEN'T HEARD THE *LAST* OF ME!

SPOKEN LIKE A TRUE MASKED VILLAIN! YOU PROFESSIONAL BAD GUYS MUST ALL STUDY YOUR SPEECHES OUT OF THE SAME TEXT-BOOKS!

TWENTY MINUTES LATER, THE COLORFUL ADVENTURER IS BACK AT F.F. HEAD-QUARTERS, PERFORMING A WELDING JOB WHICH EVEN A *SIGHTED* EXPERT WOULD BE PROUD OF!

THERE! RICHARDS' SAFE IS AS GOOD AS NEW AGAIN!

NOW I'LL START WORK ON THE LEASE, AND... *TOO LATE!* I HEAR THE FANTASTI-CAR NEARBY!

RACING FROM THE BAXTER BUILDING TOWER LIKE A SILENT WRAITH, DAREDEVIL QUICKLY CHANGES BACK TO HIS EVERY-DAY IDENTITY, AND... WITHIN MINUTES...

ANYONE KNOW WHERE A FELLA CAN FIND A GOOD LAWYER?

HI, MATT! EVERY-THING ALL TAKEN CARE OF?

MR. MURDOCK! YOU'RE BACK!

BUT, BEFORE THE HANDSOME ATTORNEY CAN ANSWER...

MURDOCK, WE WANNA *SUE* SOME-BODY! WHILE WE WERE GONE, SOME NUT BUSTED OUR SKYLIGHT, AND...

OH *NOOOO!* NOT *AGAIN!!*

MR. GRIMM, WHY DON'T YOU TRY WRITING US A *LETTER* NEXT TIME?!

IT..IT'S THE *THING,* MR. MURDOCK!

THANKS, KAREN! BUT SOME-HOW I FEEL I WOULD HAVE *GUESSED* THAT!!

CRUNCH

WE'LL *REPLACE* THAT DOOR FOR YOU, MURDOCK! AND NOW, MAY WE HAVE YOUR REPORT ABOUT OUR LEASE?

I'M SORRY, MR. RICHARDS! I, EH, JUST DIDN'T HAVE A CHANCE TO *GET* TO IT, YET!

IS ZAT SO? WHAT DO THEY *CALL* YOUR OUTFIT ANYWAY...THE *LIGHTNIN'* BOYS??

NOW, NOW! IF YOU'LL JUST BE PATIENT, I'M SURE MY PARTNER CAN EXPLAIN!

NEVER MIND! WE'LL FIND SOME OTHER LAWYERS...WHO WORK A BIT FASTER!

MATT...*HOW* COULD YOU LOSE US FOUR FAMOUS CLIENTS LIKE *THEM*??

IT WASN'T *EASY,* PARTNER! BELIEVE ME!!

POOR MATT! HIS CLIENTS GONE...HIS PARTNER DISAPPOINTED...ELECTRO OUT TO GET HIM...AND THIS WAS A *SUCCESSFUL* ADVENTURE! IMAGINE IF HE EVER *FAILED!* ANYWAY, MORE THRILLS, GUEST STARS, AND SURPRISES NEXT ISH! DAREDEVIL WILL BE EXPECTING YOU!!

The End

22.

HERE COMES...

DAREDEVIL

APPROVED BY THE COMICS CODE AUTHORITY

IND.

3
AUG.

MARVEL COMICS GROUP 12¢

THE MAN WITHOUT FEAR!

MARVEL'S NEWEST SENSATION IS TRAPPED BY...

THE OWL,

OVERLORD OF CRIME!

DAREDEVIL BATTLES THE OWL, OMINOUS OVERLORD OF CRIME!

A MOVIE-LENGTH ACTION THRILLER PRESENTED WITH PRIDE BY THE MIGHTY MARVEL COMICS GROUP!

WRITTEN WITH RAW REALISM BY: **STAN LEE**

ILLUSTRATED WITH DARING DRAMA BY: **JOE ORLANDO**

INKED WITH ACTUAL ARTISTRY BY: **VINCE COLLETTA**

LETTERED WITH PERFECT PRECISION BY: **S. ROSEN**

X-733

THIS IS WALL STREET, HEART OF NEW YORK'S FINANCIAL DISTRICT, WHERE FORTUNES ARE MADE AND LOST BY THE WORLD'S GREATEST FINANCIAL WIZARDS! AND, WITHIN THE CANYONS OF THIS STREET, WE ARE ABOUT TO FIND ONE CERTAIN MAN...

...A MERCILESS MAN...A MAN WITH NO FRIENDS...NO LOVED ONES... NOTHING TO CONNECT HIM WITH THE HUMAN RACE SAVE THE FACT OF HIS BIRTH! LET US FOLLOW THIS MAN...

LET US STUDY HIM AS HE WALKS INTO A TOWERING OFFICE BUILDING, HIS HEAVY FOOTSTEPS REVERBERATING THROUGH THE HUGE MARBLE LOBBY! FOR WE SHALL SEE MUCH OF THIS MAN ON THE PAGES THAT FOLLOW...

HE WALKS SLOWLY, BUT WITH A SURE, STEADY TREAD... LOOKING NEITHER TO THE RIGHT NOR THE LEFT... IGNORING THOSE HE PASSES AND THOSE WHO PASS HIM!

BUT HE HIMSELF CANNOT READILY BE IGNORED BY OTHERS! HIS VERY PRESENCE SEEMS SO FRAUGHT WITH EVIL, WITH MENACE, THAT HIS FELLOW HUMANS SHRINK BACK FROM THE MERE SIGHT OF HIM!

THERE ARE SOME WHO RECOGNIZE HIM... WHO SPEAK HIS NAME IN WHISPERS... FOR HIS WEALTH IS SAID TO BE LEGENDARY, AND HIS POWER ALMOST BEYOND MEASURE!

BUT THERE IS *ANOTHER* WITH EQUAL POWER WHO SITS DARINGLY PERCHED ON A ROOFTOP ACROSS THE STREET, HIS INCREDIBLY SHARP SENSES WAITING FOR THE SLIGHTEST CALL FOR HELP, WHICH WILL INSTANTLY BRING *DAREDEVIL* INTO ACTION!

EVERYTHING IS QUIET BELOW! THE CITY IS AT PEACE! I AM NOT YET NEEDED!

BUT FATE IS SHAPING EVENTS IN SUCH A WAY THAT DAREDEVIL SOON *WILL* BE NEEDED!... AND ALL BECAUSE OF THE MAN WE HAVE BEEN FOLLOWING...

...THE MAN WHOSE LEGAL NAME IS LONG SINCE FORGOTTEN, FOR HE IS KNOWN TO THE WORLD AT LARGE ONLY AS... *THE OWL*, THE MOST RUTHLESS FINANCIAL WIZARD OF ALL TIME!

ARROGANTLY HE ENTERS HIS PALATIAL OFFICES AS A TIMOROUS FEMALE VOICE INFORMS HIM...

YOU HAVE A CALLER, SIR! MR. GREY IS WAITING IN THE CONFERENCE ROOM!

GREY? THAT SPINELESS MILKSOP?! WHAT CAN *HE* WANT?

I HIRED HIM AS MY ACCOUNTANT SO THAT *HE* WOULD TAKE THE BLAME IF EVER MY ILLEGAL BUSINESS DEALINGS WERE EXPOSED! CAN HE FINALLY HAVE WISED UP?

CONFERENCE ROOM

OWL, I NEED YOUR HELP! THE INCOME TAX PEOPLE ARE ACCUSING ME OF FRAUD.... BECAUSE OF *YOU*! BUT I'M INNOCENT ... *YOU* KNOW THAT!

OF *COURSE* I KNOW IT! YOU FOOL! *I* *FRAMED* YOU!

YOU *FRAMED* ME ?? BUT...

I'VE MADE MY FORTUNE BY CROOKED BUSINESS DEALS AND DODGING TAXES! BUT I *KNEW* THE LAW WOULD CATCH UP WITH ME...THAT'S WHY I NEEDED A *FALL GUY!*

I'VE CAREFULLY ARRANGED MY AFFAIRS SO THAT *YOU* WILL GET THE BLAME FOR WHAT I'VE DONE! AND NOW... *GET OUT!!*

AFTER ALL...A SUCCESSFUL BUSINESSMAN LIKE THE *OWL* CANNOT AFFORD TO ASSOCIATE WITH A MAN WHO'LL SOON BE A *JAILBIRD!*

SLOWLY, THE PALE, HAGGARD MAN RISES FROM THE TABLE! SILENTLY HE TURNS AND SHUFFLES OUT OF THE ROOM WITHOUT A BACKWARD GLANCE...

HIS WORLD HAS CRASHED DOWN AROUND HIS EARS! BECAUSE HE HAD BEEN WILLING TO WORK FOR A SCOUNDREL...BECAUSE HE HAD BEEN WILLING TO SHUT HIS EYES TO THE ILLEGAL THINGS HE HAD SEEN...HE NOW MUST PAY THE PRICE!

SCANT MINUTES LATER, THE UN-BELIEVABLY KEEN EARS OF *DARE-DEVIL* HEAR THE SOUND OF A FAINT IMPACT BELOW, FOLLOWED BY THE PIERCING WAIL OF A SIREN, AS HE LEAPS INTO SPELLBINDING ACTION...

WHEEEEE!

A SIREN SPELLS *TROUBLE!* AND THAT MEANS *DARE-DEVIL* MAY BE NEEDED!

ALTHOUGH HIS EYES ARE SIGHTLESS, FOR HE HAS BEEN BLIND SINCE THE AGE OF FIFTEEN, DAREDEVIL'S *OTHER* SENSES ARE SO SHARP, SO UNFAILING, THAT HE CAN PERFORM BREATH-TAKING FEATS WHICH EVEN A SIGHTED PERSON CANNOT MATCH!

PING!

LUCKILY, MY BUILT-IN *RADAR SENSE* TELLS ME HOW FAR I AM FROM A SOLID OBSTACLE...SO I ALWAYS KNOW WHEN TO DODGE AND WHEN TO GRASP!

YOU'RE TOO LATE THIS TIME! EVEN *YOU* CAN'T HELP THAT POOR MAN!

LOOK!! HERE COMES *DARE-DEVIL!!*

HIS SENSES TELL HIM THAT A HUMAN FORM IS LYING IN FRONT OF HIM, BUT HE HEARS NO PULSE...NO HEARTBEAT...AND HE INSTANTLY REALIZES...

THIS MAN IS *DEAD!* HOW DID IT HAPPEN ??

HE WALKED RIGHT IN FRONT OF A SPEEDING CAR...AS THOUGH...HE DIDN'T *CARE!!*

I *RECOGNIZE* HIM! IT'S GEORGE GREY! HE'S UNDER INDICTMENT FOR FRAUD! HE WORKS FOR THE *OWL!*

THE *OWL!* I'VE *HEARD* OF HIM!!

3.

52

A FEW MINUTES LATER...

LET'S GO, OWL! THEY WANT TO ASK YOU SOME QUESTIONS AT HEADQUARTERS, CONCERNING GEORGE GREY!

YOU MAY BRING A LAWYER IF YOU WISH!

I DON'T *NEED* A LAWYER...AND YOU *KNOW* IT! YOU'VE GOT NOTHING ON ME! I HAD NOTHING TO DO WITH GREY'S DEATH!

WE *KNOW*, OWL! BUT WE FOUND SOME PAPERS LINKING YOU WITH SOME FRAUDULENT BUSINESS DEALINGS!

WE'VE ALWAYS *KNOWN* YOU WERE CROOKED, OWL...BUT WE HAD NO PROOF...TILL *NOW!* AT LAST WE'RE GOING TO BE ABLE TO PULL YOUR FINANCIAL EMPIRE DOWN AROUND YOUR EARS!

BUT, UPON REACHING HEADQUARTERS...

OWL, WITH THE EVIDENCE WE'RE UNEARTHING ABOUT YOU, I SUGGEST YOU *DO* GET YOURSELF A LAWYER!

ALL RIGHT, I *WILL!* BUT ONLY TO PROVE HOW *FLIMSY* YOUR CASE IS! I WON'T EVEN USE AN EXPENSIVE, HIGH-POWERED LAWYER!

I'LL PICK OUT ANY NAME AT RANDOM...AND I'LL STILL BE OUT OF HERE WITHIN THE HOUR! GET ME A PHONE BOOK!

OPENING THE CLASSIFIED DIRECTORY, THE OWL CARELESSLY POINTS TO THE FIRST NAME THAT CATCHES HIS EYE...

HERE...I'LL HIRE *THIS* FIRM... NELSON AND MURDOCK!

NELSON AND MURDOCK Attorneys a...

HELTADO, IRVING Attorney-at-law

AND SECONDS LATER, A COLORFUL COSTUMED FIGURE DARINGLY SWINGS IN THROUGH A BACK WINDOW OF THAT VERY SAME LAW FIRM, AS HIS PARTNER, FRANKLIN "FOGGY" NELSON, IS CONCLUDING A PHONE CALL...

SORRY, OWL! I'M NOT INTERESTED IN REPRESENTING ANYONE WITH *YOUR* REPUTATION, AND I DON'T THINK MY *PARTNER* WOULD BE, EITHER!

FOGGY'S TALKING TO THE *OWL!!*

CHANGING CLOTHES WITH DAZZLING SPEED, DAREDEVIL RETURNS TO HIS NORMAL IDENTITY OF MATT MURDOCK, BLIND ATTORNEY, AS HE MANAGES TO GRASP THE PHONE BEFORE HIS STARTLED PARTNER CAN HANG UP!

OH! MR. MURDOCK MUST HAVE COME IN THROUGH THE BACK DOOR!

SAY! WHAT'S THE *RUSH*, MATTHEW, OL' PAL?

I DON'T BELIEVE IN TURNING DOWN *ANY* CASES, FOGGY! *I'LL* HANDLE THIS ONE IF YOU DON'T WANT TO! HELLO, OWL?? I'LL BE IN COURT IN TEN MINUTES!

BRIMMING WITH EXCITEMENT, MATT MURDOCK LEAVES THE OFFICE, CHANGING BACK TO *DAREDEVIL* AS SOON AS HE IS SAFELY OUT OF SIGHT! AND THEN, ROLLING HIS WRINKLE-PROOF SUIT INTO A TIGHT BALL, HE RACES TOWARDS HIS GOAL AT BREAKNECK SPEED...

I'VE BEEN ANXIOUS TO LEARN MORE ABOUT THE MYSTERIOUS *OWL*... AND THIS IS THE CHANCE OF A LIFETIME!

I'VE *TRIED* TO EXPLAIN TO FOGGY THAT *EVERY* MAN IS ENTITLED TO A LAWYER! IF WE ATTORNEYS REFUSE TO HELP ACCUSED PEOPLE BECAUSE WE THINK THEY'RE GUILTY, THEN WE'RE JUDGING THEM WITHOUT TRIAL!

BESIDES, THE OWL INTRIGUES ME! I WANT TO LEARN MORE ABOUT HIM!

AH, I HEAR THE COURT HOUSE BELL CHIMING! IT'S TIME FOR ME TO CHANGE BACK TO MATT MURDOCK AND CALL UPON MY NEW CLIENT!

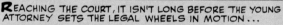

REACHING THE COURT, IT ISN'T LONG BEFORE THE YOUNG ATTORNEY SETS THE LEGAL WHEELS IN MOTION...

VERY WELL, COUNSELOR, I WILL FREE YOUR CLIENT ON A WRIT OF HABEAS CORPUS!

BUT HE IS TO REPORT TO THIS COURT TOMORROW MORNING AT TEN FOR FURTHER DISPOSITION!

THANK YOU, SERGEANT! AND NOW, IF I MAY MEET MY CLIENT...?

HE'S RIGHT OVER HERE, MR. MURDOCK!

TURNING SLOWLY, MATT MURDOCK INVOLUNTARILY RECOILS IN SHOCK AS AN AURA OF UNMISTAKABLE *VILLAINY* SEEMS TO SURROUND HIS RAZOR-SHARP SENSES...

I AM THE OWL!

IT'S INCREDIBLE!! I CAN TELL BY THE SOUND OF HIS HEART-BEAT, HIS PULSE RATE, HIS LABORED BREATHING... THE MAN IS CHARGED WITH SHEER ANIMAL POWER... WITH ALMOST LIMITLESS ENERGY... ALL OF IT DIRECTED INTO EVIL CHANNELS!

5.

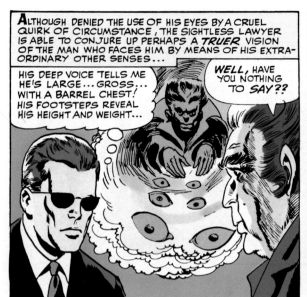

ALTHOUGH DENIED THE USE OF HIS EYES BY A CRUEL QUIRK OF CIRCUMSTANCE, THE SIGHTLESS LAWYER IS ABLE TO CONJURE UP PERHAPS A *TRUER* VISION OF THE MAN WHO FACES HIM BY MEANS OF HIS EXTRAORDINARY OTHER SENSES...

HIS DEEP VOICE TELLS ME HE'S LARGE...GROSS... WITH A BARREL CHEST! HIS FOOTSTEPS REVEAL HIS HEIGHT AND WEIGHT...

WELL, HAVE YOU NOTHING TO *SAY*??

SORRY! I WAS, EH, THINKING! YOU'RE TO RETURN HERE TOMORROW MORNING AT TEN!

OF COURSE! I'LL SEE YOU THEN! GOODBYE!!

HE DOESN'T REALIZE I CAN HEAR HIS PULSE! IT'S LIKE HAVING A BUILT-IN LIE DETECTOR! HIS PULSE RATE SPEEDED UP UNNATURALLY! HE HAS NO INTENTION OF BEING HERE TOMORROW!

I CAN HEAR HIM CACKLING TO HIMSELF AS HE LEAVES! BUT IT DOESN'T MATTER! HE ISN'T GETTING AWAY WITH ANYTHING! NOW THAT I'VE FORMED A MENTAL IMAGE OF HIM, I'LL BE ABLE TO FIND HIM AGAIN *ANYWHERE*!

THE NEXT MORNING, AT TEN O'CLOCK, AS MATT MURDOCK APPEARS IN COURT...

YOUR CLIENT HAS NOT SHOWN UP, COUNSELOR! I SHALL ISSUE A SUMMONS FOR HIS IMMEDIATE ARREST! THAT IS ALL!

VERY WELL, YOUR HONOR!

WHAT DOES THE OWL EXPECT TO *GAIN* BY THIS? HE MUST KNOW HE'LL BE FOUND SOONER OR LATER!

LATER, AS THE MAN WITHOUT FEAR RETURNS TO HIS OFFICE...

I HAVE A FEELING THAT IT WILL SOON BE TIME FOR *DAREDEVIL* TO GO INTO ACTION AGAIN, AND I'VE JUST THOUGHT OF A WAY TO IMPROVE THE EFFICIENCY OF MY COSTUME!

...I'M GOING TO DESIGN A *HOOD* FOR MY SHOULDERS...THEN I'LL BE ABLE TO FOLD MY STREET CLOTHES AND CONCEAL THEM UNDER IT SO THEY'LL ALWAYS BE HANDY!

AND, UPON JOINING KAREN AND FOGGY AGAIN...

I'M GOING TO TAKE KAREN *BOWLING* TONIGHT, MATT! HOW ABOUT JOINING US?

NO, THANKS, FOGGY! I'M AFRAID I WOULDN'T BE ABLE TO APPRECIATE IT! A SPARE AND A NEAR-STRIKE SOUND ABOUT THE SAME TO ME!

POOR MATT! MY HEART GOES OUT TO HIM FOR HIS HANDICAP! IF ONLY I COULD TAKE HIM IN MY ARMS...!

6.

ANYONE LOOKING INTO MATT MURDOCK'S APARTMENT THAT NIGHT WOULD SEE THE INCREDIBLE SIGHT OF A MAN THREADING A NEEDLE AND SEWING IN THE DARK!

IT'S AMAZING HOW MY *OTHER* SENSES CAN COMPENSATE FOR MY LACK OF SIGHT! MY SENSE OF TOUCH IS SO ACUTE THAT THIS IS CHILD'S PLAY FOR ME!

THERE! IT SEEMS TO FIT PERFECTLY! AND I CAN CLOSE IT EASILY BY USING ONE OF THOSE NEW CONTACT-TYPE ZIPPERS! NOW TO SEE IF ALL MY OUTER CLOTHES WILL FIT!

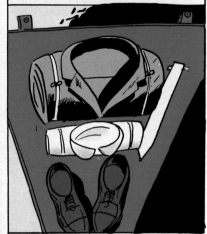

AND FIT THEY *DO!* AGAIN GUIDED BY HIS UNCANNY SENSE OF TOUCH, THE SIGHTLESS ADVENTURER IS ABLE TO CONTAIN A COMPLETE CHANGE OF CLOTHES WITHIN HIS CLEVERLY DESIGNED NEW SHOULDER POUCH!

MINUTES LATER, WE FIND THE DAZZLING *DAREDEVIL* TRAVELING AT BREAKNECK SPEED THROUGH THE GREAT CITY'S MAZE OF DARK, TWISTING UNDERGROUND TUNNELS...

I'VE COVERED EVERY IMPORTANT ARTERY! WHEREVER THE OWL IS HIDING, IT ISN'T BELOW THE SURFACE!

NEXT, THE MAN WITHOUT FEAR TAKES TO THE AIR...

I'LL COVER THE BRIDGES LEADING OUT OF THE CITY! IF HE'S CROSSED ANY OF THEM, THE SCENT OF HIS UNUSUAL HAIR TONIC SHOULD STILL BE DETECTABLE TO ME!

AND, AS THE LONG EVENING HOURS CRAWL BY...

THIS IS MY FINAL STOP! NO TRACE OF THE OWL HAVING PASSED THROUGH ANY BRIDGE OR TRAIN STATION! THAT CAN ONLY MEAN TWO THINGS...

EITHER HE'S STILL SOMEWHERE IN THE CITY... IN WHICH CASE I'LL PICK UP HIS TRAIL SOONER OR LATER...OR ELSE HE LEFT BY *BOAT!* IF HE *DID*, THERE ARE TOO MANY SMALL CRAFT FOR ME TO INVESTIGATE THEM ALL!

THIS SHOULD TEACH ME NOT TO BECOME TOO OVER-CONFIDENT! I WAS SO *SURE* I COULD FIND HIM EASILY WHENEVER I WANTED TO! BUT, IT SEEMS THAT EVEN A MAN WITH SUPER-KEEN SENSES ISN'T INFALLIBLE!

7.

MEANTIME, WHERE *IS* THE MYSTERIOUS OWL? ALTHOUGH HE DOESN'T YET KNOW IT, DAREDEVIL'S *SECOND* GUESS WAS THE CORRECT ONE! FOR, ACROSS THE HUDSON, PERCHED HIGH ABOVE THE PALISADES CLIFFS, IS ONE OF THE STRANGEST RESIDENCES IN THE NATION! IT IS THE OWL'S *AERIE!* LOOKING LIKE NOTHING MORE THAN A JAGGED PART OF THE SCENERY WHEN VIEWED FROM THE RIVER, THIS COMPLEX STRUCTURE SEEMS TO EXUDE THE SAME AIR OF MENACE AS THE MAN WHO INHABITS IT!

RRRING!

AH, MY ALARM BELL! THAT MEANS THE TWO "GUESTS" I INVITED HAVE ARRIVED! I MUST GO TO WELCOME THEM!

SEATING HIMSELF UPON A CHAIR WHICH RESEMBLES SOME FANTASTIC VERSION OF AN OWLISH THRONE, THE MILLIONAIRE FUGITIVE WATCHES TWO COLD-EYED MEN SLOWLY ENTER!

SO! "SAD SAM" SIMMS, AND "APE" HORGON! I HAVE HEARD THAT YOU ARE TWO OF THE UNDERWORLD'S MOST DANGEROUS MEN! WE SHALL SEE IF YOU ARE DANGEROUS ENOUGH TO SERVE THE *OWL!*

YOU USED TO PRETEND TO BE *LEGIT* UNTIL NOW, OWL! YOU ALWAYS WORKED *ALONE!* WHAT *HAPPENED?*

I MADE A CARELESS MISTAKE! NOW THERE IS NO FURTHER NEED FOR PRETENSE! THE WORLD NOW *KNOWS* I AM A CRIMINAL, SO I HAVE PLANNED A *NEW* CAREER FOR MYSELF!

8.

BUT FIRST, I MUST *TEST* YOU! THEY SAY YOU ARE THE *BEST* GUNMAN IN THE EAST, SAD SAM! WE SHALL NOW FIGHT A *DUEL* AND SEE!

DON'T BE ALARMED! THESE ARE MERELY *WAX* BULLETS!

MOVING WITH UNEXPECTED SPEED FOR ONE SO LARGE, THE UNCANNY OWL ACTUALLY DRAWS HIS GUN *FIRST!* BUT, BEFORE HIS FINGER CAN SQUEEZE THE TRIGGER, THE MAN KNOWN AS SAD SAM RECOVERS FROM HIS SURPRISE, AND THEN MOVES WITH LIGHTNING-LIKE PRECISION!

WHOO! WHOOO!

CRACK!

EXCELLENT! EXCELLENT! YOU ACTUALLY HIT THE MUZZLE OF MY *OWN* GUN, PREVENTING ME FROM FIRING! YOU ARE JUST THE MAN I WANT!

AND NOW, APE... ARE YOU READY FOR *YOUR* TEST?

SURE! I'M STRONG ENOUGH TO DO *ANYTHING!* I AIN'T WORRIED!

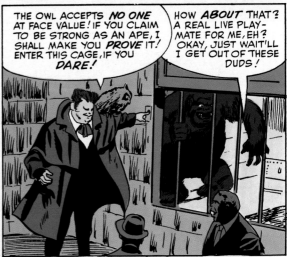

THE OWL ACCEPTS *NO ONE* AT FACE VALUE! IF YOU CLAIM TO BE STRONG AS AN APE, I SHALL MAKE YOU *PROVE* IT! ENTER THIS CAGE, IF YOU *DARE!*

HOW *ABOUT* THAT? A REAL LIVE PLAY-MATE FOR ME, EH? OKAY, JUST WAIT'LL I GET OUT OF THESE DUDS!

MINUTES LATER, THE MAN KNOWN AS "APE" HURLS HIMSELF INTO BATTLE AGAINST THE SNARLING, SAVAGE BEAST WITHIN THE HEAVILY BARRED CAGE! AND, AS THE OWL AND HIS NEW GUNMAN WATCH IN AMAZEMENT...

THIS OVERGROWN CHIMP MAY BE AS STRONG AS I AM... BUT HE DON'T KNOW THE *RASSLIN'* HOLDS I KNOW! WHAT SHOULD I *DO* WITH 'IM NOW? THIS IS GETTIN' *BORING!*

RELEASE HIM! YOU'VE PROVED YOUR POINT!

RRRRR RRRR!

WITH A MARKSMAN LIKE SAD SAM WORKING FOR ME... AND A POWERFUL BRUTE LIKE *YOU*... I'LL BE THE UNDISPUTED OVERLORD OF CRIME!

9.

AND NOW...I SHALL DEMONSTRATE MY *OWN* POWER--- TO MAKE SURE YOU NEVER DARE THINK YOU CAN DOUBLE-CROSS YOUR MASTER!

IF YOU ASK *ME*, HE'S SOME KINDA *NUT!*

SHUDDUP... TILL WE KNOW MORE ABOUT HIM!

STAND WHERE YOU ARE! *GOOD!* NOW LISTEN CLOSELY...I HAVE MANAGED TO SAVE A *FORTUNE* OVER THE YEARS... MONEY WHICH I'VE SPENT TO INCREASE MY POWERS! THAT IS WHY I'M READY TO COME OUT INTO THE OPEN AT LAST...TO BATTLE THE FORCES OF LAW AND ORDER!

BUT WHAT POWERS ARE YOU *TALKIN'* ABOUT??

YOU SHALL SEE FOR YOURSELF WITHIN SECONDS!

NOT FOR *NOTHING* DO I CALL MYSELF THE *OWL!* NOT MERELY BECAUSE I BEAR A SLIGHT PHYSICAL RESEMBLANCE TO THE NOCTURNAL BIRD OF PREY WHICH YOU SEE PERCHED UPON MY SHOULDER! NO...THERE IS *ANOTHER* REASON!

AND *NOW*... YOU SHALL LEARN WHAT IT *IS!!* ALL I NEED DO IS PRESS THIS CONTROL BUTTON...

WE WERE STANDIN' ON A *TRAP DOOR!!*

HE'S TRYIN' TO *KILL* US!! WE'RE *FALLIN'!!* HELLLP!

THEN, AS THE TWO STARTLED CRIMINALS PLUNGE DOWNWARD, A LOUD, CACKLING, SPINE-CHILLING LAUGH FOLLOWS THEM DOWN, AND DOWN, AND DOWN...

HEE HE

YAAAAAAA

HA HA! HA HA!

HO HO!

HA HA!

10.

AND THEN, THE OWL RUSHES OUTSIDE, SHOUTING...

DON'T PANIC! THE AIR CURRENTS WILL SLOW YOUR DESCENT LONG ENOUGH FOR ME TO SAVE YOU!

SAVE US? ...HOW??

NOT BOTHERING TO ANSWER, THE UNCANNY MASTER CRIMINAL HURLS HIMSELF OFF THE TOP OF THE CLIFF, TOWARDS THE TWO FALLING MEN...

THIS IS THE POWER I MENTIONED!! THE POWER TO GLIDE WITH THE AIR CURRENTS... TO DRIFT AND SWOOP, AND PLUNGE...LIKE THE BIRD WHICH IS MY NAMESAKE!

AIDED BY THE INGENIOUS CUT OF HIS CAPELIKE GARMENT, THE OWL IS ABLE TO PLUMMET DOWNWARD FASTER THAN THE OTHERS, CATCHING THEM BEFORE THEY REACH THE SWIRLING RIVER! AND THEN, SOARING WITH THE AIR CURRENTS, TAKING ADVANTAGE OF THEM LIKE A BIRD OF PREY, HE GLIDES UPWARDS AGAIN, UNTIL...

SEE TO IT THAT YOU NEVER FORGET THIS LITTLE LESSON, MY FRIENDS! NO MATTER HOW POWERFUL YOU ARE...THE OWL IS YOUR MASTER!!

OKAY, OKAY! YOU SURE PROVED YOUR POINT! WHAT DO WE DO NEXT?

NOW WE CROSS THE RIVER AND RETURN TO THE HEART OF THE CITY! WE HAVE A LITTLE VISIT TO PAY!

BEFORE BEGINNING MY CRIME CAREER IN EARNEST, I NEED ONE MORE THING! A MOUTHPIECE! A LAWYER WHO IS WEAK ENOUGH, AND GULLIBLE ENOUGH, SO THAT HE WILL ACT AS A FRONT FOR ME!

AND I KNOW JUST THE MAN! THE BLIND MATTHEW MURDOCK! HE'S YOUNG, INEXPERIENCED, HELPLESS! WE'LL USE HIM AS A GO-BETWEEN! THE POLICE WOULD NEVER SUSPECT HIM!

11.

MEANWHILE, WHAT OF THAT "HELPLESS" LAWYER WHOM THE OWL IS SEEKING? LET US JOIN HIM ONCE AGAIN IN THE LAW OFFICES OF NELSON AND MURDOCK...

WHAT'S WRONG, MATT?? YOU'VE BEEN LOOKING DOWNHEARTED ALL DAY! ANYTHING WORRYING YOU, PARTNER?

I THINK YOU'VE BEEN WORKING TOO HARD, MR. MURDOCK! PERHAPS IF YOU...

NO, I'M OKAY! FORGET IT! I CAN'T VERY WELL TELL THEM HOW DISTURBED I AM THAT I LET THE OWL GET AWAY FROM ME! I FEEL LIKE A FOOL!

MR. MURDOCK, I KNOW YOU DON'T LIKE ME TO MENTION THIS, BUT I CAN'T STOP WISHING YOU'D CHANGE YOUR MIND ABOUT NOT WANTING AN EYE OPERATION! IF THERE'S A CHANCE OF YOUR REGAINING YOUR SIGHT, ISN'T IT WORTH TAKING?

I KNOW YOU MEAN WELL, KAREN! AND I APPRECIATE IT! BUT...I'VE LEARNED TO LIVE WITH MY AFFLICTION! PERHAPS WE CAN DISCUSS THIS SOME OTHER TIME!

RIGHT NOW IT'S PAST QUITTING TIME! SO YOU JUST RUN ALONG! THERE'S NOTHING FOR YOU TO WORRY ABOUT!

VERY WELL! I REALIZE I HAD NO RIGHT TO OFFER YOU PERSONAL ADVICE! I'M SORRY IF I SPOKE OUT OF TURN! IT WON'T HAPPEN AGAIN!

IF ONLY I COULD FORGET HIM! WHY DO I TORTURE MYSELF SO? I MEAN LESS THAN NOTHING TO HIM!

HER PULSE RATE IS ALWAYS SPEEDING UP WHEN SHE'S NEAR ME! I CAN HEAR IT! I WONDER...?

NO...IT'S IMPOSSIBLE! HOW COULD SHE EVER BE INTERESTED IN ME?? AND YET...!

WAIT! THAT ODOR! THE SCENT OF A BIRD!...AN OWL! COMING FROM THE OTHER SIDE OF THE WALL! BUT THAT OFFICE IS VACANT!

CAN'T TAKE ANY CHANCES! I HATE TO LIE, BUT I'VE GOT TO GET FOGGY OUT OF HERE... SO I CAN CHANGE!

DIDN'T YOU HEAR KAREN'S TONE OF VOICE WHEN SHE LEFT, FOGGY? EVEN I COULD TELL SHE WAS DISAPPOINTED BECAUSE YOU DIDN'T OFFER TO WALK HER HOME!

REALLY, MATT?! GOSH, I'LL GO RIGHT AFTER HER! MAYBE I CAN STILL CATCH HER! YOU'RE A REAL PAL!

AND, NO SOONER DOES MATT MURDOCK HEAR THE DOOR CLOSE IN THE ANTEROOM, THAN...

AND NOW... EXIT MATT MURDOCK, ATTORNEY-AT-LAW... BECAUSE... HERE COMES... DAREDEVIL!!

12.

AS SURE-FOOTED AS A PUMA... AS SILENT AS A LEOPARD... AS FEARLESS AS A TIGER... THE MASKED ADVENTURER STEPS OUT UPON THE NARROW LEDGE WHICH ENCIRCLES THE UPPER FLOORS OF HIS OFFICE BUILDING, AND THEN, EVERY SENSE KEYED TO ITS HIGHEST PITCH, HE INCHES TOWARDS THE ADJOINING OFFICE WINDOW...

THE MUFFLED WHISPERS FROM THE NEXT OFFICE ARE LIKE ROARING SHOUTS TO ME! THERE ARE THREE MEN IN THERE... AND ONE IS, WITHOUT ANY DOUBT, THE *OWL!*

THE HEARTBEATS ARE SLIGHTLY TO MY RIGHT... ABOUT FIVE FEET AWAY!

JUDGING BY THE DEPTH AND PITCH OF THE BREATHING, THE MEN WITH THE OWL ARE OPPOSITES! ONE, TALL AND THIN... THE OTHER, SHORT AND HUSKY!

IT'S *DAREDEVIL!!*

CRASH!

I DUNNO WHAT HE'S *DOIN'* HERE, BUT YOU WANT *ME* TO TAKE CARE OF HIM, OWL?

LET *ME* DO IT, BOSS! I HAVEN'T HAD ANY *PRACTICE* FOR A WHILE!

THEY CALL HIM "BOSS"... SO THEY'RE IN HIS EMPLOY! BUT WHAT ARE THEY DOING *HERE*... NEXT DOOR TO MATT MURDOCK!??

HE'S UP FOR GRABS, BOYS! YOU CAN *BOTH* HAVE HIM! NO CORNY MASKED ACROBAT IS GOING TO STOP THE *OWL* FROM GETTING HIMSELF A LAWYER!

SO *THAT'S* IT! HE'S HERE TO TRY TO MAKE MATT MURDOCK HIS LAWYER!

YOU BACK ME UP, SAD SAM! *I'LL* TACKLE 'IM FIRST!

OKAY... GO AHEAD!

A GUY WHO CAN BEAT A *GORILLA* WITH HIS BARE HANDS WON'T HAVE ANY TROUBLE WITH ONE COSTUMED CLOWN!

THAT'S WHAT *YOU* THINK, FELLA! I'M A LOT HARDER TO *CATCH* THAN ANY OF YOUR GORILLA FRIENDS!!

13.

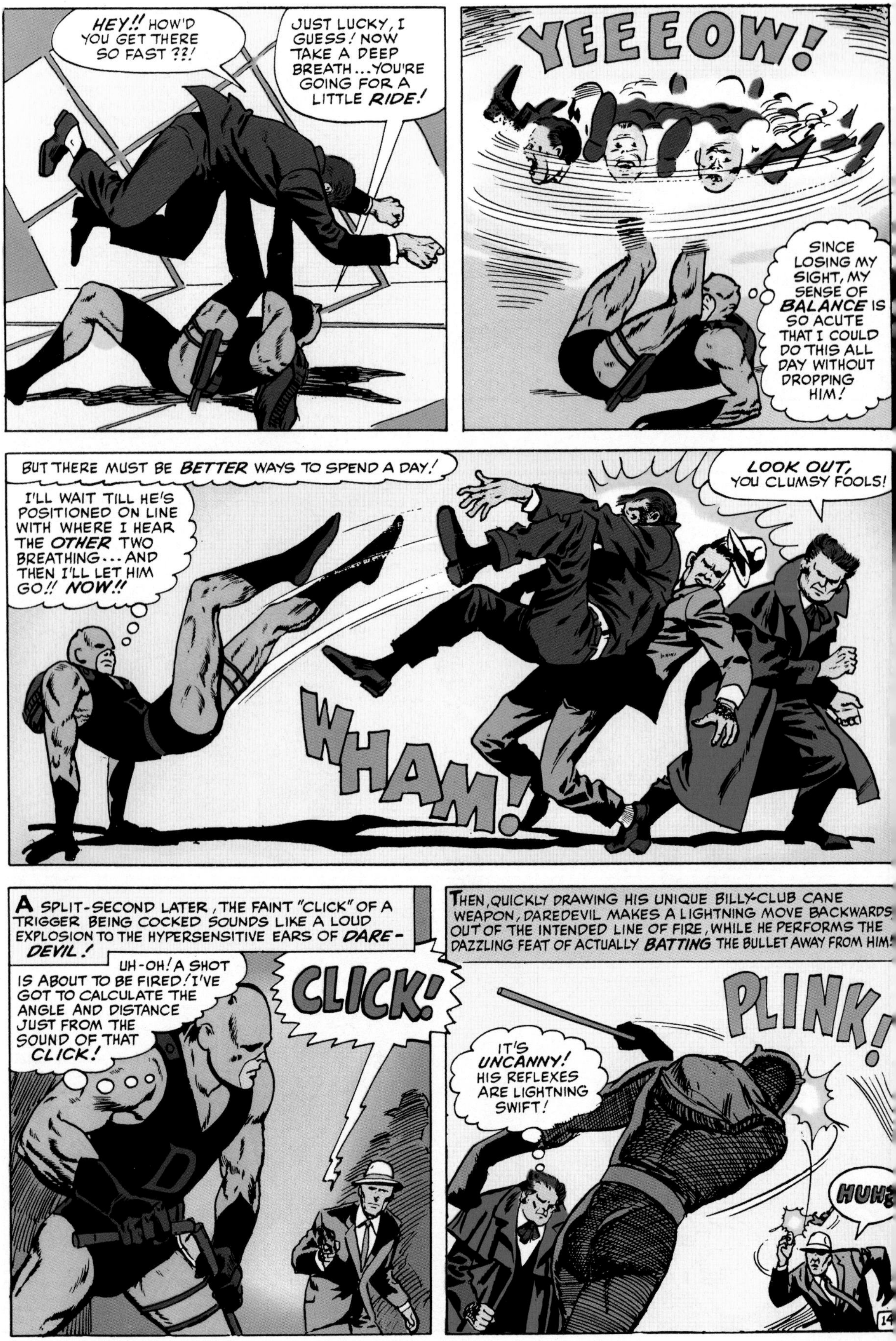
HEY!! HOW'D YOU GET THERE SO FAST ??!
JUST LUCKY, I GUESS! NOW TAKE A DEEP BREATH ... YOU'RE GOING FOR A LITTLE RIDE!
YEEEOW!
SINCE LOSING MY SIGHT, MY SENSE OF BALANCE IS SO ACUTE THAT I COULD DO THIS ALL DAY WITHOUT DROPPING HIM!
BUT THERE MUST BE BETTER WAYS TO SPEND A DAY!
I'LL WAIT TILL HE'S POSITIONED ON LINE WITH WHERE I HEAR THE OTHER TWO BREATHING... AND THEN I'LL LET HIM GO!! NOW!!
LOOK OUT, YOU CLUMSY FOOLS!
WHAM!
A SPLIT-SECOND LATER, THE FAINT "CLICK" OF A TRIGGER BEING COCKED SOUNDS LIKE A LOUD EXPLOSION TO THE HYPERSENSITIVE EARS OF DARE-DEVIL!
UH-OH! A SHOT IS ABOUT TO BE FIRED! I'VE GOT TO CALCULATE THE ANGLE AND DISTANCE JUST FROM THE SOUND OF THAT CLICK!
CLICK!
THEN, QUICKLY DRAWING HIS UNIQUE BILLY-CLUB CANE WEAPON, DAREDEVIL MAKES A LIGHTNING MOVE BACKWARDS OUT OF THE INTENDED LINE OF FIRE, WHILE HE PERFORMS THE DAZZLING FEAT OF ACTUALLY BATTING THE BULLET AWAY FROM HIM!
PLINK!
IT'S UNCANNY! HIS REFLEXES ARE LIGHTNING SWIFT!
HUH?
14

BUT, SENSATIONAL THOUGH HE IS, THE MAN WITHOUT FEAR CANNOT ANTICIPATE *EVERYTHING!* AND SO IT IS THAT THE EVENTS OF THE NEXT FEW SECONDS ARE ABOUT TO TURN HIS NEAR VICTORY INTO ONE OF HIS MOST BITTER *DEFEATS!* FOR, AT THAT VERY MOMENT, *KAREN PAGE* ENTERS THE SCENE...

I LEFT MY PURSE ON MY DESK! IT'S LUCKY I REMEMBERED... *OHH!*

A *FIGHT!*... IN THE OFFICE NEXT DOOR!! WHAT'S GOING ON...??!

A GIRL!!

KAREN'S VOICE!! I'VE GOT TO GET HER *OUT* OF HERE!!

KAREN! RUN!! DON'T WASTE A MINUTE!! BEFORE THEY GET YOU... *RUN!!*

BUT THE BEWILDERED GIRL, TRANSFIXED BY SHOCK AND UNCERTAINTY, STANDS ROOTED TO THE SPOT, UNTIL THE QUICK-THINKING *OWL* REACHES OUT, AND...

SHE IS, DAREDEVIL... BUT I CAN SENSE THE *CONCERN* IN YOUR VOICE! SO, SURRENDER TO ME *IMMEDIATELY*... OR ELSE!

GOOD WORK, BOSS!

LET ME *DOWN!* NO! DON'T... *HELP!!*

AND THEN, REALIZING THE GRAVE DANGER THE INNOCENT GIRL IS IN, DAREDEVIL'S VOICE GRIMLY UTTERS THE TWO WORDS HE HAD NEVER EXPECTED TO SAY WHILE A SPARK OF LIFE REMAINED WITHIN HIM!

I SURRENDER!

AND ONCE MORE, THE MAD, SPINE-CHILLING CHORTLE OF THE *OWL* FILLS A ROOM WITH DEMONIAC MENACE!!

HEE-HEE WHOOO WHOOO HEE!

DAREDEVIL! YOU KNEW MY NAME! HOW? WHERE DID WE...??

NO TIME FOR THAT NOW! I'LL EXPLAIN LATER!

I'VE GOT TO BE MORE CAREFUL! I FORGOT THAT *DAREDEVIL* ISN'T SUPPOSED TO KNOW KAREN PAGE! I ALMOST GAVE MYSELF AWAY!

I'LL USE YOUR OWN BLASTED BILLY CLUB TO KEEP THESE ROPES TIGHT, WISE GUY!

15.

LATER, BACK AT THE AVIARY OF THE OWL...

I'M IN SOME SORT OF LARGE *CAGE!* JUDGING BY THE SLIGHT AIR MOVEMENT ABOVE ME, IT'S DANGLING EXACTLY EIGHT AND A HALF FEET FROM THE CEILING... AND FROM THE SOUND OF THE OWL'S VOICE, IT'S TEN FEET FROM THE FLOOR!

ESTIMATING THE TIME IT TAKES AN *ECHO* TO BOUNCE BACK FROM THE WALLS, IT'S A HUGE ROOM, ROUGHLY 325 FEET IN DIAMETER! THAT TELLS ME ALL I NEED TO KNOW... FOR *NOW!*

I HOPE MY TWO GUESTS WILL BE COMFORTABLE! IF THERE'S ANYTHING YOU NEED, JUST RING FOR *ROOM SERVICE!*

WITHOUT ANOTHER WORD, THE OMINOUS OWL TURNS ON HIS HEEL AND LEAVES THE LARGE CHAMBER! MOMENTS LATER, WE FIND HIM ON HIS PERCH, OVER-LOOKING THE HUDSON, AS HE PLANS HIS NEXT SINISTER MOVES...

ONCE THE UNDERWORLD LEARNS THAT I HAVE CAPTURED THE FEARLESS *DAREDEVIL*, NO OTHER CRIMINAL WOULD DARE TO DISPUTE MY LEADER-SHIP! SOON, EVERYONE WILL ACKNOWLEDGE ME AS THE OVERLORD OF CRIME!

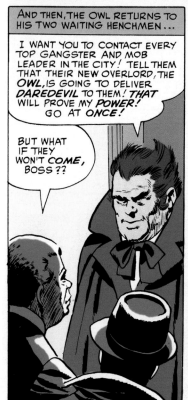

AND THEN, THE OWL RETURNS TO HIS TWO WAITING HENCHMEN...

I WANT YOU TO CONTACT EVERY TOP GANGSTER AND MOB LEADER IN THE CITY! TELL THEM THAT THEIR NEW OVERLORD, THE OWL, IS GOING TO DELIVER *DAREDEVIL* TO THEM! *THAT* WILL PROVE MY *POWER!* GO AT *ONCE!*

BUT WHAT IF THEY WON'T *COME*, BOSS??

YOU BRAINLESS FOOL!! YOU ARE *NEVER* TO QUESTION THE OWL'S ORDERS! WHEN THEY HEAR THAT I HAVE CAPTURED *DAREDEVIL*, *NOTHING* WILL KEEP THEM AWAY! NOW *GO!!*

WITH THOSE SCATHING WORDS, THE OWL AGAIN DEPARTS, AS THE MAN WITHOUT FEAR THINKS QUICKLY...

SO! HE INTENDS TO HAND ME OVER TO THE UNDERWORLD, IN ORDER TO BECOME THEIR CHIEF! I'M NOT WORRIED ABOUT *MYSELF*, NO MATTER WHAT THE ODDS, BUT...

...I CAN'T LET ANY HARM COME TO *KAREN!* I'VE GOT TO SET HER FREE, SOMEHOW!

16.

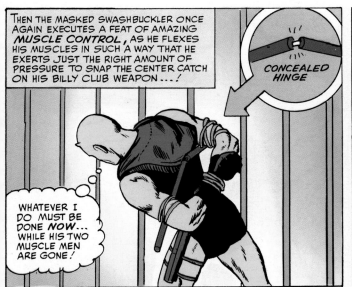

THEN THE MASKED SWASHBUCKLER ONCE AGAIN EXECUTES A FEAT OF AMAZING *MUSCLE CONTROL*, AS HE FLEXES HIS MUSCLES IN SUCH A WAY THAT HE EXERTS JUST THE RIGHT AMOUNT OF PRESSURE TO SNAP THE CENTER CATCH ON HIS BILLY CLUB WEAPON....!

CONCEALED HINGE

WHATEVER I DO MUST BE DONE *NOW*... WHILE HIS TWO MUSCLE MEN ARE GONE!

THEN, ONCE THE PRESSURE HAS BEEN SLACKENED, IT'S A SIMPLE MATTER FOR THE SUPERBLY TRAINED *DAREDEVIL* TO SNAP THE NOW-LOOSENED CORDS...

IT'S LUCKY THAT HE DIDN'T SUSPECT MY CANE WEAPON IS HINGED IN THE CENTER!

SNAP!

I ALWAYS *KNEW* THIS THIN FLEXIBLE COTTER PIN WOULD COME IN HANDY SOME DAY! I'VE GOT TO REMOVE IT CAREFULLY... CAREFULLY... MUSTN'T DROP IT! AHHH, THERE!

THOUGH HIS EYES ARE SIGHTLESS, DAREDEVIL'S HYPERSENSITIVE FINGERS QUICKLY FEEL THE PERIMETER OF THE CAGE UNTIL THEY REACH A SMALL KEYHOLE! THEN, WITH THE UNERRING PRECISION OF A TRAINED LOCKSMITH, HE MANIPULATES THE PIN, UNTIL...

CLICK!

I *DID* IT! IT'S *OPEN*!

LEAVING HIS CAGE WITH ONE EFFORTLESS, SILENT SWING, THE FEARLESS CRIMEFIGHTER REALLY BEGINS TO HIT HIS STRIDE!

DON'T WORRY, KAREN! I'LL HAVE YOU OUT OF THERE IN *SECONDS*!

THE SOUND OF HER BREATHING, COUPLED WITH HER HEARTBEAT, TELL ME WHERE SHE IS JUST AS UNERRINGLY AS A RADAR SIGNAL GUIDES A PILOT IN THE THICKEST FOG!

THE FLOOR IS *WIRED*! IF YOU STEP ON IT, YOU'LL SET OFF AN ALARM!

17.

THAT WAS *CARELESS* OF ME! I SHOULD HAVE THOUGHT TO *CHECK* FOR BOOBY-TRAPS!! BUT I CAN *STILL* OVERCOME THAT OBSTACLE!

THANKS, *KAREN!* AND NOW, IF I CAN'T REACH YOU VIA THE *FLOOR...*

...I'LL DO IT *THIS* WAY!

ALL I HAVE TO DO IS KEEP SWINGING BACK AND FORTH, TILL I BUILD UP ENOUGH MOMENTUM, AND THEN...

I-I WOULDN'T HAVE *BELIEVED* IT!

IMAGINE HOW MUCH *MORE* AMAZED SHE'D BE IF SHE KNEW A *BLIND MAN* WAS PERFORMING THIS FEAT!

BUT NOW THAT YOU'RE *HERE*... HOW WILL YOU BE ABLE TO OPEN THE CAGE?

DON'T WANT TO USE MY CANE'S COTTER PIN AGAIN! BEING SO CLOSE TO IT THIS TIME, KAREN MIGHT RECOGNIZE IT AS MATT MURDOCK'S WALKING STICK!

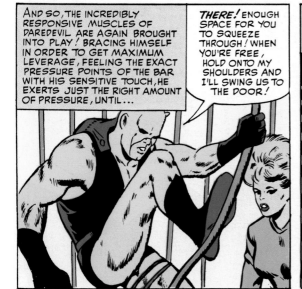

AND SO, THE INCREDIBLY RESPONSIVE MUSCLES OF DAREDEVIL ARE AGAIN BROUGHT INTO PLAY! BRACING HIMSELF IN ORDER TO GET MAXIMUM LEVERAGE, FEELING THE EXACT PRESSURE POINTS OF THE BAR WITH HIS SENSITIVE TOUCH, HE EXERTS JUST THE RIGHT AMOUNT OF PRESSURE, UNTIL...

THERE! ENOUGH SPACE FOR YOU TO SQUEEZE THROUGH! WHEN YOU'RE *FREE,* HOLD ONTO MY SHOULDERS AND I'LL SWING US TO THE DOOR!

THEN, SILENTLY BUT SURELY, THE FEARLESS ADVENTURER LEADS THE BRAVE GIRL DOWN A WINDING FLIGHT OF STEPS, AS HE UNERRINGLY FOLLOWS THE ODOR OF *GASOLINE,* WHICH GROWS STRONGER WITH EVERY STEP THEY TAKE...

THE OWL *MUST* HAVE A GARAGE SOMEWHERE NEAR-BY! YOU'LL TAKE A CAR AND HEAD FOR THE POLICE... WHILE *I* WRAP THIS LITTLE EPISODE UP!

18.

MINUTES LATER... BUT, WHAT ABOUT *YOU*? WHAT IF THE OWL RETURNS AND FINDS YOU?

THEN HE'LL BE THE *UNHAPPIEST* LITTLE OWL YOU EVER DID SEE! NOW DON'T STOP FOR ANYTHING UNTIL YOU REACH THE POLICE, HEAR?

BUT YOU STILL HAVEN'T *EXPLAINED*! THE OWL WAS A CLIENT OF MY BOSS, MATT MURDOCK! WHAT DID HE *WANT*? HOW DID *YOU* GET INVOLVED? HOW DO YOU *KNOW* ME?

THE *LAST* QUESTION IS THE EASIEST! I'VE SEEN YOU IN MY DREAMS SINCE I CAN REMEMBER, KAREN!

STRANGE... WHEN YOU SAY THAT, SOMETHING IN YOUR VOICE REMINDS ME OF...

MY *SECOND* CARELESS MISTAKE! I FORGOT TO MUFFLE MY VOICE!

HOLD IT! I *HEAR* SOMETHING!!!

BUT, BECAUSE OF CONCENTRATING SO INTENTLY UPON KAREN PAGE, DAREDEVIL'S HEARING SENSE WAS A SECOND TOO SLOW, AND...

YOU CAN'T ESCAPE *ME*! ONCE I PULL THIS LEVER, THE GARAGE DOOR WILL BE SEALED SHUT, AND YOU'LL BE MY PRISONERS AGAIN!

IGNORE HIM! KAREN! START *DRIVING!*

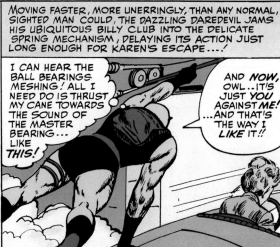

MOVING FASTER, MORE UNERRINGLY, THAN ANY NORMAL, SIGHTED MAN COULD, THE DAZZLING DAREDEVIL JAMS HIS UBIQUITOUS BILLY CLUB INTO THE DELICATE SPRING MECHANISM, DELAYING ITS ACTION JUST LONG ENOUGH FOR KAREN'S ESCAPE....!

I CAN HEAR THE BALL BEARINGS MESHING! ALL I NEED DO IS THRUST MY CANE TOWARDS THE SOUND OF THE MASTER BEARING... LIKE *THIS!*

AND *NOW*, OWL... IT'S JUST *YOU* AGAINST *ME!* ...AND THAT'S THE WAY I *LIKE* IT!!

YOU'RE A FAR MORE DANGEROUS FOE THAN I SUSPECTED, DAREDEVIL... BUT I'M *STILL* YOUR MASTER! I'M HEAVIER... MORE POWERFUL... MORE CUNNING! AND REMEMBER... WE'RE FIGHTING ON *MY* HOME GROUNDS!

I'VE PLANNED TOO LONG, TOO CAREFULLY... I'VE TOO MUCH AT STAKE, TO LET YOU STOP ME *NOW!*

I'VE GOT A LITTLE SOMETHING AT STAKE, *TOO*... MY *LIFE!!*

19.

ALTHOUGH FIGHTING A HEAVIER, POWERFUL, MORE DESPERATE OPPONENT, THE YEARS OF TRAINING AND BODYBUILDING WHICH MATT MURDOCK SPENT AS A YOUTH PAY OFF FOR HIM NOW!

ALL I NEED DO IS SHIFT MY WEIGHT QUICKLY, GRAB HIS FREE RIGHT ARM, AND BEND FORWARD SUDDENLY FROM THE WAIST!

WHATEVER I DO MUST BE DONE *QUICKLY!* THERE'S NO TELLING HOW SOON THE OWL'S TWO HENCHMEN WILL RETURN WITH THE GANG LEADERS THEY WERE SENT TO BRING BACK!

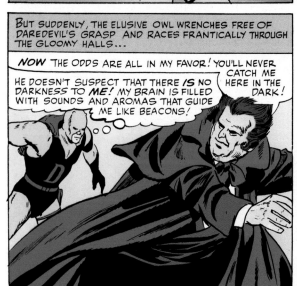

BUT SUDDENLY, THE ELUSIVE OWL WRENCHES FREE OF DAREDEVIL'S GRASP AND RACES FRANTICALLY THROUGH THE GLOOMY HALLS...

NOW THE ODDS ARE ALL IN MY FAVOR! YOU'LL NEVER CATCH ME HERE IN THE DARK!

HE DOESN'T SUSPECT THAT THERE *IS* NO DARKNESS TO *ME!* MY BRAIN IS FILLED WITH SOUNDS AND AROMAS THAT GUIDE ME LIKE BEACONS!

IT'S ALMOST OVER NOW! I CAN HEAR HIS HEART POUNDING FROM HIS EXERTION! HE CAN'T RUN MUCH FURTHER! HIS *WEIGHT* HAS TIRED HIM OUT... HE'S ALMOST EXHAUSTED!

BUT, REACHING THE TOP OF THE STAIRS, THE OWL'S HAND SUDDENLY DARTS OUT, TOUCHING A CONCEALED LEVER...

HAH! YOU DIDN'T *EXPECT* THOSE STEPS TO *FLATTEN* INTO ICY SMOOTHNESS BENEATH YOUR FEET, DID YOU?!! HAPPY LANDINGS, YOU FOOL!

CAN'T KEEP MY FOOTING! I'M PLUNGING BACK! THERE'S A SLIGHT DRAFT BENEATH ME... A *TRAP-DOOR* HAS BEEN OPENED...!!

AND THEN...

SPLASH!

WATER!! HE'S CAUSED ME TO DROP RIGHT DOWN INTO THE RIVER! I'VE GOT TO SURFACE QUICKLY... THE WATER DEADENS MY HEARING SENSE!

20.

I'VE ELUDED HIM FOR NOW, BUT I CAN TAKE NO FURTHER CHANCES! HE'S FAR STRONGER THAN I THOUGHT!

I'VE GOT TO BUILD A NEW AVIARY... WITH NEW DEFENSES! I'VE A FORTUNE HIDDEN AWAY... I CAN STILL ACCOMPLISH ANYTHING!

AND THEN, THE HULKING OWLISH FIGURE HEARS THE DISTANT WAIL OF SCREAMING SIRENS...COMING EVER CLOSER...

THE *POLICE!!* THEY'RE SURROUNDING MY AVIARY!! BUT THEY'LL NEVER FIND ME!!

SO LONG AS I REMAIN *THE OWL,* I ALWAYS HAVE ONE LAST MEANS OF ESCAPE LEFT TO ME!

I'VE PLANNED *PERFECTLY...* THOUGHT OF EVERYTHING!

MY FULLY-FUELED POWER LAUNCH IS DOCKED BELOW, READY FOR JUST SUCH AN EMERGENCY!

HAD ANY EYES BEEN ABLE TO PIERCE THE GLOOM OF NIGHT, THEY WOULD HAVE SEEN THE AWESOME SIGHT OF A GROSS HUMAN FIGURE *GLIDING* THROUGH THE AIR LIKE A NOCTURNAL BEAST OF PREY... LIKE A MARAUDING *OWL!!*

HOW *EASY* IT IS...FOR *ME!*

BUT, A SCANT TWO SECONDS LATER, THE DRAMATIC HEAD OF *DAREDEVIL* BREAKS THE SURFACE ...HEARING THE SPEEDBOAT'S MOTOR AND ESTIMATING ITS SPEED AND DIRECTION IN THE SPACE OF A SINGLE HEARTBEAT...

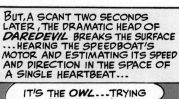

IT'S THE *OWL*...TRYING TO ESCAPE!

MOVING WITH THE SPEED OF THOUGHT, THE SIGHTLESS MAN DUCKS BENEATH THE SURFACE, AND... AS THE SPEEDING CRAFT PASSES OVER HIM...

I'LL USE MY CANE TO JAM HIS PROPELLER!!

...*NOW!!*

THE MOTOR SPUTTERS...DIES...AND THEN THERE IS SILENCE!

I CAN DETECT NO HEARTBEAT... NO SOUND OF BREATHING! BUT THE OWL *MIGHT* BE SWIMMING UNDER THE SURFACE! WATER ACTS AS A MUFFLER TO MY SENSES...I'LL NEVER BE ABLE TO FIND HIM NOW!

21.

FRUSTRATED AT NOT KNOWING WHETHER HIS FOE IS ALIVE OR DEAD, THE WEARY ADVENTURER STEALTHILY CLIMBS ONTO THE NEARBY DOCK, REASSURED BY THE KNOWLEDGE THAT THE OWL'S PLAN HAS BEEN COMPLETELY SHATTERED!

I'D BETTER CHANGE BACK TO MATT MURDOCK WHILE I CAN! I'LL TELL KAREN THAT I CAME HERE BECAUSE THE OWL SENT FOR ME, TO DISCUSS SOME LEGAL MATTERS!

AND SO, A FEW MINUTES LATER...

OH, MATT... YOU'RE LUCKY THAT YOU DIDN'T GET HERE *EARLIER!* YOU'VE NO *IDEA* WHAT A DANGEROUS CREATURE THE *OWL* IS!!

BETTER TAKE HIM BACK TO THE CITY, MA'AM! IF THOSE RACKET BOSSES ARE ON THEIR WAY HERE, THIS'LL BE NO PLACE FOR A BLIND MAN!!

THANK YOU, OFFICER! I SUPPOSE IT *IS* NEEDLESSLY DANGEROUS FOR ME TO REMAIN HERE!

BUT I WON'T MISS THE EXCITEMENT *ANYWAY!* I CAN HEAR THE MOBSTERS' CARS APPROACHING THE AVIARY *NOW!*

IN FACT, THEY SOUND AS THOUGH THEY'RE JUST RIDING THROUGH THE GATE, PAST THE PLAINCLOTHESMEN WHO ARE STATIONED ON EITHER SIDE!

JUDGING BY THE AMOUNT OF PULSEBEATS I HEAR, THE POLICE GOT THEM ALL... INCLUDING *APE* AND *SILENT SAM!* IT'S THE BIGGEST HAUL SINCE APPALACHIAN!

THEY'RE TAKING ALL THE MOBSTERS BACK TO TOWN IN PADDY WAGONS, MR. MURDOCK! AND, WITH THE OWL VANISHED, IT SEEMS YOU'VE LOST A CLIENT!

FROM WHAT I'VE *HEARD* OF HIM, KAREN, IT'S NOT MUCH OF A LOSS! I'M NOT REALLY CUT OUT FOR ALL THIS COPS AND ROBBERS STUFF!

IT'S ODD... EVEN THOUGH YOU *SAY* THAT... YOU REMIND ME SOMEHOW OF *ANOTHER* MAN... A MAN WHO IS SO TOTALLY *DIFFERENT!*

OH, WELL, EH... I GUESS WE'D BETTER BE GETTING HOME NOW...

AND, AFTER REACHING THE CITY, AS MATT SLOWLY WALKS AWAY...

I *MUST* BE FALLING IN LOVE WITH HIM! WHY ELSE WOULD SUCH A SHY, QUIET, HANDICAPPED MAN REMIND ME OF... OF ALL PEOPLE... THE MAN CALLED *DAREDEVIL??!*

22.

THE END

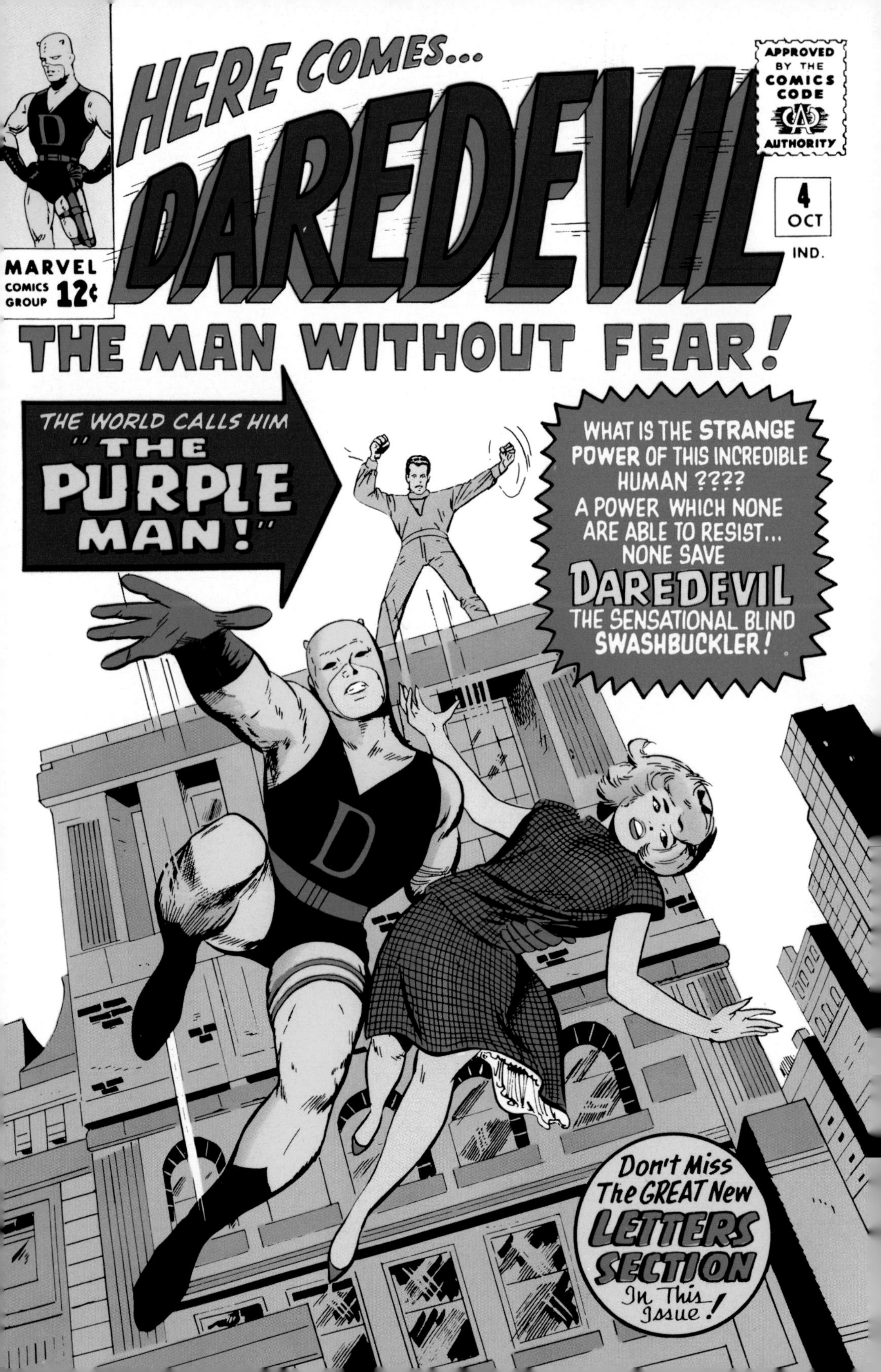

HERE COMES...
DAREDEVIL
THE MAN WITHOUT FEAR!
MARVEL COMICS GROUP 12¢
APPROVED BY THE COMICS CODE AUTHORITY
4 OCT
IND.
THE WORLD CALLS HIM "THE PURPLE MAN!"
WHAT IS THE STRANGE POWER OF THIS INCREDIBLE HUMAN ???? A POWER WHICH NONE ARE ABLE TO RESIST... NONE SAVE DAREDEVIL THE SENSATIONAL BLIND SWASHBUCKLER!
Don't Miss The GREAT New LETTERS SECTION In This Issue!

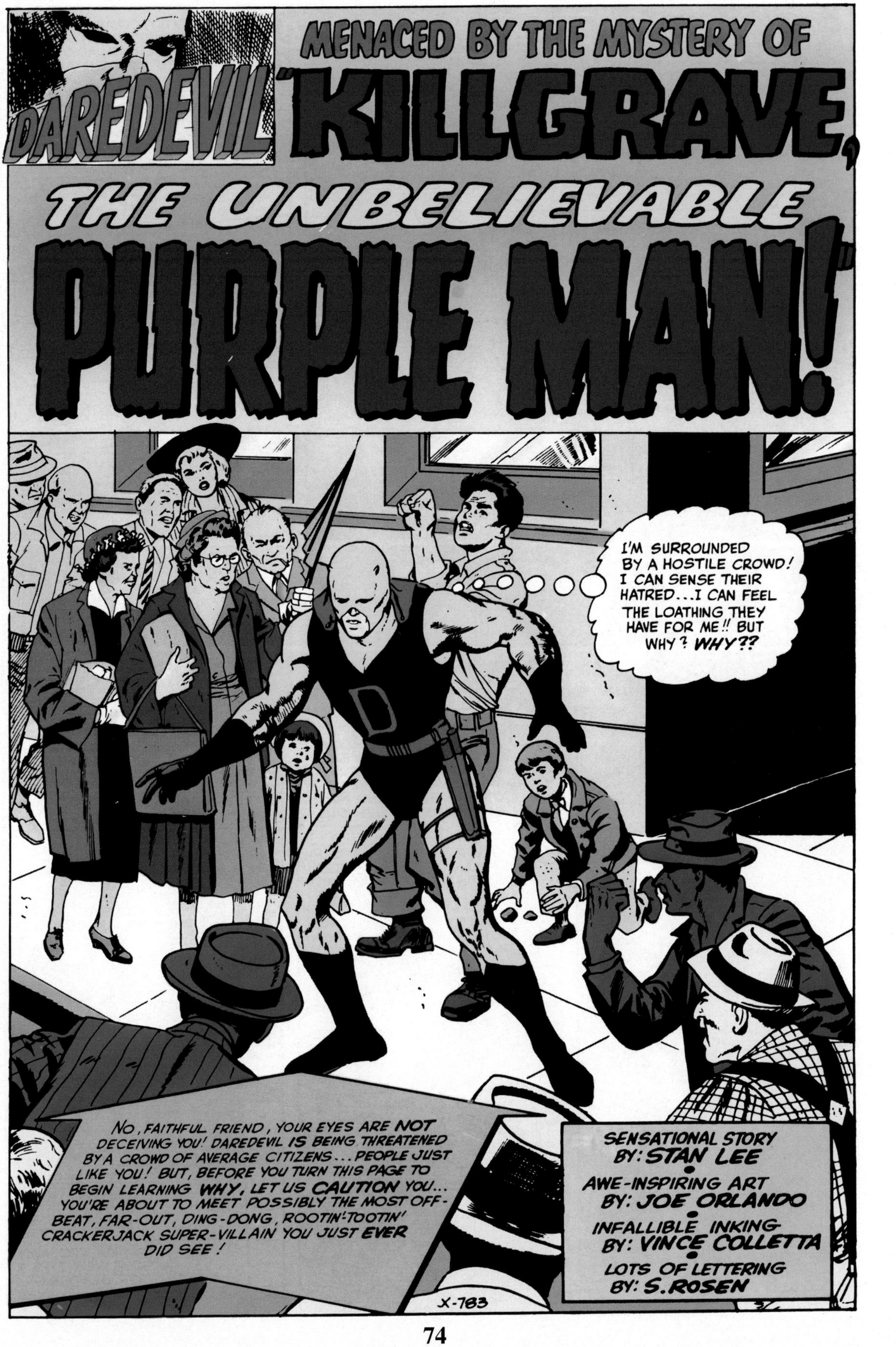

DAREDEVIL
MENACED BY THE MYSTERY OF
"KILLGRAVE, THE UNBELIEVABLE PURPLE MAN!"
I'M SURROUNDED BY A HOSTILE CROWD! I CAN SENSE THEIR HATRED...I CAN FEEL THE LOATHING THEY HAVE FOR ME!! BUT WHY? WHY??
NO, FAITHFUL FRIEND, YOUR EYES ARE NOT DECEIVING YOU! DAREDEVIL IS BEING THREATENED BY A CROWD OF AVERAGE CITIZENS... PEOPLE JUST LIKE YOU! BUT, BEFORE YOU TURN THIS PAGE TO BEGIN LEARNING WHY, LET US CAUTION YOU... YOU'RE ABOUT TO MEET POSSIBLY THE MOST OFF-BEAT, FAR-OUT, DING-DONG, ROOTIN'-TOOTIN' CRACKERJACK SUPER-VILLAIN YOU JUST EVER DID SEE!
SENSATIONAL STORY BY: STAN LEE
AWE-INSPIRING ART BY: JOE ORLANDO
INFALLIBLE INKING BY: VINCE COLLETTA
LOTS OF LETTERING BY: S. ROSEN
X-783

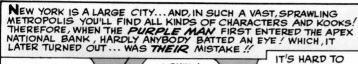
NEW YORK IS A LARGE CITY... AND, IN SUCH A VAST, SPRAWLING METROPOLIS YOU'LL FIND ALL KINDS OF CHARACTERS AND KOOKS! THEREFORE, WHEN THE *PURPLE MAN* FIRST ENTERED THE APEX NATIONAL BANK, HARDLY ANYBODY BATTED AN EYE! WHICH, IT LATER TURNED OUT... WAS *THEIR* MISTAKE!!

THIS SEEMS TO BE A LIKELY PLACE!

LOVELY DAY, ISN'T IT, MR. SMATHERS?

IT'S HARD TO TELL FROM IN HERE, MRS. PERKINS!

CALMLY, PATIENTLY, COMPLETELY RELAXED, THE PURPLE MAN STANDS BEHIND THE LITTLE OLD LADY, AS HE POLITELY AWAITS HIS TURN! AND THEN...

NEXT!

PLEASE FILL THIS CASE WITH HUNDRED DOLLAR BILLS! ONLY *NEW* ONES, IF YOU DON'T MIND! I LIKE THEM NICE AND CRISP!

YES, SIR!

WITHOUT A MOMENT'S HESITATION, THE TELLER DOES AS HE IS TOLD, WHILE THE PURPLE MAN CASUALLY STANDS AND WATCHES THE OPERATION... BETRAYING NO SIGN OF WORRY OR NERVOUSNESS!

DON'T STUFF IT TOO FULL, PLEASE! IT'S A NEW BRIEFCASE, AND I DON'T WANT THE SEAMS TO SPLIT!

I THINK THAT WILL BE ENOUGH NOW, THANK YOU!

VERY WELL, SIR! I HOPE THIS WILL DO!

THEN, SECURELY TUCKING THE BULGING BAG UNDER HIS ARM, THE PURPLE MAN TURNS AND SLOWLY WALKS THROUGH THE DOOR TO THE STREET, WITH A SATISFIED SMILE ON HIS PURPLE FACE...

SUCH A PLEASANT INSTITUTION TO DO BUSINESS WITH!

WHAT AN ODD-LOOKING MAN!

HMMPH... PROBABLY SOME NEW TYPE OF BEATNIK!

2.

BUT, A FEW MINUTES AFTER THE SOFT-SPOKEN STRANGER HAS LEFT THE BANK, THE STARTLED TELLER SUDDENLY *SEEMS* AWARE FOR THE FIRST TIME...OF WHAT HE HAS *DONE!*

GOOD HEAVENS! I MUST HAVE BEEN OUT OF MY *MIND!* I HANDED A PERFECT STRANGER THOUSANDS OF DOLLARS IN NEW HUNDRED-DOLLAR BILLS!!

THEN, I LET HIM CALMLY WALK *OUT* WITH THE MONEY!

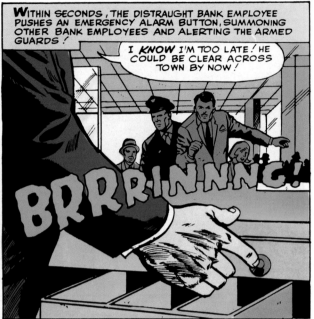

WITHIN SECONDS, THE DISTRAUGHT BANK EMPLOYEE PUSHES AN EMERGENCY ALARM BUTTON, SUMMONING OTHER BANK EMPLOYEES AND ALERTING THE ARMED GUARDS!

I *KNOW* I'M TOO LATE! HE COULD BE CLEAR ACROSS TOWN BY NOW!

BRRRINNNG!

BUT, STRANGELY ENOUGH, THE PURPLE MAN HAS MADE NO ATTEMPT TO FLEE! AND SO, A SCANT THREE BLOCKS AWAY WE FIND...

THERE HE IS! *HE'S* THE ONE!

HALT! STOP, OR I'LL *SHOOT!*

IT'S JUST TOO NICE A DAY TO TAKE A TAXI! I'D RATHER WALK!

THERE'S THE BAG WITH THE MONEY! WE'VE GOT YOU DEAD TO RIGHTS!

DIDN'T THINK WE'D *FIND* YOU, EH?

TAKE YOUR HANDS OFF ME! I *DETEST* PHYSICAL CONTACT!

HAND OVER THAT CASE, MAC! YOU'VE GOT A DATE WITH THE JUDGE!

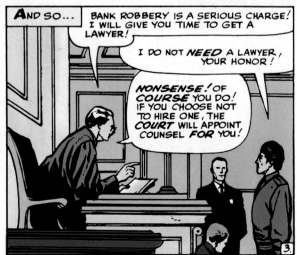

AND SO...

BANK ROBBERY IS A SERIOUS CHARGE! I WILL GIVE YOU TIME TO GET A LAWYER!

I DO NOT *NEED* A LAWYER, YOUR HONOR!

NONSENSE! OF *COURSE* YOU DO! IF YOU CHOOSE NOT TO HIRE ONE, THE *COURT* WILL APPOINT COUNSEL *FOR* YOU!

3.

AND NOW, FOR THOSE OF YOU WHO WERE WONDERING WHEN, IF EVER, WE'D BE SEEING OUR *HERO*, WE NEXT GO TO THE OFFICES OF *NELSON AND MURDOCK*, WHERE WE FIND...

MR. MURDOCK IS SO HANDSOME... SO CAPABLE... IT'S HARD TO BELIEVE HE'S *BLIND!*

WHAT'S THAT? THE COURT WANTS US TO DEFEND A MAN ACCUSED OF BANK ROBBERY? WELL, I'M INVOLVED IN SOME OTHER LITIGATION RIGHT NOW, BUT PERHAPS MY PARTNER...

SAY NO MORE, FOGGY! I'LL *TAKE* THE CASE!

GET ALL THE DETAILS YOU CAN FOR OL' MATTHEW!

IF YOU'D LIKE ME TO COME ALONG AND TAKE NOTES...?

I'D *LOVE* IT, LITTLE LADY! GET YOUR COAT!

KAREN HAS NEVER *BEEN* TO COURT WITH US! I GUESS SHE'S CURIOUS TO SEE LAWYERS ACTUALLY AT WORK!

DON'T KEEP HER TOO LONG, MATT! I'VE GOT A LOT OF DICTATION TO FINISH OFF!

AND SO THEY REACH THE COURTHOUSE, WITH MATT LITTLE DREAMING THAT HE *HIMSELF* IS THE ATTRACTION FOR KAREN PAGE, RATHER THAN THE LURE OF THE TRIAL!

YOU WALK THE STEPS SO *QUICKLY*, MR. MURDOCK! YOU MUST COME HERE OFTEN!

I'M GETTING CARELESS! MUSTN'T LET ON THAT MY EXTRA-KEEN SENSES TAKE THE PLACE OF MY EYESIGHT!

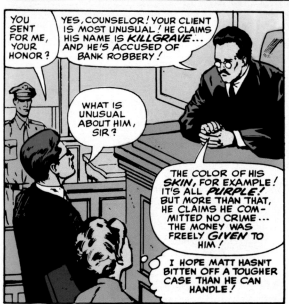

YOU SENT FOR ME, YOUR HONOR?

YES, COUNSELOR! YOUR CLIENT IS MOST UNUSUAL! HE CLAIMS HIS NAME IS *KILLGRAVE*... AND HE'S ACCUSED OF BANK ROBBERY!

WHAT IS UNUSUAL ABOUT HIM, SIR?

THE COLOR OF HIS *SKIN*, FOR EXAMPLE! IT'S ALL *PURPLE!* BUT MORE THAN THAT, HE CLAIMS HE COMMITTED NO CRIME... THE MONEY WAS FREELY *GIVEN* TO HIM!

I HOPE MATT HASN'T BITTEN OFF A TOUGHER CASE THAN HE CAN HANDLE!

THIS WAY, MR. MURDOCK... HE'S IN CELL BLOCK 14!

I SEEM TO SENSE A STRANGE SINISTER PRESENCE ALREADY!

WHAT A DEPRESSING PLACE!

4.

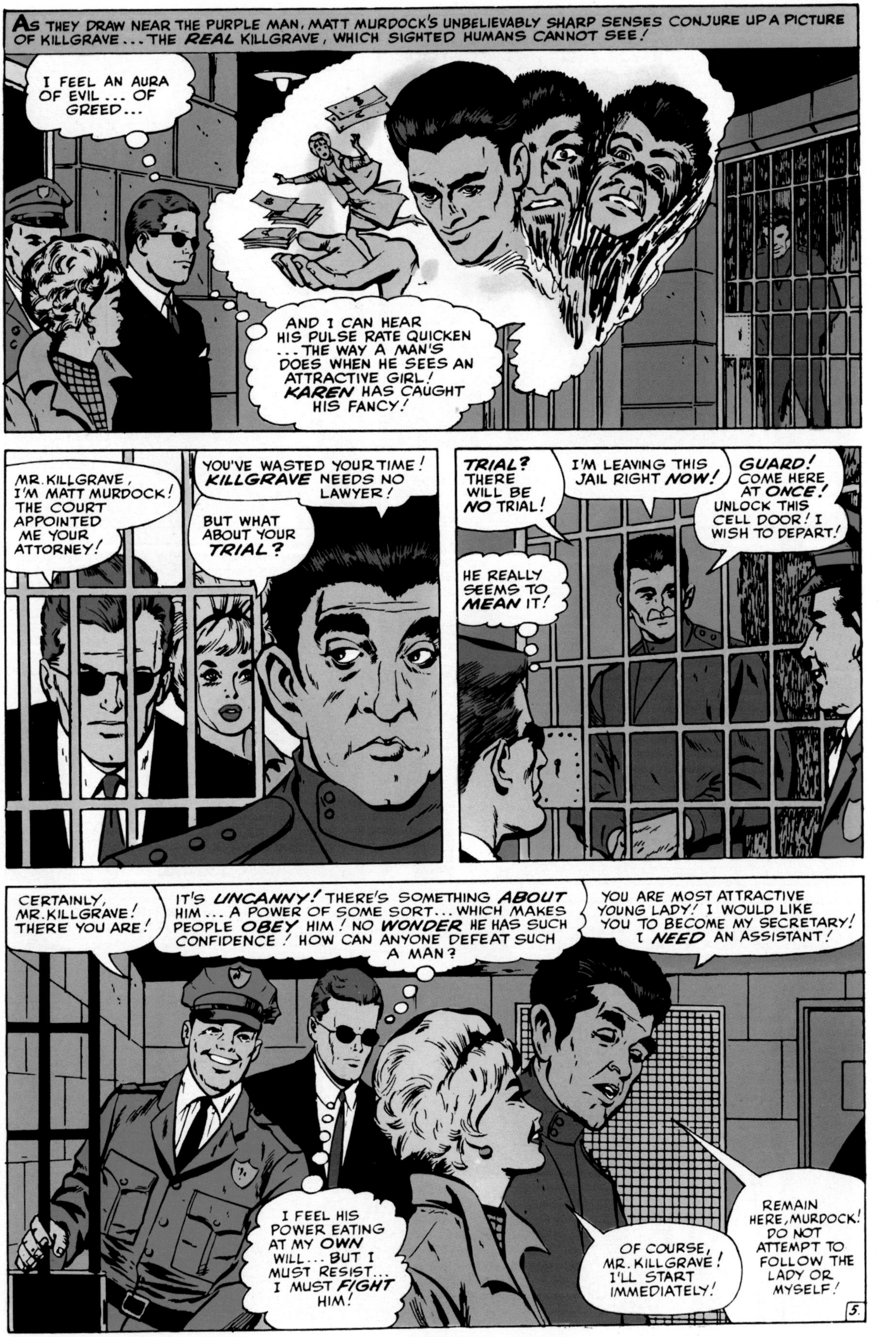
AS THEY DRAW NEAR THE PURPLE MAN, MATT MURDOCK'S UNBELIEVABLY SHARP SENSES CONJURE UP A PICTURE OF KILLGRAVE ... THE REAL KILLGRAVE, WHICH SIGHTED HUMANS CANNOT SEE!
I FEEL AN AURA OF EVIL ... OF GREED ...
AND I CAN HEAR HIS PULSE RATE QUICKEN ... THE WAY A MAN'S DOES WHEN HE SEES AN ATTRACTIVE GIRL! KAREN HAS CAUGHT HIS FANCY!
MR. KILLGRAVE, I'M MATT MURDOCK! THE COURT APPOINTED ME YOUR ATTORNEY!
YOU'VE WASTED YOUR TIME! KILLGRAVE NEEDS NO LAWYER!
BUT WHAT ABOUT YOUR TRIAL?
TRIAL? THERE WILL BE NO TRIAL!
I'M LEAVING THIS JAIL RIGHT NOW!
GUARD! COME HERE AT ONCE! UNLOCK THIS CELL DOOR! I WISH TO DEPART!
HE REALLY SEEMS TO MEAN IT!
CERTAINLY, MR. KILLGRAVE! THERE YOU ARE!
IT'S UNCANNY! THERE'S SOMETHING ABOUT HIM ... A POWER OF SOME SORT ... WHICH MAKES PEOPLE OBEY HIM! NO WONDER HE HAS SUCH CONFIDENCE! HOW CAN ANYONE DEFEAT SUCH A MAN?
YOU ARE MOST ATTRACTIVE YOUNG LADY! I WOULD LIKE YOU TO BECOME MY SECRETARY! I NEED AN ASSISTANT!
I FEEL HIS POWER EATING AT MY OWN WILL ... BUT I MUST RESIST ... I MUST FIGHT HIM!
OF COURSE, MR. KILLGRAVE! I'LL START IMMEDIATELY!
REMAIN HERE, MURDOCK! DO NOT ATTEMPT TO FOLLOW THE LADY OR MYSELF!
5.

ALTHOUGH ORDERED TO REMAIN BEHIND, MATT MURDOCK DOES NOT HAVE THE REACTIONS OF AN ORDINARY HUMAN! WITH HIS EVERY SENSE RAZOR SHARP... HIS INDOMITABLE WILL SHRUGS OFF KILLGRAVE'S COMMAND, AND, AS THE ALARM IS FINALLY SOUNDED...

KILLGRAVE IS *GONE*!!

SEND OUT AN ALL-POINTS ALARM! DON'T JUST *STAND* THERE, MAN!

I'VE GOT TO FIND A PRIVATE CORNER... WHERE I CAN MAKE A QUICK CHANGE!

AND, FIND IT HE *DOES*... AS, SECONDS LATER, THE WORLD'S MOST FEARLESS ADVENTURER THUNDERS INTO ACTION!

I'LL *FIND* HIM! NO MATTER *WHERE* HE'S HIDING, I'LL HEAR HIS HEARTBEAT... HIS BREATHING...

TO ME, THEY'RE AS DISTINCTIVE AS HIS *VOICE*!

AND, WITHIN MINUTES...

THAT PULSE... IT'S *HIM*!!

HOLD IT, KILLGRAVE!

DARE-DEVIL!!

AT LAST, I CAN PROVE MY SUPERIORITY OVER A MERE COSTUMED CRIME-FIGHTER!

YOU DON'T WANT TO PURSUE ME! YOU'VE MADE A *MISTAKE*! *I'M* NOT THE ONE YOU WANT!

HE ALMOST HAS ME *CONVINCED*! WHAT CAN HIS POWER *BE*?? IT ISN'T *HYPNOTISM*... I'M TOTALLY *BLIND*, AND YET I *FEEL* IT!!

LOOK! THERE'S THE *PURPLE MAN*... THE GUY THE *POLICE* ARE AFTER!

WHAT'S HE DOING IN THE *STREET*?

I'M NOT THE PURPLE MAN! I'M JUST A TOURIST!

WE SHOULD HAVE KNOWN!

YEAH! WE WERE WRONG!

IT'S *AMAZING*! HE SEEMS TO HAVE THE POWER TO SAP MEN'S WILLS!

6.

OKAY, KILLGRAVE, YOUR LITTLE GAME HAS GONE ON LONG ENOUGH! NOW RELEASE THE GIRL FROM WHATEVER INFLUENCE YOU'VE EXERTED ON HER... AND COME BACK TO JAIL WITH ME... OR DO I HAVE TO TAKE YOU THE *HARD* WAY??

SO! I'VE FINALLY ENCOUNTERED SOMEONE WHO CAN *RESIST* MY POWER! THAT IS TOO BAD... FOR *YOU*! NOW I'LL HAVE TO DEFEAT YOU... *PERMANENTLY*!

HIS POWER LIES WITHIN HIS *BODY*, SOMEHOW! I'VE NEVER SENSED ANYTHING *LIKE* IT! WHAT TYPE OF FREAK CAN HE *BE*?

YOUR WILL IS TOO STRONG FOR ME! BUT I HAVE *OTHER* METHODS!

I'LL LET THE *CROWD* TAKE CARE OF YOU! THEY'LL DO ANYTHING I ASK!

STAY BY MY SIDE, GIRL!

OF COURSE I WILL, KILLGRAVE!

THEN, BEFORE DAREDEVIL CAN MAKE ANOTHER MOVE, THE PURPLE MAN ASKS THE CROWD TO *ATTACK* THE FEARLESS ADVENTURER! AND UNHESITATINGLY, THEY OBEY!!

IT IS TIME FOR US TO LEAVE NOW! COME, MY DEAR!

BUT, YOU ASKED THE PEOPLE TO ATTACK DAREDEVIL! SHOULDN'T I *HELP* THEM?

DOWN WITH DAREDEVIL!

DAREDEVIL IS OUR *ENEMY*!

STOP! YOU DON'T KNOW WHAT YOU'RE *DOING*!!

7.

80

REALIZING HIS PLIGHT IS HOPELESS, THE SIGHTLESS ADVENTURER RESORTS TO NIMBLE *FLIGHT!*

STOP HIM! DON'T LET HIM ESCAPE US!!

DEATH TO DAREDEVIL!!

I CAN'T REASON WITH THEM...AND DON'T WANT TO *HURT* ANYONE, SO THIS IS THE ONLY WAY!

IT'S AMAZING! I CAN SENSE THE HATRED... THE LOATHING...WHICH KILLGRAVE SO EASILY INSTILLED IN THEM!

WHAT'S GOING *ON* HERE? *BREAK IT UP!* BREAK IT UP!

I HEAR AN OFFICER TRYING TO CALM THE CROWD! HE ARRIVED TOO LATE TO BE AFFECTED BY KILLGRAVE...BUT EVEN *HE* CAN'T BREAK THE PURPLE MAN'S SPELL!

BUT THEN...

LUCKY I HEARD THE WIND MAKING THE LEAVES OF THIS TREE RUSTLE! I'LL BE SAFE WITHIN SECONDS!

SOMEONE GRABBED MY HOOD--- RIPPED IT!

RIPP!

I REALIZE NOW THAT IT'S TOO DANGEROUS TO KEEP MY STREET SUIT HIDDEN IN THAT HOOD! IT'S TOO EASY FOR AN ENEMY TO GRAB...TO SLOW ME UP!

LOOK! HE'S GETTING AWAY!

CAN'T ANYONE *STOP* HIM ??!

8.

AND, IF ANYONE EVER **FOUND** MY STREET SUIT, THEY'D HAVE A CLUE TO MY REAL IDENTITY!

SO THE HOOD MUST **GO**!

WHAT WERE WE SO **EXCITED** ABOUT?

I-I CAN'T **REMEMBER**!

SECONDS LATER, AS HE SWINGS AWAY TO FREEDOM, THE DASHING DAREDEVIL REALIZES...

I SENSED THE ANGRY MOOD FADING FROM THE CROWD! THAT MEANS KILLGRAVE'S POWER CAN ONLY BE EFFECTIVE WHEN HE HIMSELF IS NEAR! THE FURTHER HE WENT FROM THE CROWD, THE MORE HIS SPELL WEAKENED!

BY NOW, THE CROWD MUST BE COMPLETELY BACK TO NORMAL!

BUT **MY** JOB IS JUST BEGINNING! I'VE GOT TO FIND **KAREN**... TO FREE HER FROM KILLGRAVE'S EVIL INFLUENCE!

BUT, AFTER SEARCHING THE CITY FOR HOURS...

IT'S NO USE! I'VE LOST HIS TRAIL! HE HAD TOO MUCH TIME IN WHICH TO HIDE!

WELL, I CAN'T KEEP PROWLING THE ROOFTOPS ALL DAY! I'M JUST WASTING TIME! KILLGRAVE WON THE FIRST ROUND, AND I CAN'T **DENY** IT!!

BUT I WON'T REST TILL KAREN'S SAFE! ...AND TILL I'VE FOUND A WAY TO DESTROY HIS UNCANNY POWER!

MINUTES LATER, A HANDSOME UNSEEING MAN ENTERS THE TOP OF AN OFFICE BUILDING STAIRWELL, FROM THE ROOF, AFTER LISTENING CAREFULLY TO MAKE SURE NOBODY IS ON THE OTHER SIDE OF THE DOOR TO SEE HIM!

DAREDEVIL CAN DO NO MORE FOR THE PRESENT!

SO IT'S TIME FOR **MATT MURDOCK** TO RETURN TO HIS LAW OFFICE, AND TRY TO FIGURE OUT A WAY TO BRING KILLGRAVE TO HIS KNEES!

THUS, A DEJECTED, SOMBER MATT MURDOCK ENTERS THE LAW OFFICES OF NELSON AND MURDOCK, DREADING THE EXPLOSIVE MOMENT WHEN HE WILL HAVE TO TELL HIS UNSUSPECTING PARTNER WHAT HAS HAPPENED...

I HEAR HIM IN HIS CHAIR... FACING ME! HIS HEARTBEAT IS CALM, NORMAL! BUT NOW IT'S SPEEDING UP, AS HE REALIZES THAT *KAREN* IS NOT WITH ME!

HI, MATTHEW, BOY! GLAD YOU GOT BACK IN TIME TO...

SAY! WHERE'S *KAREN*? I *TOLD* YOU I NEEDED HER TO FINISH SOME DICTATION!

I DON'T QUITE KNOW HOW TO *TELL* YOU THIS, FOGGY... WE HAD SOME *TROUBLE* WITH THE MAN NAMED KILLGRAVE! HE ESCAPED FROM JAIL...AND...HE TOOK KAREN *WITH* HIM!

HE TOOK KAREN WITH HIM?? JUST LIKE *THAT*??! HOW CAN YOU SIT THERE SO *CALMLY*?? *WHERE* DID HE TAKE HER?? HOW DID IT *HAPPEN*??

HIS PULSE RATE IS FANTASTIC NOW! ONLY A MAN WHO'S WORRIED ABOUT ONE HE *LOVES* COULD REACT THAT WAY!

THEN, AFTER MATT HAS SOBERLY EXPLAINED...

I NEVER REALIZED HE FELT THAT WAY ABOUT HER! THIS COULD CAUSE... COMPLICATIONS!

WELL, I GUESS I SHOULDN'T YELL AT *YOU*, MATT! AFTER ALL, IT WASN'T *YOUR* FAULT!

IT WAS *MY* FAULT! I SHOULD HAVE KNOWN BETTER THAN TO LET HER VISIT A DANGEROUS CRIMINAL WITH *YOU*! IT WAS TOO *RISKY*!

HE FEELS MY *BLINDNESS* PREVENTED ME FROM AIDING KAREN!

WAIT, HERE! I'LL SEE WHAT *I* CAN DO!

HIS REACTION IS UNDERSTANDABLE! I WOULD FEEL THE SAME WAY IN HIS SHOES! HE STILL CAN'T REALIZE HOW IMPOSSIBLE IT IS FOR ANY NORMAL PERSON TO DEFY THE PURPLE MAN!

BUT THERE IS *ONE* WHO IS *NOT* A NORMAL PERSON! ONE WHO CALLS HIMSELF... *DAREDEVIL!*

MEANWHILE, LET US TURN OUR ATTENTION TO A LARGE GYMNASIUM, ON THE WEST SIDE OF TOWN, WHERE WE FIND...

HEY, YOU GUYS! HOLD IT! *HOLD IT!* SOMEONE WANTS TO *TALK* TO YA!

NOW STEP ASIDE! I'LL HANDLE THIS!

10

As Killgrave speaks, the husky muscle-men immediately fall under his spell, except for one known as "Punchy" who is too slow-witted to react at normal speed...

FROM THIS MOMENT ON, YOU ARE ALL WORKING FOR ME! YOU WILL SERVE AS MY BODYGUARDS, AND PROTECT ME WITH YOUR LIVES!

YOU'RE NUTS! WHO DO YOU THINK YOU ARE?

NOBODY CAN TELL PUNCHY WHAT TO DO, SEE? I'LL SHOW YOU WHO'S GONNA WORK FOR WHO!!

UNHAND ME! I LOATHE PHYSICAL VIOLENCE! PROTECT ME, MY BODYGUARDS! REMEMBER, YOUR MASTER MAY NOT BE HARMED!

AND, A SPLIT-SECOND LATER... THE MASTER MAY NOT BE HARMED!

LET GO OF KILLGRAVE!

ENOUGH! DO NOT HURT HIM!!

AND NOW, MARCH DOWN THE STAIRS! I HAVE WORK FOR YOU TO DO!!

SNAP!

And so, the Purple Man leads his small but powerful army brazenly through the street, knowing that no one who gets close enough to stop him can resist his uncanny spell...

OUR DESTINATION IS THE RITZ PLAZA HOTEL. MARCH!

11

LATER, THE NEXT IN A SERIES OF INCREDIBLE EVENTS OCCURS! GUARDED BY HIS INTENSELY LOYAL GYMNASTS, THE PURPLE MAN CONFIDENTLY APPROACHES THE STARTLED DESK CLERK AND DEMANDS...

EVICT ALL YOUR TENANTS FROM THE TOP FLOOR! MY STAFF AND I SHALL USE IT AS OUR HEADQUARTERS!

OF COURSE, SIR! I'LL ORDER ALL THE TOP FLOOR TENANTS TO LEAVE WITHIN THE HOUR!

THAT WILL NOT BE SATISFACTORY! I WANT THEM OUT IMMEDIATELY!

CERTAINLY, SIR! I'M SORRY I MISUNDERSTOOD YOU!

AND SO, THE INCREDIBLE OCCURS! THE WEALTHY TENANTS OF THE HOTEL'S FASHIONABLE TOP FLOOR ARE ALL USHERED OUT OF THE BUILDING, UPON THE WORD OF ONE MYSTERIOUS MAN!

I'LL SUE SOMEBODY FOR THIS! THIS IS UNPARDONABLE!

ORDER ME OUT, WILL THEY? I'LL NEVER COME BACK HERE AGAIN!

I WONDER WHY THEY'RE DOING THIS? THEY GAVE US NO REASON!

AND, FINALLY...

I'VE DONE IT! I'VE PROVEN MYSELF TO BE UNBEATABLE! THERE IS NOTHING I CANNOT ACCOMPLISH! BEFORE I'M DONE, THE ENTIRE WORLD WILL BE AT THE FEET OF KILLGRAVE, THE ALL-POWERFUL PURPLE MAN!

THERE WAS ONLY ONE WHO SEEMED ABLE TO RESIST MY POWER! BUT, I'LL FIND A WAY TO DEFEAT HIM, TOO! IT IS MY DESTINY TO TRIUMPH! I WAS MEANT TO CONQUER ALL!

12.

MEANWHILE, WHAT OF THE MAN WHOM KILLGRAVE WAS REFERRING TO ?? BACK AT THE LAW OFFICES OF NELSON AND MURDOCK, WE FIND HIM RAPIDLY SCANNING HIS BRAILLE LAW BOOKS, EVEN THOUGH HIS SUPER-SENSITIVE FINGERS COULD "READ" ORDINARY PRINT IF HE WISHED, MERELY BY FEELING THE IMPRESSION OF THE *INK* ON THE PAGE!

IT'S JUST AS I *THOUGHT*!

KILLGRAVE ACTUALLY SEEMS TO HAVE BROKEN NO LAW!

I CAN FIND NO LAW WHICH PROHIBITS A MAN FROM *ASKING* FOR THINGS!

AND IF PEOPLE CHOOSE TO *OBEY* HIM, THAT'S THEIR PRIVILEGE! I CAN PROVE NO USE OF UNDUE *FORCE* ON KILLGRAVE'S PART!

NOT ONLY MUST I OUT-*FIGHT* HIM, BUT I MUST ALSO OUT-*THINK* HIM! MMM... I SEEM TO REMEMBER A BLUFF I PULLED WHEN I WAS BATTLING THE *FIXER*, NOT LONG AGO!*

I HAVE A MINIATURE TAPE RECORDER CONCEALED IN MY BILLY CLUB! IT'LL TELL THE POLICE ALL THEY NEED TO KNOW!

* SEE DAREDEVIL #1... EDITOR.

THAT GIVES ME AN IDEA OF A WAY TO BEAT THE PURPLE MAN! IT'S A LONG CHANCE, BUT I'VE *GOT* TO TAKE IT!

WHAT WAS MERELY A *BLUFF* IN THE CASE OF THE FIXER, WILL BE A *REALITY* IN THE CASE OF *KILLGRAVE*! THIS MINIATURIZED SPY-TYPE RECORDER IS JUST WHAT I NEED!

THEN, AFTER AN HOUR OF LONG PREPARATION...

PERFECT! THIS CHEMICALLY TREATED PLASTIC SHEET SNAPS OPEN AND CLOSED WITHIN MY CANE BY MEANS OF A TAUT SPRING, LIKE A MODIFIED WINDOW SHADE!

ZIP!

13.

AND NOW, WITH MY BILLY CLUB SHEATHED IN ITS HOLSTER...AND UNHAMPERED BY MY BULKY HOOD...I'M READY FOR ONE OF THE TOUGHEST MISSIONS OF MY CAREER!

THIS TIME I WON'T STOP SEARCHING THE CITY TILL I *FIND* KILLGRAVE! NO MATTER HOW LONG IT TAKES...NO MATTER HOW DIFFICULT IT IS!

HEEDLESS OF THE RISKS... IGNORING THE DANGERS... HIS EVERY SENSE OPERATING AT PEAK EFFICIENCY...THE DAZZLING SIGHTLESS *DAREDEVIL* COMBS THE CITY...

...LISTENING FOR VOICES, HEARTBEATS... *ANY* CLUE AT ALL...

FOR, ONCE HAVING STOOD NEAR THE PURPLE MAN, DAREDEVIL'S RAZOR-SHARP SENSES COULD IDENTIFY HIS VOICE, HIS PULSE RATE, HIS FOOTSTEPS, THE ODOR OF HIS HAIR TONIC, FROM AMONG MILLIONS OF OTHERS! FOR, TO THE SIGHTLESS CRUSADER, SUCH THINGS ARE AS DISTINCTIVE...AS UNFAILING...AS A MAN'S *FINGER-PRINTS!*

ALL THAT DAREDEVIL REQUIRES IS TO BE WITHIN APPROXIMATELY ONE CITY BLOCK OF HIS QUARRY, AND HE WILL BE ABLE TO REACH HIS TARGET UNFAILINGLY!

BUT, THIS TIME HIS TASK IS EASIER THAN USUAL... FOR KILLGRAVE, CONFIDENT OF HIS GROWING POWER, HAS TAKEN NO PAINS TO CONCEAL HIS WHEREABOUTS! IN FACT, THROUGH THE MAGIC OF T.V. AND RADIO COVERAGE, THE ENTIRE *NATION* IS KEEPING ABREAST OF EACH NEW DEVELOPMENT!

ACCORDING TO THE RADIO NEWS BROADCAST I HEARD THROUGH THE WINDOW I JUST PASSED, KILLGRAVE HAS JUST TAKEN POSSESSION OF THE TOP FLOOR OF THE RITZ PLAZA HOTEL! I SHOULD BE THERE IN *MINUTES!*

ALTHOUGH UNABLE TO SEE, DAREDEVIL'S SENSE OF DIRECTION IS COMPLETELY FLAWLESS! HE IS POSSIBLY THE ONLY HUMAN ALIVE WHO CAN TELL WHERE *NORTH* IS BY SENSING THE MAGNETIC PULL OF THE POLE*...OR WHO CAN *HEAR* THE DIRECTION OF THE VERY CURRENTS OF THE AIR ITSELF!

I'VE REACHED MY GOAL! THE RITZ PLAZA IS DIRECTLY ACROSS THE STREET! I HEAR VANS BELOW...MOVING MEN...THEY'RE UNLOADING CAMERA EQUIPMENT!

...IT REMINDS ME OF THE JACK RUBY CASE IN DALLAS! WHATEVER HAPPENS NEXT MAY WELL OCCUR WITH THE EYES OF THE WORLD *WITNESSING* THE ENTIRE TABLEAU!

* WITH THE POSSIBLE EXCEPTION OF *MAGNETO*, HOMO SUPERIOR MUTANT LEADER OF THE *X-MEN'S* MOST DEADLY FOES! — EDITOR.

AND, UNAWARE THAT THE ONE MAN ABLE TO BATTLE HIM IS NEARBY, *KILLGRAVE* DISCUSSES HIS FUTURE PLANS WITH HIS "CAPTIVE AUDIENCE"...

I NOW HAVE A SMALL BUT POWERFUL PROTECTIVE FORCE, TO GUARD ME IF I SHOULD EVER BE CAUGHT UNAWARES!

I HAVE KAREN PAGE TO SERVE AS MY CONTACT WITH THE OUTER WORLD, AND AS MY RECORDING SECRETARY AND BIOGRAPHER!

OUR HEADQUARTERS ARE SECURE... SO IT IS TIME WE *BRANCHED OUT*...THERE IS MUCH YET TO BE DONE!

KAREN, I WANT YOU TO CONTACT...WHAT'S *WRONG*?? WHAT DO YOU SEE ON THE TERRACE??

BEFORE THE STARTLED GIRL CAN REPLY, A NIMBLE, SMOOTH-MUSCLED FIGURE BURSTS INTO THE ROOM, AS CONFIDENTLY AS IF HE CAN ACTUALLY *SEE* THE DANGERS THAT AWAIT HIM!

THEY'RE STANDING IN A SEMI-CIRCLE...KILLGRAVE IS IN THE CENTER! KAREN'S SOFTER BREATHING IS COMING FROM MY LEFT...BEHIND KILLGRAVE!

IT'S *DAREDEVIL*! DON'T LET HIM *TOUCH* ME!

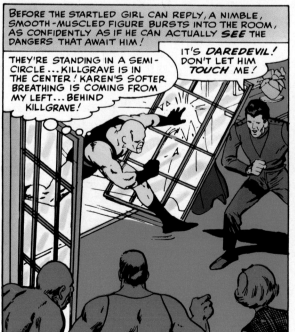

THEIR SOFT FOOTSTEPS ARE COMING CLOSER... PREPARING TO ATTACK! HEARTBEATS HAVEN'T SPEEDED UP ENOUGH YET...THEY WON'T RUSH ME FOR AT LEAST FIVE SECONDS!

ATTACK HIM ALL AT *ONCE*!! HE IS MORE POWERFUL THAN YOU SUSPECT!

C'MON, YOU GUYS! WE HAVE TO PROTECT THE *MASTER*!

15.

NOW! THEIR PULSE RATES ARE SHARPLY ACCELERATED! THEY'RE PREPARING TO LUNGE FORWARD! I'VE JUST TIME TO UNSHEATH MY BILLY CLUB!

WELL, WHAT ARE WE WAITIN' FOR??

LET'S GET 'IM!

BUT "GETTING" THE MAN WITHOUT FEAR IS SOMEWHAT MORE DIFFICULT THAN IT SOUNDS! MOVING WITH THE LIGHTNING-LIKE PRECISION OF ONE WHO HAS SPENT HIS LIFE IN TRAINING, DAREDEVIL BALANCES HIMSELF UPON HIS UPRIGHT BILLY CLUB, AND SPINS AROUND WITH THE FORCE OF A WHIRLWIND!

WHAM!

HE'S TOO FAST TO TACKLE LIKE THIS! BUT A BULLET WILL SURE ENOUGH STOP 'IM!

THE SOUND OF A PISTOL HAMMER BEING COCKED! I MUST TIME MY MOVE TO THE MICRO-SECOND! --NOW!

CRACK!

CLUMSY FOOL! YOU MISSED HIM!

NOT IF I CAN HELP IT!

RELAX! MY NEXT SHOT'LL GET HIM!

CLICK!

BY SNAPPING MY BILLY CLUB INTO POSITION AT A 90 DEGREE RIGHT ANGLE, I CAN HURL IT LIKE A BOOM-ERANG!

AND I CAN PIN-POINT MY TARGET BY THE UN-MISTAKABLE ODOR OF GUN-POWDER!

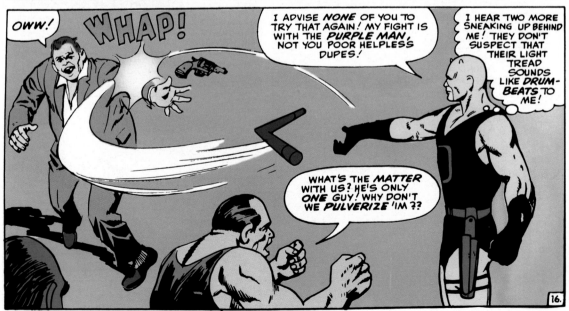

OWW!

WHAP!

I ADVISE NONE OF YOU TO TRY THAT AGAIN! MY FIGHT IS WITH THE PURPLE MAN, NOT YOU POOR HELPLESS DUPES!

I HEAR TWO MORE SNEAKING UP BEHIND ME! THEY DON'T SUSPECT THAT THEIR LIGHT TREAD SOUNDS LIKE DRUM-BEATS TO ME!

WHAT'S THE MATTER WITH US? HE'S ONLY ONE GUY! WHY DON'T WE PULVERIZE 'IM??

16.

89

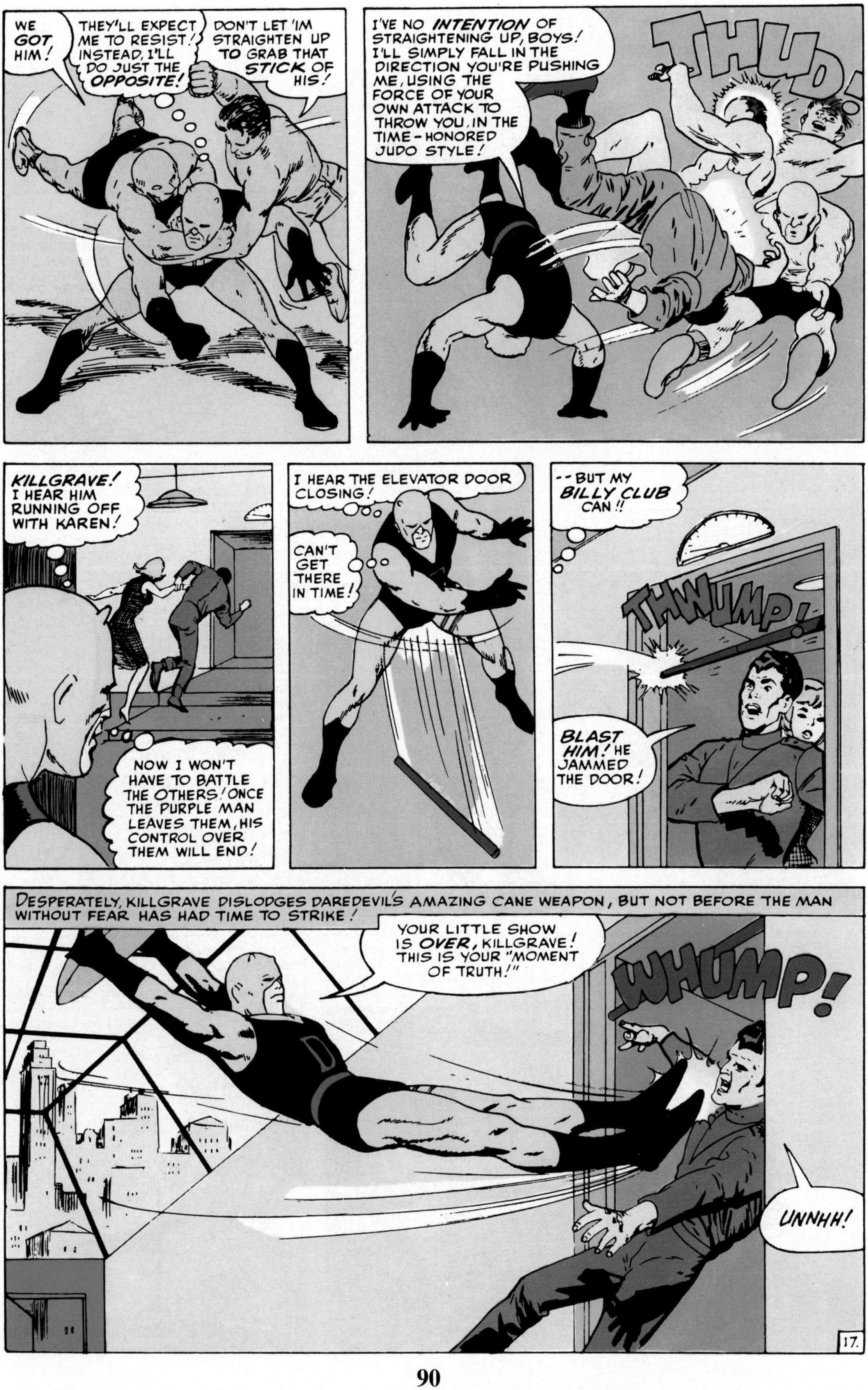

WE GOT HIM!
THEY'LL EXPECT ME TO RESIST! INSTEAD, I'LL DO JUST THE OPPOSITE!
DON'T LET 'IM STRAIGHTEN UP TO GRAB THAT STICK OF HIS!
I'VE NO INTENTION OF STRAIGHTENING UP, BOYS! I'LL SIMPLY FALL IN THE DIRECTION YOU'RE PUSHING ME, USING THE FORCE OF YOUR OWN ATTACK TO THROW YOU, IN THE TIME-HONORED JUDO STYLE!
THUD!
KILLGRAVE! I HEAR HIM RUNNING OFF WITH KAREN!
NOW I WON'T HAVE TO BATTLE THE OTHERS! ONCE THE PURPLE MAN LEAVES THEM, HIS CONTROL OVER THEM WILL END!
I HEAR THE ELEVATOR DOOR CLOSING!
CAN'T GET THERE IN TIME!
--BUT MY BILLY CLUB CAN!!
THWUMP!
BLAST HIM! HE JAMMED THE DOOR!
DESPERATELY, KILLGRAVE DISLODGES DAREDEVIL'S AMAZING CANE WEAPON, BUT NOT BEFORE THE MAN WITHOUT FEAR HAS HAD TIME TO STRIKE!
YOUR LITTLE SHOW IS OVER, KILLGRAVE! THIS IS YOUR "MOMENT OF TRUTH!"
WHUMP!
UNNHH!
17.

BUT, BEFORE THE MASKED CRUSADER CAN CONSOLIDATE HIS ADVANTAGE, THE PURPLE MAN RESORTS TO HIS ONE ACE-IN-THE-HOLE...

KAREN! STAND AT THE EDGE OF THE ROOF! AT MY NEXT COMMAND... HURL YOURSELF TO THE STREET BELOW!

NO! DON'T DO IT, KILLGRAVE!

WHETHER I ORDER HER TO DO IT OR NOT, DEPENDS ON YOU, DAREDEVIL!

I CAN'T AFFORD TO GAMBLE WITH A HUMAN LIFE! ESPECIALLY... HERS! THIS ROUND IS YOURS!

THERE YOU ARE WRONG, MY DEFEATED FOOL! I HAVE WON EVERY ROUND...FOR THIS IS THE FINAL ONE!

WHAT I CANNOT ACCOMPLISH WITH MY UNCANNY POWER, I CAN CERTAINLY ACHIEVE WITH THIS GUN!

AND NOW, YOUR RASH DEFIANCE HAS FORCED ME TO DO WHAT I DID NOT WISH TO DO! BUT YOU LEAVE ME NO CHOICE! I CANNOT ALLOW ANYONE TO LIVE WHO CAN RESIST MY POWER!

BEFORE YOU SQUEEZE THAT TRIGGER...TELL ME...WHAT IS YOUR POWER? HOW DID YOU OBTAIN IT?

"YES, IT IS ONLY FITTING THAT YOU DO KNOW...BEFORE THE END COMES! IT BEGAN SOME MONTHS AGO, WHEN I STOLE INTO AN ARMY ORDNANCE DEPOT! FOR YOU SEE, I WAS FORMERLY A SPY FOR A FOREIGN POWER!"

THIS IS WHERE THE DREADED "NERVE GAS" IS STORED!

HOLD IT, YOU!

I'VE BUNGLED! A GUARD SPOTTED ME!

I CAN'T LET HIM CATCH ME! THE PENALTY COULD BE DEATH!

PUT DOWN THAT GUN! DON'T BE A FOOL! YOU CAN'T...UHH!

CRACK!

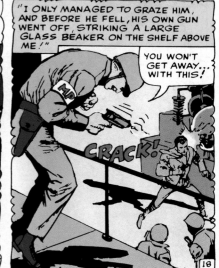

"I ONLY MANAGED TO GRAZE HIM, AND BEFORE HE FELL, HIS OWN GUN WENT OFF, STRIKING A LARGE GLASS BEAKER ON THE SHELF ABOVE ME!"

YOU WON'T GET AWAY... WITH THIS!

CRACK!

18

"BEFORE I COULD MOVE, THE CONTENTS OF THE BEAKER...CONTAINING A STRANGE PURPLE NERVE GAS, POURED OVER ME...DYEING MY ENTIRE BODY INDELIBLY! AND, BY THEN, *OTHER* GUARDS HAD SURROUNDED ME!"

WE CAUGHT YOU DEAD TO RIGHTS!

"DAZED, FRIGHTENED, I MUMBLED A WEAK STORY ABOUT BEING INNOCENT...ABOUT IT BEING AN *ACCIDENT!* BUT, TO MY ASTONISHMENT, THEY *BELIEVED* ME!"

IF YOU SAY YOU'RE INNOCENT, SIR, WE'RE SORRY WE ACCUSED YOU!

FOR SOME REASON, THEY BELIEVE WHATEVER I SAY!

"THEN, AS TIME WENT BY, AND MORE SUCH INCIDENTS OCCURRED, I KNEW THE TRUTH! IN SOME INEXPLICABLE WAY, THE PURPLE NERVE GAS HAD FUSED WITH MY OWN BODY ACIDS, GIVING ME A POWER GREATER THAN ANY HUMAN HAS EVER POSSESSED...THE POWER TO *COMMAND MEN'S WILLS!*"

ONLY *YOU* HAVE BEEN ABLE TO RESIST ME...AND, FOR THAT REASON, YOU CAN NO LONGER BE PERMITTED TO LIVE!

THANK YOU, KILLGRAVE!

THANK ME?? FOR *WHAT*??

FOR FURNISHING ME WITH THE EVIDENCE THE POLICE WILL NEED TO *CONVICT* YOU FOR TREASON!

IT'S ALL DOWN ON MY CONCEALED *TAPE RECORDER!*

AS FOR THAT INEFFECTUAL *GUN* OF YOURS, YOU DIDN'T *REALLY* THINK I'D BE A SITTING DUCK FOR YOU, DID YOU??

IT *WORKED!* I HAD TO GAMBLE THAT THE SHOCK OF REALIZING HIS CONFESSION WAS DOWN ON TAPE WOULD SLOW HIS REFLEXES ENOUGH TO ALLOW ME TO STRIKE!

WHAP!

AND THEN, WITHOUT PAUSING TO CATCH A BREATH, THE DAZZLING DAREDEVIL HURLS HIMSELF RIGHT OVER THE EDGE OF THE ROOF, GRABBING THE STILL-ENTRANCED KAREN PAGE AS HE DOES SO!

HE MUST HAVE GONE *MAD!* HE'S THROWING HIMSELF TO HIS *DEATH*... AND TAKING THE GIRL *WITH* HIM!

19.

NO! IT'S **I** WHO WAS MAD! I ALLOWED HIM TO ESCAPE RIGHT UNDER MY NOSE! HE KNEW THERE WAS A **SCAFFOLD** THERE!

I'LL GET YOU **YET!!** YOU'RE **DOOMED!**

THERE ARE REPORTERS DOWN BELOW... CAMERAMEN... POLICE! BUT THEY CAN'T STOP **ME!** ONCE I'M NEAR THEM, THEY'LL BE IN MY POWER... LIKE EVERY-ONE **ELSE!**

ONLY **DAREDEVIL** CAN RESIST MY PURPLE POWER... HE MUST BE DESTROYED... NO MATTER **WHAT!!**

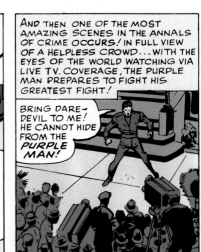

AND THEN ONE OF THE MOST AMAZING SCENES IN THE ANNALS OF CRIME OCCURS! IN FULL VIEW OF A HELPLESS CROWD... WITH THE EYES OF THE WORLD WATCHING VIA LIVE T.V. COVERAGE, THE PURPLE MAN PREPARES TO FIGHT HIS GREATEST FIGHT!

BRING DARE-DEVIL TO ME! HE CANNOT HIDE FROM THE **PURPLE MAN!**

BUT NOW, ONE OF THE MOST DRAMATIC, THE MOST DARING, THE MOST DAZZLING ADVENTURERS OF ALL TIME STEPS FORWARD TO **MEET** THE CHALLENGE... ARMED ONLY WITH HIS SUPER-SHARP SENSES... HIS UNIQUE BILLY CLUB... AND, MOST IMPORTANT OF ALL, HIS MATCHLESS, UNFAILING **COURAGE!**

DAREDEVIL HIDES FROM NO ONE!! NOW WE SHALL **SEE** WHOSE POWER IS TRULY THE **GREATEST!**

HAVE YOU FORGOTTEN SO **SOON??** ALTHOUGH **YOU** CAN RESIST MY COMMANDS, THE **CROWD** CANNOT! **THIS** TIME YOU ARE HELPLESSLY SURROUNDED! AND I SHALL **REMAIN** HERE, TO DIRECT YOUR DEFEAT!

DAREDEVIL IS YOUR **ENEMY!** SMASH HIM! SLAY HIM! HE MUST NOT ESCAPE **ALIVE!**

HIS HOLD OVER OTHERS IS AS STRONG AS EVER! BUT, I **EXPECTED** HIM TO DO THIS...

NOW, IT REMAINS TO BE SEEN IF MY GAMBLE WILL PAY OFF!

20.

THEN, MOVING WITH STAGGERING SPEED, BEFORE THE HOSTILE CROWD CAN REACH HIM, DAREDEVIL SPINS AROUND, FACING KILLGRAVE, AND RELEASES THE SNAP CATCH OF HIS CANE, WHERE HE HAD ROLLED HIS SPECIALLY-PREPARED PLASTIC SHEET...

SWISH!

WHA..??

SNAP!

IT'S NOW... OR *NEVER!*

EXACTLY AS PLANNED, THE CHEMICALLY-TREATED MATERIAL COMPLETELY ENSHROUDS THE TRAPPED PURPLE MAN, COVERING EVERY BIT OF HIS DYED, STRANGELY-POTENT SKIN!

I NO LONGER FEEL THE UNCANNY EMANATIONS FROM KILLGRAVE! THE PLASTIC SHEET HAS EFFECTIVELY CUT THEM OFF, AS I HOPED IT WOULD!

WHAT'S GOING *ON* HERE?

WHO IS THAT MAN COVERED BY THE PLASTIC SHEET?

WITH HIS PURPLE SKIN COVERED UP, THE CROWD HAS RETURNED TO NORMAL! *NOW* WE KNOW THE WAY TO THWART KILL-GRAVE'S POWER!

WITHIN SECONDS, THE PLASTIC SHEET IS SECURELY TIED AROUND THE HAPLESS PRISONER, AS THE POLICE CLOSE IN TO TAKE OVER...

LOOK! ISN'T THAT *DAREDEVIL?* THE MAN THE NEWSPAPERS REFER TO AS BEING ABSOLUTELY FEARLESS!?

THAT'S *HIM,* ALL RIGHT! THIS IS PROBABLY THE FIRST TIME HE'S ALLOWED A CROWD OF PEOPLE TO GET SO CLOSE TO HIM!

GOOD WORK, DAREDEVIL! WITH THAT SPOOL OF MAGNETIC TAPE YOU GAVE US, WE HAVE ENOUGH EVIDENCE ON KILLGRAVE TO PUT HIM AWAY FOR A LONG LONG TIME!

C'MON, SAM! GET THAT TRUCK CLOSER! THIS IS OUR CHANCE TO GET AN EXCLUSIVE *INTERVIEW* WITH DAREDEVIL!

TRY TO GET THE CROWD TO STAND ASIDE! IT'S HARD TO FOCUS ON HIM!

LET'S GO, GANG! LET'S GET DARE-DEVIL'S *AUTO-GRAPH* WHILE WE CAN!

HOLD IT, DAREDEVIL! WE WANT A FEW MORE SHOTS OF YOU IN THAT POSE!

HOW ABOUT A *SMILE,* FELLA? TURN MORE THIS WAY, WILL YOU?

21

BUT THEN, BEFORE THE EAGER CROWD CAN CLOSE IN ANY FURTHER...

I'VE GOT TO GET AWAY BEFORE I'M *MOBBED*!

WAIT! WE WANT YOUR *AUTO-GRAPH*!

COME *BACK*! JUST FOR A FEW MORE *PICTURES*!

AND, WHILE THE SIGHTLESS ADVENTURER TAKES HIS LEAVE, FRANKLIN "FOGGY" NELSON PUSHES HIS WAY THROUGH THE MILLING CROWD...

KAREN! IT'S *ME!* I WAS WATCHING TV... I *SAW* YOU! I RUSHED TO GET YOU...!

FOGGY... IT'S ALL *RIGHT!* KILLGRAVE IS *BEATEN!*

AS, FROM A SECOND STORY WINDOW, ABOVE THE COUPLE...

I HEAR KAREN AND FOGGY BELOW! I'LL CHANGE AND BEAT THEM BACK TO THE OFFICE!

I WAS SO WORRIED ABOUT YOU, KAREN! BUT, THANKS TO *DARE-DEVIL*...

...I WISH I KNEW WHO HE REALLY *IS!* HE'S *SOME* BALL OF FIRE!

WHAT ABOUT *MATT!* IS HE ALL RIGHT?

REACHING THE OFFICE A SHORT TIME LATER, KAREN RECEIVES THE ANSWER TO HER QUESTION...

MATT, YOU SIMPLY WOULDN'T *BELIEVE* WHAT HAPPENED?! THAT HORRIBLE PURPLE MAN HAD ME UNDER SOME SORT OF SPELL! HE SEEMED IMPOSSIBLE TO DEFEAT... UNTIL *DAREDEVIL* CAME ALONG!

SORRY I LOST MY TEMPER WITH YOU, PARTNER! I WAS JUST KIND OF UPSET! I REALIZE IT WASN'T *YOUR* FAULT!

NO HARD FEELINGS, FOGGY! WE *BOTH* WERE WORRIED ABOUT KAREN!

BUT, NOW THAT I KNOW HOW *FOGGY* FEELS ABOUT HER, I MUST NEVER REVEAL MY *OWN* FEELINGS! IT... JUST WOULDN'T BE RIGHT!

THERE GOES ONE OF THE GREATEST GUYS IN THE WORLD! IT SURE IS A PITY HE'S BLIND!

AND YET, FOR SOME STRANGE REASON, I SOMETIMES FEEL HE SEES MORE THAN *ANY* OF US! I GUESS I'M JUST A SILLY FEMALE!

THE END

DAREDEVIL, THE FEARLESS ADVENTURER WHOM THE WORLD HAS TAKEN TO ITS HEART, WILL THRILL AND AMAZE YOU AGAIN *NEXT* ISSUE! JOIN US THEN FOR THE ALL-NEW ACTION AND MARVEL-TYPE SURPRISES!

22.

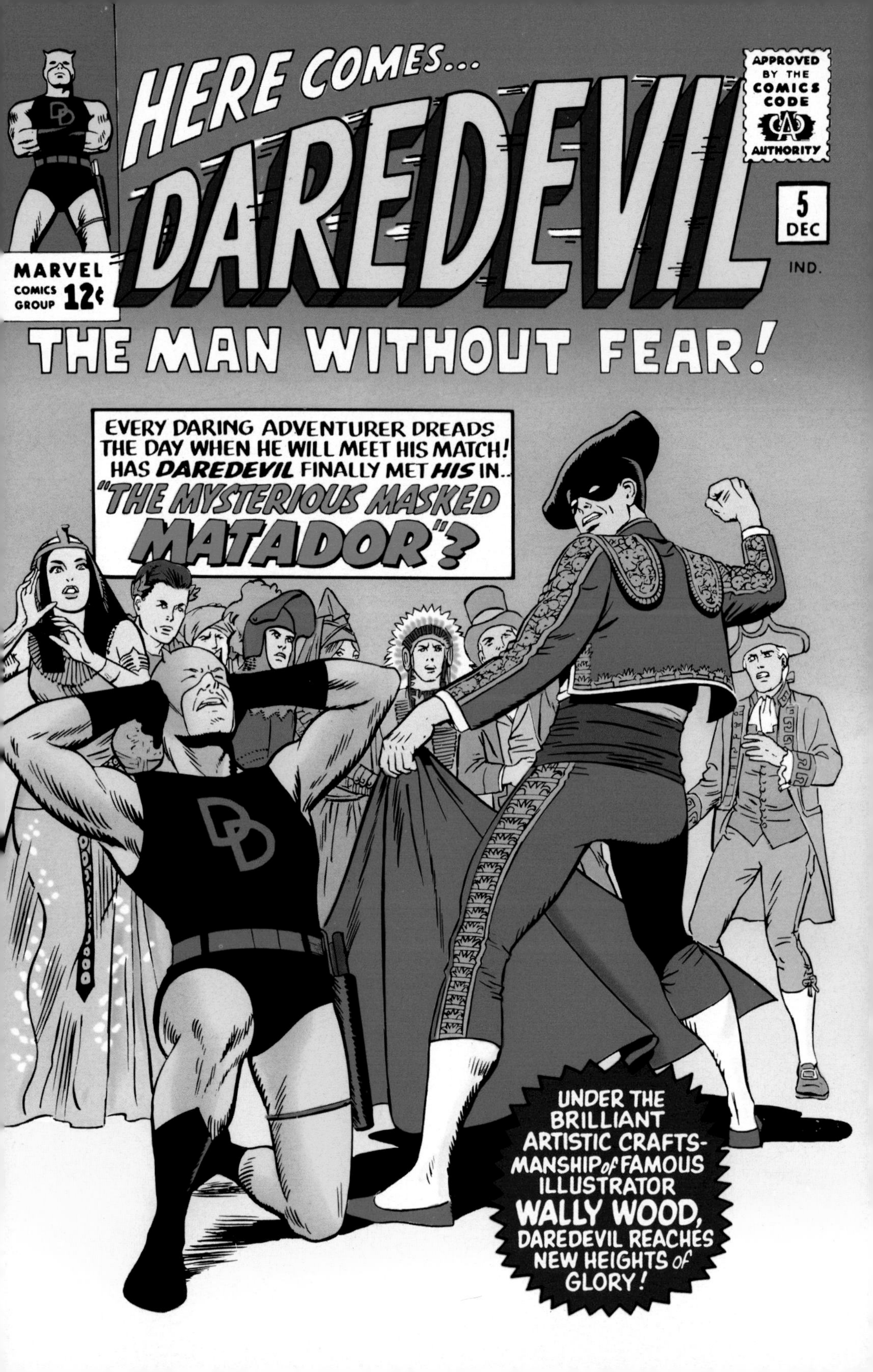
HERE COMES...
DAREDEVIL
APPROVED BY THE COMICS CODE AUTHORITY
5 DEC
IND.
MARVEL COMICS GROUP 12¢
THE MAN WITHOUT FEAR!
EVERY DARING ADVENTURER DREADS THE DAY WHEN HE WILL MEET HIS MATCH! HAS DAREDEVIL FINALLY MET HIS IN.. "THE MYSTERIOUS MASKED MATADOR"?
UNDER THE BRILLIANT ARTISTIC CRAFTS-MANSHIP of FAMOUS ILLUSTRATOR WALLY WOOD, DAREDEVIL REACHES NEW HEIGHTS of GLORY!

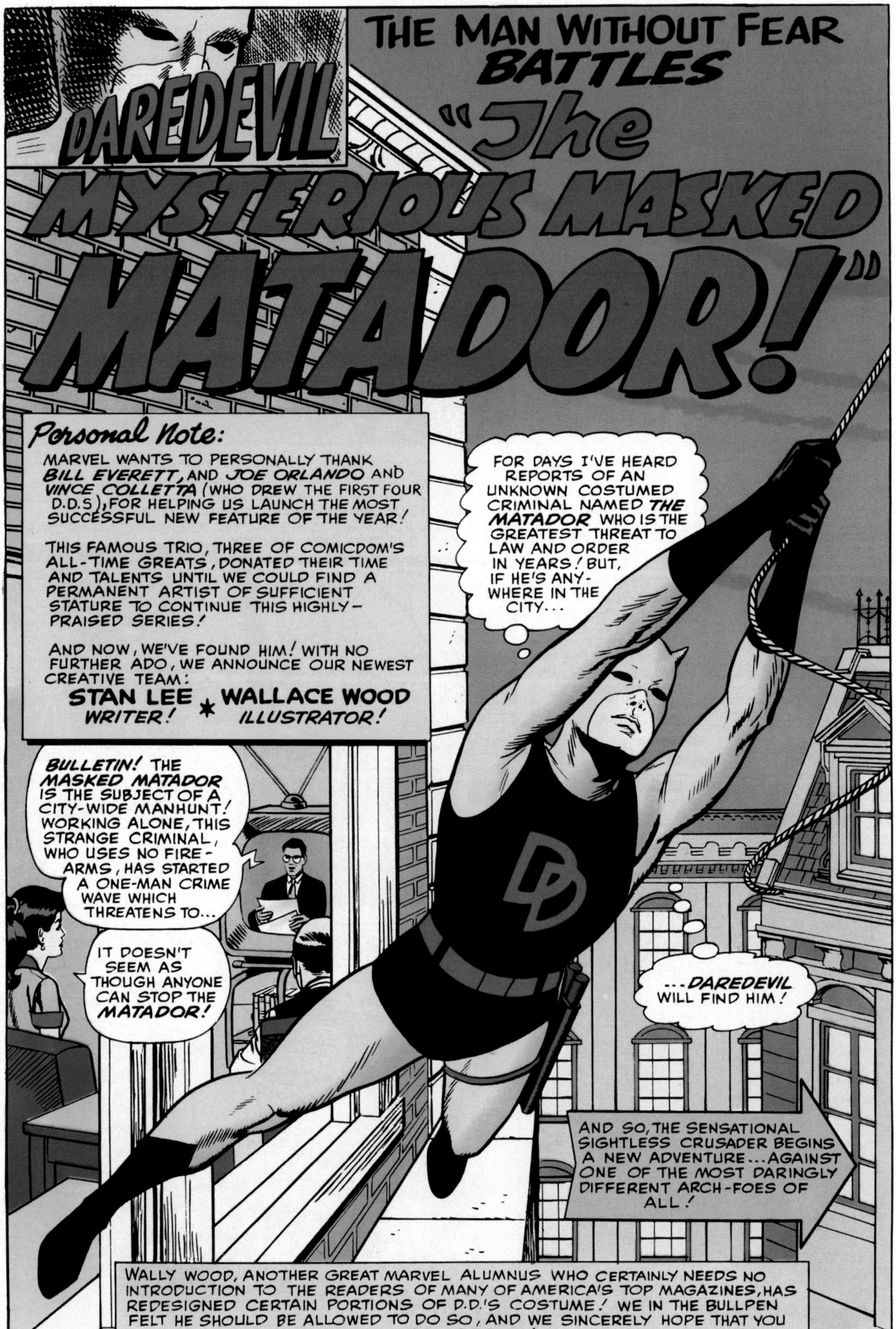
DAREDEVIL
THE MAN WITHOUT FEAR BATTLES
"The MYSTERIOUS MASKED MATADOR!"
Personal Note:
MARVEL WANTS TO PERSONALLY THANK BILL EVERETT, AND JOE ORLANDO AND VINCE COLLETTA (WHO DREW THE FIRST FOUR D.D.S), FOR HELPING US LAUNCH THE MOST SUCCESSFUL NEW FEATURE OF THE YEAR!
THIS FAMOUS TRIO, THREE OF COMICDOM'S ALL-TIME GREATS, DONATED THEIR TIME AND TALENTS UNTIL WE COULD FIND A PERMANENT ARTIST OF SUFFICIENT STATURE TO CONTINUE THIS HIGHLY-PRAISED SERIES!
AND NOW, WE'VE FOUND HIM! WITH NO FURTHER ADO, WE ANNOUNCE OUR NEWEST CREATIVE TEAM:
STAN LEE WRITER! * WALLACE WOOD ILLUSTRATOR!
FOR DAYS I'VE HEARD REPORTS OF AN UNKNOWN COSTUMED CRIMINAL NAMED THE MATADOR WHO IS THE GREATEST THREAT TO LAW AND ORDER IN YEARS! BUT, IF HE'S ANYWHERE IN THE CITY...
BULLETIN! THE MASKED MATADOR IS THE SUBJECT OF A CITY-WIDE MANHUNT! WORKING ALONE, THIS STRANGE CRIMINAL, WHO USES NO FIRE-ARMS, HAS STARTED A ONE-MAN CRIME WAVE WHICH THREATENS TO...
IT DOESN'T SEEM AS THOUGH ANYONE CAN STOP THE MATADOR!
...DAREDEVIL WILL FIND HIM!
AND SO, THE SENSATIONAL SIGHTLESS CRUSADER BEGINS A NEW ADVENTURE...AGAINST ONE OF THE MOST DARINGLY DIFFERENT ARCH-FOES OF ALL!
WALLY WOOD, ANOTHER GREAT MARVEL ALUMNUS WHO CERTAINLY NEEDS NO INTRODUCTION TO THE READERS OF MANY OF AMERICA'S TOP MAGAZINES, HAS REDESIGNED CERTAIN PORTIONS OF D.D.'S COSTUME! WE IN THE BULLPEN FELT HE SHOULD BE ALLOWED TO DO SO, AND WE SINCERELY HOPE THAT YOU WILL AGREE!
#5

DAY AFTER DAY, THE MAN WITHOUT FEAR, HAS COMBED THE CITY, SEEKING THE MATADOR! BUT NOW, AT LAST, HIS HYPER-SENSITIVE EARS DETECT THE FLUTTERING OF A LARGE CAPE ON THE STREET BELOW...

LUCKY IT'S EVENING, AND THE CITY IS HUSHED... OTHERWISE THE THOUSANDS OF OTHER NOISES MIGHT HAVE DROWNED OUT THE FAINT SOUND!

I HEAR THE CAPE BEING SLOWLY RAISED AS A HEAVY IRON VEHICLE APPROACHES IT! EVEN A BLIND MAN CAN NOW DEDUCE THAT THE MATADOR IS FACING AN ONCOMING ARMORED TRUCK!

BUT WHAT CAN ONE MAN, ARMED ONLY WITH A CAPE, DO AGAINST A STEEL-PLATED VEHICLE?

POISED FOR ACTION... HIS EVERY SENSE OPERATING AT PEAK EFFICIENCY... DARE-DEVIL WAITS, USING THE TIME-HONORED TACTIC OF EVERY TRAINED FIGHTER... WAITING TO LEARN AS MUCH AS POSSIBLE ABOUT HIS FOE, BEFORE HE STRIKES!

HEY! WHO'S THAT COSTUMED NUT BLOCKIN' OUR WAY?? LOOK OUT... YOU'LL HIT 'IM!

NUT NOTHING! DON'T YOU READ THE PAPERS?? THAT'S THE MASKED MATADOR! HE'S NOT MOVIN'! I CAN'T STOP IN TIME! I'LL HAVE TO SWERVE OUT OF THE WAY!

SCREEE!

THEN, AT THE LAST POSSIBLE SPLIT-SECOND, THE MASKED CRIMINAL MAKES HIS MOVE! EVEN THOUGH THE STARTLED DRIVER TRIES DESPERATELY TO AVOID HITTING HIM, THE MATADOR HURLS HIS CAPE AT THE WINDSHIELD, TEMPORARILY BLINDING THE TWO MEN INSIDE!

WHAT'S HE DOING?? I CAN'T SEE!

CUT 'ER SHARP! WATCH OUT! WE'RE GONNA HIT SOMETHING!

SO THAT'S HOW HE DOES IT! OKAY, MATADOR... I'VE HEARD ENOUGH!

AHHH, TORO! ONCE AGAIN I HAVE TRIUMPHED! WHAT DELICACY! WHAT ARTISTRY! WHAT MAGNIFICENT DARING! NO WONDER THE MASKED MATADOR IS UN-BEATABLE!

CRASH!

2.

99

WHAT IS *THIS*?? WHO *DARES*? AHH... THE MAN WITHOUT FEAR! *OLÉ*, DAREDEVIL!

HE'S AS FAST AS *I* AM! HE CONFUSED ME WITH HIS WAVING CAPE!

BUT THEN, BEFORE DAREDEVIL CAN FOLLOW UP HIS ATTACK...

THAT SUDDEN SOUND! A CABLE SLIPPING OUT OF ITS PULLEY! AN UNNATURAL DISPLACEMENT OF AIR ABOVE!

IF IT SIGNIFIES WHAT I *THINK*.. I'M *NEEDED*!

COME, DAREDEVIL! TO *ME*, YOU ARE NO MORE THAN A HELP-LESS *TORO*!

BUT DAREDEVIL HAS A MORE PRESSING PROBLEM TO COPE WITH! FOR, ON THE BUILDING ABOVE...

HELP! I'M *FALLING!* MY *SCAFFOLDING* BROKE!

I HEAR ONE END OF THE ROPE TRAILING ON THE GROUND! THERE'S STILL *HOPE* FOR THAT FALLING PAINTER!

ALL THOUGHT OF HIS DANGEROUS FOE TEMPORARILY FORGOTTEN, THE GALLANT GLADIATOR MOVES WITH DAZZLING SPEED...

AS THE SCAFFOLD FALLS, THE OTHER END OF THE ROPE WILL *RISE*!

IF I CAN JUST *REACH* IT IN TIME!

HOW CAN HE EXPECT TO SAVE THAT *DOOMED* MAN?

GOT IT!

NOW TO LISTEN FOR THE SOUND OF THE FALLING PAINTER!

HERE HE *COMES!*

HELP! SOMEONE... *HELP ME!!*

YOUR HAND! STRETCH OUT YOUR *HAND!* QUICKLY, MAN!

A LESSER MAN WOULD NOT HAVE HAD THE SKILL, THE SPEED, THE STRENGTH TO ACCOMPLISH SUCH AN AWESOME FEAT! BUT, THIS IS *NO* LESSER MAN... THIS IS *DAREDEVIL*, THE MAN WITHOUT FEAR!

EASY NOW... *EASY!* OUR COMBINED WEIGHT WILL BE ENOUGH TO SLOWLY LOWER US SAFELY TO THE GROUND!

YOU *DID* IT! I THOUGHT I WAS A GONER... BUT YOU *SAVED* ME!

3.

BUT, BY THE TIME THE SIGHTLESS ADVENTURER IS READY TO AGAIN FACE HIS COSTUMED ADVERSARY, HE FINDS...

I NO LONGER HEAR THE MATADOR'S CAPE WAFTING IN THE BREEZE... NOR DO I DETECT HIS DISTINCTIVE HEARTBEAT! HE HAS FLED! LOOK! IT'S DAREDEVIL!

BUT I DO HEAR OTHERS APPROACHING! I, TOO, HAD BEST FADE INTO THE SHADOWS!

SUDDENLY RACING AROUND THE CORNER, THE MAN WITHOUT FEAR IS SOON TRANSFORMED INTO MATT MURDOCK, THE BRILLIANT BLIND LAWYER!..

I'D BETTER RETURN TO THE OFFICE NOW! I'VE STILL GOT A JOB TO TAKE CARE OF!

AND SO, MATT MURDOCK ARRIVES AT THE LAW FIRM OF NELSON AND MURDOCK AS HE HEARS HIS PARTNER'S DISAPPOINTED VOICE...

YOU SAY THAT TONIGHT IS THE ONLY TIME YOU CAN MEET ME FOR THE EXAMINATION BEFORE TRIAL? WELL, I DID HAVE ANOTHER ENGAGEMENT, BUT I GUESS I CAN POSTPONE IT!

POOR FOGGY! HE'LL HAVE TO WORK LATE AGAIN!

BOY, AM I GLAD TO SEE YOU, MATT! WOULDN'T YOU KNOW IT?? I HAVE A DATE TO TAKE KAREN TO A COSTUME PARTY TONIGHT... AND NOW I'VE GOT TO HANG AROUND HERE, INSTEAD!

HOW ABOUT BEING A PAL AND TAKING HER THERE FOR ME... UNTIL I CAN FINISH UP AND MEET YOU THERE?

THAT, FOGGY, MY BOY, IS THE BEST OFFER I'VE HAD IN MANY A DAY! THE VERDICT IS YES!

I'LL TRY TO GET THERE AS SOON AS POSSIBLE, MATT! IT SHOULDN'T TAKE TOO LONG!

YOU SAID IT'S A COSTUME PARTY.. I WON'T NEED ONE, WILL I?

OH, NO! YOU CAN GO AS YOU ARE! BUT KAREN AND I PLANNED TO ATTEND AS CAESAR AND CLEOPATRA! I'LL BE CAESAR, OF COURSE!

FOGGY THINKS I'M DOING HIM A FAVOR! HE DOESN'T SUSPECT HOW I FEEL ABOUT KAREN! AND SHE MUST NEVER SUSPECT IT, EITHER!

I COULDN'T EVER BEAR THE THOUGHT OF KAREN FEELING SORRY FOR ME... OR TRYING TO BE NICE TO ME, SO AS NOT TO HURT THE FEELINGS OF A BLIND MAN!

THAT SOFT, SWEET SCENT OF PERFUME! THAT GENTLE HEARTBEAT! SHE'S HERE NOW!

HELLO, MATT! I DIDN'T KNOW YOU WERE HERE! HOW DO I LOOK, FOGGY?

BRO-THER! KAREN, HONEY, IF TWENTIETH-CENTURY FOX HAD SEEN YOU FIRST, LIZ TAYLOR WOULD PROBABLY NEVER HAVE MET DICK BURTON!

MIND IF MATT ESCORTS YOU AND I JOIN YOU LATER?

I GUESS I CAN STAND IT IF HE CAN!

AND SO...

WHY DON'T WE STOP AND FIND A COSTUME FOR YOU, MATT? YOU'D PROBABLY ENJOY REMAINING AT THE PARTY!

I MIGHT, KAREN... BUT THERE ARE TIMES WHEN THREE'S A CROWD! I DON'T THINK FOGGY EXACTLY NEEDS ANOTHER MAN HANGING AROUND WHEN HE'S AT A PARTY WITH YOU!

I KNOW I'D WANT TO BE ALL ALONE WITH YOU, IF I EVER HAD THE CHANCE, MY DARLING!

4.

A SHORT TIME LATER...

THE RUSTLE OF SILKS AND SATINS...CLINK OF ARMOR...SOUND OF MIXED, LAUGHING VOICES! I CAN PICTURE THE SCENE AS THOUGH MY EYES SEE IT!

OH, MATT! YOU CAN'T *IMAGINE* HOW LOVELY IT IS! IT'S THE BIGGEST CHARITY BALL OF THE YEAR! JUST *EVERYBODY* IS HERE!

THAT HEARTBEAT! THAT FAST, NERVOUS PULSE RATE! I'VE HEARD IT *BEFORE!* WAIT... OF *COURSE!*.. THE *MASKED MATADOR!*

I CAN HEAR THE WAY HIS FABRIC FOLDS WHEN HE MOVES! IT'S HIS MATADOR COSTUME!

HOW *CLEVER* OF HIM! A *COSTUME* PARTY IS THE ONE FUNCTION HE CAN ATTEND IN HIS CRIMINAL GUISE WITHOUT AROUSING SUSPICION! OTHERS WILL THINK HE'S ONE OF THE GUESTS!

MY RADAR SENSE INDICATES HE'S STANDING AGAINST THE *WALL* ...HIS BACK TOWARDS THE CROWD! I HEAR HIM TURNING A DIAL... SOFTLY... CAUTIOUSLY...

IT CAN ONLY MEAN *ONE* THING! HE'S *OPENING THE SAFE!* HE'S DARING A ROBBERY IN THE MIDDLE OF A PARTY....AND NO ONE YET HAS NOTICED IT!

I CAN'T REVEAL MY IDENTITY AS *DAREDEVIL*, BUT I MUST WARN THE OTHERS! THERE'S ONLY ONE THING TO DO... I'LL HAVE TO SPEAK IN A LOUD VOICE!

KAREN, I'LL BET IF THE *MATADOR* WANTED TO ROB THE WALL SAFE HERE, HE COULD DO IT WITHOUT ANYONE NOTICING!

WHAT EVER GAVE YOU *THAT* IDEA, MATT?

SAY! THERE *IS* SOMEONE HERE DRESSED LIKE THE MASKED MATADOR!

WHERE? *WAIT* ...*THERE* HE IS! *SAY!* WHY IS HE NEAR THE WALL SAFE?? WHAT'S GOING *ON?!*

5

CALL THE *POLICE!* QUICK! HE'S NO GUEST! HE *IS* THE MASKED MATADOR!

I HAD HOPED TO FINISH MY LITTLE BUSINESS WITHOUT CAUSING A DISTURBANCE, BUT ALAS, YOU LEAVE ME NO CHOICE!

STOP HIM! HOLD HIM TILL THE POLICE ARRIVE!

AH! THAT IS EASIER SAID THAN DONE, MY BRAVES! SO, YOU WOULD ATTACK THE *MATADOR!* WELL, THEN... COME AND GET ME!

THAT RIDICULOUS CLOAK CAN'T HELP HIM *NOW! GET HIM!*

AYYY, TORO! OLE!

HE'S AS SLIPPERY AS AN *EEL!*

HE'S TRYING TO RUN OFF! *AFTER HIM!* BLOCK THE DOORS!

DOORS? WHAT DOES THE *MATADOR* WANT WITH DOORS?

ALL I NEED DO IS STOP IN MY TRACKS AND TOY WITH YOU AGAIN!

IF ONLY THE *BULLS* WERE AS CLUMSY AS YOU!!

OOOF!

LET'S STOP! WE'VE GOT TO *PLAN* AN ATTACK! HE'S MAKING US LOOK LIKE *FOOLS!*

OH, MATT! THAT MAN IS *DANGEROUS!* NO ONE CAN LAY A HAND ON HIM! THERE'S NO TELLING *WHAT* HE'LL DO NEXT!

IF ONLY I HAD A CHANCE TO SECRETLY CHANGE TO *DAREDEVIL!*

THEY'RE STILL FIGHTING! IT'S TOO DANGEROUS HERE FOR A MAN WHO CAN'T SEE TO PROTECT HIMSELF! QUICK... GO INTO THE NEXT ROOM! I'LL SHUT THE DOOR BEHIND YOU! YOU'LL BE *SAFER* THERE!

PERFECT! JUST THE CHANCE I *NEED!*

BUT WHAT ABOUT *YOU?* WILL *YOU* BE SAFE?

OF *COURSE,* MATT! I WANT TO SEE WHAT *HAPPENS!* NOW HURRY!

6.

THEN, NO SOONER DOES MATT MURDOCK HEAR THE DOOR SLAM SHUT BEHIND HIM...

AT *LAST!* NOW I CAN GO INTO ACTION!

SLAM!

I'VE GOT TO CHANGE *QUICKLY,* BEFORE THE MATADOR CAN ESCAPE AGAIN!

WITH EVERYONE WATCHING THE MASKED CRIMINAL SO CAREFULLY, THEY MAY NOT NOTICE ME AS I RUSH SILENTLY OUT OF THIS ROOM AGAIN!

FROM THE SOUND OF THEIR VOICES THROUGH THE WALL, I CAN TELL THEY'RE FACING *AWAY* FROM MY DOOR!

I WAS *RIGHT!* SO FAR, SO GOOD!

GET THE MATADOR!

SOME-BODY *STOP* HIM!

LOOK OUT!!

ALL THIS NOISE... THIS SHOUTING... IT'S MAKING IT *DIFFICULT* FOR ME! IT'S HARD TO SEPARATE ONE SOUND FROM THE OTHER!

TOO MANY PEOPLE CROWDING AROUND! I CAN'T BREAK THROUGH WITHOUT INJURING SOMEBODY! NO ONE REALIZES I'M THE *REAL* DAREDEVIL!

THEY PROBABLY THINK I'M JUST ANOTHER COSTUMED *GUEST!*

BUT I CAN'T STAY IN THE BACKGROUND MUCH LONGER! I'VE GOT TO DO *SOMETHING!*

AND IF I CAN'T SHOULDER MY WAY *THROUGH* THE CROWD...

THEN I'LL HAVE TO GO FLYING OVER THEIR *HEADS*...LIKE *THIS!*

DAREDEVIL! SO ONCE AGAIN OUR PATHS CROSS, EH?

7.

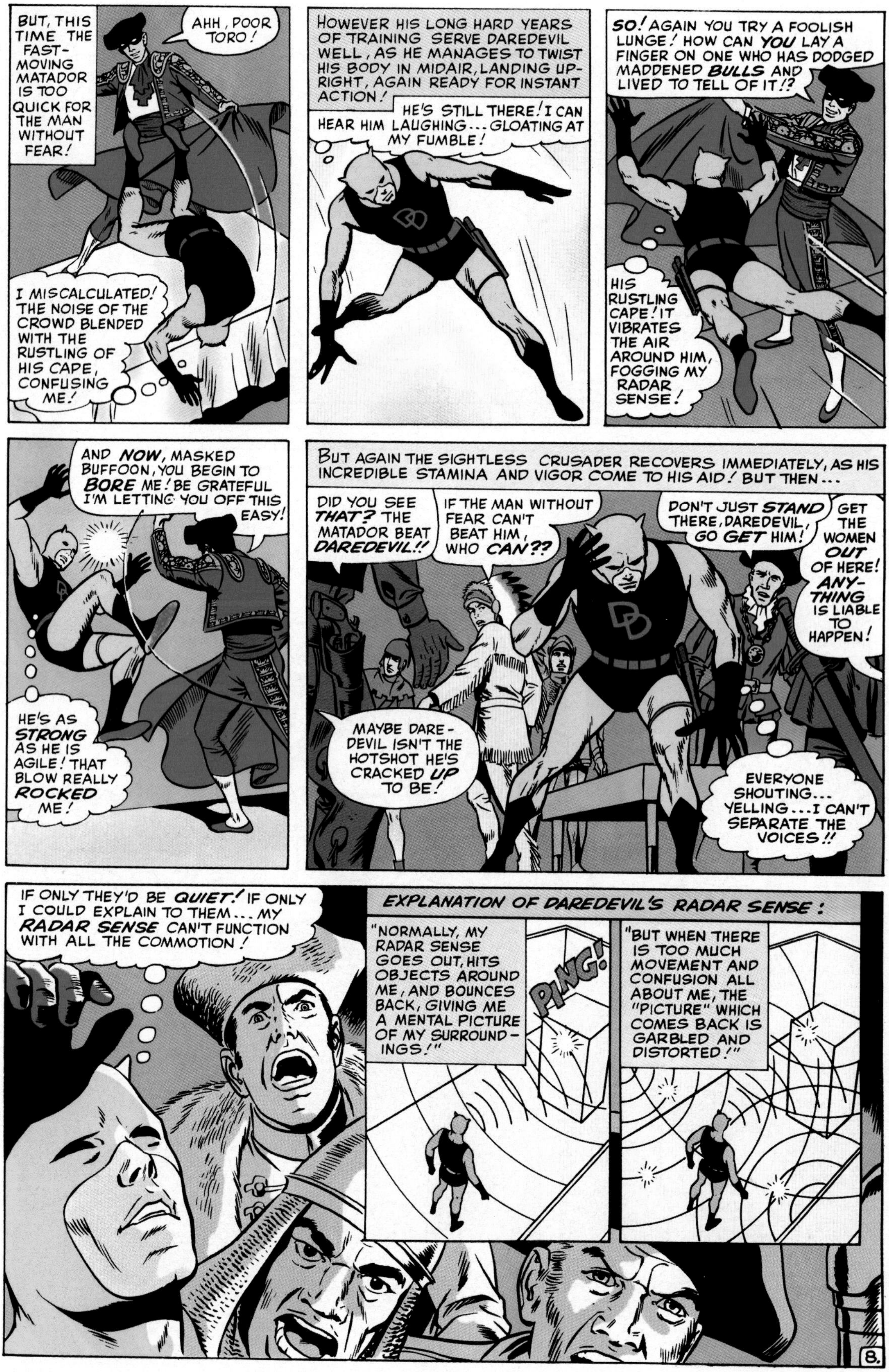
BUT, THIS TIME THE FAST-MOVING MATADOR IS TOO QUICK FOR THE MAN WITHOUT FEAR!
AHH, POOR TORO!
I MISCALCULATED! THE NOISE OF THE CROWD BLENDED WITH THE RUSTLING OF HIS CAPE, CONFUSING ME!
HOWEVER HIS LONG HARD YEARS OF TRAINING SERVE DAREDEVIL WELL, AS HE MANAGES TO TWIST HIS BODY IN MIDAIR, LANDING UPRIGHT, AGAIN READY FOR INSTANT ACTION!
HE'S STILL THERE! I CAN HEAR HIM LAUGHING... GLOATING AT MY FUMBLE!
SO! AGAIN YOU TRY A FOOLISH LUNGE! HOW CAN YOU LAY A FINGER ON ONE WHO HAS DODGED MADDENED BULLS AND LIVED TO TELL OF IT!?
HIS RUSTLING CAPE! IT VIBRATES THE AIR AROUND HIM, FOGGING MY RADAR SENSE!
AND NOW, MASKED BUFFOON, YOU BEGIN TO BORE ME! BE GRATEFUL I'M LETTING YOU OFF THIS EASY!
HE'S AS STRONG AS HE IS AGILE! THAT BLOW REALLY ROCKED ME!
BUT AGAIN THE SIGHTLESS CRUSADER RECOVERS IMMEDIATELY, AS HIS INCREDIBLE STAMINA AND VIGOR COME TO HIS AID! BUT THEN...
DID YOU SEE THAT? THE MATADOR BEAT DAREDEVIL!!
IF THE MAN WITHOUT FEAR CAN'T BEAT HIM, WHO CAN??
DON'T JUST STAND THERE, DAREDEVIL, GO GET HIM!
GET THE WOMEN OUT OF HERE! ANYTHING IS LIABLE TO HAPPEN!
MAYBE DAREDEVIL ISN'T THE HOTSHOT HE'S CRACKED UP TO BE!
EVERYONE SHOUTING... YELLING... I CAN'T SEPARATE THE VOICES!!
IF ONLY THEY'D BE QUIET! IF ONLY I COULD EXPLAIN TO THEM... MY RADAR SENSE CAN'T FUNCTION WITH ALL THE COMMOTION!
EXPLANATION OF DAREDEVIL'S RADAR SENSE:
"NORMALLY, MY RADAR SENSE GOES OUT, HITS OBJECTS AROUND ME, AND BOUNCES BACK, GIVING ME A MENTAL PICTURE OF MY SURROUNDINGS!"
PING!
"BUT WHEN THERE IS TOO MUCH MOVEMENT AND CONFUSION ALL ABOUT ME, THE "PICTURE" WHICH COMES BACK IS GARBLED AND DISTORTED!"
8.

STILL, EVEN IF MY SENSES *AREN'T* FUNCTIONING PERFECTLY, I CAN'T GIVE UP! I'VE GOT TO KEEP TRYING! I KNOW *APPROXIMATELY* WHERE HE IS... HE'S SOMEWHERE IN FRONT OF ME!

I'LL ATTACK QUICKLY! PERHAPS, IF I'M LUCKY...

SO! YOU WILL NOT ADMIT DEFEAT! YOU *FORCE* ME TO TAKE *STRONGER* MEASURES, DO YOU?

VERY WELL, THEN! I SHALL DO WHATEVER I MUST!

AYYY, TORO! DEFEND YOURSELF!

TOO SLOW! I MISCALCULATED AGAIN!

CAUSING YOU BODILY INJURY WILL AFFORD ME NO PLEASURE! IT PLEASES ME TO *HUMILIATE* YOU INSTEAD.. AS A LESSON TO *OTHERS!*

WHOP!

HE'S THROWN HIS CAPE OVER MY HEAD! NOW MY SENSES ARE *ALL* DULLED! FOR THE FIRST TIME, I FEEL THE WAY AN *ORDINARY* SIGHTLESS MAN MIGHT FEEL IN A BATTLE!

AND NOW, FAREWELL! IT IS UNLIKELY THAT WE SHALL MEET AGAIN! FOR I FEEL THE MATADOR HAS *ENDED* YOUR CAREER, MOST EMPHATICALLY!

SO SHOCKED, SO STARTLED ARE THE OTHERS AT THE SIGHT OF DAREDEVIL'S IGNOBLE DEFEAT, THAT NO ONE MAKES A MOVE TO STOP THE MATADOR AS HE FADES FROM SIGHT THROUGH AN OPEN WINDOW... AND THEN, GETTING HIS BEARINGS AGAIN, IN THE SUDDEN SILENCE, DAREDEVIL ONCE MORE MOVES QUICKLY...

I'VE GOT TO CHANGE BACK TO MATT MURDOCK.. BEFORE *KAREN* ENTERS THE ROOM!

AND BY THE TIME KAREN *DOES* APPEAR...

NEITHER WOULD *I!*

MATT! FOGGY JUST ARRIVED! HE SAW THE WHOLE THING, ALSO! IT WAS *TERRIBLE!* THAT MAN MADE A *LAUGHING STOCK* OF DAREDEVIL!

I NEVER WOULD HAVE *BELIEVED* IT, MATT!

I HEARD A LOT OF COMMOTION THROUGH THE DOOR... BUT I COULDN'T QUITE TELL WHAT WAS GOING ON!

9.

IN THE DAYS THAT FOLLOW, THE SOBER, SIGHTLESS ATTORNEY FINDS HIMSELF BROODING MORE AND MORE OVER HIS DEFEAT AT THE HANDS OF THE MASKED MATADOR! EVEN IN THE COMPANY OF THE GIRL HE SECRETLY LOVES, AS THEY RETURN TO THE OFFICE AFTER LUNCHING TOGETHER HE CAN'T FORGET...

MATT, YOU'VE BEEN SO QUIET... SO THOUGHTFUL! IS ANYTHING TROUBLING YOU? HAVE *I* DONE ANYTHING?

OF COURSE NOT, KAREN! IT'S NOTHING IMPORTANT!

COME ON, TOMMY! *I'VE* BEEN DAREDEVIL LONG ENOUGH! I WANNA BE THE *MATADOR*!

AWW, I WAS DAREDEVIL *LAST* TIME! JUST LET ME BE THE MATADOR A WHILE LONGER!

LISTEN! CHILDREN PLAYING! THEY'RE MAKING A *HERO* OF THE MATADOR! THEY *SNEER* AT DARE-DEVIL!

IT'S A PERFECT *SHAME!*

I'LL BET THE *MATADOR* COULD LICK DAREDEVIL WITH ONE HAND TIED BEHIND HIM!

WHEN I THINK HOW *WONDERFUL* DAREDEVIL WAS... HOW HE RESCUED *ME* IN THE PAST... WITHOUT EVEN *KNOWING* ME...! * I COULD JUST *CRY!*

I'D HATE TO THINK THAT THE YOUNG-STERS ARE MAKING A *HERO* OF SOMEONE LIKE THE MATADOR.. AND YET, CHILDREN *DO* ADMIRE A *WINNER!*

* SEE *DAREDEVIL* #4...STAN.

"CHILDREN *DO* ADMIRE A WINNER!" THAT ONE THOUGHT SPINS 'ROUND AND 'ROUND IN THE BROODING LAWYER'S BRAIN ALL THE WAY BACK TO THE OFFICE! BUT LITTLE DOES HE SUSPECT THAT, DIRECTLY ACROSS TOWN, THE MATADOR IS PREPARING FOR THE MOST DARING CRIME OF ALL!

NO ONE HAS EVER DARED ROB A *BURGLAR ALARM* FACTORY BEFORE!

FOR *NONE* HAS THE AUDACITY OF...THE *MATADOR!*

HOW EASY IT IS FOR *ME* TO VAULT *OVER* ALL THE PROTECTIVE ELECTRIFIED FENCING!

THEN, IT IS BUT THE WORK OF A MOMENT TO OVERCOME THE WATCHMAN....!

AND, BY MEANS OF MY THIN, PLIABLE SWORD BLADE, I CAN DE-ACTIVATE THE MAIN SWITCHES, RENDERING THE COMPLEX SYSTEM OF BURGLAR ALARMS UTTERLY *USELESS!*

HOW CAN *ANYONE* EVER STOP ME?? MY TALENT, AND MY INGENUITY ARE UTTERLY WITHOUT PEER! THE WORLD SHALL LONG REMEMBER THE DEEDS OF THE *MATADOR!*

10.

THE MONEY IS NOT AS IMPORTANT TO ME AS THE *GLORY!* I SHALL DECEIVE THE WORLD INTO THINKING OF ME AS THE *UNDERDOG...* THE LONE ADVENTURER WHO PITS HIS WITS AND COURAGE AGAINST ALL OF SOCIETY'S FORCES!

IF I PLAY MY CARDS RIGHT, THE STUPID PUBLIC WILL ACTUALLY *ROOT* FOR ME! THEY'LL CALL ME THE 20TH CENTURY *ROBIN HOOD!*

AND, MY CRIMES SHALL BE THE TYPE TO MAKE MEN GASP IN AWE! ONLY THE *MATADOR* WOULD DARE INVADE A PLANT WHICH SPECIALIZES IN BURGLAR ALARMS!

AND, ONLY THE MATADOR WOULD STEAL THEIR OWN ALARM FROM THE WALL! I'LL USE IT TO GUARD THE STOLEN TREASURES WHICH SHALL SOON BE MINE!

WHAT A MOMENT OF *TRIUMPH* THIS IS FOR ME! FIRST, MY RESOUNDING VICTORY OVER DAREDEVIL... AND NOW, *THIS!*

THEN.... NEXT MORNING, THE STARTLING NEWS IS FEATURED ON FRONT PAGES THROUGHOUT THE NATION...

EXTRA! MATADOR STRIKES AGAIN! ALL NEW! EXTRA!

Journal and Tribune

EXTRA

MATADOR ROBS BURGLAR ALARM CO.

ADDITIONAL DETAILS ON BACK PAGE.

"MOST DARING CRIME OF THE CENTURY!" SAYS PUBLIC! POLICE HUNT FOR CLUES. PROMINENT CRIMINOLOGISTS SUMMONED FOR CONSULTATION.

STORES REPORT RECORD SALES ON MATADOR SUITS.

AND, IN HIS PRIVATE OFFICE AT *NELSON AND MURDOCK*, THE MAN WITH THE MOST SENSITIVE TOUCH IN THE WORLD ALSO "READS" THE MORNING PAPER BY FEELING THE MINISCULE IMPRESSION OF THE NEWLY-PRINTED INK ON THE SURFACE OF THE PAGE...

THE MATADOR HAS STRUCK AGAIN! AND THROUGHOUT THE NATION, THE YOUNG PEOPLE, AND THE FOOLISH, UNTHINKING ADULTS, WILL SOON START MAKING A *HERO* OF HIM!

HE MUST BE *STOPPED!* HE CAN'T ESCAPE FOREVER! THE POLICE WILL GET HIM SOONER OR LATER...

BUT, HOW MUCH MORE DRAMATIC IT WOULD BE IF *DAREDEVIL* COULD DEFEAT HIM *FIRST!* NOT MERELY FOR MY PRIDE... BUT TO SHOW THE WORLD THAT *JUSTICE* IS MIGHTIER THAN CRIME!

AND THEN, THERE IS SOMETHING *ELSE* I MUST DO! FOR I CAN REMAIN SILENT NO LONGER! I *MUST* TELL KAREN OF MY LOVE... NO MATTER *WHAT* HER ANSWER MAY BE!

HOWEVER, AT THAT VERY MOMENT...

MATT, GOT A MINUTE? I'D LIKE YOUR ADVICE ABOUT SOMETHING!

SURE, FOGGY!

HIS PULSE RATE SOUNDS UNUSUALLY FAST! HE SEEMS TO BE HAVING AN EMOTIONAL DILEMMA!

CAN YOU FEEL WHAT THIS IS, MATT?

A RING! MANY-FACETTED, OBVIOUSLY A DIAMOND! MY SENSE OF TOUCH CAN PIN-POINT THE WEIGHT AT EXACTLY 4½ CARATS! IT'S SQUARE CUT... AND BY LISTENING TO THE FAINT SOUND WHEN I TAP MY FINGERNAIL AGAINST IT, IT IS ABSOLUTELY FLAWLESS!

IT SEEMS TO BE A RING OF SOME SORT!

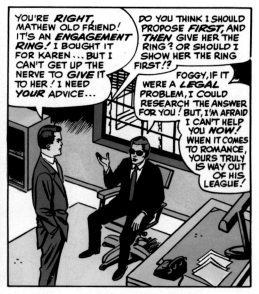

YOU'RE RIGHT, MATHEW OLD FRIEND! IT'S AN ENGAGEMENT RING! I BOUGHT IT FOR KAREN... BUT I CAN'T GET UP THE NERVE TO GIVE IT TO HER! I NEED YOUR ADVICE...

DO YOU THINK I SHOULD PROPOSE FIRST, AND THEN GIVE HER THE RING? OR SHOULD I SHOW HER THE RING FIRST!?

FOGGY, IF IT WERE A LEGAL PROBLEM, I COULD RESEARCH THE ANSWER FOR YOU! BUT, I'M AFRAID I CAN'T HELP YOU NOW! WHEN IT COMES TO ROMANCE, YOURS TRULY IS WAY OUT OF HIS LEAGUE!

I GUESS YOU'RE RIGHT! ONLY I CAN MAKE THE DECISION! BUT I'M SO CRAZY ABOUT THAT GAL THAT I CAN'T EVEN THINK STRAIGHT! WELL, SEE YOU LATER, FELLA...I'M GONNA GO INSIDE AND TOSS A COIN!

OH, NO! MY BEST FRIEND...MY PARTNER ...WANTS TO MARRY THE SAME GIRL AS I DO!

HOW CAN I PROPOSE TO HER NOW? WHY DID FOGGY HAVE TO TELL ME?? IF ONLY I DIDN'T KNOW! BUT I CAN'T NOW...I CAN'T!

THERE'S ONLY ONE THING TO DO! I'VE GOT TO PUT HER OUT OF MY MIND...FORGET HER! PERHAPS IT'S BEST THIS WAY!

AFTER ALL, CAN DAREDEVIL OFFER A GIRL THE TYPE OF LIFE ALL BRIDES DREAM OF? NO... THIS MUST BE FATE'S WAY OF TELLING ME THAT I'M DESTINED TO ALWAYS BE...A LONER!

MINUTES LATER...

WHERE DAREDEVIL WALKS, HE MUST WALK ALONE!

THUS DO I ACCEPT MY LONELY FATE!

THEN, THE SIGHTLESS ADVENTURER PUTS ALL OTHER THOUGHTS OUT OF HIS MIND, AS HE BEGINS TO CONCENTRATE ON THE JOB AT HAND...THE DEFEAT OF THE MATADOR!

MY FIRST STOP MUST BE THE PUBLIC LIBRARY! IT'S CLOSED AT THIS HOUR, BUT THAT WON'T STOP DAREDEVIL!

12.

 MOST COSTUMED ADVENTURERS WOULD GO OUT OF BUSINESS WITHOUT THESE *SKY-LIGHTS* TO DROP THROUGH!

 NOW, LET ME SEE...I'VE GOT TO FEEL MY WAY TO THE NEWSPAPER ARCHIVE ROOM...

QUIET

 MMM...I MUST HAVE TAKEN A WRONG TURN SOMEWHERE!

I'D BETTER REMOVE MY GLOVE AND MAKE IT EASIER FOR MY SENSE OF TOUCH!

 FINALLY... AH...THIS IS WHAT I WANT!

NOW TO GO THROUGH THE SPORTS SECTIONS OF THE INTER-NATIONAL EDITIONS!

 THEN, THERE IN THE SEMI-DARKNESS, "READING" FASTER THAN ANY SIGHTED PERSON COULD HOPE TO, DAREDEVIL'S INCREDIBLY SENSITIVE FINGERTIPS SCAN PAGE AFTER PAGE, UNTIL...

I'D BE GREAT FOR THAT CLASSIFIED PHONE BOOK AD THAT SAYS: "LET YOUR *FINGERS* DO THE WALKING"!

HERE'S WHAT I'M AFTER! I *KNEW* I'D FIND IT! IT'S FROM A PAPER DATED APRIL 6TH, 1964! "MANUEL ELOGANTO, THE WORLD-FAMOUS BULL-FIGHTER HAS MYSTERIOUSLY *VANISHED!*"

 "FOR YEARS, ELOGANTO WAS THE MOST FAMOUS, MOST CONTRO-VERSIAL BULL-FIGHTER IN ALL OF SPAIN! HIS MASTERY OF THE BULLS WAS UNQUESTIONED, BUT..."

ANOTHER VICTORY FOR ELOGANTO!

 "...HIS CRUELTY, AND HIS BRUTALI-TY TOWARDS THE BULLS MADE THE CROWDS HATE HIM! IN FACT, DURING HIS LAST PUBLIC APPEAR-ANCE, THE AUDIENCE ACTUALLY WAS HEARD TO CHEER FOR THE BULL!"

VIVA EL TORO!

LEAVE THE ARENA, MATADOR!

OLE, TORO!

TORO!! TORO!!

 "THIS SO INFURIATED THE TEMPERA-MENTAL MATADOR, THAT HE TURNED TO HURL AN EPITHET BACK AT THE JEERING CROWD! AND THAT WAS HIS GREATEST MISTAKE!"

PEASANTS! BRAINLESS ONES! EVEN THE BULL HAS MORE COURAGE, MORE INTELLI-GENCE, THAN THOSE WHO MOCK ME!

13.

"FOR THEN, DISASTER STRUCK!"

"MANUEL ELOGANTO WAS RUSHED TO THE NEAREST HOSPITAL, WHERE PROMPT MEDICAL ATTENTION SAVED HIS LIFE! BUT, HE WAS HEARD TO BLAME HIS INJURIES ON HIS FELLOW MAN, AND TO VOW *REVENGE* UPON ALL MANKIND! THEN, AFTER HIS RELEASE, HE *DISAPPEARED*!"

NOW I KNOW WHO MY ENEMY IS!

EARLY THE NEXT MORNING...

HELLO, ASSOCIATED PRESS! THIS IS MATT MURDOCK, COUNSELOR-AT-LAW! I'M CALLING A PRESS CONFERENCE TO ANNOUNCE THE *IDENTITY* OF THE MATADOR!

NO, THIS ISN'T A CRANK CALL! SEND SOMEONE TO THE OFFICE OF NELSON AND MURDOCK AT ELEVEN SHARP!

THERE! THAT'S THE FINAL CALL! NOW FOR STEP TWO!

BY ELEVEN A.M., PUZZLED REPRESENTATIVES OF ALL THE MAJOR NEWS SERVICES HAVE GATHERED IN MATT'S OFFICE, TO HEAR...

THE ANSWER IS SO SIMPLE, THAT I'M SURPRISED NO ONE ELSE HAS FIGURED IT OUT! ONLY *ONE* MAN HAS THE SKILL AND ABILITY TO DUPLICATE THE MATADOR'S FEATS... BEYOND THE SHADOW OF A DOUBT, THE MATADOR IS... *DAREDEVIL*!

DAREDEVIL!??

BUT, THE MATADOR HIMSELF HAD FOUGHT... AND *BEATEN*... DAREDEVIL!

YES! HOW DO YOU ACCOUNT FOR *THAT* FACT, COUNSELOR?

SIMPLE! HOW EASY IT WOULD BE FOR DAREDEVIL TO HAVE SOMEONE *IMPERSONATE* HIM, SO IT WOULD *SEEM* THE MATADOR HAD BEATEN HIM... TO THROW SUSPICION OFF HIMSELF! AFTER ALL, DIDN'T THE MATADOR WIN *TOO* EASILY!?

YOU MAY *HAVE* SOMETHING THERE, MR. MURDOCK!

ANYWAY, IT'LL MAKE A *GREAT* STORY!

THEN, AFTER THE NEWSMEN HAVE LEFT...

IF I HAVE JUDGED THE MATADOR CORRECTLY, ALL I NEED DO NOW IS *WAIT*!

LATER, THE EVENING EDITIONS HIT THE STANDS...

LATE EVENING — The New York Bu...

MATADOR IS DAREDEVIL, CLAIMS PROMINENT N.Y. ATTORNEY!

AND, WITHIN MINUTES...

MATT! WHAT GOT *INTO* YOU?? WHY WOULD YOU ISSUE A PUBLIC STATEMENT LIKE *THAT*?? WHAT DO *YOU* KNOW ABOUT THE MATADOR... OR ABOUT DAREDEVIL *EITHER*, FOR THAT MATTER??

I'M ENTITLED TO MY OPINION, FOGGY!

14.

BUT YOU'RE A PARTNER IN OUR LAW FIRM! WHATEVER YOU SAY OR DO REFLECTS UPON *NELSON AND MURDOCK!* YOU SHOULD CONSULT *ME* BEFORE YOU HOLD A NEWS CONFERENCE!

PERHAPS YOU'RE RIGHT, FOGGY! BUT I MEANT NO HARM! I'LL ASK YOU TO *TRUST ME!* I HAD MY *REASONS* FOR WHAT I DID!

WELL, I'LL ADMIT YOU'VE BEEN THE BRAINS OF THIS COMBO *TILL* NOW, SO I'LL GO ALONG WITH YOU! BUT I STILL CAN'T UNDERSTAND YOUR MOTIVES!

AND IT'S LUCKY FOR ME YOU *CAN'T!*

BY THE WAY, FOGGY... DID YOU... DID YOU MAKE UP YOUR MIND ABOUT... KAREN?

I HOPED YOU WOULDN'T ASK, MATT! NO, I.. I JUST COULDN'T MUSTER UP THE NERVE!

THAT NIGHT, AFTER THE OFFICE HAS BEEN CLOSED AND DESERTED...

THIS IS THE PLACE!

MURDOCK! ARE YOU *HERE?* SHOW *YOURSELF!* THIS IS THE *MATADOR!*

YOU DARE TRY TO STEAL MY GLORY... MY FAME?? YOU DARE GIVE THE CREDIT TO *DARE-DEVIL!* YOU'LL *PAY* FOR THAT, MURDOCK!

HOW DIS-APPOINT-ING! HE IS NOT *HERE!*

YOU ARE *RIGHT,* MATADOR! ...MURDOCK IS GONE!

BUT WILL *I* DO?

DAREDEVIL!!!

15

NOW I SEE IT! THAT STORY IN THE PAPER WAS A *PLANT*...A RUSE TO BRING ME HERE! YOU MUST BE IN *LEAGUE* WITH THE LAWYER MURDOCK!

BUT HAVE YOU FORGOTTEN SO SOON HOW I *BEAT* YOU TWICE ?? *THIS* TIME SHALL BE THE *LAST*,... FOR MY PATIENCE HAS COME TO AN END !!

IT *WILL* BE OUR FINAL FIGHT, MATADOR ... BUT THE RESULT MAY BE DIFFERENT THAN YOU EXPECT!

THERE ARE NO OTHER NOISES TO CONFUSE ME NOW! IT'S JUST THE TWO OF US ---MY SENSES AGAINST HIS SKILLS! TO THE *FINISH*, IF NEED BE!

DAREDEVIL IS FASTER THAN I THOUGHT! I BARELY AVOIDED HIS LUNGE!

BUT THE BULLS *TOO* ARE FAST...AND NEVER HAS ONE BEATEN ME, WHILE I WAS *LOOKING*!

COME, TORO! OLE! OLE! CLOSER... CLOSER! TOHKK TOHKK!

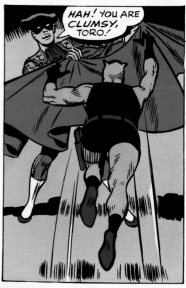

HAH! YOU ARE *CLUMSY*, TORO!

THE GREAT DAREDEVIL! HE IS HIS OWN WORST ENEMY! IT IS TO *LAUGH*!

HE DOESN'T REALIZE I *PURPOSELY* DID THIS! I CAN FIGHT BETTER *OUTSIDE*, WHERE I HAVE ROOM TO RUN, AND LEAP AND SWING! NOW TO GET HIM TO FOLLOW ME!

YOU HAVEN'T BEATEN ME *YET*! I'LL ESCAPE AND REACH THE *POLICE*! YOU CAN'T STOP ME!

FOOL! YOU'LL GET NO FURTHER THAN THE NEXT LANDING! *I'LL* SEE TO THAT!

GOOD! IT'S LUCKY HE'S EASY TO *TAUNT*!

16.

113

AH, MY FEARFUL ONE! EVEN THE *BULLS* HAVE MORE COURAGE THAN *YOU*! NEVER DID THEY FLEE ME WITH SUCH ABJECT COWARDICE!

PERFECT! HE'S GROWING DANGEROUSLY OVERCONFIDENT! DANGEROUSLY FOR *HIM*!

THE SOUND OF A THIN STEEL BLADE STRIKING THE IRON STAIR! HE HAS DRAWN HIS *SWORD*!

AND *I'LL* DRAW *MY* WEAPON!

WHAT! YOU THINK TO CHALLENGE MY *SWORDSMANSHIP* WITH A MERE *WOODEN STICK?!*

HAS YOUR COWARDLY PANIC CAUSED YOU TO TAKE LEAVE OF YOUR SENSES?

HE'D THINK I WAS *REALLY* INSANE IF HE KNEW I'M ATTEMPTING TO DEFEAT HIM WITHOUT BENEFIT OF *SIGHT*!

BUT, TO MY HYPER-SENSITIVE EARS, HIS BLADE WHIPPING ABOUT CAUSES AIR CURRENTS WHICH ARE LIKE LOUD RADAR BLIPS TO ME!

SO! NOW YOU TURN AND ATTEMPT TO FIGHT! *GOOD!* IT SHALL MAKE MY VICTORY THE MORE SATISFYING!

LOOK! DAREDEVIL... AND THE *MATADOR!*

QUICKLY! LET'S RUN AND CALL THE POLICE!

I HEARD AN ONLOOKER SAY SHE'LL SEND FOR THE POLICE! I MUST SCORE A VICTORY BEFORE THEY ARRIVE! ONLY IN THAT WAY CAN I SHOW THE WORLD THAT *DAREDEVIL* CAN VANQUISH THE *MATADOR*!

THIS IS YOUR *FINISH,* DAREDEVIL! BY COVERING YOUR EYES WITH MY CAPE, I PREVENT YOU FROM SEEING MY BLADE! AND SO... I SHALL NOW DISARM YOU!

HE DOESN'T SUSPECT HOW *USELESS* MY EYES ARE TO ME! HIS BLINDING CAPE CANNOT AFFECT ME AT *ALL!*

HOLA!

YOU *PARRIED* MY THRUST! BUT... *HOW?*

YOU WOULDN'T *BELIEVE* ME IF I TOLD YOU!

YOU WONDERED WHAT MY BILLY CLUB COULD DO AGAINST YOUR SWORD, MATADOR!

CRACK!

DOES *THIS* ANSWER YOUR QUESTION!

17.

THEN, AS THE BATTLE PROGRESSES, MORE AND MORE NEIGHBORHOOD RESIDENTS BECOME *AWARE* OF IT!

WOW! WHAT A PUNCH! *ATTA BOY*, DARE-DEVIL!

GOOD! WE HAVE AN AUDIENCE OF ONLOOKERS! THAT IS WHAT I WANT!

THERE MUST BE *WITNESSES* TO THE MATADOR'S DEFEAT!

AND *I* THOUGHT DAREDEVIL WAS ALL WASHED-UP!

WHOP!

THAT NEWS-PAPER STORY WAS *NUTS!* THERE'S *DARE-DEVIL*, FIGHTING THE MATADOR... RIGHT BEFORE OUR EYES... AND HE'S *WINNING!*

YIPPEE! GIVE IT TO 'IM, DAREDEVIL! I *KNEW* YOU WEREN'T REALLY THE MATADOR!

AGAIN HE ATTACKS! BUT I SHALL ENSNARE HIM IN MY CAPE WHEN HE COMES WITHIN REACH!

BUT THE MATADOR IS DOOMED TO DISAPPOINTMENT! FOR IT IS NOT AT *HIM* THE FEARLESS ONE LEAPS...

HE'S WAVING HIS NET... BUT I'LL LEAP *ABOVE* IT!

AS SOON AS I HEARD THE WIND WHISTLING PAST THIS T.V. ANTENNA, I KNEW IT WAS JUST WHAT I NEEDED!

NOW WHAT IS HE DOING??

STAY WHERE YOU *ARE* ELOGANTO! I'LL BE RIGHT WITH YOU!

ELOGANTO! HE *KNOWS* MY NAME!

SO STARTLED IS THE MATADOR THAT HE STANDS STOCK STILL FOR A SECOND...

HOW DOES HE KNOW ME?? *HOW??*

AND, THAT PAUSE IS HIS UNDOING...

THUD!

18.

115

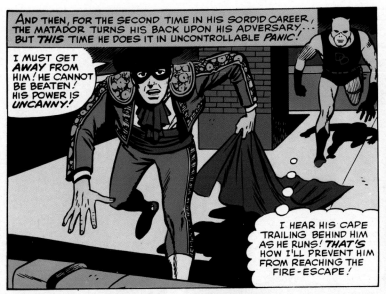

AND THEN, FOR THE SECOND TIME IN HIS SORDID CAREER, THE MATADOR TURNS HIS BACK UPON HIS ADVERSARY... BUT *THIS* TIME HE DOES IT IN UNCONTROLLABLE *PANIC!*

I MUST GET *AWAY* FROM HIM! HE CANNOT BE BEATEN! HIS POWER IS *UNCANNY!*

I HEAR HIS CAPE TRAILING BEHIND HIM AS HE RUNS! *THAT'S* HOW I'LL PREVENT HIM FROM REACHING THE FIRE-ESCAPE!

SCRUNCH!

MOMENTARILY THROWN OFF BALANCE, THE MATADOR WAVERS AT THE EDGE OF THE ROOF FOR A SPLIT-SECOND, UNTIL...

THAT'S *IT*, ELOGANTO... FALL BACK... RIGHT INTO MY WAITING ARMS!

WHERE IS YOUR CRY OF *AY TORO!* NOW?

WHERE ARE YOUR DISDAINFUL *HOLAS*... OR YOUR OTHER SNEERING TAUNTS?

NO! NO MORE! *STOP!* DON'T... *OHHHH!*

WHUMP!

AND WHERE IS YOUR MUCH-HERALDED *COURAGE*, MATADOR?? OR IS IT ONLY SOMETHING TO BE DISPLAYED WHEN ALL THE ODDS ARE IN *YOUR* FAVOR??

WH-WHAT DO YOU PLAN TO DO *NOW??*

NOW?? NOW I SHALL *END* THIS ONE-SIDED DUEL...IN THE ONLY WAY IT *CAN* BE ENDED...

19.

116

As with *all* such contests...there must always be a reckoning! There must always be... *a moment of truth!*

WHOP!

You forgot *one* important thing, Matador..

...sometimes, even the *bull* may win!

Look, Irv...that phone tip was *right!* It *is* Daredevil and the Matador!

And no matter who the Matador *is*...we can bet he *isn't* the Man Without Fear!

Not long afterwards...

Oh, Matt...I'm so glad the Matador has been captured...and by that *wonderful* Daredevil! It's like poetic justice!

Careful, Karen! It almost sounds as though you have a *crush* on Daredevil! And you know how jealous *Foggy* is!

Aww, I'd never be jealous of *him!* I'll bet he wears a mask because he's ugly as sin underneath it!

Oh, Matt...I wish you could *see* it... there are masked Matador costumes in so many trash cans! None of the children are making a hero of that criminal any more!

Then that's enough reward for me! That makes it *all* worthwhile!

By the way, counselor... I just *thought* of something...!

Aren't you *sorry* now that you gave out that statement to the press without asking *me* first? You must feel kinda foolish after saying you were sure that the Matador was really Daredevil!

Oh, Foggy! I don't think you should rub it in! I'm sure Matt *meant* well!

Well, I might as well *admit* it...when I make a mistake, it's usually a *beaut!*

But luckily, Matt's mistakes can be *Daredevil's* triumphs!

More thrills and drama with the most fascinating adventurer of all next ish! *Don't dare miss it!!*

20.

A MARVEL MASTERWORK PiN-UP

RAPIDLY BECOMING TWO OF THE WORLD'S MOST FAMOUS INITIALS...

"DD"

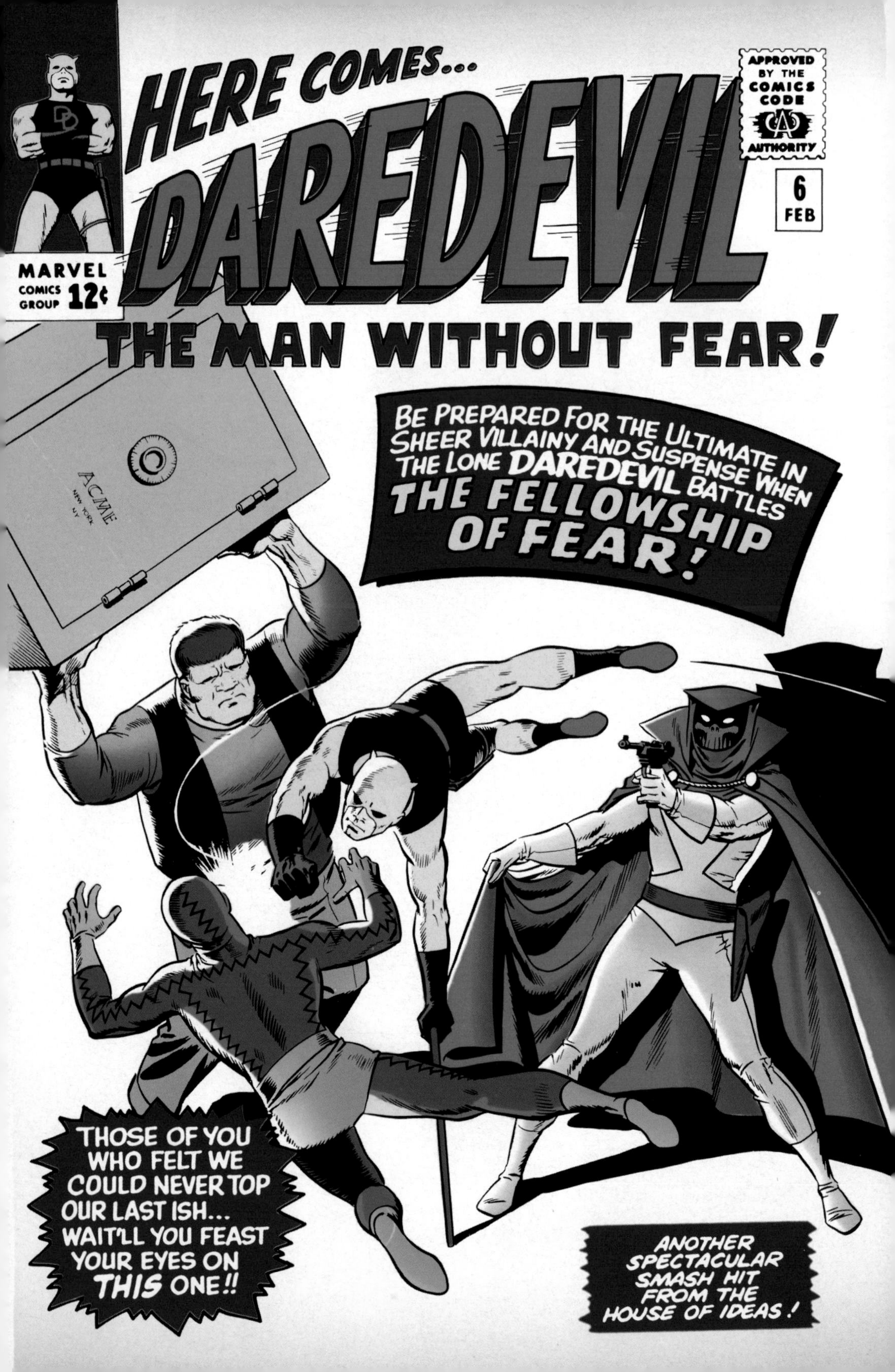
HERE COMES...
DAREDEVIL
THE MAN WITHOUT FEAR!
MARVEL COMICS GROUP 12¢
APPROVED BY THE COMICS CODE AUTHORITY
6 FEB
BE PREPARED FOR THE ULTIMATE IN SHEER VILLAINY AND SUSPENSE WHEN THE LONE DAREDEVIL BATTLES THE FELLOWSHIP OF FEAR!
ACME NEW YORK NY
THOSE OF YOU WHO FELT WE COULD NEVER TOP OUR LAST ISH... WAIT'LL YOU FEAST YOUR EYES ON THIS ONE!!
ANOTHER SPECTACULAR SMASH HIT FROM THE HOUSE OF IDEAS!

DAREDEVIL

THE MAN WITHOUT FEAR LEARNS FOR THE FIRST TIME WHAT IT MEANS TO BE TRULY **AFRAID** WHEN HE IS

"TRAPPED BY...

THE FELLOWSHIP OF FEAR!"

REMEMBER "THE PURPLE MAN" IN D.D. #4? WELL, WE HAVE A HUNCH THAT THIS MONTH'S VILLAIN WILL REMIND YOU OF HIM IN SOME WAYS! BUT, THOUGH THEIR METHODS MAY BE SOMEWHAT SIMILAR, YOU'LL FIND THAT OUR "MR. FEAR" IS FAR, FAR *DIFFERENT* THAN YOU FIRST SUSPECT!

THE VERY **NEWEST** AND POSSIBLY THE **GREATEST** SAGA IN THE EARLY CAREER OF MARVEL'S SENSATIONAL BLIND SWASHBUCKLER!
★★★★★★
SEE DAREDEVIL FIGHT ONE OF THE STRANGEST TRIO OF VILLAINS EVER ASSEMBLED!

WRITTEN WITH THE FABULOUSLY FLAWLESS FANTASY OF...
Stan Lee
—
ILLUSTRATED IN THE MAGNIFICENTLY MODERN MANNER OF...
Wally Wood
—
LETTERED IN THE SCREAMINGLY SOPHISTICATED STYLE OF...
Sam Rosen

LIKE A BROODING WINGLESS EAGLE, THE DAZZLING **DAREDEVIL** STALKS THE CITY'S ROOFTOPS, EVER ALERT, EVER VIGILANT, HIS SUPER-SHARP SENSES PROBING THE NIGHT, SEARCHING FOR ADVENTURE!

But, tonight all seems peaceful! Only the sounds of a movie-making crew, shooting a film on location in the street, break the placid silence...

Voices calling camera directions! I hear the words FADE OUT...PAN ACROSS...DOLLY FORWARD! Obviously a movie is being filmed below me!

And yet, why do I hear no script girl's voice? No sound of police, holding back the crowd? Something about the scene below does not ring TRUE to me!

Now for the big scene! We're all ready to roll!

Excellent! If I didn't know better, I'd think you were the GENUINE criminals you're portraying...the OX and the EEL! Okay... ROLL 'EM! Let's make this robbery look GOOD!

SKRAK!

Those are REAL iron bars! How can he rip 'em out so easy?

And, three stories above, Daredevil's suspicions turn into CERTAINTIES!

NO normal actor could pull iron bars from a locked store door so effortlessly! That is no ordinary film scene!

Seconds later, inside the store, as the cameras begin to grind...

WHAT a foolproof scheme! The camera crew and director we hired suspect nothing... and no one would think of interfering!

ACME

Finally...

It WORKED! Like the boss SAID it would! Now let's pay off those dumb cameramen and I am outta here!

I was RIGHT! They don't realize their softest whisper is like a shout to ME!

Okay, billy club...we've got ourselves a little JOB to do!

If there isn't a lamppost on this corner, I'm gonna be a mighty sorry Daredevil! But a fella has to take SOME chances!

AHH! There it IS!...and here I GO!

Heavy footsteps, directly below... starting to leave! I'm just in time!

HOLD IT, boys! How about an autograph for a movie fan?

DAREDEVIL!!

Where'd HE come from?

2.

SURPRISED, LITTLE FELLA? IT'LL TAKE MORE THAN *YOU* TO TACKLE THE *OX!*

IT WAS LIKE HITTING A STONE WALL! HE'S THE *REAL* OX... ONE OF THE NOTORIOUS *ENFORCERS!*

THE M.M.M.S. WANTS *YOU*

HE MUST HAVE BEEN PAROLLED BEFORE THE OTHERS!*

*LAST SEEN IN *SPIDER-MAN* #14..STAN.

WHOOM!

LUCKY FOR ME HE'S SO BULKY AND SLOW-MOVING!

YOU WON'T ESCAPE US, YOU FLEA! ONCE I GET MY HAND FREE....!

THAT REMINDS ME! THERE'S *ANOTHER* ONE! I HEAR HIS HEARTBEAT! BUT, HE'S NOT MOVING! *WHY?*

DO YOU THINK YOUR CLUMSY LEAP CAN HARM THE *EEL?*

HAH! THE TIGHTER YOU GRAB ME, THE EASIER I CAN SLIDE FROM YOUR GRIP!

HE'S COATED WITH SOME SORT OF UNIQUE *GREASE!* I CAN'T *HOLD* HIM!

THE *OX..* RUSHING UP BEHIND ME! I'VE GOT TO *DUCK!*

WHH...!

NICE TRY, BIG MAN!

HOLD *STILL,* BLAST YOU!

SORRY, OX..I'M MORE THE *NERVOUS* TYPE!

BUT SUDDENLY, DAREDEVIL TURNS AND STRIKES OUT, WITH ALL THE FORCE OF HIS SUPERB FIGHTING SKILL! BUT, SO INTENT IS HE UPON HIS HUGE FOE, THAT...

HE DOESN'T KNOW I'M BEHIND HIM! *NOW* WE'LL GET HIM!

TRY AGAIN, LITTLE MAN!

I'VE *GOT* 'IM, OX! HURRY! ONE BLOW IS ALL IT'LL TAKE!

YOU'RE NOT *KIDDIN!* EEL!

I'LL WAIT TILL I HEAR HIS FIST MOVING TOWARDS ME, AND THEN...!

THERE! YOU *FORGOT,* EEL... THE VERY GREASE-LIKE COATING WHICH MAKES IT HARD TO HOLD YOU, *ALSO* MAKES IT HARD FOR *YOU* TO HOLD ANYONE *ELSE!*

ONE WAY

WOC

EEL! LOOK OUT!

3.

MEANTIME, SUCH A SPECTACULAR BATTLE CANNOT GO UNNOTICED, AND SO...

OPERATOR, *QUICK!* GET ME THE *POLICE!* IT'S AN *EMERGENCY!!*

IF YOU'D ONLY STAY STILL LONG ENOUGH...!

GOT TO TRY SOMETHING ELSE! HE'S TOO POWERFUL!

A *CLICK!* THE SOUND OF A *PISTOL* BEING COCKED!

BOSS! AM I GLAD *YOU'RE* HERE!

WHAT A FIGHT! KEEP THOSE CAMERAS GRINDING! IT'LL BE WORTH A *FORTUNE!*

DAREDEVIL IS ALL *NERVE*... BUT HE HASN'T A *CHANCE* AGAINST THE *OX!*

THERE'S *ANOTHER* ONE! GET THOSE CAMERAS *OUT* OF HERE! IT'S TOO *DANGEROUS!*

HOW *LUCKY* I AM TO ENCOUNTER THE GREAT *DAREDEVIL* WHILE COMMITTING MY FIRST MAJOR CRIME! WHAT FAME THIS VICTORY SHALL GIVE TO... *MR. FEAR!*

MR. *FEAR??*

SIDESTEPPING WITH UNCANNY SPEED, DAREDEVIL SAVES HIMSELF FROM THE POINT-BLANK SHOT! BUT, IT WAS NOT A *BULLET* THAT WAS FIRED... RATHER A SMALL *PELLET,* WHICH BREAKS UPON CONTACT WITH THE WALL BEYOND!

FUMES! HE FIRED A *GAS* PELLET AT ME!

BUT, IT ISN'T *TEAR GAS!* NOR IS IT POISONOUS! WHAT CAN IT *BE?*

SUDDENLY, THE SIGHTLESS ADVENTURER TURNS, MAKING A FRANTIC EFFORT TO *FLEE!*

HOLD 'M, EEL!

TOO MANY OF THEM! I'VE GOT TO ESCAPE WHILE I STILL *CAN!*

CAN'T HANG ON... BUT WE'RE FORCING HIM TOWARDS THE *WALL!*

THIS IS THE END OF THE LINE, DAREDEVIL!

BOTH OF THEM... ABOUT TO ATTACK ME!

NO! STAY BACK!

DON'T *COUNT* ON IT, CHUM!

AN AIR CURRENT!...DIRECTLY ABOVE ME! THAT MEANS AN *OPENING!*

IT'S MY ONE CHANCE! IF I CAN SWING OVER IN TIME!

HE'S GETTING *AWAY!*

STOP 'IM!

I JUST *MADE* IT!

UHHH!

MISSED 'IM!

WHA AP

4.

A SHORT TIME LATER... OFFICER, WE WERE *DUPED!* WE WERE HIRED TO FILM A SHORT COMMERCIAL FILM DEALING WITH A DARING ROBBERY! BUT IT WAS *REAL!*

ALL RIGHT, MISTER! CALM DOWN! LET ME HAVE THE WHOLE STORY, FROM THE BEGIN-NING!

IT WAS THE *EEL* AND THE *OX!* BUT WE THOUGHT THEY WERE *ACTORS,* MADE UP TO *LOOK* LIKE CROOKS!

LUCKILY, *DAREDEVIL* CAME BY! HE SLOWED THEM DOWN... ALMOST CAUGHT THEM! BUT THEY WERE TOO MUCH FOR HIM!

TOWARDS THE END, A *THIRD* ONE APPEARED! DRESSED IN AN OUTLANDISH COSTUME! HE CALLED HIMSELF *MR. FEAR!* SEEMED TO BE THE *LEADER!*

WE GOT MOST OF IT ON *FILM!* WE'LL PLAY IT BACK FOR YOU!

MEANWHILE, ALONE IN HIS ROOM, WE FIND...

IT NEVER HAPPENED TO ME BEFORE! BUT I CAN'T DENY IT TO MYSELF... I WAS AFRAID! I WAS *SCARED STIFF!*

IT WAS RIGHT AFTER MR. FEAR FIRED THAT PELLET AT ME! ALL OF A SUDDEN, I BECAME ALMOST *PETRIFIED!* ALL I COULD THINK OF WAS TRYING TO ESCAPE!

WHAT'S *HAPPENED* TO ME? HAVE I TURNED... *COWARD?*

THE NEXT DAY, AT THE OFFICES OF *NELSON AND MURDOCK,* ATTORNEYS-AT-LAW...

GOOD MORNING, MATT! HAVE YOU HEARD ABOUT...? OH, I SEE YOU HAVE THE MORNING NEWS PROGRAM ON *NOW!*

YES, KAREN! I'VE JUST BEEN HEARING THE PLAY-BACK OF THE FILM SHOWING DAREDEVIL'S BATTLE WITH MR. FEAR AND HIS TWO STRANGE PARTNERS!

BATTLE? IT WAS MORE LIKE A *ROUT!* I UNDER-STAND THAT DARE-DEVIL REALLY TURNED CHICKEN AT THE END!

YES, THAT SEEMS TO BE THE CONSENSUS OF OPINION..!

I CAN'T EVEN DENY IT TO *MYSELF!* I *KNOW* IT'S TRUE!

WE'VE SEEN DAREDEVIL BRAVELY FIGHTING HOPELESS ODDS BEFORE! HE *CAN'T* BE DIFFERENT NOW! THERE *MUST* BE AN EXPLANATION!

PERHAPS THERE *IS,* KAREN! BUT I'M AFRAID THAT ONLY TIME WILL TELL!

I HEAR HER PULSE QUICKEN AS SHE SPEAKS TO ME! IF ONLY IT MEANT THAT SHE LOVES ME...!

I WONDER WHO *MR. FEAR* REALLY IS??

BUT IT MUST ONLY BE HER FEELING FOR *DAREDEVIL!*

NOT ONLY LOVELY KAREN PAGE WONDERS WHO MR. FEAR IS, BUT THE ENTIRE *WORLD* ASKS THAT QUESTION! AND, FOR THE INCREDIBLE ANSWER, LET'S GO BACK A FEW MONTHS, BACK TO A SMALL, DINGY SIDE-STREET WAX-MUSEUM...

IT'S TIME TO CONTINUE MY *EXPERIMENTS* AGAIN!

WAX MUSEUM

MY WAX MUSEUM IS A *FAILURE!* EVEN THOUGH I HAVE MODELS OF THE MOST FAMOUS HEROES... THE MOST NOTORIOUS VILLAINS OF ALL TIME, NOBODY COMES TO SEE THEM!

BUT WHEN MY *EXPERIMENTS* ARE COMPLETED, THINGS WILL BE *DIFFERENT!* THEN, THE WORLD SHALL ACCLAIM THE GENIUS OF *ZOLTAN DRAGO!*

5.

ZOLTAN DRAGO, ALAS, HAD ONE FAULT! ALTHOUGH HE WAS A TALENTED SCULPTOR AND MODEL MAKER, HE WAS ALSO... SLIGHTLY *MAD*!

SOONER OR LATER I'LL DISCOVER A WAY TO BRING MY WAX FIGURES TO *LIFE*!! AND THEN, THE ENTIRE *WORLD* WILL BE AT MY FEET!

I'VE EXPERIMENTED FOR *YEARS*, WITHOUT SUCCESS! I'VE MIXED ALL SORTS OF POTIONS, ALL TYPES OF CHEMICALS! BUT I'LL NEVER GIVE UP!

SOONER OR LATER I'LL FIND THE RIGHT FORMULA...EVEN IF IT'S BY ACCIDENT! IT WILL MAKE NO DIFFERENCE, SO LONG AS I *SUCCEED*!

GO 'WAY, KITTY! I MUST NOT BE DISTURBED NOW...BY *ANYONE*!

THE OBEDIENT FELINE OBEYS ITS MASTER'S COMMAND, BUT, IN SO DOING, SPILLS A SMALL JAR FROM THE SHELF ABOVE ---

IT LANDED ON MY BUNSEN BURNER, CAUSING *FUMES* TO APPEAR!!

UNABLE TO HELP HIMSELF, ZOLTAN DRAGO *INHALES* THE STRANGE FUMES AND SUDDENLY... AN UNEXPECTED REACTION SETS IN, AS DREAD, NAMELESS *FEAR* FILLS HIS HEART!!

STAY BACK, KITTY! DON'T *HURT* ME!

I'M SORRY I YELLED AT YOU! I DIDN'T *MEAN* IT!! DON'T COME NEAR ME! STAY BACK!

THE FUMES ARE EVAPORATING! MY FEAR IS LEAVING ME!

I *DID* DISCOVER SOMETHING *AFTER ALL*! SOMETHING I NEVER EXPECTED!

I'VE FOUND A WAY TO FILL ANY FOE WITH INDESCRIBABLE *FEAR*!!

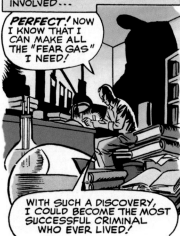

FOR LONG WEEKS, THE STRANGE, HAUNTED MAN WORKED, REFINING HIS DISCOVERY, LEARNING ALL HE COULD ABOUT THE CHEMICALS INVOLVED...

PERFECT! NOW I KNOW THAT I CAN MAKE ALL THE "FEAR GAS" I NEED!

WITH SUCH A DISCOVERY, I COULD BECOME THE MOST SUCCESSFUL CRIMINAL WHO EVER LIVED!

THEN, SOME DAYS LATER...

I'VE MODIFIED AN ORDINARY PISTOL TO FIRE MY NEW "FEAR PELLETS"!

AND NOW, FOR PSYCHOLOGICAL PURPOSES, I'LL CREATE A *COSTUME*--- THE PERFECT DISGUISE FOR ONE WHO SHALL HENCEFORTH BE KNOWN AS...

MR. FEAR!!

AND NOW, BEFORE I BEGIN, THERE IS ONE LAST DETAIL I MUST ATTEND TO...!

6

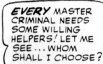

Panel 1: EVERY master criminal needs some willing helpers! Let me see... whom shall I choose?

Panel 1: DIABLO?? KRAVEN?? DOCTOR DOOM? ZEMO? NO! They are all too powerful, or too clever! Sooner or later they might find the way to gain mastery over ME!

Panel 2: BUT, THEN, FINALLY...

Panel 2: THE OX! Unbelievably powerful, but too dull-witted to challenge my leadership!

Panel 2: AND THE EEL, slippery, clever, and cunning...BUT not strong enough to defy me! They shall be the ones for me!

Panel 3: LATER, A STRANGE, FRIGHTENING FIGURE BEGAN TO MAKE THE ROUNDS OF THE CITY'S UNDER-WORLD HAUNTS...

Panel 3: I..I'LL TELL YA ANYTHING I KNOW! JUST DON'T HURT ME!

Panel 3: MY FEAR GAS NEVER FAILS! HOW EASY THIS SHALL BE! TELL ME WHERE TO FIND THE EEL...QUICKLY!!

Panel 3: SURE! WE'LL TELL YA...

Panel 4: AND SO...

Panel 4: EEL! COME UP HERE! MR. FEAR WANTS YOU!!

Panel 4: WHO ARE YOU? HOW'D YOU LEARN MY HIDING PLACE??

Panel 4: COULD THE HUMAN TORCH HAVE SENT HIM ??*

Panel 4: * REFER TO STRANGE TALES #117... STAN.

Panel 5: THEN, AFTER ONE SMALL GAS PELLET HAS BEEN FIRED...

Panel 5: SURE, I'LL WORK FOR YOU! I'LL DO WHATEVER YOU SAY! AS LONG AS I DON'T GET HURT!

Panel 5: OF COURSE! AND NOW, WE MUST FIND THE OX! I HEARD THAT HE IS NOW UP FOR PAROLE!

Panel 6: LEARNING OF THE EXACT DATE OF THE OX'S PAROLE, IT WAS A SIMPLE MATTER FOR MR. FEAR AND THE EEL TO BE WAITING OUTSIDE THE PRISON GATES!..

Panel 6: HOW DO YOU KNOW HE'LL AGREE TO WORK FOR YOU, BOSS?

Panel 6: BECAUSE NO ONE CAN RESIST MR. FEAR... NOT WHEN I USE MY LITTLE GAS PELLETS TO URGE THEM!

Panel 7: AND SO, WITHOUT FURTHER ADO, WE RETURN TO THE PERILOUS PRESENT...!

Panel 7: IT'S A GOOD THING YOU USED YOUR FEAR GUN ON DAREDEVIL, BOSS! HE ALMOST GOT THE UPPER HAND OVER ALL OF US!

Panel 7: PERHAPS! BUT I SHALL NOT PERMIT HIS CHALLENGE TO GO UNANSWERED! WE MUST SOME DAY FIND HIM, AND DISPOSE OF HIM!

Panel 7: IF SOMEONE'LL HOLD 'IM FOR ME LONG ENOUGH, BOSS, I'LL TAKE CARE OF THAT LITTLE MATTER!

BUT HOW CAN YOU *FIND* A CHARACTER LIKE THAT? NOBODY HAS ANY IDEA WHO HE IS!... OR WHERE HE HANGS HIS HAT!

I'M WAY *AHEAD* OF YOU! I'VE *ALREADY* ARRANGED A *TRAP* FOR HIM! AND *THIS* SHALL BE THE *BAIT!*

WHAT'S *THAT,* BOSS?

COULDN'T YOU *GUESS?* IT'S A NEW WAX FIGURE... OF *DAREDEVIL!*

HE'S BOUND TO COME TO SEE IT WHEN HE LEARNS THAT IT'S HERE!

AND NOW, BACK AGAIN TO OUR TWO INTREPID LEGAL EAGLES...

IT WAS NICE OF FOGGY TO GET ME THIS PUSH-BUTTON TAPE-RECORDER, SO I COULD DICTATE WITHOUT SEEING!

BUT, I WONDER WHAT HE'D SAY IF HE KNEW I CAN USE THE MOST DELICATE ELECTRONIC EQUIPMENT MORE CAPABLY THAN A SIGHTED MAN?

DON'T WORRY, COLLINS! I'LL HAVE THAT BRIEF PREPARED FOR YOU BY TUESDAY MORNING!

FROM THE SOUND OF HER BREATHING, I KNOW KAREN IS LOOKING AT ME! SHE'S PITYING BLIND MATT MURDOCK, I SUPPOSE!

OH, MATT, I LOVE YOU SO! IF ONLY YOU'D GIVE ME SOME ENCOURAGEMENT! JUST A WORD... OR A GESTURE! BUT, I CAN SEE THAT YOU SIMPLY DON'T CARE!

IT'S HARD TO THINK WHEN SHE'S SO NEAR ME! IF ONLY *FOGGY* DIDN'T LOVE HER, I'D MAKE A PITCH MYSELF... EVEN THOUGH IT WOULD BE HOPELESS! BUT SHE MUST NEVER KNOW HOW I FEEL ABOUT HER!

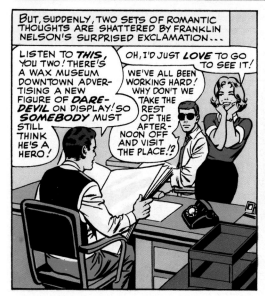

BUT, SUDDENLY, TWO SETS OF ROMANTIC THOUGHTS ARE SHATTERED BY FRANKLIN NELSON'S SURPRISED EXCLAMATION...

LISTEN TO *THIS,* YOU TWO! THERE'S A WAX MUSEUM DOWNTOWN ADVERTISING A NEW FIGURE OF *DAREDEVIL* ON DISPLAY! SO *SOMEBODY* MUST STILL THINK HE'S A HERO!

OH, I'D JUST *LOVE* TO GO TO SEE IT!

WE'VE ALL BEEN WORKING HARD! WHY DON'T WE TAKE THE REST OF THE AFTERNOON OFF AND VISIT THE PLACE!?

AND SO...

MY RADAR SENSE TELLS ME IT'S RIGHT IN FRONT OF ME, TALL AND NOBLE-LOOKING! IF ONLY I COULD FORGET ABOUT MY COWARDLY BEHAVIOR THE OTHER DAY!

OH, MATT, IT'S SO *HANDSOME!* I WISH YOU COULD *SEE* IT!

8.

127

THE PLACE IS FILLING UP NOW! I GUESS THERE ARE A **LOT** OF PEOPLE WHO ARE STILL INTERESTED IN DAREDEVIL, KAREN!

TO **ME**, HE'LL ALWAYS BE ONE OF THE MOST WONDERFUL, HEROIC MEN IN THE WORLD!

WELL, I SUPPOSE WE'D BETTER BE LEAVING NOW!

I JUST CAUGHT THE WHIFF OF A FAMILIAR SCENT! IT'S THE SAME **GAS** THAT MR. FEAR FIRED AT ME THE OTHER NIGHT!! BUT... WHY IS IT **HERE**?

SHUT THAT DOOR, YOU FOOL!! DO YOU WANT THE ODOR OF MY FEAR GAS TO TRICKLE INTO THE HALL ??!

SORRY, BOSS! I WANTED TO SEE IF **DARE-DEVIL** SHOWED UP! BUT THERE AIN'T A SIGN OF 'IM!

HE'LL BE HERE SOONER OR LATER! WE CAN AFFORD TO WAIT!

BUT, THEN, AS THE OX IS SHUTTING THE DOOR...

I COULD **SWEAR** THAT'S THE **OX**... THE ONE THE POLICE ARE SEEKING!

THAT HEAVY BREATHING! THE SCENT OF CHEAP HAIR TONIC! IT'S THE **OX**!

THAT'S WHY I DETECTED THE GAS ODOR! **MR. FEAR** MUST BE HERE!

I WON'T ALARM MATT OR KAREN! I'LL COME BACK ALONE, LATER, AND SEE IF I WAS RIGHT!

I MUST SAY NOTHING TO FOGGY! I'LL RETURN TONIGHT.. AS **DAREDEVIL!!**

THEN, AFTER THE MUSEUM HAS CLOSED FOR THE NIGHT...

WE WILL REMAIN! HE STILL MAY BE HERE!

AND, MR. FEAR'S PREDICTION PROVES TO BE CORRECT! FOR, WHEN DARKNESS FALLS, THE MAN WITHOUT FEAR APPROACHES THE GLOOMY BUILDING IN HIS OWN INIMITABLE MANNER ...

I HOPE I SHALL NOT BE TOO LATE!

I'VE **GOT** TO LEARN THE SECRET OF HIS GAS PELLET... AND I MUST SOMEHOW PROVE TO MYSELF THAT I **HAVEN'T** REALLY TURNED COWARD!

WOODWORTH

THE MUSEUM IS DIRECTLY AHEAD, AND THE SOUND OF THE SOFTLY MOVING AIR CURRENTS TELLS ME THAT I'M APPROACHING AN OPEN WINDOW!

9.

STRANGE! ALTHOUGH I HEAR BREATHING, I CAN DETECT NO MOTION! PERHAPS THOSE WITHIN ARE ASLEEP!

NO! THAT ISN'T THE ANSWER! THE BREATHING IS TOO HIGH... IT COMES FROM TWO NEARBY STANDING FIGURES!

THE HAIR TONIC AGAIN! THE PULSE RATES! IT'S OX... AND THE EEL!

OF COURSE! IT'S OBVIOUS! THINKING I CAN SEE, THEY'RE TRYING TO FOOL ME INTO BELIEVING THEY'RE MERELY WAX DUMMIES!!

NOW THAT I'VE PASSED THEM, THEY'RE STIRRING.. FACING ME... ABOUT TO ATTACK!

NOW WE GOT YA!

HEY! HOW'D HE KNOW TO DUCK??

WHAT'S THE DIFFERENCE? WE'VE GOT 'IM NOW!

THE EEL... BEHIND ME! I'VE GOT TO MOVE FAST!

SO FAR, SO GOOD!! BUT WHERE'S MR. FEAR??

WHUP!

UNHHH..!!

MEANTIME, NOT SUSPECTING WHAT IS TRANSPIRING INSIDE, FOGGY NELSON SOFTLY MOUNTS THE STEPS OUT FRONT...

I WOULDN'T WANT TO CALL THE POLICE UNTIL I'M CERTAIN! I'LL SAY I THINK I LEFT MY HAT HERE, AND TRY TO LOOK AROUND!

I'M IN LUCK! THE DOOR SEEMS TO BE OPEN!

DAREDEVIL!! FIGHTING ALL THREE OF THEM! HE NEEDS HELP!!

NOW I SENSE MR. FEAR! HE JUST ENTERED THE ROOM IN FRONT OF ME!

BUT I HEAR ANOTHER NEW-COMER!! OH, NO!! IT'S FOGGY!!

I HOPED YOU'D BLUNDER INTO MY TRAP, DAREDEVIL!!

10.

129

THE ONE IN COSTUME... ABOUT TO SHOOT DAREDEVIL! IF ONLY I CAN *STOP* HIM...!

ALL RIGHT, BOYS! HE'S ALL YOURS!

NO! I'M TOO LATE!

SOMEONE *ELSE* ATTACKING ME! WHERE DID *HE* COME FROM?

HE MUST BE A *DETECTIVE!* THEY'RE *ON* TO US!

THAT UNEXPECTED FEELING OF STARK *FEAR* AGAIN! CAN'T FIGHT IT! IT'S LIKE A DRUG!

IF I CAN SEE WHO THIS CHARACTER *IS*, MAYBE I'LL BE LUCKY ENOUGH TO GET AWAY SAFELY AND ALERT THE LAW!

MY MASK! OX, TO MY *SIDE*... I *NEED* YOU!

OBEYING HIS SUMMONS WITH THE THOUGHTLESS INSTINCTS OF THE SLOW-WITTED, THE HULKING *OX* BRUSHES DAREDEVIL ASIDE, AND...

TRY TO ATTACK THE *BOSS,* WILLYA ?? YOU'RE GONNA BE REAL *SORRY,* MISTER!

CAN'T ESCAPE! WHAT DO I DO *NOW* ??

A SPLIT SECOND LATER, FRANKLIN "FOGGY" NELSON'S UNSPOKEN QUESTION IS DRAMATICALLY *ANSWERED,* WITH ONE POWERFUL SWEEP OF THE OX'S OPEN HAND!

ENOUGH, OX! WE'VE GOT TO RUN! IF HE'S A COP, THE PLACE WILL BE *SWARMING* WITH POLICE WITHIN MINUTES! LET'S GO!

WHAP!

BUT... I THOUGHT WE WERE GONNA FINISH OFF *DAREDEVIL* ?!!

NO *TIME* FOR THAT NOW! WE CAN'T LET THE COPS GRAB US! DAREDEVIL CAN'T EVER THREATEN US AGAIN! YOU *SAW* HOW EASILY I CAN STOP HIM! COME ON, EEL... FOLLOW THE OX!

MINUTES LATER, AFTER THE FEAR GAS HAS BEEN DISSIPATED...

THE PANIC HAS *LEFT* ME AGAIN ... BUT MR. FEAR AND THE OTHERS HAVE GONE! WAIT! THAT WEAK, MUFFLED BREATHING! THAT FAINT HEARTBEAT! IT'S *FOGGY!* HE'S BEEN *INJURED!*

NOW I REMEMBER! HE CAME TO MY AID! BUT... HE'S *HURT!*

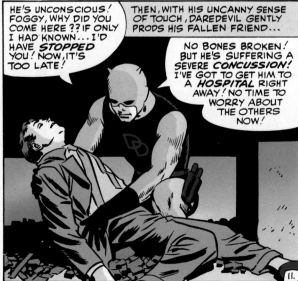

HE'S UNCONSCIOUS! FOGGY, WHY DID YOU COME HERE ?? IF ONLY I HAD KNOWN... I'D HAVE *STOPPED* YOU! NOW, IT'S TOO LATE!

THEN, WITH HIS UNCANNY SENSE OF TOUCH, DAREDEVIL GENTLY PRODS HIS FALLEN FRIEND...

NO BONES BROKEN! BUT HE'S SUFFERING A SEVERE *CONCUSSION!* I'VE GOT TO GET HIM TO A *HOSPITAL* RIGHT AWAY! NO TIME TO WORRY ABOUT THE OTHERS NOW!

11.

130

LIFTING THE INERT FIGURE AS EFFORTLESSLY AS ONE MIGHT LIFT A PAPER DOLL, THE SUPERBLY CONDITIONED ADVENTURER RACES TO THE STREET...

DID HE FOLLOW ME? DID HE GUESS MY IDENTITY?

NO! IT CAN'T BE THAT! I'D HAVE SENSED IT! HE STILL SUSPECTS NOTHING!

LUCKILY, THE SIGHT OF THE SWIFTLY RUNNING COSTUMED FIGURE SOON ATTRACTS THE ATTENTION OF A CRUISING PATROL CAR, AND THEN...

IT'S DAREDEVIL!

THIS MAN NEEDS HOSPITALIZATION IMMEDIATELY! I'LL EXPLAIN LATER!

THAT'S GOOD ENOUGH FOR US, FELLA! PUT HIM IN THE BACK SEAT!

THUS, MINUTES LATER...

YOUR GUESS WAS RIGHT! IT'S A SEVERE CONCUSSION! I SUGGEST YOU NOTIFY HIS IMMEDIATE FAMILY AS SOON AS POSSIBLE!

I CAN'T! THEY'RE VACATIONING IN EUROPE! BUT, THERE IS ONE...

AND, AT KAREN'S APARTMENT, WHERE SHE PONDERS HER MOST DIFFICULT DECISION...

I KNOW FOGGY WANTS TO MARRY ME!...AND HE'D MAKE A WONDERFUL HUSBAND! BUT...I CAN'T STOP LOVING MATT! YET, A GIRL CAN'T THROW AWAY HER LIFE FOR A MAN WHO'LL NEVER PROPOSE...!

WHO COULD BE CALLING AT THIS HOUR?

RRING!

WHAT?!! FRANKLIN NELSON... IN EMERGENCY...AT MUNICIPAL HOSPITAL!! I..I'LL BE RIGHT THERE!

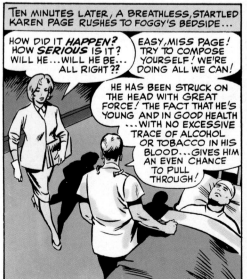

TEN MINUTES LATER, A BREATHLESS, STARTLED KAREN PAGE RUSHES TO FOGGY'S BEDSIDE...

HOW DID IT HAPPEN? HOW SERIOUS IS IT? WILL HE...WILL HE BE... ALL RIGHT??

EASY, MISS PAGE! TRY TO COMPOSE YOURSELF! WE'RE DOING ALL WE CAN!

HE HAS BEEN STRUCK ON THE HEAD WITH GREAT FORCE! THE FACT THAT HE'S YOUNG AND IN GOOD HEALTH ...WITH NO EXCESSIVE TRACE OF ALCOHOL OR TOBACCO IN HIS BLOOD...GIVES HIM AN EVEN CHANCE TO PULL THROUGH!

AND THEN...

I TOOK A TAXI AS SOON AS I HEARD THE NEWS! HE MUST RECEIVE THE BEST OF CARE! CALL IN SPECIALISTS...CONSULTANTS...ANYTHING! YOU'VE GOT TO SAVE HIM!

MATT! THEY'RE DOING EVERYTHING THEY CAN FOR HIM! ALL WE CAN DO IS...HOPE, AND PRAY!

YOU'D BETTER LOOK AFTER MR. MURDOCK, MISS! HE SEEMS TO BE UNDER A VERY GREAT STRAIN!

12.

131

BUT, MATT MURDOCK'S "STRAIN" MIGHT BE EVEN *GREATER*, IF HE COULD SEE THE OCCUPANTS OF A SPEEDING SEDAN, RAPIDLY APPROACHING THE HOSPITAL...

WE'VE GOT TO *SILENCE* THAT MEDDLER BEFORE HE RECOVERS CONSCIOUSNESS AND REVEALS MY IDENTITY TO THE POLICE!

GOOD THING YA HEARD ON THE RADIO WHERE THEY *TOOK* 'IM!

WHILE, BACK IN THE HOSPITAL...

OH, MATT, I ALWAYS TOOK FOGGY SO MUCH FOR GRANTED! BUT NOW...NOW THAT HE'S IN DANGER... I REALIZE HOW MUCH I *CARE* FOR HIM...!

I *KNEW* IT! SHE *DOES* LOVE HIM! NOW I CAN *NEVER* TELL HER HOW *I* FEEL... *NEVER!*

I..I'D BETTER GO NOW, KAREN! BUT, I'LL BE BACK IF YOU NEED ME!

YES, I *CARE* FOR FOGGY, MATT...BUT... IT'S *YOU* I LOVE! IF ONLY YOU WEREN'T SO COLD...SO UNEMOTIONAL ...OH, MATT...MATT...

MINUTES LATER...

EVEN *NOW*, WITH FOGGY IN SUCH DANGER, MATT IS PROBABLY BACK IN THE OFFICE, PORING OVER HIS BRAILLE LAW BOOKS! WHY IS THERE NO WAY TO REACH HIS HEART? HAS HE NO FEELINGS?? DOES HE THINK ONLY OF HIMSELF?

IF THAT STRANGE "FELLOWSHIP OF FEAR" INJURED FOGGY BEFORE, THEY MIGHT TRY TO RETURN, TO FINISH THE JOB! I DON'T DARE LEAVE HIM ALONE!

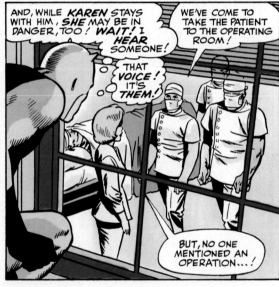

AND, WHILE *KAREN* STAYS WITH HIM, *SHE* MAY BE IN DANGER, TOO! *WAIT!* I *HEAR* SOMEONE!

WE'VE COME TO TAKE THE PATIENT TO THE OPERATING ROOM!

THAT *VOICE!* IT'S *THEM!*

BUT, NO ONE MENTIONED AN OPERATION...!

CRASH!

KAREN, *RUN!* YOU'RE IN *DANGER!*

DAREDEVIL!

HOW DID HE KNOW WHO WE *WERE?*

WHAT'S THE *DIFFERENCE,* YOU FOOL?? *GET HIM,* BEFORE HE RECOVERS HIS BALANCE!

BUT DAREDEVIL'S SUPER-HEARING, COUPLED WITH HIS INCREDIBLE AGILITY, ENABLE HIM TO DODGE THE CLUMSY ATTACK OF THE POWERFUL *OX!*

YOU TELEGRAPHED THAT BLOW BY A *MILE,* BIG MAN!

EEL...HELP THE *OX!* WE'LL *SURROUND* DAREDEVIL!

13.

"HE MOVES TOO *FAST!* USE YOUR *FEAR GUN* ON 'IM, BOSS!"

"*FEAR GUN?!!* SO *THAT'S* THE ANSWER! THOSE PELLETS HE FIRED AT ME IN THE PAST... THEY CAUSED MY *UNREASONING* PANIC!"

"I FORGOT TO *BRING* IT! BUT, WE'RE *THREE* AGAINST ONE! HE HASN'T A CHANCE!"

"YOU'RE *WRONG!* IT'S *NOT* THREE AGAINST ONE! IT'S THREE AGAINST *DAREDEVIL!* THERE'S A MIGHTY BIG *DIFFERENCE!*"

"I'LL GET HIM, AND... UHHH! HE DUCKED TOO FAST!"

"THE *EEL!* BUT *WITHOUT* HIS GREASED COSTUME!"

MOVING LIKE A HUMAN TORNADO, THE SIGHTLESS CRUSADER GRABS THE EEL'S LEGS BEFORE HE CAN LEAP SAFELY PAST, AND THEN...

"ALL RIGHT, GENTS! IF YOU *WANT* ME..."

"LOOK OUT! STAY *BACK!*"

"COME 'N' *GET* ME!"

WHHOOSH!

THEN, RELEASING THE EEL, AND DRAWING HIS BILLY CLUB...

"MY RADAR SENSE DETECTS A *LIGHT SWITCH* BEHIND THE *OX!*"

"JUST STAY WHERE YOU *ARE,* MUSCLE MAN!"

"SAY! YOU'RE PRETTY GOOD AT *SHADOW BOXING!* YOU OUGHTTA TRY SPARRING WITH A *REAL* FOE SOME TIME!"

CLICK!

"UNHHH!"

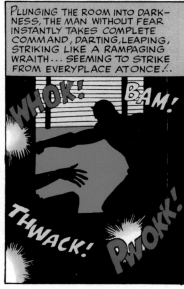

PLUNGING THE ROOM INTO DARKNESS, THE MAN WITHOUT FEAR INSTANTLY TAKES COMPLETE COMMAND, DARTING, LEAPING, STRIKING LIKE A RAMPAGING WRAITH... SEEMING TO STRIKE FROM EVERYPLACE AT ONCE!..

WHOK! BAM! THWACK! PWOKK!

"EEL! GRAB HIM! HOLD HIM! GIVE THE *OX* A CHANCE TO CONNECT! LET... MMMPFF!"

"HOW?? WE CAN'T *SEE* ANYTHING! WE CAN'T *FIND* 'IM... OWW!"

"HOW CAN *HE* SEE US?? HE'S HITTING US AS THOUGH THE *LIGHTS* ARE ON! WE CAN'T... UGHHH!"

THUD! WHAM! KRAK!

14.

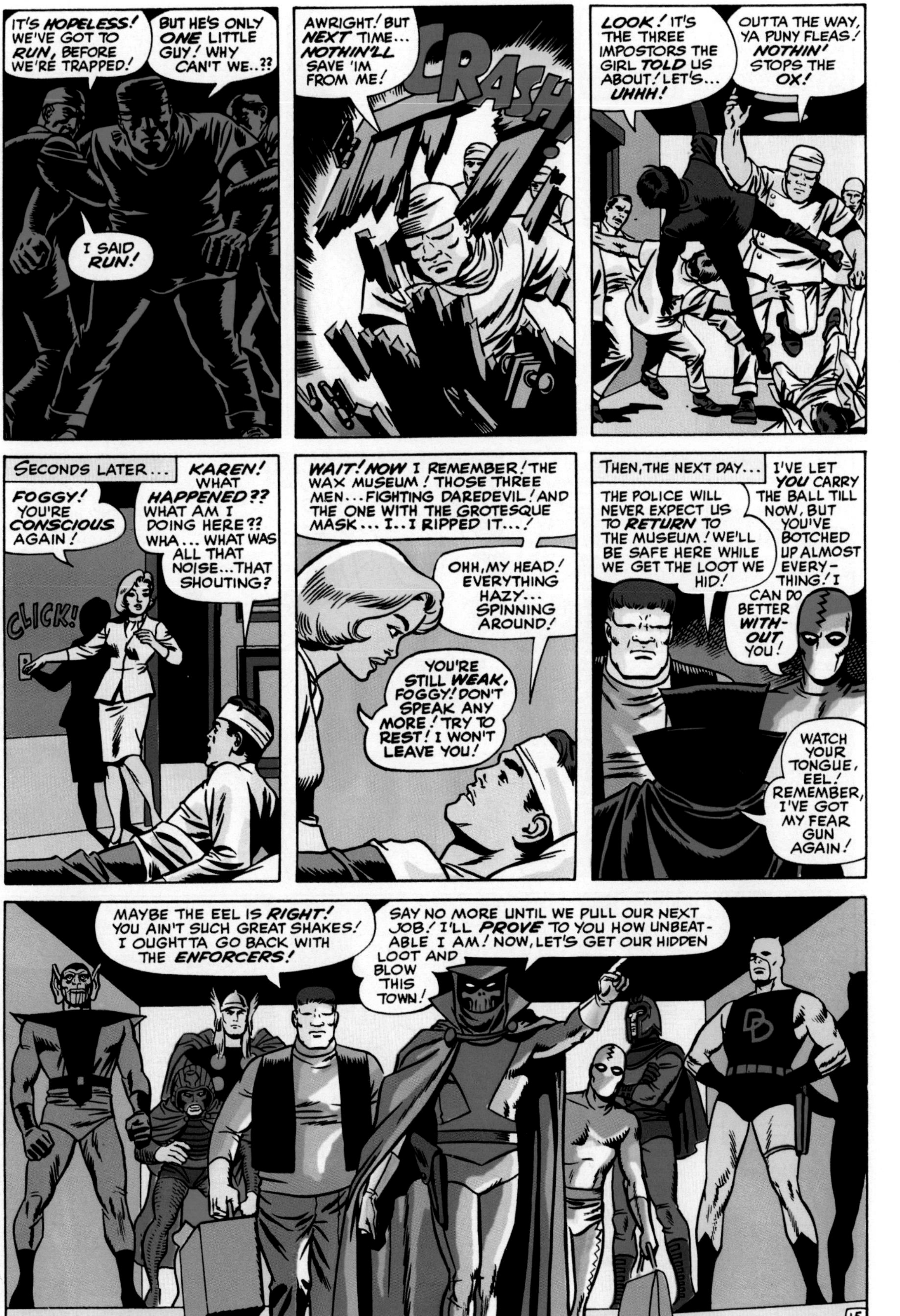
IT'S HOPELESS! WE'VE GOT TO RUN, BEFORE WE'RE TRAPPED!
BUT HE'S ONLY ONE LITTLE GUY! WHY CAN'T WE..??
I SAID RUN!
AWRIGHT! BUT NEXT TIME... NOTHIN'LL SAVE 'IM FROM ME!
CRASH!
LOOK! IT'S THE THREE IMPOSTORS THE GIRL TOLD US ABOUT! LET'S... UHHH!
OUTTA THE WAY, YA PUNY FLEAS! NOTHIN' STOPS THE OX!
SECONDS LATER...
FOGGY! YOU'RE CONSCIOUS AGAIN!
KAREN! WHAT HAPPENED?? WHAT AM I DOING HERE?? WHA... WHAT WAS ALL THAT NOISE...THAT SHOUTING?
CLICK!
WAIT! NOW I REMEMBER! THE WAX MUSEUM! THOSE THREE MEN... FIGHTING DAREDEVIL! AND THE ONE WITH THE GROTESQUE MASK... I..I RIPPED IT...!
OHH, MY HEAD! EVERYTHING HAZY... SPINNING AROUND!
YOU'RE STILL WEAK, FOGGY! DON'T SPEAK ANY MORE! TRY TO REST! I WON'T LEAVE YOU!
THEN, THE NEXT DAY...
THE POLICE WILL NEVER EXPECT US TO RETURN TO THE MUSEUM! WE'LL BE SAFE HERE WHILE WE GET THE LOOT WE HID!
I'VE LET YOU CARRY THE BALL TILL NOW, BUT YOU'VE BOTCHED UP ALMOST EVERY-THING! I CAN DO BETTER WITH-OUT YOU!
WATCH YOUR TONGUE, EEL! REMEMBER, I'VE GOT MY FEAR GUN AGAIN!
MAYBE THE EEL IS RIGHT! YOU AIN'T SUCH GREAT SHAKES! I OUGHTTA GO BACK WITH THE ENFORCERS!
SAY NO MORE UNTIL WE PULL OUR NEXT JOB! I'LL PROVE TO YOU HOW UNBEAT-ABLE I AM! NOW, LET'S GET OUR HIDDEN LOOT AND BLOW THIS TOWN!
15.

DON'T FORGET, MY *FEAR GUN* CAN MAKE *ANYONE* MY SLAVE! I'VE ONLY *BEGUN* MY CAREER!! DAREDEVIL WAS MERELY A PASSING INTERLUDE!

AN INTERLUDE THAT HASN'T YET *ENDED!*

WHO *SAID* THAT??

I WAS *HOPING* YOU'D ASK! IT GETS MIGHTY TIRESOME STANDING LIKE A STATUE ALL THAT TIME!

IT'S *DAREDEVIL!* NOW I'LL *PROVE* MY SUPERIORITY! *HOLD HIM,* EEL!

YOU AIN'T GONNA HAVE A CHANCE TO PROVE *ANYTHING!* I'M GONNA SMASH 'IM NOW!

WIGGLIN' AROUND AIN'T GONNA HELP YA, DAREDEVIL! THIS IS *IT!*

YOU'RE *RIGHT,* BUT, NOT THE WAY YOU *THINK!*

STAY *STILL,* BLAST YOU!

THOK!

HAPPY LANDINGS, BIG MAN!

AND, LEST *YOU* FEEL NEGLECTED, MY SLIPPERY FRIEND, HERE'S A LITTLE TAP FOR *YOU,* TOO!

UHH!!

THOSE FUTILE THEATRICS CANNOT SAVE YOU FROM MY *FEAR GUN!*

I WAS *WAITING* FOR YOU TO TRY THAT!

THEN, BEFORE THE POTENT FUMES CAN REACH HIM...

IT'S NOT BY *ACCIDENT* THAT I ARRANGED TO BE STANDING NEAR THIS BUILT-IN *EXHAUST FAN!* ALL I NEED DO IS PRESS THE *REVERSE* BUTTON...!

CLICK!

AND NOW, WHILE THE FUMES ARE BLOWN BACK TO *YOU,* WE'LL WRAP THIS UP FOR *GOOD!*

WHIRR!

16.

WAFTING SPEEDILY BACK AGAIN, THE FEAR FUMES CAUSE TEMPORARY PANIC AMONGST THE OX AND THE EEL...

RUN! RUN!

DON'T LET HIM GET US!

MY GUN! I MUST RETRIEVE MY GUN!

THE FUMES DIDN'T AFFECT MR. FEAR! HIS MASK MUST PROTECT HIM!

SINCE YOUR LITTLE PELLET SHOOTER DOESN'T AFFECT YOU, WE'LL JUST CARRY ON WITHOUT IT!

THAT WON'T HELP YOU! YOU'RE DOOMED, ANY-WAY!!

MINUTES AGO, HE HAD THE ADVANTAGE OF SURPRISE! BUT NOW, WE'RE READY FOR HIM!

STAND BACK! HE'S MINE!

BROOM!

DON'T YOU EVER GIVE UP, OX ??

YOU DODGED HIM, BUT I WON'T BE SO EASY!

BUT I DON'T WANT TO DODGE YOU, EEL!

I JUST WANT TO BE ABLE TO HOLD ON TO YOU... AND THIS'LL DO THE TRICK !!

NOTHING CAN HELP YOU TO HOLD ME! MY COSTUME IS COATED WITH THE SLIPPERIEST SOLVENT KNOWN TO... HEY!

NO MATTER WHAT YOU'RE COVERED WITH, THIS LAYER OF SAND WILL STOP MY FIST FROM GLANCING OFF YOU!

AND, IN CASE YOU STILL DON'T BELIEVE ME, HERE'S A LITTLE DEMONSTRATION! PARDON MY GLOVE, SON!

I CAN'T AFFORD ANY SLIP-UPS NOW! THIS IS THE PAYOFF! I HEAR THE OX COMING UP BEHIND ME...!

17.

136

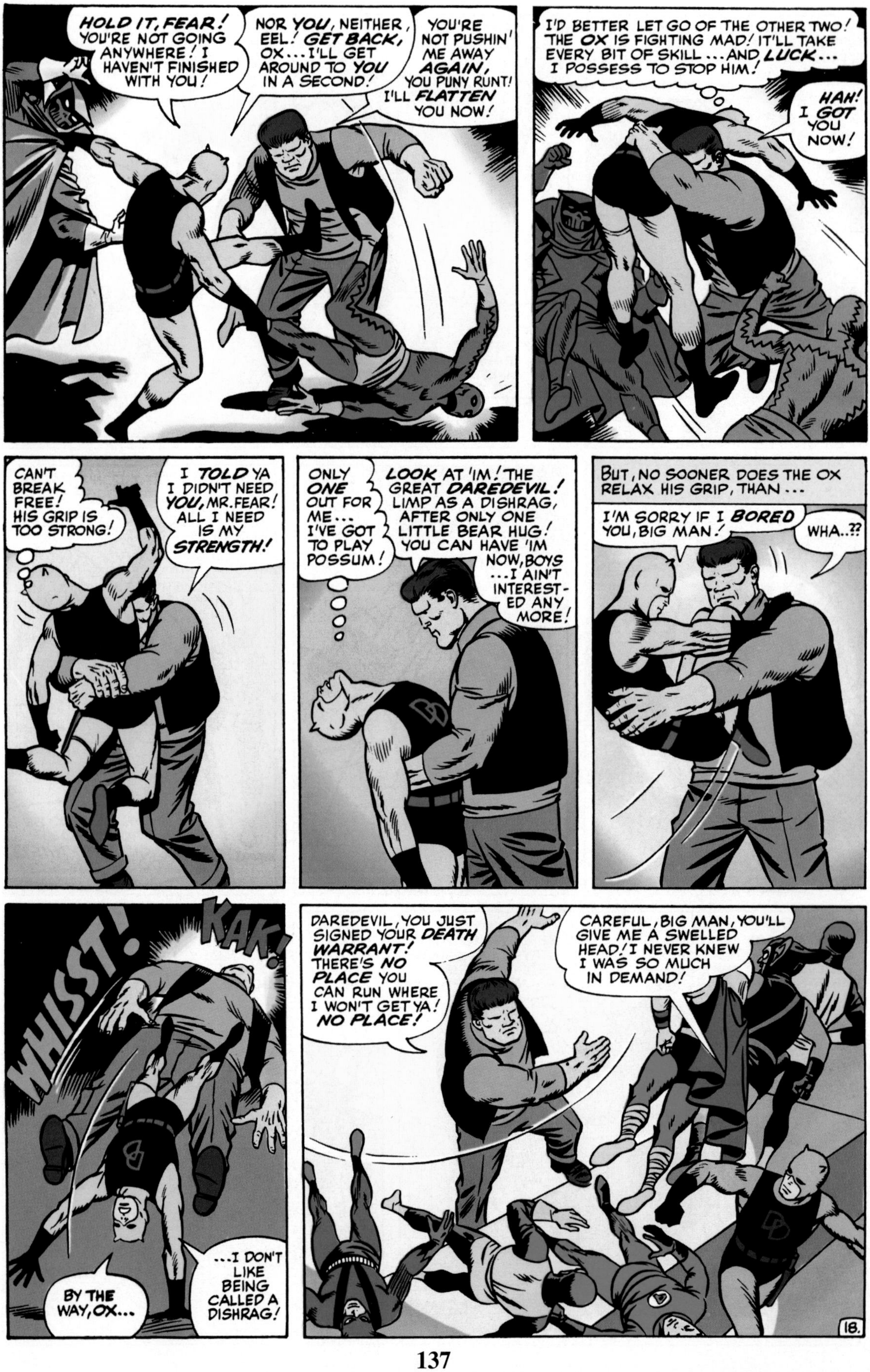
HOLD IT, FEAR! YOU'RE NOT GOING ANYWHERE! I HAVEN'T FINISHED WITH YOU!
NOR YOU, NEITHER, EEL! GET BACK, OX... I'LL GET AROUND TO YOU IN A SECOND!
YOU'RE NOT PUSHIN' ME AWAY AGAIN, YOU PUNY RUNT! I'LL FLATTEN YOU NOW!
I'D BETTER LET GO OF THE OTHER TWO! THE OX IS FIGHTING MAD! IT'LL TAKE EVERY BIT OF SKILL... AND LUCK... I POSSESS TO STOP HIM!
HAH! I GOT YOU NOW!
CAN'T BREAK FREE! HIS GRIP IS TOO STRONG!
I TOLD YA I DIDN'T NEED YOU, MR. FEAR! ALL I NEED IS MY STRENGTH!
ONLY ONE OUT FOR ME... I'VE GOT TO PLAY POSSUM!
LOOK AT 'IM! THE GREAT DAREDEVIL! LIMP AS A DISHRAG, AFTER ONLY ONE LITTLE BEAR HUG! YOU CAN HAVE 'IM NOW, BOYS ...I AIN'T INTEREST-ED ANY MORE!
BUT, NO SOONER DOES THE OX RELAX HIS GRIP, THAN...
I'M SORRY IF I BORED YOU, BIG MAN!
WHA..??
WHISST!
KAK!
BY THE WAY, OX...
...I DON'T LIKE BEING CALLED A DISHRAG!
DAREDEVIL, YOU JUST SIGNED YOUR DEATH WARRANT! THERE'S NO PLACE YOU CAN RUN WHERE I WON'T GET YA! NO PLACE!
CAREFUL, BIG MAN, YOU'LL GIVE ME A SWELLED HEAD! I NEVER KNEW I WAS SO MUCH IN DEMAND!
18.

DUCKIN' AROUND THAT CORNER WON'T HELP YA! IT'S A BLIND ALLEY! THERE'S NO PLACE ELSE TO RUN!

GOOD! I'M GETTING TIRED, ANY-WAY!

THAT'S IT! STAY THERE... THIS AIN'T GONNA TAKE LONG!

I'M SURPRISED AT YOU, OX! I THOUGHT ONE DUMMY COULD EASILY RECOGNIZE ANOTHER!

BRAM!

AND NOW, ALTHOUGH I HATE TO END OUR LITTLE PERIOD OF FUN AND GAMES, IT IS GETTING LATE AND THE EEL AND MR. FEAR MIGHT BE FEELING NEGLECTED...!

WROOM!

KLOP! SKAK! WUP!

YOU DIDN'T THINK YOU COULD SNEAK UP ON ME, DID YOU??

TH WIP!

THEN, WHEELING ABOUT WITH THE SPEED OF THOUGHT, DAREDEVIL SEIZES THE NOW-HELPLESS MR. FEAR!..

DON'T! YOU CAN'T HIT A DEFENSELESS MAN! NO!

PERHAPS I SHOULDN'T...BUT, IF EVER I HELD A TEMPTING TARGET..!

I'LL RETURN THE STOLEN LOOT! GIVE MYSELF UP! ANYTHING! BUT...DON'T HIT ME!

BOY! YOU DON'T NEED TO INHALE YOUR FEAR GAS! YOU'RE JUST A PLAIN, NATURAL-BORN COWA...

WELL! WELL! LOOK WHO'S BACK FOR A RETURN ENGAGE-MENT!

I WAS SURE I'D BEATEN HIM! HE'S WALKING SO SLOWLY! IS HE REALLY THAT CONFIDENT, OR...

19.

I WAS *RIGHT*! HE *WAS* BEATEN! BUT IT TOOK HIM TILL NOW TO *REALIZE* IT!

TIMM-BER!

UNNHHH...

SCANT SECONDS LATER...

OPERATOR, GET ME POLICE HEAD-QUARTERS! NO, IT ISN'T AN EMERGENCY! YOU CAN TAKE YOUR TIME! I'VE A LITTLE "PACKAGE" FOR THEM TO PICK UP...AND IT ISN'T GOING ANYWHERE!

FINALLY...

SO MUCH FOR THE DEFEATED FELLOWSHIP OF FEAR! NOW TO RETURN TO THE HOSPITAL AND SEE HOW *FOGGY* IS!

HE'S CONSCIOUS! HIS PULSE AND RESPIRATION ARE ALMOST NORMAL! GOOD OLD FOGGY... HE'S GOING TO BE OKAY!

MATT! I'M SO GLAD YOU CAME! THE DOCTOR SAID FOGGY WILL BE ALL RIGHT!

SURE! THEY CAN'T KEEP A GOOD MAN DOWN!

I WOULD HAVE COME SOONER... BUT I WAS BUSY...

I DON'T UNDER-STAND YOU, MATT! WEREN'T YOU EVEN *CONCERNED* ABOUT YOUR FRIEND AND PARTNER??

DON'T SAY IT, KAREN! IT'S OKAY! THAT'S WHAT MAKES MATT THE GREAT *LAWYER* HE IS! HE'S COLD AND UNEMOTIONAL! HE HASN'T ANY ROOM FOR SENTIMENT!

AFTER ALL, THERE WASN'T ANYTHING *I* COULD DO, WAS THERE?

AND, THE NEXT DAY...

THE POLICE NOW BELIEVE THAT DAREDEVIL MERELY *PRETENDED* TO BE AFRAID OF MR. FEAR AND HIS COHORTS, IN ORDER TO LATER TRAP THEM! THE STOLEN GOODS HAVE BEEN RECOVERED AND THE CAPTURED TRIO ARE BEING HELD IN A HALF-MILLION DOLLARS BOND...

I NEVER WOULD HAVE BUTTED IN MYSELF IF I'D KNOWN *DAREDEVIL* WOULD BE THERE! GOSH, I'D LIKE TO KNOW WHO HE REALLY *IS*!

≷SIGH!≷ SO WOULD *I*!

I'LL BET HE'S NOT *NEARLY* AS GLAMOROUS AS YOU TWO *IMAGINE* HE IS! AND NOW, SUPPOSE WE ALL GET BACK TO WORK!

AFTER ALL, *ONE* THING WE CAN BE SURE OF IS...HE'S *NOT* ONE OF US.

The End

20.

139

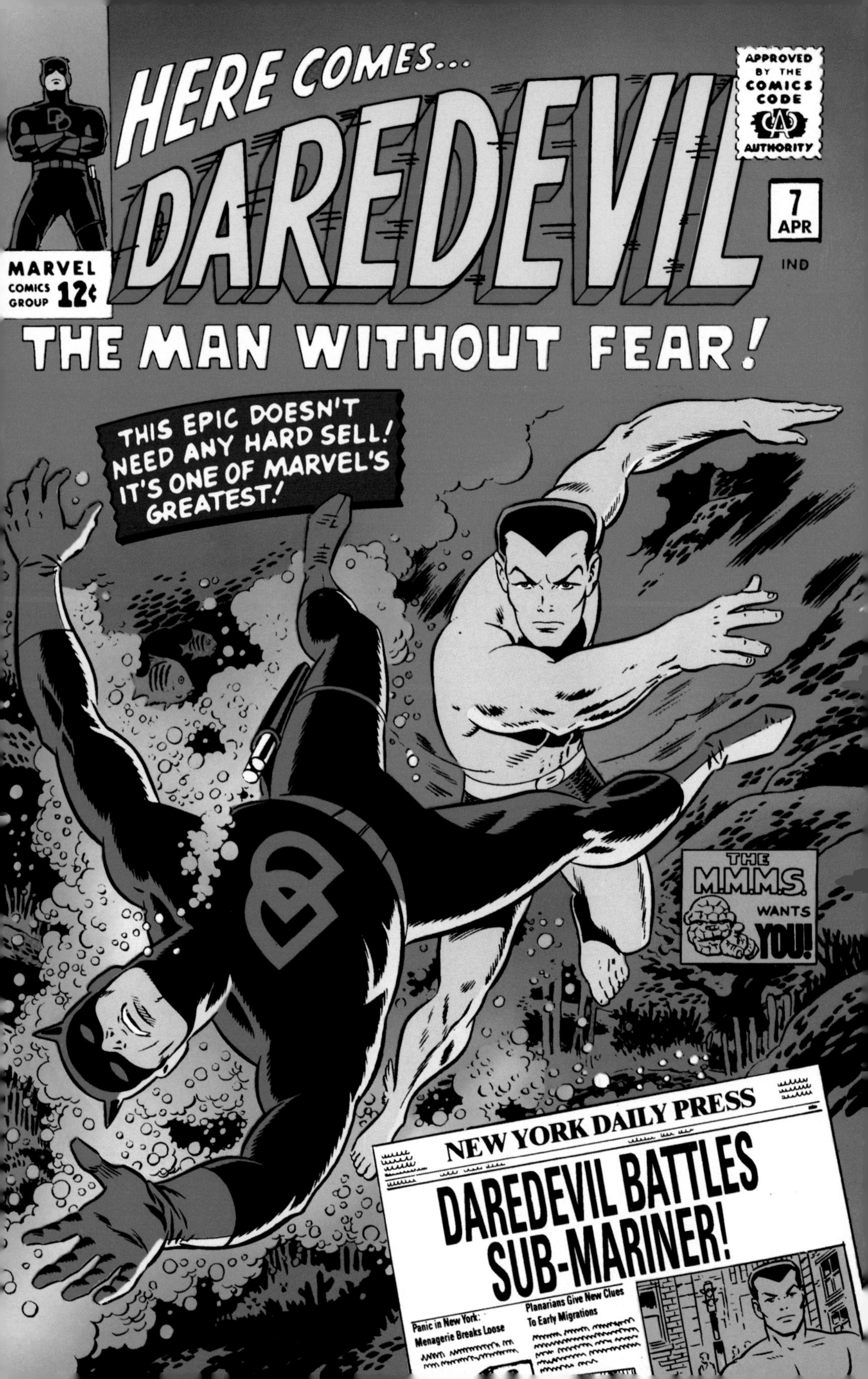

HERE COMES...
DAREDEVIL
APPROVED BY THE COMICS CODE AUTHORITY
7 APR
IND
MARVEL COMICS GROUP 12¢
THE MAN WITHOUT FEAR!
THIS EPIC DOESN'T NEED ANY HARD SELL! IT'S ONE OF MARVEL'S GREATEST!
THE M.M.M.S. WANTS YOU!
NEW YORK DAILY PRESS
DAREDEVIL BATTLES SUB-MARINER!
Panic in New York: Menagerie Breaks Loose
Planarians Give New Clues To Early Migrations

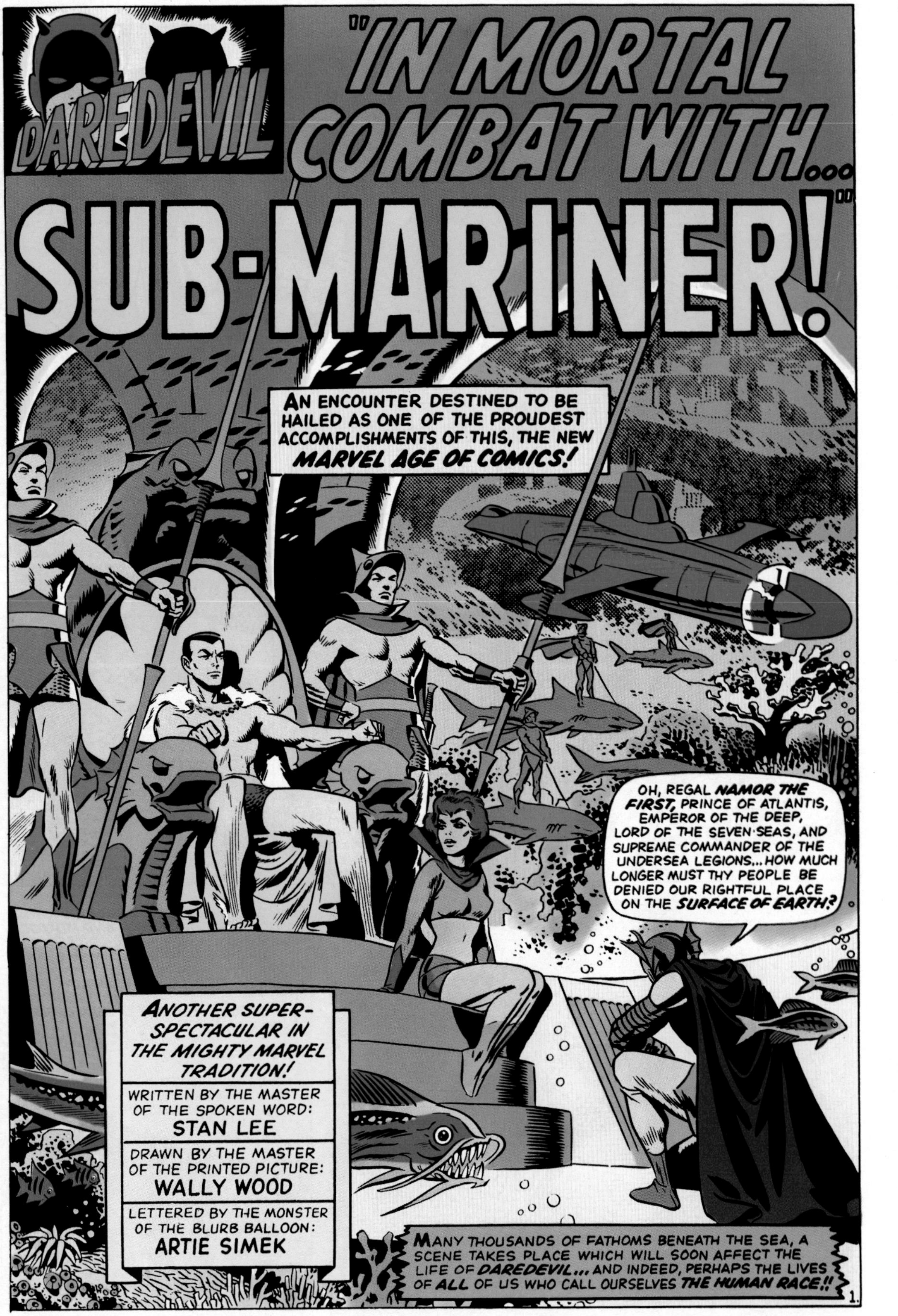
DAREDEVIL
"IN MORTAL COMBAT WITH... SUB-MARINER!"
AN ENCOUNTER DESTINED TO BE HAILED AS ONE OF THE PROUDEST ACCOMPLISHMENTS OF THIS, THE NEW MARVEL AGE OF COMICS!
OH, REGAL NAMOR THE FIRST, PRINCE OF ATLANTIS, EMPEROR OF THE DEEP, LORD OF THE SEVEN SEAS, AND SUPREME COMMANDER OF THE UNDERSEA LEGIONS... HOW MUCH LONGER MUST THY PEOPLE BE DENIED OUR RIGHTFUL PLACE ON THE SURFACE OF EARTH?
ANOTHER SUPER-SPECTACULAR IN THE MIGHTY MARVEL TRADITION!
WRITTEN BY THE MASTER OF THE SPOKEN WORD: STAN LEE
DRAWN BY THE MASTER OF THE PRINTED PICTURE: WALLY WOOD
LETTERED BY THE MONSTER OF THE BLURB BALLOON: ARTIE SIMEK
MANY THOUSANDS OF FATHOMS BENEATH THE SEA, A SCENE TAKES PLACE WHICH WILL SOON AFFECT THE LIFE OF DAREDEVIL... AND INDEED, PERHAPS THE LIVES OF ALL OF US WHO CALL OURSELVES THE HUMAN RACE!!
1.

YOUR SUBJECTS GROW RESTLESS, MY LORD! THEY LONG TO BASK IN THE HEAT OF THE SUN, TO GAZE UPON THE COUNTLESS STARS, TO RETURN TO THE LANDS FROM WHICH WE FLED MANY AGES AGO!

YOU SPEAK *HALF-TRUTHS*, KRANG! THE SURFACE *IS* OUR RIGHTFUL HERITAGE, BUT--

--OUR PEOPLE DO NOT WISH TO SHED ANY MORE BLOOD IN BATTLE WITH THE HUMANS!

IT IS *YOU*, MY *WARLORD*, WHO HUNGERS FOR COMBAT-- WHOSE SOUL LONGS FOR NEW CONQUESTS!

AND YET, I WOULD NOT BE TRUE TO MY ROYAL TRUST IF I DO NOT TRY TO REGAIN THE SURFACE WORLD FOR ATLANTIS! BUT, THERE MUST BE *ANOTHER* WAY-- A WAY SHORT OF *WAR*!

DO NOT HEED THE WORDS OF *KRANG*, MY LORD! HIS HEART IS AS EVIL AS THE *BARRACUDA*!

SILENCE, LADY DORMA! KRANG IS A *WARRIOR*! HE DOES HIS DUTY! THAT IS ALL THAT MATTERS!

I SHALL VISIT THE SURFACE AGAIN, WAR-LORD! I SHALL PRESENT NEW DEMANDS TO THE HUMAN RACE!

BUT, WHY *ALERT* THEM? LET US ATTACK WITHOUT WARNING!

AND BESMIRCH THE HONOR OF FAIR ATLANTIS?? *NEVER*!

IF MY LEGIONS ARE NEEDED, I SHALL SUMMON YOU! BUT FIRST, I SHALL RELY ON REASON, AND INTERNATIONAL LAW! FAREWELL!

THE *FOOL*! THE HUMANS WILL *DESTROY* HIM-- AND THEN *I* SHALL SEIZE POWER AND RULE ATLANTIS IN HIS STEAD!

KRANG THINKS I AM UNAWARE OF HIS RUTHLESS AMBITION, HIS UNQUENCHABLE DESIRE FOR MY CROWN, AND FOR THE HAND OF LADY DORMA!

BUT I AM *NAMOR*, THE AVENGING SON! *NONE* CAN TAKE WHAT IS MINE BY DIVINE RIGHT!

KRANG IS MY ABLEST WARLORD, AND SO I TOLERATE HIS PETTY DECEPTIONS! AND NOW-- TO THE *SURFACE WORLD*!

SOME TIME LATER, IN THE MIDTOWN LAW OFFICES OF *NELSON AND MURDOCK*, KAREN PAGE, THEIR LOVELY SECRETARY, CRIES OUT IN AMAZEMENT...

MATT! IN THE STREET BELOW-- IT'S ALMOST *UNBELIEVABLE!*

WHAT *IS* IT, KAREN? WHAT DO YOU SEE?

I HEAR PEOPLE SHOUT-ING-- THE SOUND OF RUNNING FOOTSTEPS-- BUT I CANNOT YET SENSE THE *CAUSE* OF SUCH ALARM!

2

AND, IN THE STREET BELOW...

THEY RECOGNIZE ME! THEY FLEE IN PANIC! SHALL SUCH AS *THESE* RULE OVER EARTH INSTEAD OF *NAMOR*??!

IT'S *PRINCE NAMOR!!* THE *SUB-MARINER!!*

IT COULD BE THE START OF ANOTHER UNDERSEA *INVASION!*

TAKE COVER! GET OFF THE STREETS!

BUT, ONCE THE FIRST SUDDEN SHOCK HAS PASSED -- ONCE IT IS CLEAR THAT NAMOR IS ALONE AND UNARMED, THE PEOPLE STAND THEIR GROUND, WATCHING IN SILENT BEWILDERMENT....!

BEFORE RESORTING TO *FORCE*, I SHALL ADOPT THE METHODS OF THE SURFACE DWELLERS! I SHALL PRESS MY CLAIM *LEGALLY!*

BUT, I AM UNFAMILIAR WITH SURFACE CUSTOMS -- I KNOW NOTHING OF THE HUMANS' LAW! SO, I SHALL ENGAGE THE SERVICES OF AN *ATTORNEY!*

BETTER STAND ASIDE -- GIVE HIM ROOM! HE WALKS AS CONFIDENTLY AS IF WE DON'T EVEN EXIST!

ANY LAWYER WILL DO! THERE MUST BE DOZENS WITHIN AN OFFICE BUILDING AS LARGE AS THIS ONE!

BUT, WHAT MANNER OF DOOR IS *THIS*? I CANNOT FATHOM ITS PURPOSE!

NO MATTER -- I SHALL PAY FOR WHATEVER DAMAGE I DO AT SOME LATER DATE!

DIRECTORY

2-12

NOW FOR THE FIRST ATTORNEY I FIND! *AH!* NELSON AND MURDOCK! I'M CERTAIN THEY WILL DO AS WELL AS ANY OTHERS!

THEN, AFTER WAITING IMPATIENTLY FOR THE ELEVATOR...

THE LORD OF ATLANTIS WAITS FOR *NOTHING!*

CRUNCH!

THE CAR IS NOT BEHIND THE DOORS! PERHAPS IT IS ON A FLOOR ABOVE --!

WHEN *NAMOR* IS RULER OF THE SURFACE WORLD, THERE SHALL BE AN *END* TO SUCH PRIMITIVE, UNSATISFACTORY DEVICES!

3

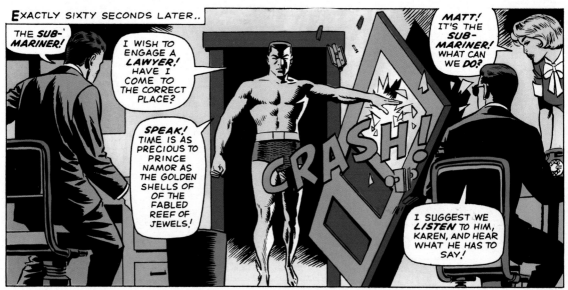

EXACTLY SIXTY SECONDS LATER..

THE **SUB-MARINER!**

I WISH TO ENGAGE A **LAWYER!** HAVE I COME TO THE CORRECT PLACE?

SPEAK! TIME IS AS PRECIOUS TO PRINCE NAMOR AS THE GOLDEN SHELLS OF THE FABLED REEF OF JEWELS!

MATT! IT'S THE **SUB-MARINER!** WHAT CAN WE **DO?**

I SUGGEST WE **LISTEN** TO HIM, KAREN, AND HEAR WHAT HE HAS TO SAY!

CRASH!

MY PEOPLE HAVE DWELLED BENEATH THE SEA SINCE TIME IMMEMORIAL! NOW, WE DEMAND OUR RIGHTFUL PLACE ON THE **SURFACE** OF EARTH!

I WISH TO **SUE** THE ENTIRE HUMAN RACE FOR DEPRIVING US OF OUR **BIRTHRIGHT!**

I'M AFRAID THAT WOULD BE **IMPOSSIBLE!** THERE IS NO LEGAL PRECEDENT FOR IT.! ALSO, THERE IS NO ONE NATION WHICH REPRESENTS THE HUMAN RACE!

YOU WEARY ME WITH DETAILS! A **PRINCE** DOES NOT CONCERN HIMSELF WITH PETTY PROBLEMS!

BUT, DON'T YOU UNDERSTAND? YOU HAVE NO **CASE!** YOU CANNOT COME TO COURT WITHOUT **EVIDENCE!** YOU'D MAKE A **LAUGHING STOCK** OF YOURSELF!

MIND YOUR TONGUE, SURFACE MAN! YOU ARE ADDRESSING A PRINCE OF THE BLOOD!

MY PARTNER IS **RIGHT,** NAMOR! WE'D **LOVE** TO TAKE YOUR CASE-- IT WOULD MAKE US THE MOST FAMOUS LAWYERS ON EARTH! BUT, WITHOUT A LEGAL BASIS FOR LAWSUIT, THEY'D KICK US OUT OF COURT!

YOUR WORDS HAVE THE RING OF **TRUTH** TO THEM! I KNOW YOU BELIEVE WHAT YOU SAY!

BUT I **MUST** PRESENT MY CLAIM! I **MUST** BE HEARD! OTHERWISE, OUR TWO RACES SHALL FIGHT A WAR TO THE DEATH--A WAR WHICH **NEITHER** CAN WIN!

I SHALL **FORCE** THEM TO TAKE ME TO COURT! AND THEN, THE WORLD WILL **HAVE** TO LISTEN!

FORCE THEM?? WHAT DO YOU **MEAN??**

4

YOU SHALL *SEE*, SOON ENOUGH!

THE SUB-MARINER WILL *SUMMON* YOU WHEN READY!

CRASH!

WHEN DAD SENT ME TO COLLEGE TO STUDY CORPORATION LAW AND CIVIL COURTS PROCEDURE, I WONDER IF HE EVER THOUGHT THERE'D BE DAYS LIKE *THIS??*

OH, MATT! IF YOU COULD HAVE *SEEN* HIM! SO ARROGANT, SO MERCILESS, AND SO SUPREMELY CONFIDENT OF HIS *POWER!*

STRANGE! I SENSED A MAN OF GREAT HONOR-- OF INTENSE PRIDE AND INNATE NOBILITY!

I WONDER-- WHICH IS THE *REAL* SUB-MARINER?

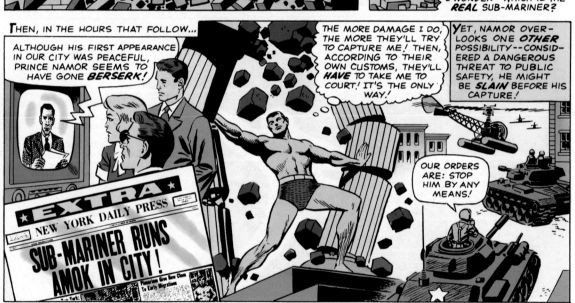

THEN, IN THE HOURS THAT FOLLOW...

ALTHOUGH HIS FIRST APPEARANCE IN OUR CITY WAS PEACEFUL, PRINCE NAMOR SEEMS TO HAVE GONE *BERSERK!*

THE MORE DAMAGE I DO, THE MORE THEY'LL TRY TO CAPTURE ME! THEN, ACCORDING TO THEIR OWN CUSTOMS, THEY'LL *HAVE* TO TAKE ME TO COURT! IT'S THE ONLY WAY!

YET, NAMOR OVER-LOOKS ONE *OTHER* POSSIBILITY-- CONSIDERED A DANGEROUS THREAT TO PUBLIC SAFETY, HE MIGHT BE *SLAIN* BEFORE HIS CAPTURE!

OUR ORDERS ARE: STOP HIM BY ANY MEANS!

EXTRA
NEW YORK DAILY PRESS
SUB-MARINER RUNS AMOK IN CITY!

BUT, IN THE NOW LONELY, DARKENED OFFICE, WHERE ONCE A BLIND LAWYER HAD STOOD, *ANOTHER* BEGINS TO TAKE HIS PLACE...

I'VE SECRETLY WORKED FOR MONTHS TO REDESIGN MY FIGHTING COSTUME-- TO MAKE IT MORE COMFORTABLE-- MORE DISTINCTIVE! BUT, I NEVER EXPECTED TO WEAR IT AGAINST SUCH A FANTASTIC FOE!

AND THEN, WITH THE SKILL OF A TRAINED ACROBAT, THE STEALTH OF A JUNGLE STALKER, AND THE COURAGE OF A-- *DAREDEVIL,* THE SIGHTLESS ADVENTURER TAKES TO THE ROOF-TOPS....!

UNTIL...

NO TRACE OF HIM YET!

WAIT! THE SOUND OF A LOW-FLYING SMALL PLANE ENGINE! COMING THIS WAY!

RRRRR

5

IT MUST BE A MILITARY OBSERVER PLANE, SEEKING PRINCE NAMOR! HE'LL REACH HERE IN SECONDS!

THERE'S A TV ANTENNA ON THE ROOF BELOW! IF I TIME THIS JUST RIGHT...!

MADE IT! AND NOW, USING THE FLEXIBLE STEEL AS A MAKESHIFT SPRINGBOARD...

--AND, GUIDED BY THE SOUND OF THE ROARING ENGINE...

--THIS IS AS EASY A FEAT AS ANY I'VE EVER ATTEMPTED!

LOOKS LIKE WE PICKED UP AN AIRBORNE HITCH-HIKER, CAPTAIN!

IT'S DAREDEVIL! KEEP HER FLYING STEADY, PHIL! WE DON'T WANT ANYTHING TO SHAKE HIM LOOSE!

HOLD IT! THERE'S A REPORT COMING IN ON THE RADIO!

ATTENTION ALL SEARCH UNITS! ENEMY SIGHTED AT WATERFRONT-- VICINITY OF PIER 94! PROCEED WITH CAUTION!

I WOULDN'T WORRY ABOUT HIM, SIR! EVEN IF HE FELL OFF, HE'D FIND SOME WAY TO BOUNCE RIGHT BACK AGAIN!

I'M IN LUCK! HE'S BEEN FOUND AGAIN!

MOMENTS LATER...

WHEN WILL YOU PUNY HUMANS REALIZE NONE OF YOU IS A MATCH FOR THE SUB-MARINER ?!!

I SEE HIM-- RIGHT BELOW US, CAPTAIN!

LOOK! DAREDEVIL JUST RELEASED HIS GRIP!

THIS IS WHAT I'VE BEEN WAITING FOR!

6

IF I CALCULATED THE PLANE'S SPEED AND DIRECTION PERFECTLY, THERE'S A HANGING TRAFFIC LIGHT DIRECTLY BELOW ME!

AND, IF I MADE A MISTAKE, IT'LL BE TOO BAD FOR POOR FOGGY! HE'LL HAVE TO FIND HIMSELF ANOTHER LAW PARTNER!

—WHEW!— WHAT A STROKE OF LUCK FOR FOGGY!

I HEAR NAMOR JUST BELOW ME! HIS HEARTBEAT IS SO STRONG IT'S ALMOST DEAFENING TO MY HYPER-SENSITIVE EARS!

THE M.M.M.S. WANTS YOU!

THE FIRST THING I'VE GOT TO DO IS SLOW HIM DOWN-- SOFTEN HIM UP LONG ENOUGH TO TALK SOME SENSE INTO HIM!

YOU DARE??!

THUP!

WHUKK

NOW SIMMER DOWN, NAMOR, I'VE SOMETHING TO SAY TO YOU!

I SPEAK TO NO COSTUMED ATTACKER! YOU MUST PAY FOR YOUR INSOLENCE!

C'MERE, LITTLE BILLY CLUB! I'M GONNA NEED YOU!

JUST IN TIME! HIS BLOW IS LIKE A BATTERING RAM! ONE SLIP COULD BE MY LAST!

7

MAYBE IF I TRICK HIM OFF THE PIER, A DASH OF COLD WATER WILL COOL HIM OFF AND MAKE HIM LISTEN!

I'LL WAIT TILL HE THROWS A BLOW, AND THEN LEAP TO SAFETY-- LIKE NOW!

UNHHH!

HE WAS TOO FAST FOR ME! HE GRABBED MY ANKLE!

HIS GRIP IS LIKE A STEEL VISE!

NOW I'M IN FOR IT! IN THE WATER, HE'S COMPLETELY INVINCIBLE!

HE HAS NO WAY OF KNOW- ING THAT I CAN HEAR HIM! BUT, A FAT LOT OF GOOD IT DOES ME!

THOUGH YOU CANNOT HEAR MY WORDS BENEATH THE SURFACE, I MUST SAY THEM! I KNOW NOT WHO YOU ARE, BUT I RESPECT YOUR COURAGE!

IT IS A PITY THAT I MUST PUT AN END TO IT FOREVER!

HERE, UNDER THE WATER, HE CAN TOY WITH ME AS THOUGH I'M A RAG DOLL IN HIS SUPER- POWERFUL HANDS!

TAKING A HUMAN LIFE PROBABLY MEANS NO MORE TO HIM THAN-- UGHHHH!

I CANNOT, I MUST NOT BE KEPT FROM MY GOAL BY ANYONE! I HAVE A WORLD TO WIN!

THEY'RE RIGHT BELOW US-- BUT IF WE DROP ANY EXPLOSIVES, WE'RE APT TO HIT DAREDEVIL! WE CAN ONLY WAIT!

8

NOW TO FINISH WHAT I'VE BEGUN!

BUT, THE HUMAN IS NOT BREATHING! HE PLUMMETS TOWARDS THE BOTTOM!

I CANNOT PERMIT ONE SO VALIANT TO DIE-- EVEN THOUGH HE IS MY ENEMY!

WARLORD *KRANG* WOULD THINK ME A FOOL--- PERHAPS WITH GOOD REASON! BUT, I DO NOT DESIRE TO CAUSE HARM TO THE WEAKER SURFACE MEN! I ONLY SEEK TO REGAIN WHAT IS TRULY MINE!

BACK TO THE SURFACE, MASKED ONE! SUCH VALOR AS YOURS DOES NOT DESERVE TO PERISH!

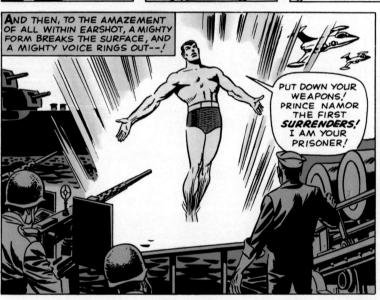

AND THEN, TO THE AMAZEMENT OF ALL WITHIN EARSHOT, A MIGHTY FORM BREAKS THE SURFACE, AND A MIGHTY VOICE RINGS OUT--!

PUT DOWN YOUR WEAPONS, PRINCE NAMOR THE FIRST *SURRENDERS!* I AM YOUR PRISONER!

NAMOR--SURRENDERING! *WHY?* ALL HE HAD TO DO WAS SWIM TO SAFETY BENEATH THE WAVES!

IT MUST BE A *TRICK!* DON'T TAKE YOUR EYES OFF HIM! RADIO HEADQUARTERS FOR FURTHER INSTRUCTIONS!

HE SAVED ME! HE COULD HAVE LEFT ME TO DIE-- BUT HE *SAVED* ME!

DON'T TRY ANY SUDDEN MOVES, WATER MAN!

ONCE I SNAP THESE 'CUFFS ON HIM HE'LL BE EASIER TO HANDLE!

CHAINS??! FOR THE LORD OF THE SEVEN SEAS?? *NEVER!*

CLIK

I SHALL ACCOMPANY YOU TO YOUR COURT OF LAW--BUT *NEVER* IN CHAINS!

CRACK!

THE NEXT MORNING, *NELSON AND MURDOCK* RECEIVE THE PHONE CALL THEY HAVE BEEN EXPECTING...

PRINCE NAMOR WANTS *US* TO REPRESENT HIM? VERY WELL, WE'LL BE THERE!

SO HE'LL *HAVE* HIS DAY IN COURT, AFTER ALL! *YOU'D* BETTER HANDLE IT, MATT!

9

THUS, THE SIGHTLESS MATT MURDOCK, POSSIBLY THE MOST BRILLIANT TRIAL LAWYER OF HIS GENERATION, BEGINS HIS OPENING PLEA...

YOUR HONOR, BEFORE THIS TRIAL BEGINS, MY CLIENT WISHES TO FILE A *COUNTER-CHARGE* AGAINST THE ENTIRE HUMAN RACE!

NAMOR MANAGES TO MAKE ANY CHAIR HE SITS UPON SEEM LIKE A ROYAL *THRONE!*

YOU'RE OUT OF ORDER, COUNSELOR! THE BENCH WILL ENTERTAIN NO SUCH MOTIONS UNTIL THIS TRIAL HAS ENDED!

THE DISTRICT ATTORNEY MAY BEGIN HIS OPENING ARGUMENT!

IF IT PLEASE THE COURT, THE STATE SHALL PROVE THE DEFENDANT TO BE GUILTY OF OUTRAGEOUS ASSAULT, ATTEMPTING TO OVERTHROW THE GOVERNMENT BY FORCE, ALIEN SEDITION, WILFUL DESTRUCTION OF PROPERTY, AND A HOST OF OTHER ATTENDANT CRIMES!

WEIGH *YOUR* WORDS CAREFULLY, COUNSELOR! YOU SPEAK OF THE PRINCE OF ATLANTIS!

YOUR HONOR, I REQUEST THAT YOU ORDER THE DEFENDANT TO REMAIN SILENT, OR ELSE HAVE HIM *GAGGED* WHILE I SPEAK!

YOU INSOLENT CLOD--!

YOUR HONOR, A CASE LIKE THIS CALLS FOR SPECIAL UNDERSTANDING! MY CLIENT IS THE SUPREME MONARCH OF HIS PEOPLE! HIS WORD IS THE SPOKEN LAW! WE CANNOT EXPECT HIM TO CONSENT TO BEING TREATED LIKE A COMMON CRIMINAL!

YOUR POINT IS WELL-TAKEN, MR. MURDOCK! I SHALL ORDER A *RECESS* WHILE I DELIBERATE ABOUT THIS MATTER!

BUT, AT THAT MOMENT, ALL EYES TURN TO THE REAR, AS A DRAMATIC FEMALE FIGURE ENTERS THE COURTROOM...

I AM THE LADY DORMA!

I MUST SPEAK WITH MY LORD, ON A MATTER OF GREAT URGENCY!

WE'RE GOING TO NEED A WHOLE NEW SET OF LAW BOOKS BEFORE *THIS* CASE IS FINISHED!

MY PRINCE--WARLORD KRANG HAS STARTED A *REBELLION* IN YOUR ABSENCE! HE SEEKS TO USURP YOUR RIGHTFUL THRONE!

THAT IS WHY HE WANTED ME GONE!

UNHAND ME! MY PLACE IS WITH MY *PEOPLE*, IN MY UNDERSEA DOMAIN!

SORRY, FELLA! YOUR PLACE IS IN A *CELL* UNTIL THE TRIAL BEGINS AGAIN!

NOW TAKE IT EASY, NAMOR! DON'T MAKE US GET TOUGH!

10

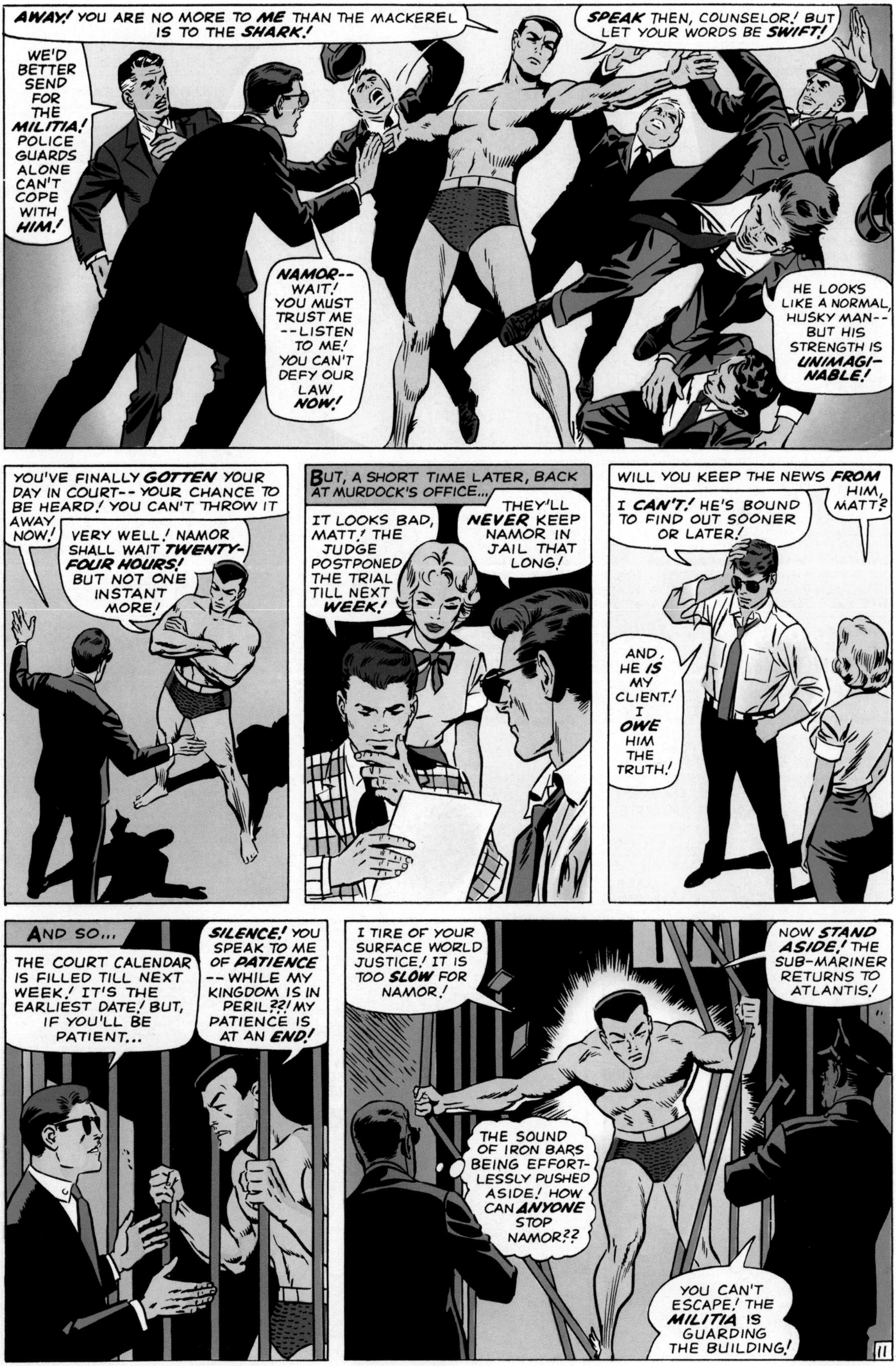
AWAY! YOU ARE NO MORE TO ME THAN THE MACKEREL IS TO THE SHARK!
SPEAK THEN, COUNSELOR! BUT LET YOUR WORDS BE SWIFT!
WE'D BETTER SEND FOR THE MILITIA! POLICE GUARDS ALONE CAN'T COPE WITH HIM!
NAMOR-- WAIT! YOU MUST TRUST ME --LISTEN TO ME! YOU CAN'T DEFY OUR LAW NOW!
HE LOOKS LIKE A NORMAL, HUSKY MAN-- BUT HIS STRENGTH IS UNIMAGINABLE!
YOU'VE FINALLY GOTTEN YOUR DAY IN COURT-- YOUR CHANCE TO BE HEARD! YOU CAN'T THROW IT AWAY NOW!
VERY WELL! NAMOR SHALL WAIT TWENTY-FOUR HOURS! BUT NOT ONE INSTANT MORE!
BUT, A SHORT TIME LATER, BACK AT MURDOCK'S OFFICE...
IT LOOKS BAD, MATT! THE JUDGE POSTPONED THE TRIAL TILL NEXT WEEK!
THEY'LL NEVER KEEP NAMOR IN JAIL THAT LONG!
WILL YOU KEEP THE NEWS FROM HIM, MATT?
I CAN'T! HE'S BOUND TO FIND OUT SOONER OR LATER!
AND, HE IS MY CLIENT! I OWE HIM THE TRUTH!
AND SO...
THE COURT CALENDAR IS FILLED TILL NEXT WEEK! IT'S THE EARLIEST DATE! BUT, IF YOU'LL BE PATIENT...
SILENCE! YOU SPEAK TO ME OF PATIENCE --WHILE MY KINGDOM IS IN PERIL?? MY PATIENCE IS AT AN END!
I TIRE OF YOUR SURFACE WORLD JUSTICE! IT IS TOO SLOW FOR NAMOR!
NOW STAND ASIDE! THE SUB-MARINER RETURNS TO ATLANTIS!
THE SOUND OF IRON BARS BEING EFFORTLESSLY PUSHED ASIDE! HOW CAN ANYONE STOP NAMOR??
YOU CAN'T ESCAPE! THE MILITIA IS GUARDING THE BUILDING!
11

MILITIA?? WHAT ARE MILITIAMEN TO THE *SUB-MARINER!*

LOOK OUT! HE'S LIKE A HUMAN *BULLDOZER!*

NAMOR IS *MORE* THAN MERELY HUMAN! FAR, FAR *MORE!*

HOLD IT, MISTER! STOP, OR I'LL *SHOOT!*

FIRE, BILL! DON'T LET HIM GET ANY *CLOSER!*

BUT, BEFORE THE STARTLED GUARDSMAN'S FINGER CAN SQUEEZE HIS TRIGGER, TWO MIGHTY ARMS SEIZE THE AUTOMATIC WEAPON AS THOUGH IT'S MERELY A PAPER TOY...

WILL YOU *NEVER* LEARN?? NONE MAY THREATEN THE ROYAL PERSON OF PRINCE NAMOR!

SKRUNNNNCH!

THEN, AS THE AMPHIBIOUS MONARCH LEAPS TO FREEDOM, THE SIGHTLESS LAWYER MAKES A FINAL, VAIN ATTEMPT TO HALT HIM...

NAMOR--STOP! I'LL ARRANGE FOR *BAIL* FOR YOU! I'LL HAVE YOU FREED *LEGALLY* BEFORE NIGHTFALL!

IT'S TOO LATE! HE WON'T LISTEN TO REASON! HIS MIND'S MADE UP!

BUT, THEY WON'T *LET* HIM ESCAPE THAT EASILY! HE CAN'T FLY VERY FAR WITH HIS SMALL ANKLE WINGS! THEY'LL BE *WAITING* FOR HIM WHEN HE LANDS!

IF HE CHOOSES TO *FIGHT,* THERE COULD BE BLOODSHED! UNLESS-- PERHAPS-- *DAREDEVIL* CAN FIND A WAY TO PREVENT IT!

AND, JUST AS MATT HAD PREDICTED, WHEN NAMOR LANDS...

YOU'LL NEVER REACH THE SEA, FISHMAN! SURRENDER NOW-- DON'T FORCE US TO SHOOT TO KILL!

IF YOU THREATEN ME WITH *FORCE*...

...THEN, I SHALL *ANSWER* YOUR THREATS IN KIND-- WITH *GREATER* FORCE!

HE'LL *NEVER* GIVE UP! WE'VE NO OTHER CHOICE THAN TO USE THE *TANKS!*

12

153

BUT, BEFORE THE HEAVILY-ARMED TANK, WAITING NEARBY, CAN BRING ITS DEADLY CANNON INTO PLAY...

I STRIKE FOR *ATLANTIS!* LET NO MAN STAND IN MY WAY!

CRASH!

HUMAN OR *NOT*-- A GRENADE WILL STOP HIM!

BUT AGAIN, NAMOR'S BLINDING SPEED AND WINGED FEET HURTLE HIM TO SAFETY,...!

NEXT TIME I SHALL NOT BE SO *MERCIFUL* TO MY ATTACKERS!

WHOOOM!

HOWEVER, *ANOTHER* DRAMATIC FIGURE NOW APPEARS ON THE ROOFTOPS-- THE FIGURE OF A MAN WITHOUT FEAR!

I'VE BEEN *WAITING* FOR A CHANCE TO TRY OUT MY NEW *CANE CABLE!* SO, HERE *GOES....!*

ALL I NEED DO IS WIELD IT, AS A FLY- CASTING FISHERMAN WOULD, TOWARDS ANY BUILDING WITHIN REACH OF ITS MINIATURE GRAPPLING HOOK--!

IT'S SILENT, SWIFT, AND SIMPLE ENOUGH TO BE COMPLETELY FOOLPROOF!

THUS, I CAN TRAVEL THRU THE CITY AT *TWICE* MY NORMAL SPEED, NO LONGER HAVING TO SLOW DOWN UNTIL I CAN FIND FLAGPOLES OR OTHER OBJECTS TO SWING UPON!

I HEAR THE RUMBLING OF A *TANK* BELOW ME! I MUST BE NEAR MY OBJECTIVE AT LAST!

STOP! I MUST SPEAK TO YOUR OFFICER-IN- CHARGE!

IT'S *DAREDEVIL!* HOLD IT UP, MEN, TILL WE SEE WHAT HE WANTS!

13

YOU CANNOT STOP NAMOR WITHOUT CASUALTIES! HE IS TOO POWERFUL! BUT, PERHAPS, *I* CAN FIND A WAY TO BRING HIM BACK-- WITHOUT ANYONE BEING INJURED!

YOU HAVE NOTHING TO LOSE! CONTINUE YOUR VIGIL.! HOLD YOUR FIRE FOR THE NEXT FEW MINUTES!

IT'S A *DEAL*, DAREDEVIL! BUT, WHAT CAN *YOU* DO, SINGLE-HANDED, AGAINST A WALKING POWERHOUSE LIKE THE SUB-MARINER.!

I WISH I *KNEW!* BUT, I CAN'T TELL *HIM* THAT!

AHH, I HEAR HIM TREADING SOFTLY BELOW! I *THOUGHT* HE'D BE JUST AHEAD OF THE TANKS!

AND NOW FOR THE *SECOND* NEW DEVICE I'VE ADDED TO MY TRUSTY LITTLE BILLY CLUB....!

IT WAS SIMPLE ENOUGH TO CONSTRUCT...

...JUST A FEW LITTLE GAS PELLETS, A CONTROL BUTTON, AND *PRESTO*--

...AN *INSTANT* SMOKE SCREEN!

YOU-- AGAIN ?!!

NAMOR LASHES OUT ANGRILY, BUT--

THE SMOKE BLINDED HIM! HE *MISSED* ME!

THIS IS THE ONLY WAY I CAN NULLIFY THE ADVANTAGE OF HIS INCALCULABLE *STRENGTH!!*

I'VE GOT TO KEEP HIM OFF-BALANCE --CONFUSE HIM!

HERE I AM, PAL! COME 'N *GET* ME!

YOU MAY BE A *WHIZ* IN ATLANTIS, SUBBY, BUT YOU'LL HAVE TO DO BETTER THAN *THAT* HERE!

WHEW! IF THAT HAD *CON-NECTED*-- GOODBYE, D.D.!

WROOOM!

14

155

INSOLENT HUMAN! WHEN I *FIND* YOU, I SHALL TEACH YOU THE FOLLY OF-- *WHA--??!*

SOMETHING HAS GRASPED MY ANKLE! IT TWINES AROUND MY LEG!

MY SMOKE PELLETS ARE USED UP NOW! I'VE GOT TO HAVE A *PLAN* OF ACTION FOR WHEN HE CAN *SEE* ME!

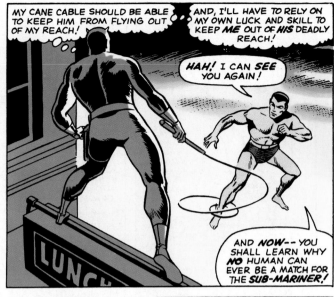

MY CANE CABLE SHOULD BE ABLE TO KEEP HIM FROM FLYING OUT OF MY REACH!

AND, I'LL HAVE TO RELY ON MY OWN LUCK AND SKILL TO KEEP *ME* OUT OF *HIS* DEADLY REACH!

HAH! I CAN *SEE* YOU AGAIN!

AND *NOW*-- YOU SHALL LEARN WHY *NO* HUMAN CAN EVER BE A MATCH FOR THE *SUB-MARINER!*

LUNCH

FOR, YOU ARE ALL PRISONERS OF THE SURFACE OF YOUR PLANET... WHILE *I*--

--I AM EQUALLY AT HOME IN THE SEA--OR IN THE *SKY!*

HE'S FLYING UPWARDS! I DIDN'T COUNT ON *THIS!!* BUT, I CAN'T JUST DANGLE HERE HELP-LESSLY!

ANY TIME I WISH, I CAN EXECUTE ENOUGH INTRICATE MANEUVERS TO CAUSE YOU TO LOSE YOUR HOLD, AND SEND YOU PLUMMETTING TO YOUR DEATH BELOW!

BUT, I SHALL GIVE YOU ONE LAST CHANCE! SWEAR TO CEASE BATTLING ME, AND I'LL ALLOW YOU TO LIVE!

I'VE ONLY SECONDS TO DO ONE THING WHICH HE DOESN'T *EXPECT!* I'LL CLIMB RIGHT *UP* TO HIM!

DID IT! AND NOW FOR A REAL LONG SHOT....!

MY CARE-LESSNESS IS *UNPARDON-ABLE!* WHILE *I* BOASTED, *HE* ACTED!

YOU'RE AS HELPLESS AS *I* AM NOW, SUBBY! YOU CAN'T STAY AIRBORNE IF I HOLD ONTO YOUR ANKLE WINGS!

15

156

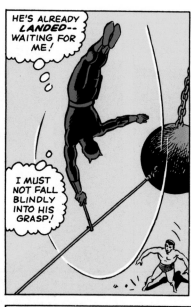

A SPLIT-SECOND LATER, BOTH FIGURES HURTLE EARTHWARD--- AND THEN, AT THE LAST INSTANT, SENSING AN OBJECT BELOW, DAREDEVIL'S BILLY CLUB CANE LASHES OUT, AS THE BLIND CRUSADER RELEASES HIS GRIP ON NAMOR'S ANKLES...

HE'S ALREADY *LANDED*-- WAITING FOR ME!

I MUST NOT FALL BLINDLY INTO HIS GRASP!

OBVIOUSLY I'M AT A CONSTRUCTION SITE-- AND THIS BATTERING-RAM IRON BALL IS JUST WHAT THE DOCTOR ORDERED!

AHHH! NOW I CAN *SOAR* AGAIN! BUT, *YOU*--!

DON'T WORRY ABOUT *ME*, NAMOR! I'M A BIG BOY NOW!

CAUTION CONSTRUCTION SITE

HIS ANKLE WINGS ARE STARTING TO FLAP--HE'S ABOUT TO LEAP UP! I'VE GOT TO TIME THIS *PERFECTLY!*

YOU *WANT* ME, NAMOR? OKAY--ALL YOU'VE GOT TO DO IS COME AND *GET* ME!

I'LL DRIVE YOUR TAUNTING WORDS BACK INTO YOUR THROAT FOREVER, COSTUMED ONE!

NO NEED TO BE SO *FORMAL*, SUBBY! THE NAME'S *DAREDEVIL!* I'VE GOT A HUNCH YOU'RE GOING TO *REMEMBER* IT AFTER TODAY!!

HE'S FLYING TOWARDS THE *RIGHT*--TRYING TO AVOID THE BALL--I'VE GOT TO SHIFT MY WEIGHT JUST A BIT--!

OKAY, FELLA! READY OR NOT-- HERE I *COME!*

BULLSEYE!

I JUST HOPE THIS'LL TAKE THE WIND OUT OF HIS SAILS LONG ENOUGH FOR ME TO *REASON* WITH HIM--TO GET HIM TO RETURN PEACEFULLY TO THE JAIL!

WHOOMF!

16

157

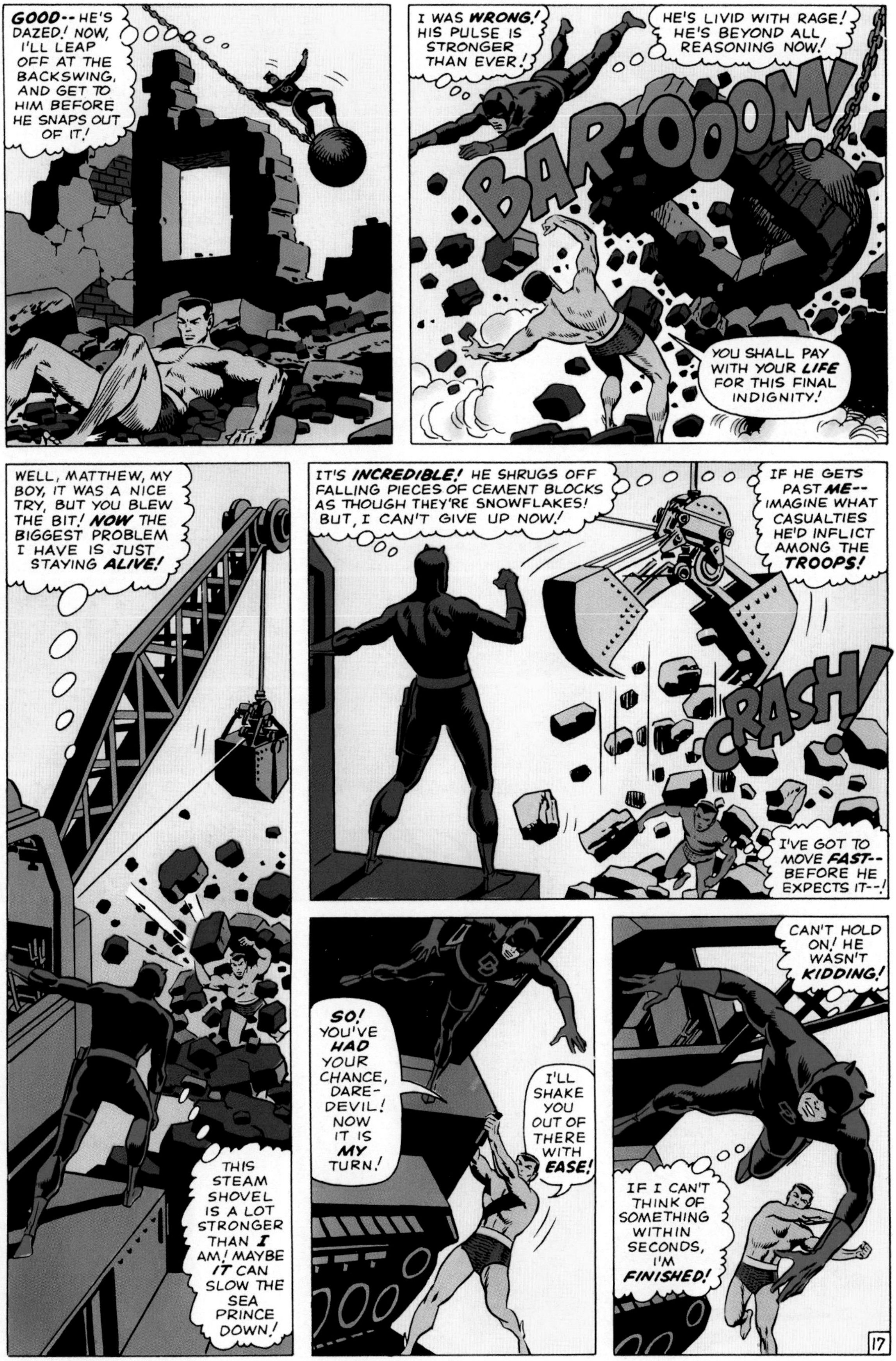
GOOD-- HE'S DAZED! NOW, I'LL LEAP OFF AT THE BACKSWING, AND GET TO HIM BEFORE HE SNAPS OUT OF IT!
I WAS WRONG! HIS PULSE IS STRONGER THAN EVER!
HE'S LIVID WITH RAGE! HE'S BEYOND ALL REASONING NOW!
BAR-OOOM!
YOU SHALL PAY WITH YOUR LIFE FOR THIS FINAL INDIGNITY!
WELL, MATTHEW, MY BOY, IT WAS A NICE TRY, BUT YOU BLEW THE BIT! NOW THE BIGGEST PROBLEM I HAVE IS JUST STAYING ALIVE!
THIS STEAM SHOVEL IS A LOT STRONGER THAN I AM! MAYBE IT CAN SLOW THE SEA PRINCE DOWN!
IT'S INCREDIBLE! HE SHRUGS OFF FALLING PIECES OF CEMENT BLOCKS AS THOUGH THEY'RE SNOWFLAKES! BUT, I CAN'T GIVE UP NOW!
IF HE GETS PAST ME-- IMAGINE WHAT CASUALTIES HE'D INFLICT AMONG THE TROOPS!
CRASH!
I'VE GOT TO MOVE FAST-- BEFORE HE EXPECTS IT--!
SO! YOU'VE HAD YOUR CHANCE, DARE-DEVIL! NOW IT IS MY TURN!
I'LL SHAKE YOU OUT OF THERE WITH EASE!
CAN'T HOLD ON! HE WASN'T KIDDING!
IF I CAN'T THINK OF SOMETHING WITHIN SECONDS, I'M FINISHED!
17

BUT, LUCKILY FOR THE SIGHTLESS ADVENTURER, HE SENSES A *LAMPPOST* NEARBY, AND...

NO! YOU WON'T ESCAPE ME *THAT* WAY!

WELL, IF YOU KNOW ANY *BETTER* WAYS, I'M OPEN TO SUGGESTIONS, SUBBY!

BOY! IF I WERE ONLY *HALF* AS CONFIDENT AS I'M TRYING TO SOUND!

YOU HAVE *OUTSMARTED* YOURSELF THIS TIME! I NEED NOT EVEN HASTEN! THERE IS NO PLACE FOR YOU TO SWING TO FROM UP THERE!

HE'S *RIGHT!* I SENSE NOTHING ELSE NEAR ME!

KRRAK!

AND NOW, AT *LAST*, YOU SHALL FEEL THE POWER OF PRINCE NAMOR-- EVEN AS THE ENTIRE HUMAN RACE SHALL FEEL IT ONE DAY!

BY THE TIME CONSCIOUSNESS HAS RETURNED TO YOUR FRAIL SURFACEMAN'S BODY, I SHALL BE GONE-- BUT YOU WILL NEVER *FORGET* THE FURY OF THE *SUB-MARINER!*

UHHHH...

BLANNNG!

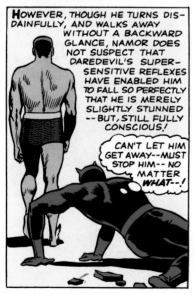

HOWEVER, THOUGH HE TURNS DISDAINFULLY, AND WALKS AWAY WITHOUT A BACKWARD GLANCE, NAMOR DOES NOT SUSPECT THAT DAREDEVIL'S SUPER-SENSITIVE REFLEXES HAVE ENABLED HIM TO FALL SO PERFECTLY THAT HE IS MERELY SLIGHTLY STUNNED --BUT, STILL FULLY CONSCIOUS!

CAN'T LET HIM GET AWAY--MUST STOP HIM-- NO MATTER *WHAT*--!

THIS ELECTRIC CORD FROM THE LAMPPOST-- IF I CAN KNOT IT IN TIME--!

NAMOR! I ORDER YOU TO *HALT!*

18

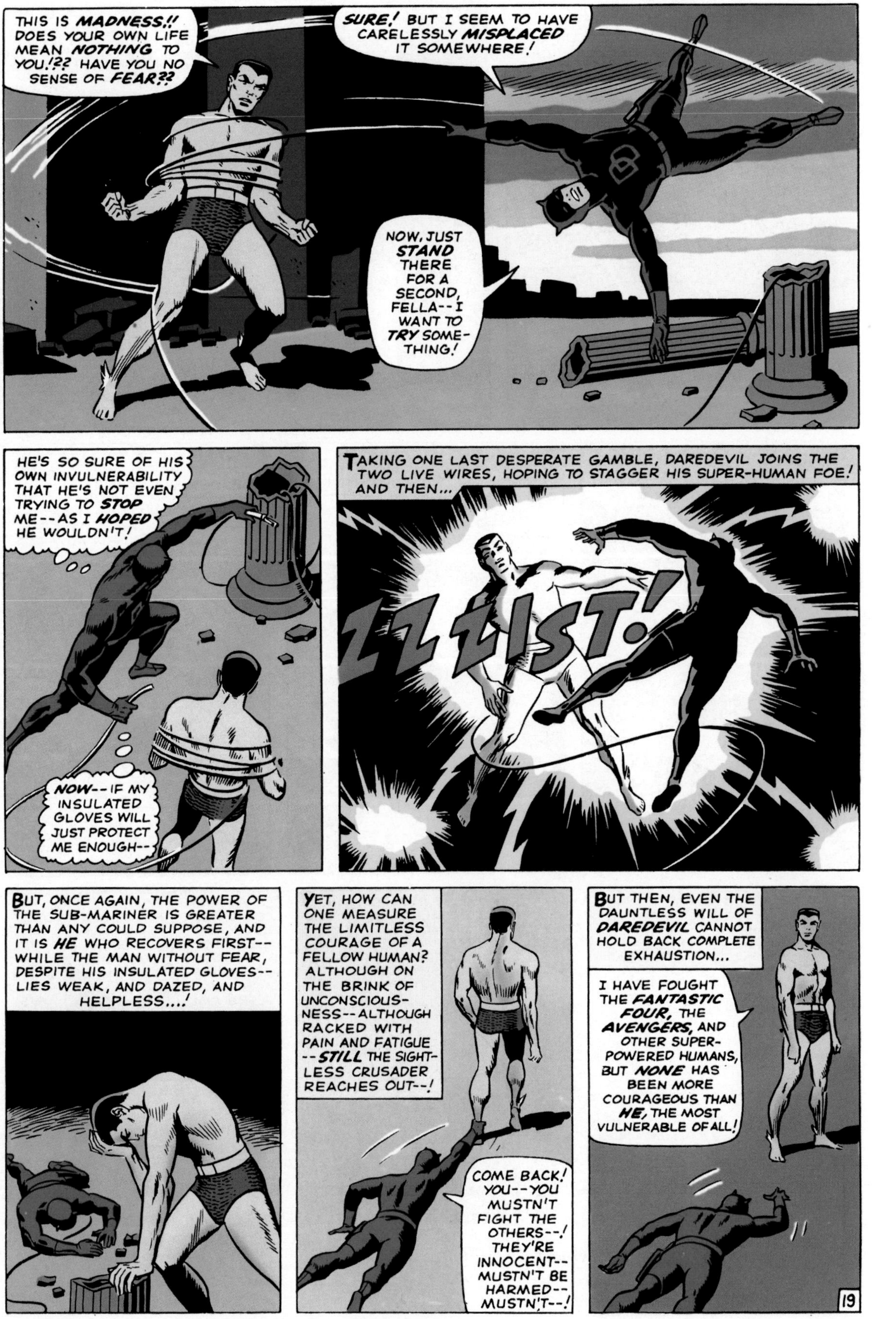
THIS IS MADNESS!! DOES YOUR OWN LIFE MEAN NOTHING TO YOU!?? HAVE YOU NO SENSE OF FEAR??
SURE! BUT I SEEM TO HAVE CARELESSLY MISPLACED IT SOMEWHERE!
NOW, JUST STAND THERE FOR A SECOND, FELLA-- I WANT TO TRY SOMETHING!
HE'S SO SURE OF HIS OWN INVULNERABILITY THAT HE'S NOT EVEN TRYING TO STOP ME--AS I HOPED HE WOULDN'T!
NOW--IF MY INSULATED GLOVES WILL JUST PROTECT ME ENOUGH--
TAKING ONE LAST DESPERATE GAMBLE, DAREDEVIL JOINS THE TWO LIVE WIRES, HOPING TO STAGGER HIS SUPER-HUMAN FOE! AND THEN...
ZZZIST!
BUT, ONCE AGAIN, THE POWER OF THE SUB-MARINER IS GREATER THAN ANY COULD SUPPOSE, AND IT IS HE WHO RECOVERS FIRST--WHILE THE MAN WITHOUT FEAR, DESPITE HIS INSULATED GLOVES--LIES WEAK, AND DAZED, AND HELPLESS...!
YET, HOW CAN ONE MEASURE THE LIMITLESS COURAGE OF A FELLOW HUMAN? ALTHOUGH ON THE BRINK OF UNCONSCIOUSNESS--ALTHOUGH RACKED WITH PAIN AND FATIGUE --STILL THE SIGHTLESS CRUSADER REACHES OUT--!
COME BACK! YOU--YOU MUSTN'T FIGHT THE OTHERS--! THEY'RE INNOCENT--MUSTN'T BE HARMED--MUSTN'T--!
BUT THEN, EVEN THE DAUNTLESS WILL OF DAREDEVIL CANNOT HOLD BACK COMPLETE EXHAUSTION...
I HAVE FOUGHT THE FANTASTIC FOUR, THE AVENGERS, AND OTHER SUPER-POWERED HUMANS, BUT NONE HAS BEEN MORE COURAGEOUS THAN HE, THE MOST VULNERABLE OF ALL!
19

AND, OUT OF RESPECT TO THE COURAGE OF DAREDEVIL, I SHALL *NOT* INJURE ANY HUMANS! I SHALL FLY *ABOVE* THE WAITING ARMED FORCES-- AND RETURN TO THE SEA WHERE I AM SUPREME!

MY FIRST DUTY IS TO MY *PEOPLE!* I SHALL CRUSH THE REBELLION OF WARLORD KRANG, AND THEN...

SOMEDAY, WHEN MANKIND LEASTS EXPECTS IT, I SHALL *RETURN* TO THE SURFACE, AND CLAIM WHAT IS RIGHTFULLY MINE-- NO MATTER *WHAT* THE COST!

THE NEXT DAY...

WANT US TO READ THE PAPER TO YOU, MATT?

NO THANKS, FOGGY! I EH HEARD THE NEWS ON THE RADIO!

OH, YOU'RE *INJURED!* WHAT *HAPPENED* TO YOU, MATT?

NEW YORK DAILY PRESS

DAREDEVIL BATTLES SUB-MARINER

I'VE *WARNED* YOU NOT TO WALK AROUND TOWN ALL ALONE THE WAY YOU DO! YOU MUST HAVE BUMPED INTO SOME-- OHH!

WATCH OUT, KAREN! YOU'LL TRIP OVER THE LEG OF THAT CHAIR!

MATT! YOU *CAUGHT* ME! BUT-- HOW COULD YOU HAVE *KNOWN?* HOW-- DID YOU MANAGE-- I MEAN--?

I HEARD YOUR SHOE KICK THE CHAIR LEG-- AND I GUESS IT WAS JUST *LUCK* THAT MADE YOU FALL INTO MY ARMS!

THE GREATEST LUCK I'VE EVER KNOWN! IF ONLY-- YOU COULD *STAY* THIS WAY-- FOREVER!

I-I KNOW IT SOUNDS FOOLISH-- BUT SOMETIMES, MATT-- I FEEL AS THOUGH YOU *CAN* SEE -- AS THOUGH YOU SEE *MORE* THAN ANYONE ELSE!

I WAS STUPIDLY CARELESS! WHEN SHE'S SO CLOSE-- I FORGET MYSELF! IT MUSTN'T HAPPEN AGAIN! SHE MUST NEVER GUESS THE *TRUTH* ABOUT ME!

CAN IT BE POSSIBLE THAT MATT REALLY *CAN*--? OH *NO!* I'M ACTING LIKE A *CHILD!* I'VE GOT TO STOP THIS WISHFUL THINKING -- GOT TO STOP TORTURING MYSELF!

WELL, PARTNER, IT LOOKS LIKE *NELSON AND MURDOCK* LOST A CLIENT, BUT I CAN'T SAY I'M SORRY TO SEE HIM GO!

IT WAS LUCKY THAT NO ONE WAS INJURED DURING NAMOR'S ESCAPE! IT *COULD* HAVE BEEN A DISASTER!

RIGHT, FOGGY! JUST LIKE YOU SAID-- IT SURE WAS *LUCKY!*

AND SO, THE CURTAIN FALLS ON ANOTHER DAZZLING *DAREDEVIL* ADVENTURE! BUT, WE'RE SURE IT WILL COME AS NO SURPRISE TO YOU THAT WE HAVE *ANOTHER* GREAT TALE IN STORE FOR NEXT ISSUE! SO, FOR THE NEXT CHAPTER IN THE LIFE OF THE WORLD'S MOST UNIQUE ADVENTURER, LET'S MEET AGAIN ON THE PAGES OF *D.D. #8*-- WE'LL BE LOOKING FOR YOU!

20

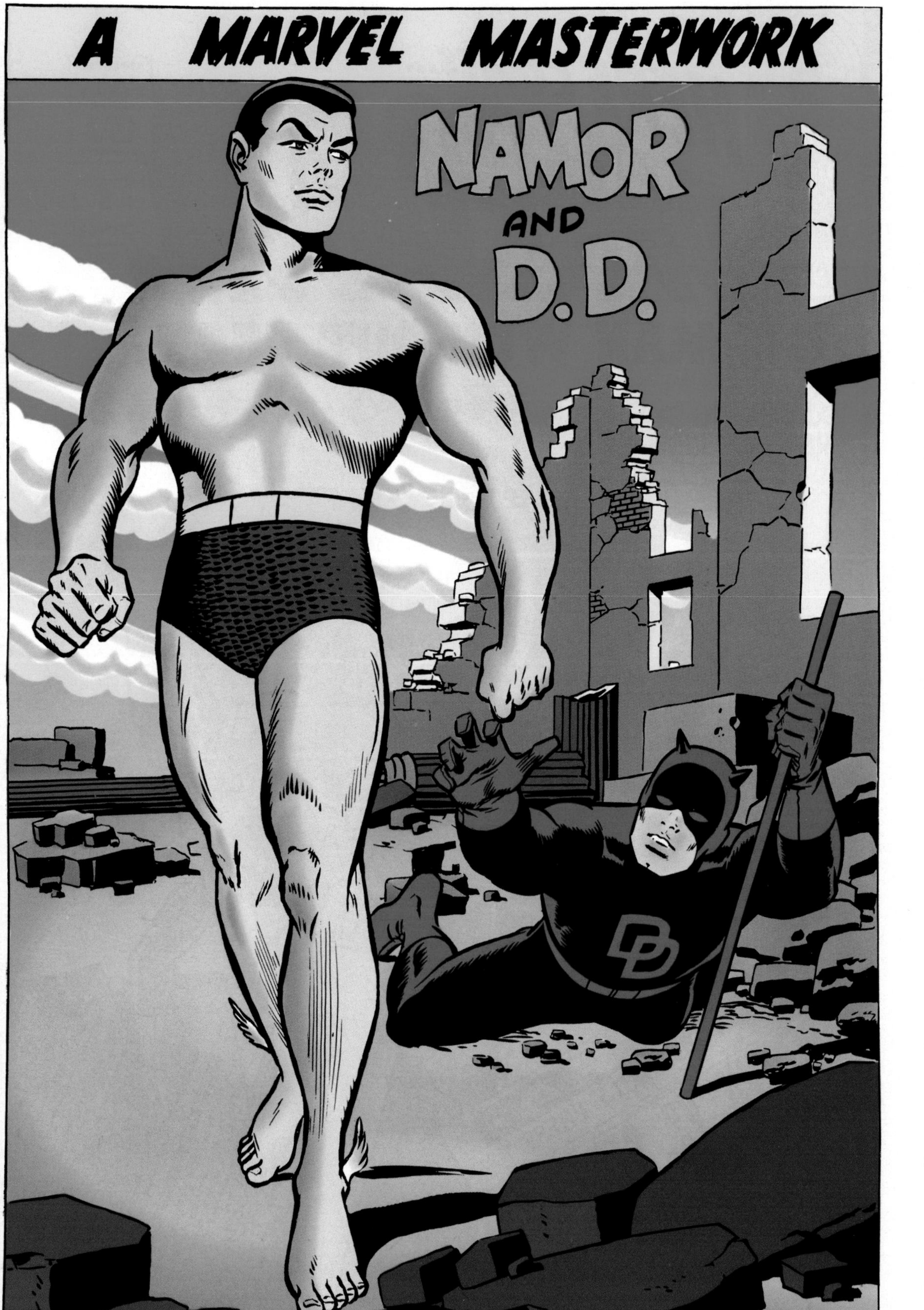
A MARVEL MASTERWORK
NAMOR
AND
D.D.

HERE COMES...

DAREDEVIL

8
JUNE

APPROVED
BY THE
COMICS
CODE
AUTHORITY

IND.

MARVEL
COMICS
GROUP 12¢

THE MAN WITHOUT FEAR!

SOARING TO STILL
GREATER HEIGHTS OF
GLORY!

★ EXTRA ★

NEW YORK DAILY PRESS

WORLD'S
FAIR
EDITION

DAREDEVIL VS. STILT MAN

EYEWITNESS
ACCOUNT OF
A FANTASTIC
ENCOUNTER
No Clue As To
Identity of Stilt
Man or Daredevil

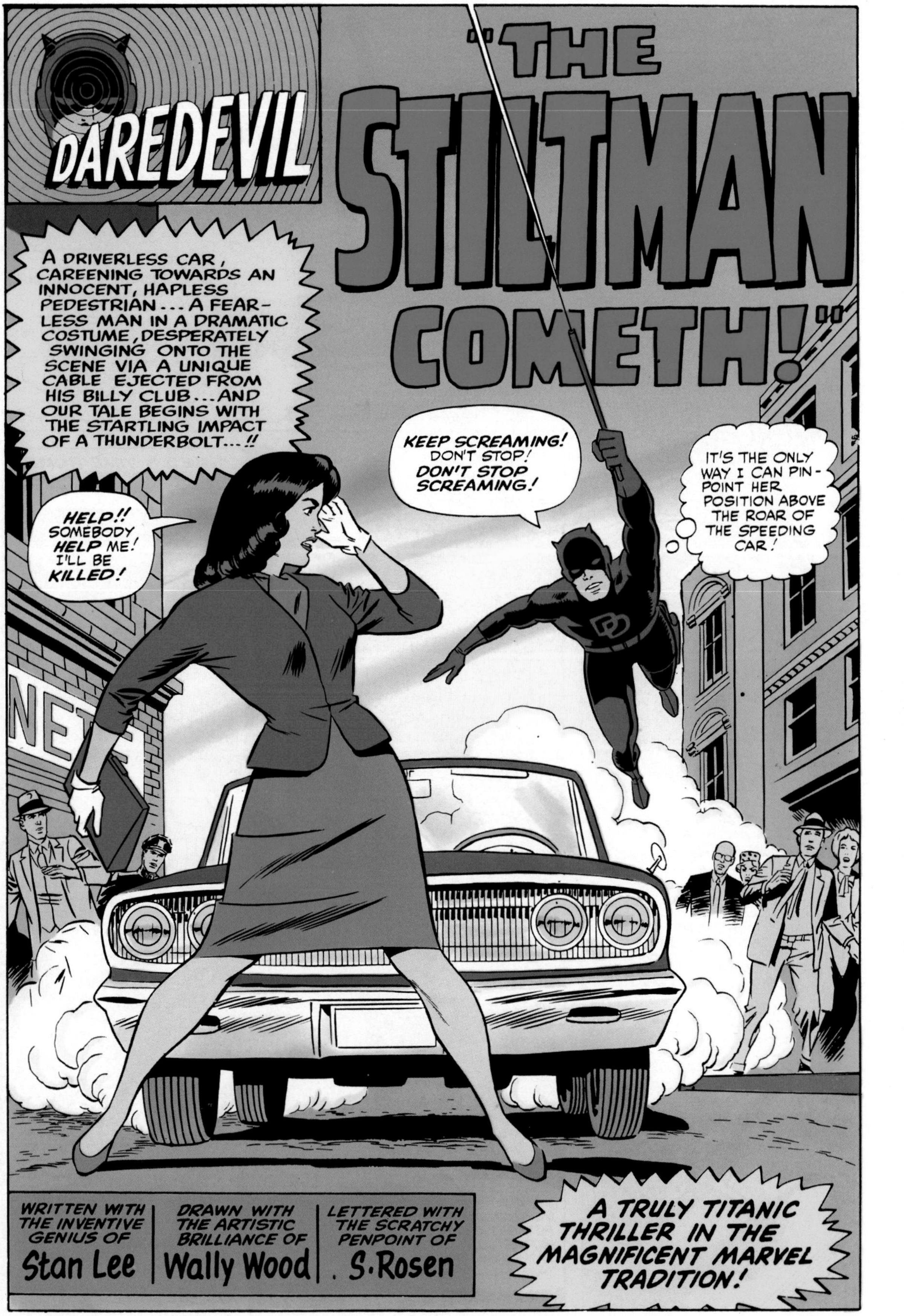
DAREDEVIL
"THE STILTMAN COMETH!"
A DRIVERLESS CAR, CAREENING TOWARDS AN INNOCENT, HAPLESS PEDESTRIAN... A FEARLESS MAN IN A DRAMATIC COSTUME, DESPERATELY SWINGING ONTO THE SCENE VIA A UNIQUE CABLE EJECTED FROM HIS BILLY CLUB... AND OUR TALE BEGINS WITH THE STARTLING IMPACT OF A THUNDERBOLT...!!
HELP!! SOMEBODY HELP ME! I'LL BE KILLED!
KEEP SCREAMING! DON'T STOP! DON'T STOP SCREAMING!
IT'S THE ONLY WAY I CAN PINPOINT HER POSITION ABOVE THE ROAR OF THE SPEEDING CAR!
WRITTEN WITH THE INVENTIVE GENIUS OF Stan Lee
DRAWN WITH THE ARTISTIC BRILLIANCE OF Wally Wood
LETTERED WITH THE SCRATCHY PENPOINT OF S. Rosen
A TRULY TITANIC THRILLER IN THE MAGNIFICENT MARVEL TRADITION!

GOOD GIRL! IT'S ALL RIGHT... YOU'LL BE SAFE NOW!

LUCKY I WAS ON A BUILDING LEDGE JUST NOW AND HEARD HER SCREAMS!

BUT, I HEAR NO HEART-BEAT FROM THE CAR BELOW... NO SOUND OF BREATHING! IT MUST BE DRIVERLESS! IT CAN STILL KILL SOMEONE!

THAT AWNING WILL BREAK YOUR FALL, MA'AM... I HAVEN'T TIME FOR FORMALITIES NOW... I DON'T DARE MISS THAT CAR!

LUCKY I KNEW THAT CORNER STORE ALWAYS HAS ITS AWNING DOWN AT THIS HOUR! WITH HER IN MY ARMS, I'D NEVER MAKE IT TO THE CAR!

THE GAS PEDAL IS NAILED TO THE FLOOR... AND THE BRAKE PEDAL HAS BEEN CUT! THIS IS NO SIMPLE ACCIDENT!! SOMEBODY PLANNED IT!

WAIT! THAT MUFFLED TICKING BENEATH THE HOOD... MY RADAR SENSE TELLS ME...

...THERE'S A TIME BOMB HIDDEN IN THE MOTOR! I'M DRIVING A DEATH TRAP!!

TICK TICK TICK TICK TICK

MEANWHILE, ON THE OTHER SIDE OF TOWN...

THIS IS THE LIFE! NO MORE DANGER OF BEING ROBBED SINCE WE'VE BEEN USING THIS WHIRLYBIRD TO DELIVER OUR PAYROLLS!

JOE! WHAT'S THAT AHEAD? ARE... ARE WE SEEING THINGS??

IT'S IMPOSSIBLE! IT CAN'T BE! B-BUT I SEE IT, TOO!

A MAN... STANDING IN MIDAIR!! TALKING TO US THROUGH A BUILT-IN LOUDSPEAKER!!

THIS IS A HOLDUP! OBEY MY INSTRUCTIONS TO THE LETTER, AND YOU WILL NOT BE HURT!

I'M SURE WE'RE IMAGININ' THIS! BUT, GET OUT THE RIFLE JUST THE SAME! WE CAN'T TAKE ANY CHANCES!

HE..HE MUST BE FOR REAL! WE ALL SEE HIM!

2.

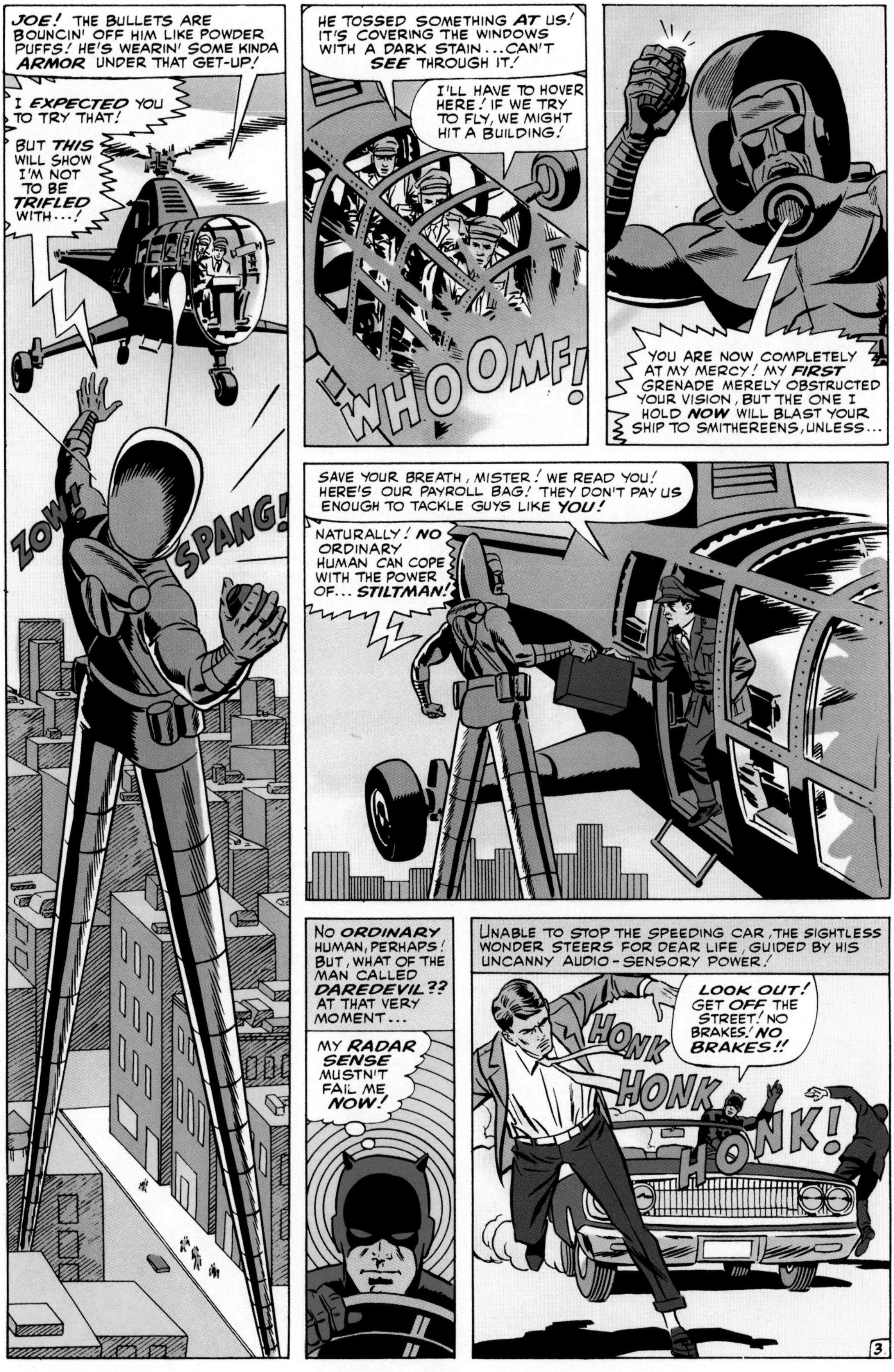
JOE! THE BULLETS ARE BOUNCIN' OFF HIM LIKE POWDER PUFFS! HE'S WEARIN' SOME KINDA ARMOR UNDER THAT GET-UP!
I EXPECTED YOU TO TRY THAT!
BUT THIS WILL SHOW I'M NOT TO BE TRIFLED WITH...!
ZOW!
SPANG!
HE TOSSED SOMETHING AT US! IT'S COVERING THE WINDOWS WITH A DARK STAIN...CAN'T SEE THROUGH IT!
I'LL HAVE TO HOVER HERE! IF WE TRY TO FLY, WE MIGHT HIT A BUILDING!
WHOOMF!
YOU ARE NOW COMPLETELY AT MY MERCY! MY FIRST GRENADE MERELY OBSTRUCTED YOUR VISION, BUT THE ONE I HOLD NOW WILL BLAST YOUR SHIP TO SMITHEREENS, UNLESS...
SAVE YOUR BREATH, MISTER! WE READ YOU! HERE'S OUR PAYROLL BAG! THEY DON'T PAY US ENOUGH TO TACKLE GUYS LIKE YOU!
NATURALLY! NO ORDINARY HUMAN CAN COPE WITH THE POWER OF... STILTMAN!
NO ORDINARY HUMAN, PERHAPS! BUT, WHAT OF THE MAN CALLED DAREDEVIL?? AT THAT VERY MOMENT...
MY RADAR SENSE MUSTN'T FAIL ME NOW!
UNABLE TO STOP THE SPEEDING CAR, THE SIGHTLESS WONDER STEERS FOR DEAR LIFE, GUIDED BY HIS UNCANNY AUDIO-SENSORY POWER!
LOOK OUT! GET OFF THE STREET! NO BRAKES! NO BRAKES!!
HONK
HONK
HONK!
3.

THE BOMB IS TICKING *LOUDER* NOW! IT'S NEARING THE INSTANT OF *DETONATION!*

BUT I CAN'T DESERT THE CAR...WITHOUT ME TO *STEER* IT, SOMEONE WILL SURELY BE HIT! I'VE GOT TO KEEP GUIDING IT...TILL THE *END!*

MY ONLY HOPE IS THE *RIVER!* IF I CAN SOMEHOW REACH THERE BEFORE IT EXPLODES, AND PLUNGE THE CAR INTO THE WATER..!

WITH IRON NERVE, WITH STEADY HANDS, THE MAN WITHOUT FEAR GUIDES THE DOOMED VEHICLE AT BREAKNECK SPEED THROUGH THE CITY STREETS, GUIDED BY HIS RADAR SENSE THE SAME AS A JETLINER FLYING THROUGH A HEAVY FOG ....!

THOUGH DAREDEVIL *"SEES"* IMAGES RATHER THAN ACTUAL *SIGHTS,* SO ACCURATE IS HIS SENSORY PERCEPTION THAT HE STEERS THE ONRUSHING CAR WITH THE SKILL AND PRECISION OF A MASTER DRIVER!

JUST A LITTLE BIT FURTHER! I'M ALMOST *THERE!*

TICK TICK TICK TICK TICK TICK

NOW!

MADE IT!

JUST BY THE SKIN OF MY CHINNY-CHIN-CHIN!!

WHROOM!

THAT CAR COULD HAVE HAD ONLY *ONE* PURPOSE... TO SERVE AS A *DECOY!*

...TO LURE ME AND ANY POLICE OFFICERS AWAY FROM SOME *OTHER* AREA!

THERE MUST BE A SERIOUS CRIME BEING COMMITTED IN SOME OTHER PART OF TOWN!

AND, IF THERE *IS,* MY *SNOOPERSCOPE* WILL HELP ME *FIND* IT!

I'LL JUST RELEASE THE DIRECTIONAL SHOTGUN MIKE FROM MY BILLY CLUB, AND POINT IT SLOWLY OVER THE CITY!!

4.

FOR THE BENEFIT OF ALL JOHNNY-COME-LATELIES, HERE IS D.D.'S BILLY CLUB CANE--

SWITCH

RETRACTABLE MICROPHONE

TRANSISTORS AND BATTERIES

MINIATURE TAPE RECORDER

SWITCH

SPRING REEL FOR CABLE

CABLE

HINGE

CHAMBER FOR PROJECTILES SUCH AS GAS PELLETS.

REFLECTOR SHIELD

ALL I HEAR ARE ORDINARY, EVERYDAY SNATCHES OF CONVERSATION...

WAIT! THAT LAST CRY! THAT MUST BE IT!

FOR PETE'S SAKE, HERMAN! TURN THAT T.V. SET DOWN, WILLYA?!

YOU TAKE THE WHITES OF TWO EGGS, MIX THEM GENTLY AND THEN ADD SAUCE...

HEY, CHARLIE, CAN YA LEND ME A SAWBUCK? I GOT A HEAVY DATE TONIGHT!

AW, MA! I DON'T WANNA GET A HAIR-CUT!

IT'S TRUE, I TELL YOU! I SEE HIM! IT'S A MAN, WALKING OVER THAT BUILDING!

QUICKLY RACING TO THE PLACE THE CRY ORIGINATED FROM, THE MAN WITHOUT FEAR FINALLY FINDS...!

THE TREAD OF HEAVY FEET A FEW YARDS AHEAD OF ME...BUT THE HEARTBEAT ACCOMPANYING THEM IS AT LEAST TEN STORIES ABOVE ME!

HOW CAN THAT BE??

I'VE GOT TO RUSH! HE'S TURNING THE CORNER!

BUT, RACING AROUND THE CORNER AFTER HIS FANTASTIC FOE, DAREDEVIL CAN HARDLY BELIEVE THE EVIDENCE OF HIS SENSES...!

HE'S GONE! BUT...IT ISN'T POSSIBLE! NOBODY THAT BIG COULD DISAPPEAR SO QUICKLY! UNLESS...CAN I...CAN I BE LOSING MY SENSES?

COMPLETELY BAFFLED, THE SIGHTLESS CRUSADER REVERTS TO HIS EVERYDAY IDENTITY, RETURNING TO THE LAW FIRM OF NELSON AND MURDOCK...

MATT, HAVE YOU HEARD THE NEWS? EVERYONE'S TALKING ABOUT THE CRIMINAL CALLED STILT-MAN!

STILT-MAN! THEN I DIDN'T IMAGINE IT! BUT, HOW DID HE VANISH?

NO, KAREN! TELL ME ALL ABOUT HIM!

I WILL, MATT, AS SOON AS I TELL YOU MY OTHER BIT OF NEWS!

I HEARD FROM DR. VAN EYCK, THE EYE SPECIALIST FROM BOSTON! HE STILL THINKS HE MIGHT HELP YOU TO SEE!

IT WOULD BE WONDERFUL TO HAVE MY SIGHT, KAREN...

TO BE ABLE TO FEAST MY EYES ON YOUR FEATURES...THAT FACE WHICH MY FINGERS TELL ME IS SO YOUNG, SO LOVELY...

MATT, IF ONLY YOU'D UNDERGO DR. VAN EYCK'S OPERATION! IF ONLY YOU COULD REGAIN YOUR SIGHT...!

5.

BUT THEN, AT THAT MOMENT, THE DOOR SUDDENLY OPENS, AND MATT MURDOCK'S PARTNER ENTERS...A PAINED EXPRESSION SUDDENLY APPEARING IN HIS BLAZING EYES....!

SAY, MATT, THERE'S SOMEONE OUTSIDE WHO WANTS TO SEE Y...

OH, SORRY! I-I DIDN'T *KNOW!*

FOGGY!

FOGGY! FOGGY... WAIT! IT...IT ISN'T WHAT YOU *THINK!*

WE'LL DISCUSS IT SOME OTHER TIME...!

I'LL LET *YOU* HANDLE THIS GENTLEMAN'S CASE!

FOGGY IS *HURT!* I WOULDN'T HAVE HAD THIS HAPPEN FOR THE WORLD! *HE* LOVES KAREN, TOO!

MR. MURDOCK, MY NAME IS WILBUR DAY!

OH, EH, COME IN, MR. DAY! WHAT CAN I *DO* FOR YOU?

I'M A MILD MAN, SIR! AND I DON'T LIKE TO CAUSE TROUBLE, BUT MY BOSS *STOLE* AN INVENTION OF MINE! I...I'VE JUST *GOT* TO GET IT BACK!

I SEE! SUPPOSE YOU START AT THE BEGINNING AND TELL ME ALL ABOUT IT!?

IT'S SO HARD TO CONCENTRATE! I CAN'T GET KAREN AND FOGGY OFF MY MIND...NOR THAT STRANGE BEING CALLED *STILTMAN!* BUT I MUST *TRY!*

YOU WERE SAYING, MR. DAY...?

I'M A SCIENTIST...AN INVENTOR! I WORK FOR KAXTON LABORATORIES! I INVENTED A NEW TYPE OF HYDRAULIC LIFT AND MY BOSS, CARL KAXTON, *STOLE* THE PATENT FROM ME!

I INVENTED IT AT HOME, ON MY OWN TIME! MY BOSS HAD NO RIGHT TO IT! I WANT TO *SUE* HIM!

JUST A MOMENT, WHILE I DOUBLE-CHECK THE LATEST PATENT LAWS...

I DON'T *NEED* THIS BRAILLE TYPE, BUT NO ONE MUST *SUSPECT* THAT!

THE LAW SEEMS TO BE ON YOUR SIDE, MR. DAY! SUPPOSE I *CALL* MR. KAXTON AND TRY TO GET HIM TO SETTLE OUT OF COURT!?

I DON'T CARE, SO LONG AS I GET MY PATENT BACK!

MR. KAXTON? THIS IS MATT MURDOCK, WILBUR DAY'S ATTORNEY...

AND, IN A LARGE, SECURELY-LOCKED LABORATORY, ON THE OTHER SIDE OF TOWN...

SETTLE OUT OF COURT? WITH THAT SNIVELING *WORM?* NOT A *CHANCE!* GO AHEAD, *SUE* ME! I *DARE* YOU!

6.

LATER THAT NIGHT, AFTER LEAVING THE OFFICE, MATT MURDOCK GOES DIRECTLY TO HIS APARTMENT! AND, FOR THE FIRST TIME, WE SHOW THE APARTMENT *BENEATH* MATT'S WHICH HE HAS SECRETLY RENTED ALSO, UNDER AN ASSUMED NAME...

THAT CARL KAXTON CERTAINLY SOUNDED ROUGH! OVER THE PHONE! I HOPE I'LL BE ABLE TO WIN WILBUR DAY'S CASE AGAINST HIM! BUT I CAN'T GET *STILTMAN* OUT OF MY MIND!

SLIDING BOOKCASE

GYM

SECRET STAIRWAY

WHO *IS* HE? HOW DID HE ESCAPE ME SO EASILY? WHAT IS HIS SECRET? ...THERE'S ONLY ONE THING TO DO WHEN MY MIND IS RACING LIKE THIS...

I'LL GO TO THE SPECIAL SOUNDPROOF GYM IN MY APARTMENT BELOW...

LAB AND ELECTRONIC WORKSHOP

THERE'S NOTHING LIKE A GOOD WORK-OUT TO MAKE A MAN RELAX AND THINK THINGS OUT CLEARLY!

SUPPOSE I *DO* CONSENT TO THE OPERATION THAT KAREN THINKS I SHOULD HAVE?

WHAT IF I *DO* REGAIN MY SIGHT...?

...BUT LOSE MY EXTRA-SENSORY POWERS IN THE PROCESS?!!

IT WOULD MEAN THE END OF *DAREDEVIL* AS A FORCE FOR JUSTICE!

BUT IT WOULD BE THE ONLY WAY I COULD DARE TRY TO MAKE KAREN MY WIFE!

FOR, I COULD NEVER ASK HER TO MARRY A SIGHT-LESS MAN!

BUT, THEN, THERE'S *FOGGY* TO CONSIDER! I KNOW HOW *HE* LOVES HER, TOO...!

BULLETIN! STILTMAN IS REPORTED AT LARGE AGAIN ON THE EAST SIDE OF TOWN!

THE *RADIO!* THIS IS MY *CHANCE!*

I WONDER IF ANYONE SEEING DAREDEVIL IN ACTION SUSPECTS THAT I HAVE A COMPLEX RADIO RECEIVER INSIDE MY HEAD COVERING...?

OR, THAT MY "DEVIL'S HORNS" ARE REALLY TWIN *ANTENNAE* TO PICK UP RADIO SIGNALS AND AMPLIFY MY OWN SUPER-SENSORY RADAR BLIPS!

7.

AND, AS DAREDEVIL RACES FROM HIS BUILDING, THE GUESTS AT A PENT-HOUSE PARTY NOT FAR AWAY, ARE STARTLED TO SEE...

IT'S STILT-MAN!

HE...HE'S THROWING SOMETHING!

LOOK OUT!

IT'S A GRENADE!! DUCK!

FOOM!

DUCKING CAN'T HELP YOU NOW, YOU SCARED RABBITS!

BUT, LUCKILY FOR YOU, THAT "GRENADE" WAS MERELY FILLED WITH SLEEP GAS!

AND NOW SINCE YOU'RE NOT USING THEM AT PRESENT, I'LL PAINLESSLY RELIEVE YOU OF YOUR LITTLE TRINKETS!

HE'S DIRECTLY AHEAD OF ME! I'D RECOGNIZE THAT ONE-IN-A-MILLION RADAR IMAGE ANYWHERE!

I'VE GOT TO REACH HIM BEFORE HE DISAPPEARS AGAIN!

WELL! WHAT HAVE WE HERE? A STOW-AWAY!

AHH, IT'S DAREDEVIL! I'M INDEED HONORED AT THE ATTENTION YOU'RE LAVISHING UPON ME...AND THEREFORE I'LL RETURN THE FAVOR!

I CAN HEAR HIS PULSE RATE! IT'S STEADY AND FIRM! NO TRACE OF FEAR OR ALARM! WHY??

A SPLIT-SECOND LATER, DAREDEVIL GETS HIS ANSWER...THE HARD WAY!

UNHHH! HE SWUNG HIS "LEG"...DASHED ME AGAINST THE WALL! I...I WAS UN-PREPARED!

AND IN THE HEADLINES NEXT DAY...

EXTRA WORLD'S FAIR EDITION

NEW YORK DAILY PRESS

STILT MAN STRIKES AGAIN!

DAREDEVIL NARROWLY ESCAPES FATAL INJURY

Penthouse Robbed

Costumed Crusader

POLICE BAFFLED, COMMISSIONER PROMISES ACTION

VIET NAM CRISIS IN

ONCE AGAIN, THE AMAZING HUMAN PHENOMENON KNOWN AS STILTMAN HAS SUCCESS-FULLY ELUDED...

8

WHILE, IN MATT MURDOCK'S OFFICE...

KAREN, ABOUT YESTERDAY...I HOPE I HAVEN'T DONE ANYTHING TO EMBARRASS YOU OR HURT FOGGY...!

OF COURSE NOT, MATT! HE JUST MISUNDERSTOOD WHEN HE CAME IN! I'LL EXPLAIN AS SOON AS I SEE HIM!

KAREN, MY DARLING... IF HE THINKS I LOVE YOU, HE *DIDN'T* MISUNDERSTAND!

EH, EXCUSE ME, MR. MURDOCK...THE DOOR WAS UNLOCKED, SO I TOOK THE LIBERTY OF ENTERING!

IT'S WILBUR DAY, MATT! I KNEW IT TWO MINUTES AGO WHEN I HEARD HIM IN THE HALL!

COME IN, MR. DAY!

MR. MURDOCK, I HAVE REASON TO BELIEVE THAT KAXTON IS WORKING ON MY INVENTIONS RIGHT *NOW!* IF WE GO TO HIS LABORATORY, WE MIGHT GET ENOUGH EVIDENCE FOR YOU!

I DON'T WORK THAT WAY, MR. DAY! I DON'T TRESPASS ON PRIVATE PROPERTY WITHOUT A WARRANT!

HOWEVER, I'VE BEEN GIVING YOUR CASE SOME SERIOUS THOUGHT!

THEN, AT THAT VERY MOMENT...

A FAINT HEARTBEAT, OUTSIDE THE DOOR! SOMEONE IS TRYING TO *EAVESDROP!*

YOU WERE SAYING..?

THUD THUD

HE'S MOVING CLOSER! ORDINARY WALLS ARE NO OBSTACLE AT ALL TO MY HYPER-ACUTE EXTRA-SENSORY "RADAR"!

I'D BETTER LEARN WHO IT IS, ALTHOUGH I'VE GOT A GOOD *HUNCH*...!

SORRY, MR. DAY! I THOUGHT I *HEARD* SOMETHING!

IN FACT, PERHAPS I'D BETTER SEE IF ANYONE'S AT THE DOOR!

COME IN, MR. KAXTON! YOU CAN HEAR BETTER FROM INSIDE!

HOW DID YOU KNOW WHO I WAS?

UH-OH! I ALMOST GAVE MYSELF AWAY THAT TIME!

MY SECRETARY SAW YOU OUT THERE AND BUZZED ME!

KAXTON! YOU DARED COME *HERE*?!

YOU *BET* I DARED COME HERE! YOU AND THAT SHYSTER LAWYER OF YOURS AREN'T GOING TO BLACKMAIL *ME* OUT OF A RED CENT, YOU LITTLE CROOK!

CALM DOWN, MR. KAXTON! THIS IS *MY* OFFICE, AND MR. DAY IS MY CLIENT!

KEEP HIM *AWAY* FROM ME!

YOU SPINELESS MILKSOP! *YOU* DIDN'T INVENT THOSE HYDRAULIC DEVICES...*I* DID! YOU WERE NO MORE THAN A SECOND-RATE *STOOGE!*

MR. MURDOCK, YOU'RE MY LAWYER! DON'T LET HIM *SAY* THAT!

LET'S TRY TO DISCUSS THIS LIKE GENTLEMEN!

9.

172

IF THEY TALK LONG ENOUGH, I'LL USE THEIR PULSE RATES LIKE A *LIE DETECTOR!*

I'M NOT AFRAID OF YOU JUST BECAUSE YOU'RE *RICH!*

YOU'RE *NOT,* EH?

YOU LITTLE *CROOK!* DO YOU THINK I'LL STAND BY AND LET YOU *ROB* ME?

YOU'RE TRYING TO ROB *ME!* *BOTH* OF THEIR PULSES HAVE SPEEDED UP!

IT'S NO USE! THEY'RE TOO CLOSE TOGETHER! I CAN'T SEPARATE THEIR PULSE BEATS!

IF YOU TRY TO SUE ME, I'LL SEE THAT YOU NEVER GET ANOTHER JOB IN ANY LAB!

NO! YOU *CAN'T!*

I *CAN'T,* EH? JUST TRY ME AND *SEE!* AND, REMEMBER THIS...

I DIDN'T GET WHERE I AM BY BEING *SOFT!* TANGLE WITH *ME,* DAY, AND I'LL *BREAK* YOU! AND THAT GOES FOR *YOU,* TOO, MURDOCK!

DAY'S HYDRAULIC INVENTION... I WONDER... COULD IT BE USED FOR SOMETHING LIKE A GIANT PAIR OF *STILTS?*

HE *MEANS* IT, MR. MURDOCK! WHAT WILL WE *DO?*

YOU WAIT HERE, MR. DAY! I HAVE A PLAN! I HAVE TO LEAVE FOR A MOMENT, AND... EH ENLIST THE AID OF A *FRIEND!*

ALL RIGHT, COUNSELOR! BUT BE CAREFUL! CARL KAXTON CAN BE A VERY DANGEROUS MAN!

MAY I HELP YOU TO THE DOOR?

NO, THANKS! I'LL BE ABLE TO MAKE IT ALL RIGHT!

SCANT SECONDS LATER, THE SAME MAN WHO HAD BEEN OFFERED HELP TO REACH A NEARBY DOOR PERCHES PERILOUSLY AT A HIGH WINDOW LEDGE...

I HEAR A CAR JUST BEGINNING TO PULL AWAY FROM THE CURB BELOW!

IN MY LINE OF WORK, A BUILDING WITHOUT A FLAGPOLE WOULD BE *SUICIDE!*

AND NOW TO LEARN A LITTLE MORE ABOUT THE TERRIBLE-TEMPERED MR. KAXTON!

10.

BUT, A BUILT-IN ALARM ON THE DASHBOARD ALERTS THE GRIM-FACED INVENTOR!

BAP! BAP! BAP BAP!

SOMEONE IS TAILING ME!

AND, CARL KAXTON IS NOT TO BE FOLLOWED LIKE ANY ORDINARY, UN-PROTECTED FOOL...

NOT WHILE I CAN DO *THIS*...!

KLIK!

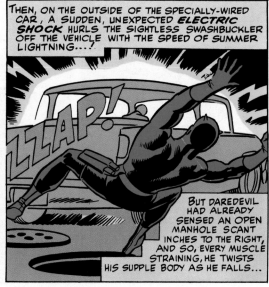

THEN, ON THE OUTSIDE OF THE SPECIALLY-WIRED CAR, A SUDDEN, UNEXPECTED *ELECTRIC SHOCK* HURLS THE SIGHTLESS SWASHBUCKLER OFF THE VEHICLE WITH THE SPEED OF SUMMER LIGHTNING...!

ZZZAP!

BUT DAREDEVIL HAD ALREADY SENSED AN OPEN MANHOLE SCANT INCHES TO THE RIGHT, AND SO, EVERY MUSCLE STRAINING, HE TWISTS HIS SUPPLE BODY AS HE FALLS...

...LANDING HARMLESSLY IN THE EXACT CENTER OF THE OPENING, WHILE HIS ARM SNAKES OUT, GRASPING FOR THE STEEL RUNGS HE KNOWS MUST BE THERE!

I WAS LUCKY THIS *TIME!* IT'S A LOT BETTER THAN LANDING ON THE HARD CONCRETE!

I'VE LOST KAXTON FOR NOW, AND I'VE NO WAY OF KNOWING WHETHER... *WAIT!* I'M PICKING UP AN EMERGENCY *POLICE CALL* ON MY BUILT-IN HEADPIECE ANTENNAE!

IT'S AN ALL-POINTS *ALERT! STILT-MAN* HAS APPEARED IN THE CITY AGAIN!

IF ONLY I HAD BEEN ABLE TO KEEP TRACK OF *KAXTON!*

BUT, GUIDED BY THE RADIO SIGNALS I'M RECEIVING, I'LL SOON FIND OUT WHAT I HAVE TO KNOW!

SWINGING, CLIMBING, RACING THROUGH THE CITY FASTER THAN ANY SIGHTED HUMAN COULD EVER HOPE TO MOVE, THE MAN WITHOUT FEAR REACHES HIS DESTINATION IN MINUTES, TO FIND...

OUR BULLETS HAVE NO EFFECT ON HIM! HE'S WEARING SOME SORT OF FINELY-TEMPERED FLEXIBLE ARMOR...!

I'VE *FOUND* HIM! *THIS* TIME HE WON'T ESCAPE ME AGAIN!!

THIK THIKK!

PUKKA-PUKKA! PUKKA! KRAK!

11.

BUT, BEFORE DAREDEVIL CAN REACH STILTMAN, HE HEARS A SQUAD CAR RACING TOWARDS ONE OF THE INCREDIBLE, TOWERING LEG-SUPPORTS...!

FASTER, SAM! IF WE CAN RAM INTO THAT NUTTY METAL STILT, IT'LL BRING HIM CRASHING DOWN TO EARTH WHERE WE CAN NAB HIM!

SAM! WHAT HAPPENED??

SO THAT'S IT! THAT MUST BE HOW HE VANISHED LAST TIME I WAS NEAR HIM!

EACH "LEG" MUST WORK BY HYDRAULIC PRESSURE! HE RAISED IT JUST IN TIME!

HE MUST HAVE TELESCOPED HIS LEGS DOWN, BECOME NORMAL-SIZED, DISCARDED HIS DISGUISE, AND WALKED AWAY UNNOTICED!

WHATEVER ELSE HE MAY BE, STILTMAN IS NO FOOL!

I'LL HAVE A BETTER CHANCE AT HIM UP HERE! HE'S COMING IN THIS DIRECTION! IF HE'LL JUST GET A LITTLE CLOSER... CLOSER...!

TZING!

ZOW

RAT TAT TAT!

NOW!!

DARE-DEVIL!

FAST AS YOU ARE, I CAN RETRACT MY HYDRAULIC LEGS STILL FASTER!

AND IN THIS LEAGUE, THERE'S NO SECOND CHANCE AT BAT!

FAREWELL, DAREDEVIL! EVEN YOU WERE NO MATCH FOR STILTMAN!

IT CAN'T END LIKE THIS! IT JUST CAN'T!!

12.

175

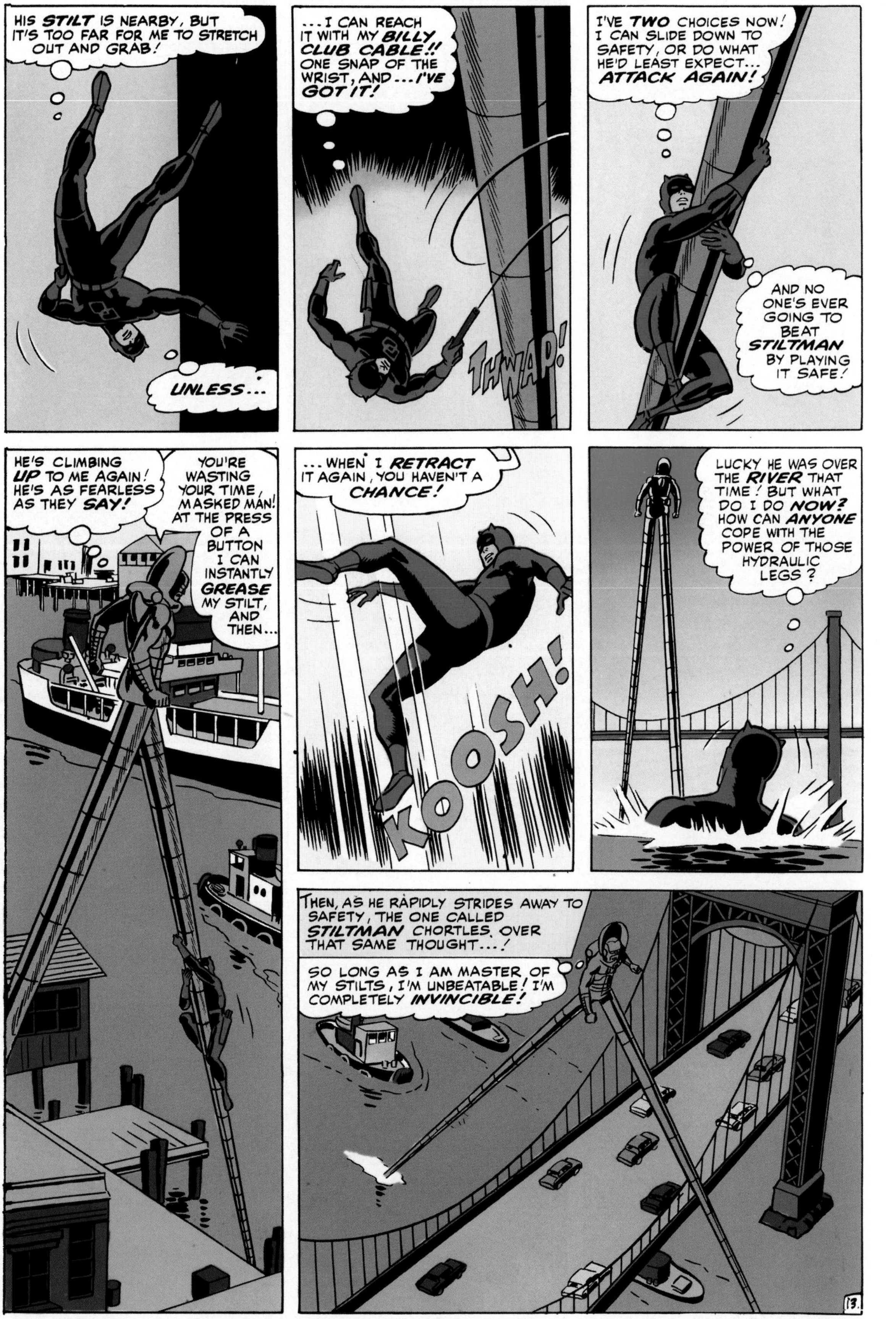
HIS STILT IS NEARBY, BUT IT'S TOO FAR FOR ME TO STRETCH OUT AND GRAB!
UNLESS...
...I CAN REACH IT WITH MY BILLY CLUB CABLE!! ONE SNAP OF THE WRIST, AND...I'VE GOT IT!
THWAP!
I'VE TWO CHOICES NOW! I CAN SLIDE DOWN TO SAFETY, OR DO WHAT HE'D LEAST EXPECT... ATTACK AGAIN!
AND NO ONE'S EVER GOING TO BEAT STILTMAN BY PLAYING IT SAFE!
HE'S CLIMBING UP TO ME AGAIN! HE'S AS FEARLESS AS THEY SAY!
YOU'RE WASTING YOUR TIME, MASKED MAN! AT THE PRESS OF A BUTTON I CAN INSTANTLY GREASE MY STILT, AND THEN...
...WHEN I RETRACT IT AGAIN, YOU HAVEN'T A CHANCE!
KOOSH!
LUCKY HE WAS OVER THE RIVER THAT TIME! BUT WHAT DO I DO NOW? HOW CAN ANYONE COPE WITH THE POWER OF THOSE HYDRAULIC LEGS?
THEN, AS HE RAPIDLY STRIDES AWAY TO SAFETY, THE ONE CALLED STILTMAN CHORTLES OVER THAT SAME THOUGHT...!
SO LONG AS I AM MASTER OF MY STILTS, I'M UNBEATABLE! I'M COMPLETELY INVINCIBLE!
13.

LATER, A RAGING, FIGHTING-MAD MATT MURDOCK RETURNS TO HIS OFFICE, A HASTILY FORMED PLAN TAKING SHAPE IN HIS BRAIN...

I HEAR DAY'S BREATHING! GOOD! I'M GLAD HE'S STILL HERE!... I MAY *NEED* HIM!

HE'S ASLEEP! NO NEED TO WAKEN HIM TILL I DOUBLE CHECK MY SCHEME WITH A PHONE CALL!

AHH, *PERFECT!* THERE'S NO ONE HOME AT KAXTON'S HOUSE!

WAKE UP, MR. DAY! I'VE GOT A VISIT TO MAKE, AND *YOU'RE* GOING WITH ME!

MURDOCK! YOU'RE *BACK!* WH-WHERE ARE WE *GOING?*

WE'RE GOING TO PAY A LITTLE CALL... AT THE HOME OF *CARL KAXTON!*

THUS, A SHORT TIME LATER...

THIS IS THE PLACE, MURDOCK! I WISH YOU COULD *SEE* IT! IT'S A *MANSION,* ALL BUILT WITH MONEY HE *STOLE* FROM OTHERS! BUT, HE WON'T ESCAPE JUSTICE FOREVER!

WOULDN'T DAY BE SURPRISED TO LEARN THAT MY RADAR SENSE ENABLES ME TO "SEE" KAXTON'S ESTATE IN MY MIND'S EYE AS CLEARLY AS HE HIMSELF SEES IT!

MURDOCK! FOLLOW ME... QUICKLY! I'VE *FOUND* SOMETHING!

WHAT *IS* IT, MR. DAY?

FEEL *THAT??* WHAT DO YOUR FINGERS TELL YOU IT *IS?*

A LARGE METAL *TUBE* OF SOME SORT!

I HEAR KAXTON'S HEARTBEAT BEHIND DAY! BUT I MUSTN'T LET ON THAT I KNOW HE'S THERE!

MY HYPER-SENSITIVE FINGERS CAN DETECT SOME SORT OF *SPRING* HIDDEN IN THESE TUBES! IF I WERE TO EXERT PRESSURE ON IT... *AHHH!* IT *WORKED!*

DON'T EITHER OF YOU *MOVE!*

MURDOCK! IT'S *KAXTON!* HE'S FOUND US... AND, HE'S GOT A *GUN!!*

SPANNG!

14

WHAT ARE YOU DOING HERE? WHY ARE YOU NEAR THOSE TUBES?? ANSWER ME!!

WHY ARE YOU WALKING AROUND WITH A RECOILLESS RIFLE, KAXTON??

I'VE GOT A RIGHT TO USE A WEAPON TO PROTECT MY PROPERTY AGAINST INTRUDERS!

WELL, YOU'LL NEVER GET A CHANCE TO USE IT AGAINST ME!!

THE LAMB HAS TURNED INTO A TIGER! DAY FELLED KAXTON WITH ONE KARATE BLOW!

THWUP!

UNHHH...!

WHY DID YOU HIT HIM, MR. DAY?

ARE YOU SERIOUS, MURDOCK? HE THREATENED OUR LIVES WITH THAT GUN, DIDN'T HE? YOU SHOULD BE GRATEFUL TO ME!

AND SURELY YOU MUST REALIZE BY NOW THAT ONLY KAXTON COULD BE STILTMAN!

HIS PULSE RATE HAS CHANGED! HE'S LYING!

HE'S ABOUT TO STRIKE OUT AT ME!

CAN'T MAKE HIM SUSPICIOUS BY DUCKING! I'LL HAVE TO TAKE THE BLOW, BUT ROLL WITH IT! IT NEEDS PERFECT TIMING... NOW!

SORRY I HAVE TO DO THIS, MURDOCK!

WITHOUT A BACKWARD GLANCE, WILBUR DAY ENTERS THE HOME LABORATORY OF CARL KAXTON, NOT NOTICING THAT THE MAN HE THOUGHT HE HAD DISPOSED OF IS GETTING TO HIS FEET OUTSIDE AND BEGINNING TO CHANGE INTO A DRAMATIC-LOOKING COSTUME!

KAXTON WAS THE GENIUS... NOT ME! IT WAS I WHO STOLE HIS IDEAS! AND THIS IS THE ONE I REALLY WANTED... HIS EXPERIMENTAL MOLECULAR CONDENSER... THE MOST VALUABLE WEAPON ON EARTH!

ALL THE HOLDER NEEDS TO DO IS FOCUS IT ON SOMETHING, AND THE OBJECT SLOWLY FADES AWAY TO NOTHINGNESS!

15.

178

BUT, BEFORE WILBUR DAY CAN MAKE ANOTHER MOVE...

NOW I KNOW WHO'S *REALLY* STILTMAN!

DAREDEVIL!

CRASH!

IF THAT MOLECULAR GADGET DOES WHAT YOU *SAID*, THEN *YOU'RE* THE LAST ONE ON EARTH TO HAVE CONTROL OF IT!

KRAK!

PWEOON!

THEN, DUE TO A ONE-IN-A-MILLION ACCIDENT, WILBUR DAY'S SUDDEN BLAST STRIKES THE STEEL CONTROL PANEL BEHIND DAREDEVIL, CAUSING IT TO TOPPLE...

WHUMP!

UHHH....!

AND, BY THE TIME THE SIGHTLESS SENTINEL CAN PULL HIMSELF TOGETHER AGAIN, HE FINDS...

DAY IS *GONE!* BUT... WHAT'S *THIS* AT MY FINGERTIPS? ...HIS RIFLE!

HE CAN'T HAVE GOTTEN FAR! IF HE'S ANYWHERE WITHIN EARSHOT, I'LL FIND HIM!

BUT, JUST OUTSIDE THE LONELY HOUSE, WILBUR DAY FRANTICALLY FITS HIMSELF WITH A *STRANGE*-LOOKING SET OF HYDRAULICALLY-POWERED SECTIONAL LIFTS....!

ONCE THESE STILTS ARE AGAIN ON MY FEET, I'M MORE THAN A MATCH FOR *ANYONE!* I MAY NEVER TAKE THEM OFF AGAIN!

KAXTON CREATED THIS HYDRAULIC DEVICE AS AN AID TO INDUSTRY! BUT ONLY A *FOOL* WOULDN'T HAVE KEPT IT FOR *HIMSELF!*

THAT'S WHY I *STOLE* IT! WILBUR DAY IS NO FOOL!

WELL, WELL! THERE'S *DARE-DEVIL!* BUT THIS TIME IT WILL BE HIS LAST OPPORTUNITY TO BOTHER ME! *THIS* TIME, HE *DIES!*

16

I DON'T KNOW HOW YOU *FOUND* ME, DAREDEVIL... BUT THAT *GUN* WILL DO YOU NO GOOD!

HE'S SHINING A BEAM ON IT! I FEEL THE INTENSITY! IT MUST BE THE *MOLECULAR CONDENSER!*

MY OWN RADAR SENSE ENABLES *ME* TO DODGE THE BEAM EASILY, BUT THE *GUN*... IT...IT'S *CHANGING!*

IT'S GETTING SMALLER... ACTUALLY FADING AWAY... FADING TO...

...ALMOST COMPLETE *NOTHINGNESS!*

AND *NOW*, DAREDEVIL, EVEN *YOUR* AGILITY WON'T HELP YOU! ALL I NEED DO IS MAKE THE BEAM *WIDER*, SO YOU CAN'T DODGE IT!

THAT SOUNDS *BAD!* IF HE MAKES THE BEAM TOO WIDE, I'LL HAVE NO SPACE LEFT TO MANEUVER IN!

HE'S *STARTED!* ONE FALSE MOVE WILL MEAN MY *DEATH!*

I'VE GOT TO STAY ONE JUMP AHEAD OF HIM *SOMEHOW!*

THEN, UTILIZING HIS RADAR SENSE, HIS LITHE, NIMBLE, MUSCULAR POWER, AND HIS DAUNTLESS COURAGE TO THE FULLEST EXTENT, THE MAN WITHOUT FEAR DARTS, AND DUCKS, AND DODGES, UNTIL...

HE'S *TIRING!* I CAN SENSE IT! IF I CAN JUST HOLD OUT SECONDS LONGER...!

I DON'T KNOW HOW MANY MORE CHARGES ARE LEFT IN THE RAY! I'D BETTER NOT WASTE THEM!

I'LL SETTLE WITH DAREDEVIL SOME *OTHER* TIME! RIGHT NOW, I'VE MORE IMPORTANT MATTERS TO ATTEND TO!

HE'S TURNING AWAY FROM ME! THAT MEANS I'M SAFE FROM THE RAY FOR NOW! HE'S UP TO SOMETHING *ELSE!*

17.

180

WELL, HE MAY BE THROUGH WITH *ME*, BUT I'M NOT FINISHED WITH *HIM!*

I HATE TO LEAVE A FIGHT UNSETTLED! IT'S LIKE WAITING FOR THE OTHER SHOE TO DROP!

BUT, IF I'M GOING TO TRAIL *STILTMAN*, I NEED A FAST WAY OF DOING IT!

AND, THAT TRAIN WHISTLE I HEAR IN THE DISTANCE, COMING CLOSER WITH EACH TOOT, IS JUST WHAT THE DOCTOR ORDERED!

SOMETIMES I THINK IT'S A GOOD THING I *CAN'T* SEE WHAT I'M DOING! I MIGHT GET SCARED STIFF!

WHEW!...IF I EVER GET CARELESS AND PUT ON SLIPPERY SHOES INSTEAD OF THESE TRUSTY OLD GUM-SOLES...

...IT'LL BE GOODBYE, DAREDEVIL!

EVEN OVER THE ROAR OF THE TRAIN, I CAN HEAR HIS HEAVY STEPS CLANGING ALONG THE ROADWAY! AS SOON AS I HEAR HIM DIRECTLY ALONGSIDE ME, I'LL MAKE MY MOVE!

18.

NOW!!

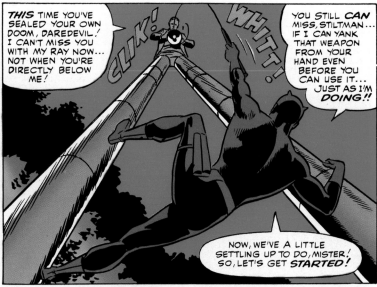

CLIK!

THIS TIME YOU'VE SEALED YOUR OWN DOOM, DAREDEVIL! I CAN'T MISS YOU WITH MY RAY NOW... NOT WHEN YOU'RE DIRECTLY BELOW ME!

WHTT!

YOU STILL **CAN** MISS, STILTMAN... IF I CAN YANK THAT WEAPON FROM YOUR HAND EVEN BEFORE YOU CAN USE IT... JUST AS I'M **DOING!!**

NOW, WE'VE A LITTLE SETTLING UP TO DO, MISTER! SO, LET'S GET **STARTED!**

BUT, BEFORE ANOTHER WORD CAN BE SAID, BEFORE ANOTHER MOVE CAN BE MADE, THE FATAL MOLECULAR RAY REVERSES ITSELF AS IT FALLS, CATCHING THE STARTLED WILBUR DAY IN THE FULL GLARE OF ITS AWESOME BEAM!!

NO! **NO!** THE **RAY**...! IT...IT'S SHINING ON **ME!!**

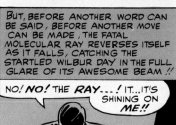

--I DIDN'T **PLAN** IT THIS WAY! IT'S AN **ACCIDENT!**

I'M GETTING **SMALLER!!** STARTING TO **FADE AWAY!** NO... **NO!** IT CAN'T BE! IT **MUSTN'T** BE! **HELP ME,** DAREDEVIL! I'LL GIVE YOU EVERYTHING I POSSESS... BUT HELP ME... **HELP ME!**

HOW **CAN** I, DAY? TELL ME, IS THERE AN **ANTIDOTE** I CAN GIVE YOU??

I DON'T **KNOW!** I **STOLE** THE RAY... I DON'T UNDERSTAND HOW IT **WORKS!**

HIS VOICE IS GETTING WEAKER AND WEAKER... HE'S SHRINKING FASTER AND FASTER!

DO SOMETHING! **HELP ME! HELP**...!

HE...HE'S **GONE!**

19.

182

NOTHING CAN COMPLETELY EVAPORATE! HE MUST BE SOMEWHERE...BUT HE'LL HAVE NO WAY TO RETURN! HE'S TRAPPED IN AN ESCAPE-PROOF PRISON OF HIS OWN MAKING!

LATER, WHEN A WEARY, SIGHTLESS ATTORNEY RETURNS TO THE LAW OFFICES OF NELSON AND MURDOCK, HE IS GREETED WITH...

KAXTON! HE'S HERE... WITH SOME OTHERS!

HE'S THE MAN! HE AND WILBUR DAY TRESPASSED ON MY PROPERTY! THEY ASSAULTED ME AND DAY STOLE A NEW EXPERIMENTAL RAY I WAS WORKING ON! I DEMAND HIS ARREST!

NOW, MR. KAXTON... SURELY WE CAN SETTLE THIS OUT OF COURT! AFTER ALL, THERE WAS NO HARM DONE!

NO HARM DONE??! I COULD NEVER DUPLICATE THAT RAY AGAIN! THE WORK OF YEARS...RUINED!

MR. KAXTON, I'VE...EH... PERSUADED MY CLIENT, WILBUR DAY, TO WITHDRAW THE CHARGES HE MADE AGAINST YOU! HE'S NOT GOING TO SUE YOU!

HE'S NOT, EH? WELL, THAT'S MORE LIKE IT! IN THAT CASE, I'M WILLING TO FORGET THIS WHOLE THING!

I DIDN'T ACTUALLY LIE! WILBUR DAY CERTAINLY ISN'T GOING TO SUE ANY-ONE FOR A LONG, LONG TIME!

MATT, I JUST DON'T UNDERSTAND YOUR ACTIONS THESE PAST FEW DAYS! YOU LOST US A CLIENT, ALMOST GOT INVOLVED IN A LAWSUIT YOURSELF! WHAT'S GOTTEN INTO YOU??

I DON'T KNOW, FOGGY! PERHAPS I JUST NEED A REST!

OH, MATT, THIS WOULD BE THE PERFECT TIME TO SEE DR. VAN EYCK, ABOUT YOUR EYE OPERATION!

NO, KAREN! I JUST CAN'T! IT'S TOO RISKY!

MATT MURDOCK, I DON'T UNDERSTAND YOU! IF YOU HAVE A CHANCE TO SEE AGAIN, HOW CAN YOU WORRY ABOUT THE RISK? ARE YOU JUST A COWARD??

HOW CAN I TELL HER I'M AFRAID OF LOSING MY SENSORY POWERS IF MY SIGHT RETURNS?!

SOMETIMES I THINK YOU JUST HIDE BEHIND YOUR HANDICAP... YOU DON'T WANT TO FACE THE WORLD...TO FACE YOUR RESPONSIBILITIES...TO... TO FALL IN LOVE...≶SOB≷!

KAREN!! NO... WAIT! KAREN... COME BACK!

CAN SHE BE RIGHT? IS THE MAN WITHOUT FEAR REALLY A COWARD... AFRAID TO RISK REGAINING HIS SIGHT? AFRAID TO ASK FOR THE HAND OF THE ONE HE LOVES??

NEXT ISSUE: DAREDEVIL FACES HIS CRUCIAL OPERATION!! YOU MUST NOT MISS IT!

the END

183

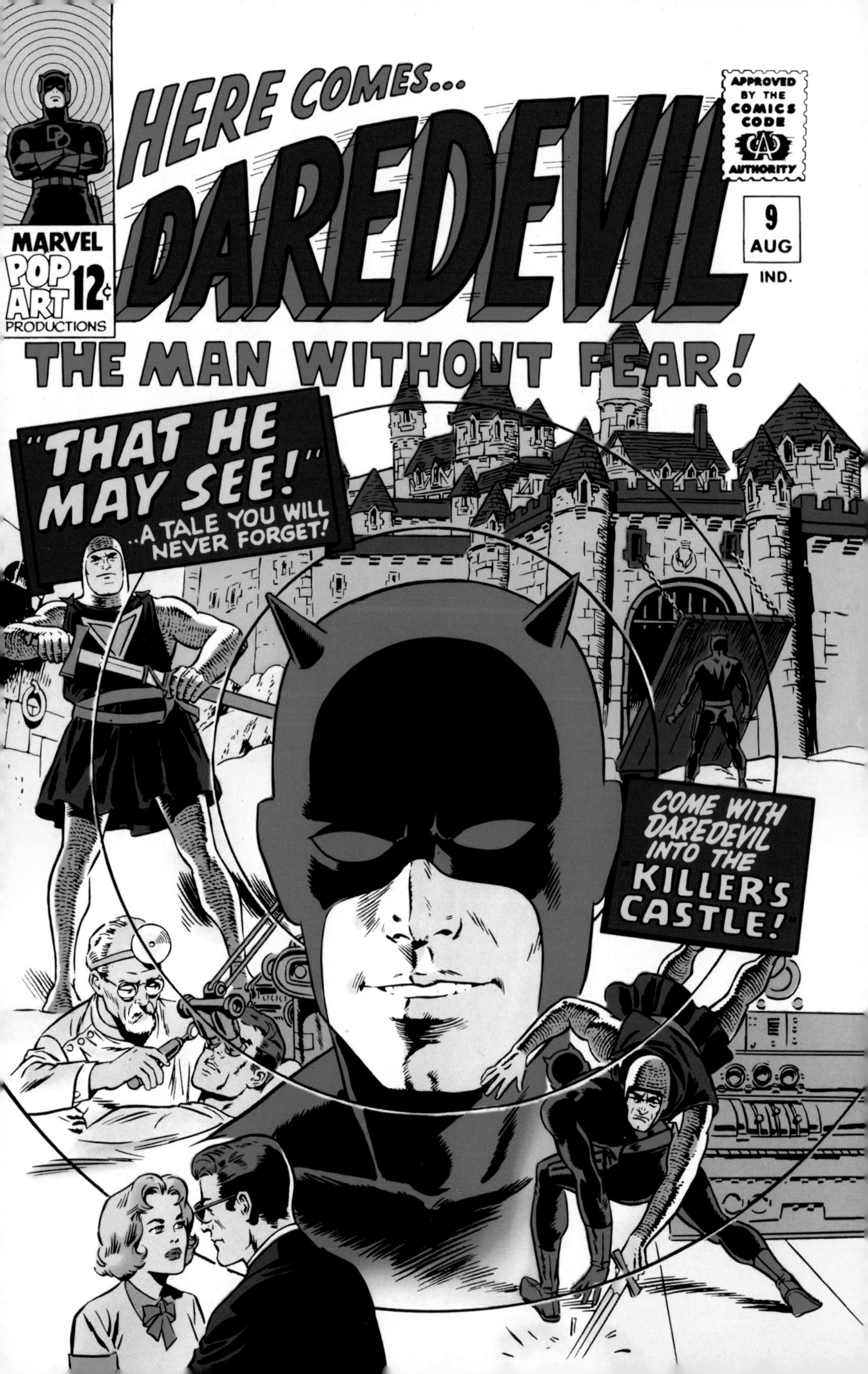
MARVEL
POP ART PRODUCTIONS
12¢
HERE COMES...
DAREDEVIL
APPROVED BY THE COMICS CODE AUTHORITY
9
AUG
IND.
THE MAN WITHOUT FEAR!
"THAT HE MAY SEE!"
..A TALE YOU WILL NEVER FORGET!
COME WITH DAREDEVIL INTO THE "KILLER'S CASTLE!"

DAREDEVIL

FEATURING: THE MURDEROUS MENACE OF... THE KILLER'S CASTLE!

"THAT HE MAY SEE!"

GOOD THING I WAS IN THE AREA! SOMEBODY'S GOT TO STOP THOSE HIJACKERS FROM ESCAPING OUT TO SEA, AND I'M NOT WEARING THIS COSTUME JUST TO CATCH FLIES!

ARE YOU THE TYPE OF READER WHO'S IMPRESSED BY LOTS OF CREDITS? IF SO, TAKE A SQUINT AT THESE!

FUNDAMENTAL PLOT and SCRIPT by SMILIN' STAN LEE
BASIC LAYOUTS and DELINEATION by WONDROUS WALLY WOOD
COMPREHENSIVE PENCILED GRAPHICS by BOUNCY BOBBY POWELL
BALLOONS, BORDERS and BLURBS by SWINGIN' SAMMY ROSEN

C'MON, NOW! DON'T DAWDLE TOO LONG OVER THIS PAGE! YOU'VE GOT A LOT OF ACTION AWAITING YOU, AND WE WANT YOU TO FACE IT ALL NICE AND REFRESHED! SO LET'S GO...!

LOOK OUT! IT'S *DAREDEVIL!!*

SHUCKS! I WANTED IT TO BE A *SURPRISE!*

BOK!

BUT, THERE'S ALWAYS *ONE* PARTY POOP...

WOK!

...WHO HAS TO OPEN HIS BIG, FLAPPIN' MOUTH!

HE'LL FINISH US *ALL* IF WE DON'T STOP 'IM, *FAST!*

THOK!

NO APPLAUSE... *PLEASE!* I'M ONLY DOING WHAT *ANY* TALENTED, HEROIC... *UNHHH!*

AWRIGHT, FUNNY MAN! LET'S SEE YA LAUGH *THAT* OFF!

I WAS *CARELESS!* HE WINGED MY ARM!

KRAK!

THIS ISN'T THE MOST GLAMOROUS EXIT SCENE, BUT IT'S BETTER THAN BEING SHOT AT AGAIN!

RRPOOO

USCG 7

ANYWAY, I HELD THEM OFF LONG ENOUGH FOR THE *COAST GUARD* TO PLAY PATTY-CAKE WITH THEM NOW!

I WONDER HOW THIS'LL READ ON THE SCORECARD? DO I GET CREDITED WITH THE WINNING PITCH?... OR WAS I KNOCKED OUT OF THE BOX IN THE LAST INNING?

USCG 78

WELL, BETTER HEAD FOR SHORE BEFORE I GET A CHILL! IT WON'T HELP MY SUPER HERO IMAGE ANY IF I'M SEEN RUNNING AROUND TOWN WITH NOSE DROPS AND KLEENEX TISSUES!

LOOKS LIKE THAT BLASTED BULLET, BIT DEEPER THAN I THOUGHT! THE ARMS STARTING TO GET *NUMB!* THIS'LL PUT A DAMPER ON MY HEROICS FOR TONIGHT, *THAT'S* FOR SURE!

TOO BAD A FELLA IN MY LINE OF WORK CAN'T JOIN *BLUE CROSS!*

2.

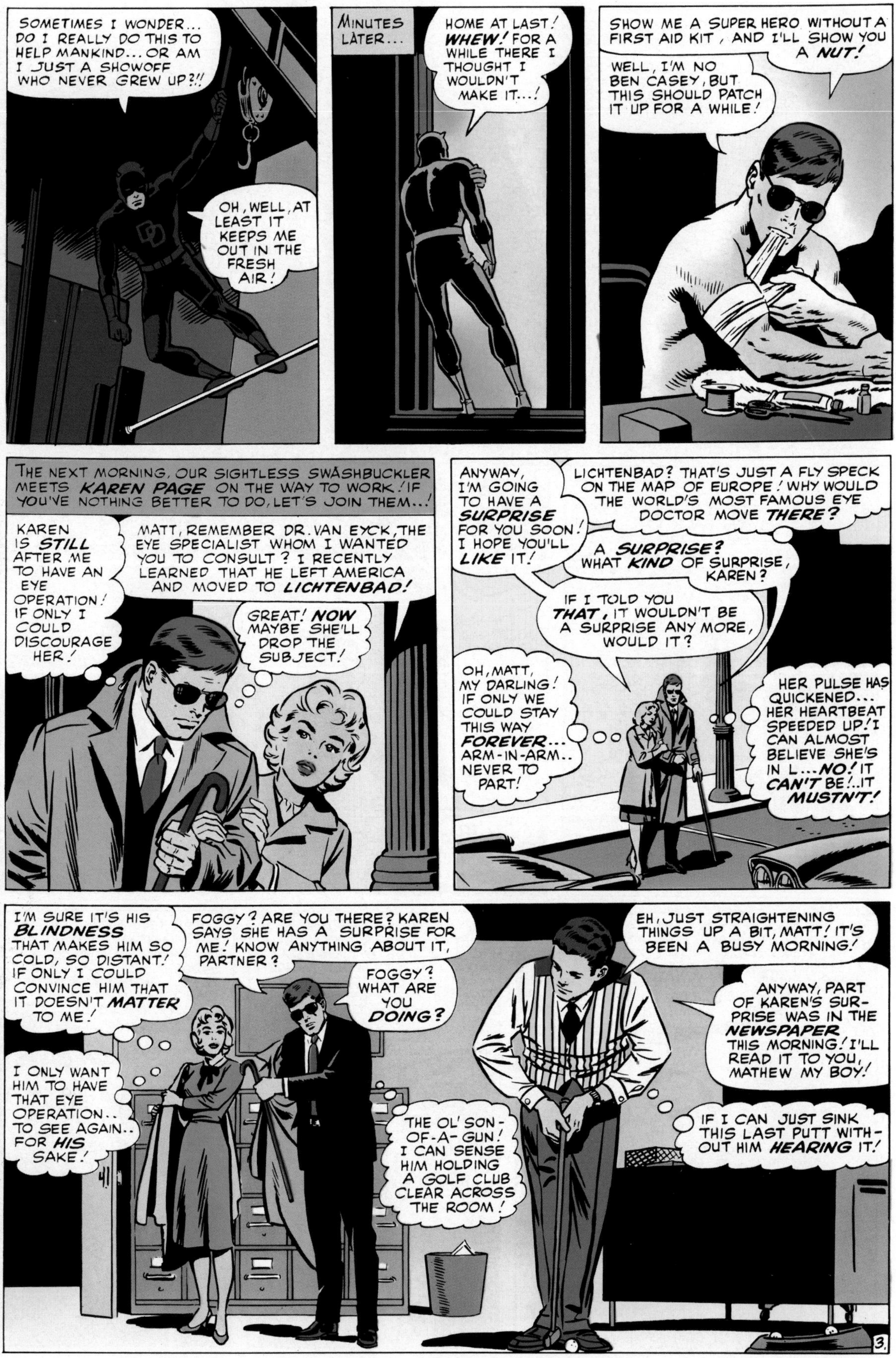
SOMETIMES I WONDER... DO I REALLY DO THIS TO HELP MANKIND... OR AM I JUST A SHOWOFF WHO NEVER GREW UP?!!
OH, WELL, AT LEAST IT KEEPS ME OUT IN THE FRESH AIR!
MINUTES LATER...
HOME AT LAST! WHEW! FOR A WHILE THERE I THOUGHT I WOULDN'T MAKE IT...!
SHOW ME A SUPER HERO WITHOUT A FIRST AID KIT, AND I'LL SHOW YOU A NUT!
WELL, I'M NO BEN CASEY, BUT THIS SHOULD PATCH IT UP FOR A WHILE!
THE NEXT MORNING, OUR SIGHTLESS SWASHBUCKLER MEETS KAREN PAGE ON THE WAY TO WORK! IF YOU'VE NOTHING BETTER TO DO, LET'S JOIN THEM...!
KAREN IS STILL AFTER ME TO HAVE AN EYE OPERATION! IF ONLY I COULD DISCOURAGE HER!
MATT, REMEMBER DR. VAN EYCK, THE EYE SPECIALIST WHOM I WANTED YOU TO CONSULT? I RECENTLY LEARNED THAT HE LEFT AMERICA AND MOVED TO LICHTENBAD!
GREAT! NOW MAYBE SHE'LL DROP THE SUBJECT!
ANYWAY, I'M GOING TO HAVE A SURPRISE FOR YOU SOON! I HOPE YOU'LL LIKE IT!
LICHTENBAD? THAT'S JUST A FLY SPECK ON THE MAP OF EUROPE! WHY WOULD THE WORLD'S MOST FAMOUS EYE DOCTOR MOVE THERE?
A SURPRISE? WHAT KIND OF SURPRISE, KAREN?
IF I TOLD YOU THAT, IT WOULDN'T BE A SURPRISE ANY MORE, WOULD IT?
OH, MATT, MY DARLING! IF ONLY WE COULD STAY THIS WAY FOREVER... ARM-IN-ARM.. NEVER TO PART!
HER PULSE HAS QUICKENED... HER HEARTBEAT SPEEDED UP! I CAN ALMOST BELIEVE SHE'S IN L... NO! IT CAN'T BE!..IT MUSTN'T!
I'M SURE IT'S HIS BLINDNESS THAT MAKES HIM SO COLD, SO DISTANT! IF ONLY I COULD CONVINCE HIM THAT IT DOESN'T MATTER TO ME!
FOGGY? ARE YOU THERE? KAREN SAYS SHE HAS A SURPRISE FOR ME! KNOW ANYTHING ABOUT IT, PARTNER?
FOGGY? WHAT ARE YOU DOING?
I ONLY WANT HIM TO HAVE THAT EYE OPERATION.. TO SEE AGAIN.. FOR HIS SAKE!
THE OL' SON-OF-A-GUN! I CAN SENSE HIM HOLDING A GOLF CLUB CLEAR ACROSS THE ROOM!
EH, JUST STRAIGHTENING THINGS UP A BIT, MATT! IT'S BEEN A BUSY MORNING!
ANYWAY, PART OF KAREN'S SURPRISE WAS IN THE NEWSPAPER THIS MORNING! I'LL READ IT TO YOU, MATHEW MY BOY!
IF I CAN JUST SINK THIS LAST PUTT WITHOUT HIM HEARING IT!
3.

FINALLY... DO YOU REMEMBER SOMEONE NAMED *KLAUS KRUGER*, MATT?

WHO? OH... *SURE*, I DO! WASN'T HE THE FOREIGN EXCHANGE STUDENT WHO WAS IN OUR CLASS FOR THE FINAL YEAR AT LAW SCHOOL?

HE'S THE ONE!

DUKE VISITS U.S.

VOL II SEC. 3

KLAUS KRUGER, HEREDITARY RULER OF THE TINY PRINCIPALITY OF LICHTENBAD, ARRIVED IN NEW YORK TODAY FOR A BRIEF VISIT. THE DUKE HAS REFUSED ALL PRESS INTERVIEWS AND DECLINED TO DIVULGE ANY...

LICHTENBAD RULER, AS HE LEFT AIRPORT.

WELL, WHEN I READ THAT HE WAS IN TOWN, I *PHONED* HIM AND TOLD HIM ABOUT... OHHH!

MURDOCK! NELSON! HOW GOOD TO SEE YOU AGAIN!

IT'S *KLAUS!* HE'S *HERE!*

COME *IN*, YOUR EXCELLENCY!

COME NOW! NONE OF THAT "YOUR EXCELLENCY" TALK BETWEEN SUCH OLD FRIENDS!

MATHEW, WHEN THIS YOUNG LADY TOLD ME YOU HAD LOST YOUR SIGHT, I KNEW I HAD TO TAKE YOU BACK TO LICHTENBAD WITH ME!

NOW I GET IT! DR. VAN EYCK IS IN LICHTENBAD... AND THEN, WHEN KAREN READ THAT *YOU* WERE HERE... *THAT'S* THE SURPRISE!

BUT, WHY WOULD KLAUS KRUGER BE INTERESTED IN ME NOW?! WE WERE NEVER REALLY THAT FRIENDLY! HE WAS A *STRANGE* ONE... A GIANT OF A MAN... BRILLIANT, ATHLETIC.. ALWAYS WITH AN AIR OF *MYSTERY* ABOUT HIM!

WHY DID DR. VAN EYCK *GO* TO LICHTENBAD, KLAUS?

HE CAME FOR A VACATION... FELL IN LOVE WITH THE BEAUTY OF THE COUNTRYSIDE... AND DECIDED TO MAKE HIS HOME THERE!

YOU *MUST* GO BACK WITH THE DUKE, MATT! YOU *CAN'T* PASS UP A CHANCE LIKE THIS...

...A CHANCE TO *SEE* AGAIN!

SHE IS *RIGHT*, MY FRIEND! YOU WILL BE *MY GUEST!* YOU SHALL *HAVE* YOUR OPERATION, AND RETURN TO AMERICA WITH YOUR VISION RESTORED!

I *WILL* GO WITH HIM! BUT, FOR A *DIFFERENT* REASON!

I CAN TELL BY HIS PULSE RATE THAT HE'S *LYING!* THE ENTIRE STORY IS A *HOAX!* BUT I DON'T KNOW *WHY!* AND ONE THING I CAN'T RESIST IS A *MYSTERY!*

4

189

THAT NIGHT... AND YET, IF ONLY I **DARED** TO REALLY **HAVE** AN EYE OPERATION! IF ONLY I DIDN'T FEAR THAT I WOULD LOSE MY SUPER-SENSES IF MY VISION RETURNED!

HOW IRONIC THAT **DAREDEVIL**, THE MAN WITHOUT FEAR, IS MORTALLY AFRAID OF EVER REGAINING HIS SIGHT!

THEN, EARLY THE NEXT MORNING...

GOOD LUCK, MATT... I PRAY THE OPERATION WILL SUCCEED! WITH ALL MY HEART, I PRAY...!

DON'T BUILD YOUR HOPES UP **TOO** MUCH, KAREN! I.. I WOULDN'T WANT YOU TO BE DISAPPOINTED!

IF ONLY I DARED TO SWEEP HER UP IN MY ARMS... TELL HER WHAT I'M LONGING TO SAY!

TAKE GOOD CARE OF HIM, KLAUS! PARTNERS LIKE **MATT** DON'T GROW ON TREES!

NOW THAT WE'RE TAKING OFF, I SENSE A **CHANGE** IN HIM! HE'S GROWN COLD, ALOOF...UTTERLY EMOTIONLESS!

WHAT IF SOMETHING GOES **WRONG!** IF THE OPERATION **FAILS?** I..I COULDN'T **BEAR** IT!!

IT'S **MATT** SHE LOVES.. NOT ME! I ALWAYS **KNEW** IT!

SHE WANTS HIM TO SEE AGAIN, SO THAT HE'LL MARRY HER! BUT, IF THE OPERATION FAILS, PERHAPS **I'LL** STILL HAVE A CHANCE...!

NO! I MUSTN'T **THINK** THAT WAY! HE'S MY **FRIEND!** WHAT'S **WRONG** WITH ME.??!

LATER, HALF A WORLD AWAY...

CAN **THIS** BE LICHTENBAD? I SENSE A **WALLED CITY**... LIKE A MEDIEVAL FORTRESS! OR, PERHAPS IT'S EVEN **MORE** LIKE A HUGE, PRESENT-DAY **PRISON!**

5.

THEN, AS THE PASSENGERS BEGIN TO DISEMBARK...

EXCELLENCY! LOOK OUT! THERE IS AN ASSASSIN... WITH A PISTOL!

TAKE YOUR HANDS OFF ME, FOOL! THE DUKE OF LICHTENBAD DOES NOT PANIC AT THE SIGHT OF A PEASANT WITH A WEAPON!

OUT OF MY WAY! HE DOES NOT FRIGHTEN ME! LET ME APPROACH HIM!

DEATH TO TYRANTS!! LONG LIVE FREEDOM!

HOW CAN YOU REMAIN STANDING?? WHY DO YOU NOT FALL?

YOUR BULLETS CANNOT HARM ME!

KRAK!

KRAK!

STAY BACK, GUARDS! ONE KARATE BLOW IS ALL I WILL NEED!

UHHH..!

THAK!

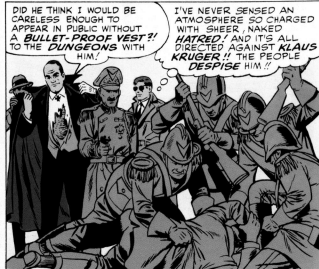

DID HE THINK I WOULD BE CARELESS ENOUGH TO APPEAR IN PUBLIC WITHOUT A BULLET-PROOF VEST?! TO THE DUNGEONS WITH HIM!

I'VE NEVER SENSED AN ATMOSPHERE SO CHARGED WITH SHEER, NAKED HATRED! AND IT'S ALL DIRECTED AGAINST KLAUS KRUGER!! THE PEOPLE DESPISE HIM!!

MOMENTS LATER, INSIDE THE DUKE'S PERSONAL HEAVILY-ARMORED CAR...

ALL THROUGH THE COUNTRYSIDE IS THAT FEELING OF HATRED... OVERSHADOWED ONLY BY AN EVEN STRONGER FEELING OF STARK FEAR!!

I SHALL TAKE YOU TO SEE DR. VAN EYCK NOW, MURDOCK!

THE SENSATION OF TERROR, SUSPICION, AND HATRED IS EVERY-WHERE! IT'S SO STRONG, SO THICK, YOU CAN ALMOST TOUCH IT!!

THERE'S NO DOUBT ABOUT IT! KLAUS HAS MADE A SLAVE STATE OF LICHTENBAD! BUT WHY?

6.

AND THEN, INSIDE A SMALL, CLOSELY GUARDED ROOM...

WHY ARE THERE **GUARDS** OUT-SIDE THE DOOR? WHY IS THE **DOCTOR** ALSO FILLED WITH FEAR?

I'LL LEAVE YOU WITH DR. VAN EYCK NOW! REPORT TO ME TOMORROW!

SO **YOU** ARE MATHEW MURDOCK? I HAVE HEARD OF YOU!

DOCTOR, WHAT IS **HAPPEN-ING** IN LICHTENBAD? WHAT IS EVERYONE **AFRAID** OF? AND, WHY ARE **YOU** HERE?

NO! **NO!** DO NOT **TALK** OF SUCH MATTERS! EVEN THE **WALLS** HAVE EARS! I KNOW NOTHING! **NOTHING!**

BUT, AS THE TREMBLING DOCTOR FEARFULLY COMPLETES HIS EXAMINATION, THE SUPER-KEEN HEARING OF MATT MURDOCK NOTES FRAGMENTS OF SPEECH FROM ALL OVER THE BUILDING...

WE MUST **REVOLT!**

BE BRAVE! WAIT FOR THE SIGNAL!

IT'S **DEATH** TO DEFY THE DUKE!

HIS **SPIES** ARE EVERY-WHERE!

I'M INNOCENT! I **SWEAR** IT!

AND SO...

VAN EYCK SAID THE X-RAYS WOULD BE READY TOMORROW! BUT, WHILE I'M WAITING, IT'S TIME FOR **DAREDEVIL** TO LEARN MORE ABOUT THIS COMIC-OPERA KINGDOM!

I'VE GOT TO BE CAREFUL, THOUGH! I STILL CAN'T USE MY RIGHT ARM! IT'S ALMOST COMPLETELY NUMB!

HMMM! WHEREVER I GO, I HEAR PEOPLE PLOTTING TO REVOLT AGAINST THE DUKE! HOW HAS HE MANAGED TO KEEP THEM ENSLAVED **TILL** NOW? WHAT **POWER** DOES HE HOLD OVER THEM?

WE CAN DELAY NO LONGER! OUR PEOPLE SUFFER MORE EACH DAY!

YOU ARE **RIGHT!** BETTER **DEATH** THAN TYRANNY! THE TIME TO STRIKE IS **NOW!**

FIRST, WE MUST FIND **ARMS!** WE NEED MORE GUNS, MORE...!!

THE DUKE'S **PALACE GUARDS!** WE'VE BEEN **BETRAYED!** WE'RE **TRAPPED!**

YOU ARE **TRAITORS, ALL!** YOU KNOW THE PENALTY FOR **TREASON!** YOU MUST COME WITH US!

NO! DON'T LET THEM TAKE US! WE MUST **FIGHT!**

7.

THE "PALACE GUARD"!.. THEY'RE **NOT MEN**.... THEY'RE **ROBOTS!!** NOTHING CAN HARM THEM... OR STOP THEM!

YOU MUST COME WITH US! THE ORDERS OF HIS EXCELLENCY, THE **DUKE**, MUST EVER BE OBEYED!

IT'S **USELESS!** THE ROBOT GUARDS ARE **EVERYWHERE!** WE **MUST** SUBMIT! WE MUST LIVE TO FIGHT **ANOTHER** DAY!

BUT, AS THE HELPLESS PRISONERS ARE BROUGHT TO THE TOWERING CASTLE OF THE DUKE OF LICHTENBAD, THERE IS ONE WHO HAS **FOLLOWED** THEM! SILENTLY, STEALTHILY, PATIENTLY WAITING... DARINGLY PLANNING...

IN THE NAME OF THE **DUKE**... LOWER THE DRAWBRIDGE!

A MOAT... ALIVE WITH SHARKS! A GIGANTIC DRAW- BRIDGE! IT'S LIKE A SCENE FROM THE CRUSADES! I CAN SENSE IT **ALL!**

AND, NO SOONER HAS THE FINAL PRISONER BEEN LED ACROSS, WHEN...

IF I LEAP **NOW**, I CAN JUST MAKE IT, UN- OBSERVED!

IT'S ALMOST A PITY THAT NOBODY'S LOOKING! THIS WOULD KNOCK 'EM DEAD ON ED SULLIVAN'S SHOW!

WELL, I CAN'T HANG AROUND ALL DAY... SO, **IN** I GO...!

I BID YOU WELCOME! YOU WILL FIND IT HARDER TO **LEAVE** THAN IT WAS TO **ENTER!**

UH-OH! THAT'S THE **DUKE'S** VOICE! HE KNOWS I'M HERE!

8.

MY RADAR SENSES CAN "SEE" THROUGH THE FLOOR BELOW ME AS THOUGH IT'S MADE OF GLASS! THIS CASTLE ISN'T AS OLD-FASHIONED AS IT SEEMS! IT'S FILLED WITH COMPLEX *ELECTRONIC* EQUIPMENT... AND ENOUGH POWER TO BLOW UP HALF A CONTINENT!

BUT I'LL WORRY ABOUT *THAT* LATER! RIGHT NOW, I'VE GOT TO CONCENTRATE ON SAVING MY OWN LITTLE HIDE!

AT THAT MOMENT, A HUGE MECHANIZED STEEL DOOR SLIDES OPEN, SUDDENLY REVEALING THE PRESENCE OF A LEERING KLAUS KRUGER, SURROUNDED BY POWERFUL PALACE GUARDS IN THE ORNATE THRONE ROOM OF LICHTENBAD....!

COME FORWARD, INTRUDER! LET ME *LOOK* AT YOU! IT IS ONLY FITTING I LEARN THE IDENTITY OF ANY I AM ABOUT TO THROW INTO MY DUNGEON!

I HAVE NOT SEEN THAT COSTUME IN MY KINGDOM BEFORE! AND, AFTER TODAY, NONE SHALL EVER SEE IT AGAIN! REMAIN *MOTIONLESS* WHEN I SPEAK TO YOU!

THERE ARE ONLY TWO HEARTBEATS IN THIS ENTIRE CHAMBER! THAT MEANS ONLY THE DUKE AND I ARE HUMAN--- EVERY GUARD IN THE CASTLE MUST BE A *ROBOT!*

KLAUS KRUGER MUST BE AFRAID TO TRUST *ANY* LIVING BEING!

YOUR COSTUMED DISGUISE CAN MEAN ONLY *ONE* THING! *YOU* MUST BE THE LEADER OF THE UNDERGROUND! *YOU* MUST BE THE ONE WHO HAS PLANNED THE REVOLT AGAINST ME! THEREFORE, YOU MUST *DIE!*

GUARDS! TO THE *DUNGEON* WITH HIM! MY PATIENCE WEARS THIN! THE VERY SIGHT OF HIM IS AN EFFRONTERY TO MY EYES!

AT LEAST HE DOESN'T YET SUSPECT WHO I REALLY *AM!*

OKAY, KIDDIES! IF YOU *WANT* ME, COME AND *GET* ME!

BUT DON'T EXPECT ME TO STAND AROUND AND WELCOME YOU WITH OPEN ARMS!! I'M MORE THE *SHY* TYPE MYSELF!

WH UP!

9.

194

I'll **ADMIT** you're a lot of laughs, gang, but it's the **DUKE** I'm after!

So, if you'll excuse me..!

One little gas projectile ought to get your mind off **DUNGEONS** for a while, sweetie!

You are a most **ABLE** fighter, my friend...

But you have **BITTEN** off more than you can chew!

No gas pellet in the world can affect a sovereign wise enough to sit behind an unseen, impenetrable **FORCE SHIELD**!

And, you should have realized that a robot may be knocked down, but...unlike a human...it is never **OUT** until it has been **DESTROYED**!

OHHHH! My injured **ARM**!

THOP!

WELL DONE, my loyal creations..! Now, throw him into the dungeon with the others...to await my pleasure!

Thus, it comes to pass that when the **MAN WITHOUT FEAR** regains consciousness, he finds himself manacled to an unbreakable post, with the sardonic sound of Klaus Kruger's laughter ringing in his ears....!

He came here to **GLOAT**...to **BRAG**! If I remain silent, he may tell me what he's **REALLY** after....!

I won't even **BOTHER** unmasking you yet! Your identity means nothing! **NO** revolt can ever succeed against **ME**!

Each passing hour, each passing day I grow **STRONGER**, as the best **BRAINS** in all the world come here to **SERVE** me!

WEEKS ago, I captured the world's greatest eye surgeon! Only yesterday I brought one of the most famous **LAWYERS** here!

He thinks I'll help him restore his sight! The **FOOL**! All I desire is to use **HIM**, as I use all the others!

10

195

LITTLE BY LITTLE, BY TRICKERY AND DECEIT, I SHALL FORCE THE GREATEST MEN IN EVERY FIELD TO SERVE ME!

AND, AIDED BY THEIR BRAINS AND TALENT... AND MY OWN WEALTH AND CUNNING, I SHALL BUILD A ROBOT ARMY WHICH SHALL CONQUER THE **EARTH!**

WHEW! HE'S AS NUTTY AS A FRUITCAKE! BUT, SO WAS A LITTLE HOUSEPAINTER NAMED HITLER, AND LOOK AT THE DAMAGE *HE* CAUSED!

YOU WILL BE SHOT AT SUN- RISE, WITH THE OTHERS!

BUT, AS SOON AS THE IRON GATE HAS SLAMMED SHUT...

I *CAN'T* LET THEM SHOOT ME AT SUN- RISE! I HATE GETTING UP SO EARLY!

IF I CAN JUST SHINNY TO THE *TOP* OF THIS POLE...!

THE MASKED MAN *DID* IT!! HE IS *FREE!*

I APPRECIATE YOUR ENTHUSIASM, MA'AM, BUT KEEP IT QUIET, HUH?

FIRST THING TO DO NOW IS GET MY HANDS IN *FRONT*, WHERE I CAN *USE* THEM!

HE IS AS NIMBLE AS A CIRCUS ACROBAT!

THANKS A HEAP, PAL! AND I DON'T EVEN BELONG TO ACTORS' EQUITY!

BUT, EVEN THOUGH YOU ARE FREE, HOW CAN YOU ESCAPE FROM THIS BARRED DUNGEON??

FUNNY, I'VE BEEN WONDERING THE SAME THING!

I HEAR A *GUARD* OUTSIDE! SHOUT FOR HIM! *HURRY!*

GUARD!! *HELP!!* COME QUICK! *GUARD...* PLEASE... *HELP!*

OKAY! OKAY! DON'T HAM IT UP!

11.

THEN, AS THE UNSUSPECTING FIGURE ENTERS THE GLOOMY DUNGEON...

ALL RIGHT... HE'S NOT GONNA BOTHER US FOR A WHILE! SOMEBODY GRAB HIS KEY RING NOW!

BUT.. EVEN IF WE CAN FLEE THE DUNGEON... HOW WILL WE GET OVER THE CASTLE MOAT? THE DRAW-BRIDGE IS ALWAYS RAISED!

YOU MUST SPEND EVERY SPARE MINUTE DREAMING UP QUESTIONS!

HERE! YOU GET STARTED BREAKING THE LEASE IN THIS PLACE, WHILE I TRY TO FIND US ALL A NEW APARTMENT!

MMM, THIS IS WHAT I WANT! I CAN HEAR THE DRONE OF ELECTRIC CIRCUITS INSIDE THIS WALL PANEL!

WHY DO YOU PAUSE ON THE STAIR THAT WAY?

I THOUGHT IT WAS A BUS STOP! WHY ELSE?

NOW YOU WASTE TIME STRIKING THE WALL?? I DON'T UNDERSTAND!

LOOK, CAN'T YOU FIND SOMEONE ELSE TO PLAY 20-QUESTIONS WITH? I'M BUSY!

THAK!

ONE KARATE BLOW OUGHT TO DO IT!

OH! NOW I SEE WHAT YOU DID!

WELL, HAPPY DAY! THIS SHORT CIRCUIT OUGHT TO LOWER THE DRAW-BRIDGE! SO MOVE!

ONE MAN ALONE... ACCOMPLISHED SO MUCH! IT IS LIKE A DREAM!

LISTEN! THE ALARMS! WE'RE NOT SAFE YET!

BRRINNG! BRRINNG! BRINNG! BRINNG!

RUN! I'LL HOLD OFF THE GUARDS!!

12.

197

HOW CAN WE EVER **THANK** YOU?

REMEMBER ME IN YOUR **WILL!** BUT, RIGHT NOW, THERE'S A **BIGGER** PROBLEM TO WORRY ABOUT!

I'LL WAIT TILL THEIR FOOTSTEPS COME **CLOSER!** MY TIMING HAS TO BE **PERFECT!**

GERONIMO!

WHONK!

AND NOW, **I'D** BETTER AMSCRAY, TOO! I'LL JUST DUCK OUT THE BACK WAY... I HATE SENTIMENTAL GOODBYES!

NOT LONG AFTERWARDS, THE SIGHTLESS ATTORNEY RETURNS TO THE OFFICE OF DR. VAN EYCK, NOT QUITE KNOWING WHAT TO EXPECT NEXT...!

IF VAN EYCK IS ACTUALLY A **PRISONER** HERE, I'VE GOT TO FIND SOME WAY TO SET HIM FREE! BUT FIRST...

I'VE GOT A LITTLE DEBT TO SETTLE WITH KLAUS KRUGER!

MR. MURDOCK, I HAVE THE RESULTS OF YOUR X-RAYS! I WOULD LIKE TO TALK TO YOU ABOUT YOUR BLINDNESS!!!

HOW **ABOUT** THAT?! IN ALL THE EXCITEMENT, I CLEAR FORGOT THE REASON I'M SUPPOSED TO BE HERE!

WHAT'S THE VERDICT DOC?

AND, AS MATT MURDOCK WAITS BREATHLESSLY FOR THE DOCTOR'S NEXT WORDS, LET'S RETURN BRIEFLY TO THE U.S., WHERE WE FIND...

KAREN, WOULD YOU GET ME THE FILE ON THE SUB-MARINER CASE, PLEASE?

YES, MATT... EH, I MEAN **FOGGY!**

SHE'S BEEN THAT WAY SINCE HE LEFT! SHE CAN'T FORGET HIM FOR A **MINUTE!**

EVEN THOUGH HE'S SIGHTLESS, IT'S **MATT** WHOM SHE LOVES! I CAN STAND RIGHT IN FRONT OF HER, AND SHE DOESN'T KNOW I'M THERE! TO KAREN I'M NOTHING... **NOTHING...!**

CR-RACK!

FOGGY! WHAT **IS** IT? WHAT **HAPPENED??** OH...YOUR HAND! DID YOU HURT YOURSELF...??

IT'S NOT MY **HAND,** THAT HURTS ME, KAREN!--IT'S MY **HEART!** BUT NOTHING CAN CHANGE THAT!

I'M ALL RIGHT! I ACCIDENTALLY BRUSHED PAST THE MIRROR BREAKING IT!

I WISH THERE WERE **NO** MATT MURDOCK! I WISH HE'D NEVER RETURN! AND I **HATE** MYSELF FOR IT!

13.

MEANWHILE BACK IN LICHTENBAD...

YOU'VE **ALREADY** EXAMINED ME, DOC! WHY THIS ROUTINE AGAIN?

SHH! LOWER YOUR VOICE! I WANT TO WARN YOU... YOU ARE IN GREAT DANGER HERE...

EVEN IF THE OPERATION IS A SUCCESS, THE DUKE WILL NEVER LET YOU LEAVE ALIVE! YOU'RE A **PRISONER**... AS **I** AM!

THERE'S ONLY ONE CHANCE! IF **YOU** CAN ESCAPE... IF YOU CAN NOTIFY THE EMBASSY... **OHHH!**

OUR **HIDDEN MICROPHONES** HAVE PICKED UP YOUR TREASONOUS REMARKS! YOU MUST BE **PUNISHED**, DOCTOR! **SEIZE HIM!**

KRUGER'S INHUMAN GUARD!!

REMAIN HERE, SIGHTLESS ONE! YOUR FATE WILL BE DECIDED LATER..!

IT'S **MY** FAULT, MURDOCK! IF ONLY I HADN'T SPOKEN!

DON'T BLAME YOURSELF, DOC! YOU DID YOUR BEST!

AND DON'T DESPAIR! THINGS MAY NOT BE AS HOPELESS AS THEY SEEM!

THEY'VE TAKEN HIM AWAY! I'M **ALONE** HERE NOW!

OKAY, KRUGER! IT'S BEEN **YOUR** BALL GAME TILL NOW... BUT IT'S TIME FOR A **CHANGE!!**

I'VE NEVER TACKLED A HEAD OF STATE BEFORE, BUT IN **THIS** CASE, I'LL MAKE AN EXCEPTION!

HERE'S WHERE **DAREDEVIL** RETURNS TO THAT KILLER'S CASTLE... FOR THE **LAST** TIME!

AND, AS THE SWASHBUCKLING MAN WITHOUT FEAR SWINGS OUT OVER THE STREETS OF LICHTENBAD, HE REALIZES...

MY TIMING IS **PERFECT!** THE PEOPLE HAVE ALREADY BROKEN OUT IN **OPEN REVOLT!**

I'VE GOT TO **HELP** THEM ANY WAY I CAN!

AND THERE'S NO TIME LIKE THE **PRESENT!**

14.

WOW! AN ENTIRE ROBOT PLATOON IS MARCHING TO ATTACK THE UNARMED CROWD!

A FEW HIGH-POTENCY MORTAR PROJECTILES, FIRED FROM MY BILLY CLUB, MIGHT SLOW THEM UP FOR A WHILE....!

FOOSH!

I WAS LIVING IN A FOOL'S PARADISE! THEY DON'T EVEN SEEM TO FEEL THE IMPACT!

KLANK!

WHEW! THAT WAS A CLOSE ONE!

WITHOUT A SECOND'S PAUSE, DAREDEVIL TURNS AND OUTDISTANCES THE SLOW-MOVING ROBOTS UNTIL HE REACHES THE MOAT SURROUNDING KLAUS KRUGER'S CASTLE...

THE ONLY WAY TO STOP THAT NUTS AND BOLTS BRIGADE IS TO STOP THE DUKE HIMSELF!

AND THAT'S JUST WHAT I'VE BEEN BUSTIN' TO DO!

THE ROBOTS ARE CONTROLLED BY KRUGER! SO IF HE'S BEATEN...

..THAT'LL BE THE END OF HIS RUSTY LITTLE ROVER BOYS, TOO!

I HATE TO DROP IN WITHOUT A FORMAL INVITATION, BUT IF I'M LUCKY, EMILY POST MAY NOT HEAR ABOUT IT!

SORRY TO DISAPPOINT THOSE SHARKS, BUT MY COSTUME WOULD ONLY GIVE THEM INDIGESTION, ANYWAY!

15.

OKAY, KLAUS, START BAKIN' A CAKE!! *COMPANY'S* HERE!

I DON'T SENSE ANY ROBOT *GUARDS* NEARBY! THIS IS *GREAT!* HE PROBABLY SENT THEM ALL INTO *TOWN!*

THAT MEANS IT'LL BE JUST THE *TWO* OF US FOR FUN AND GAMES!

AND, UNLESS MY RADAR SENSE CONKED OUT, MY ROYAL PLAY-MATE IS RIGHT BELOW ME *NOW!*

SO! YOU HAVE CHOSEN TO RETURN TO MY *CASTLE!* THUS, YOU HAVE SEALED YOUR *DOOM!*

HOW COME ALL YOU PROFESSIONAL BAD GUYS USE THE SAME CORNBALL DIALOGUE? DO YOU ALL STUDY FROM THE SAME MANUAL?

IF I CAN JUST DIVERT HIM LONG ENOUGH TO GET MY *HANDS* ON HIM...!

CLANG!

HOOO BOY!

PEASANT! YOU ARE HOPELESSLY *OUT-CLASSED* BY THE GREATEST HAND-TO-HAND FIGHTER IN EUROPE!

NONE CAN DEFEAT KLAUS KRUGER!

I WAS *BORN* TO RULE... *DESTINED* TO COMMAND! TODAY I AM MONARCH OF *LICHTENBAD!* TOMORROW... THE UN-SUSPECTING *WORLD* SHALL FALL TO MY ARMS, AND MY ROBOT LEGIONS!

NOT IF *I* CAN HELP IT, YOU PENNY-ANTE *ATTILA!*

16.

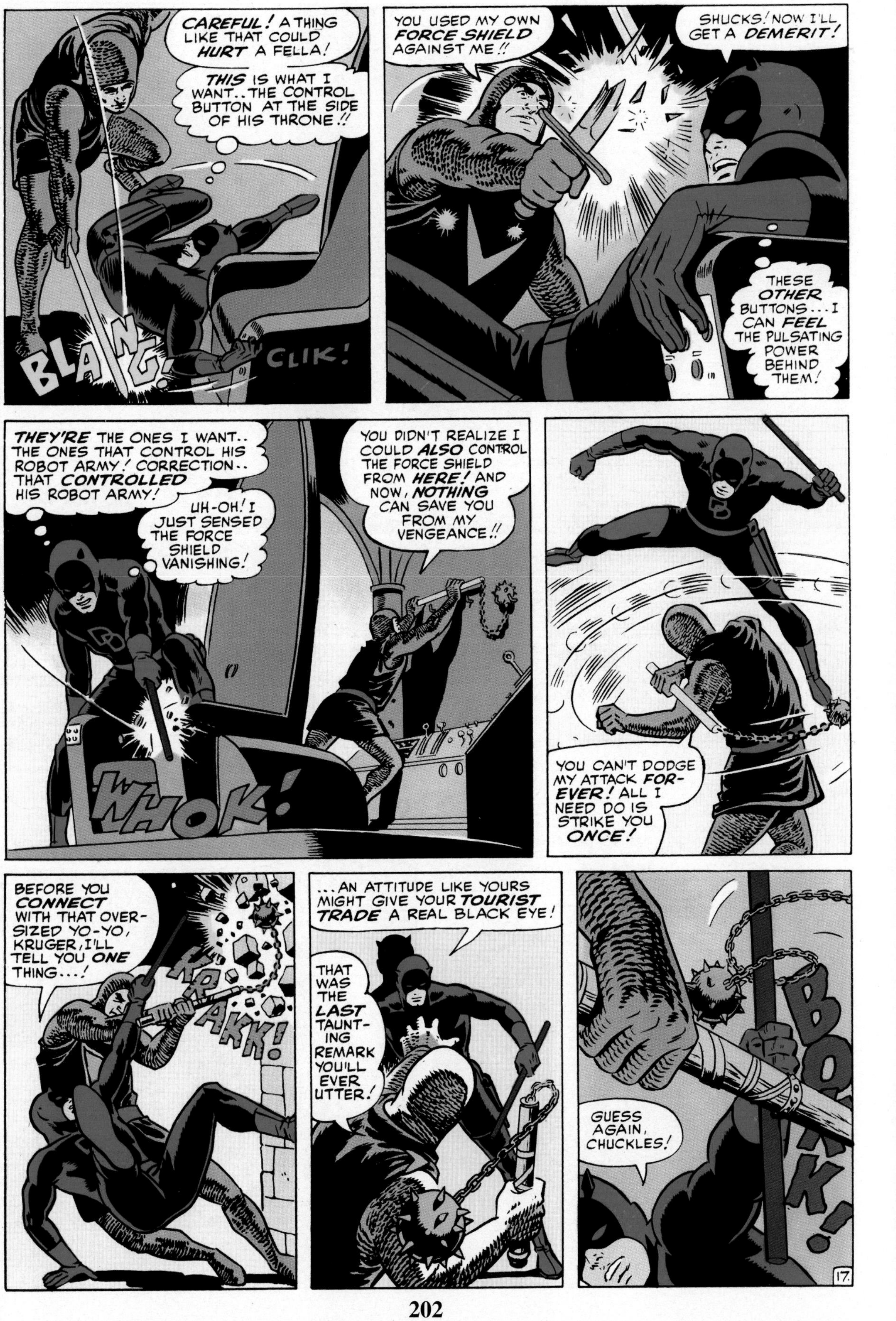
CAREFUL! A THING LIKE THAT COULD HURT A FELLA!
THIS IS WHAT I WANT.. THE CONTROL BUTTON AT THE SIDE OF HIS THRONE!!
BLANG!
CLIK!
YOU USED MY OWN FORCE SHIELD AGAINST ME!!
SHUCKS! NOW I'LL GET A DEMERIT!
THESE OTHER BUTTONS... I CAN FEEL THE PULSATING POWER BEHIND THEM!
THEY'RE THE ONES I WANT.. THE ONES THAT CONTROL HIS ROBOT ARMY! CORRECTION.. THAT CONTROLLED HIS ROBOT ARMY!
UH-OH! I JUST SENSED THE FORCE SHIELD VANISHING!
WHOK!
YOU DIDN'T REALIZE I COULD ALSO CONTROL THE FORCE SHIELD FROM HERE! AND NOW, NOTHING CAN SAVE YOU FROM MY VENGEANCE!!
YOU CAN'T DODGE MY ATTACK FOR-EVER! ALL I NEED DO IS STRIKE YOU ONCE!
BEFORE YOU CONNECT WITH THAT OVER-SIZED YO-YO, KRUGER, I'LL TELL YOU ONE THING...!
KRAKK!
...AN ATTITUDE LIKE YOURS MIGHT GIVE YOUR TOURIST TRADE A REAL BLACK EYE!
THAT WAS THE LAST TAUNT-ING REMARK YOU'LL EVER UTTER!
BOK!
GUESS AGAIN, CHUCKLES!
17

NOW, LET'S SEE HOW GOOD YOU ARE WITHOUT THAT LITTLE DOO-DOO OF YOURS, KRUGER!

ONE KARATE CHOP...THAT IS ALL IT WILL TAKE...AT THE HAND OF A MASTER SUCH AS I!

I ADMIRE YOUR ENTHUSIASM, DUKEY!! TOO BAD I CAN'T SAY AS MUCH FOR YOUR SPEED!

UNHHHH

IT'S DAREDEVIL! I READ ABOUT HIM IN AMERICA... THOUGHT HE WAS JUST A LEGEND! WHAT IS HE DOING HERE?

HEAR THAT, KRUGER?? THE SOUND OF EXPLOSIONS! THAT'S YOUR PEOPLE DESTROYING THE ROBOT ARMY WHICH I'VE DE-ACTIVATED!

I'VE WON!! YOU AND YOUR TYRANNY ARE FINISHED!

NOT YET! I STILL HAVE A TRUMP CARD...AND EVEN YOU CAN'T STOP ME FROM PLAYING IT!

THEN IT IS DAREDEVIL WHO BROKE THE ELECTRICAL CIRCUITS, FREEING ME FROM THE DUNGEON! BUT...HIS BODY IN THAT COSTUME...IT IS EXACTLY THE SAME AS THE CONFORMATION OF MATT MURDOCK'S PHYSIQUE, WHEN I EXAMINED HIM! SO THAT'S HIS SECRET!

WITHIN SECONDS, A RADIO-ACTIVE COBALT CLOUD WILL SWEEP OVER THE EARTH...!

YOU MADMAN! DON'T TOUCH THAT LEVER!

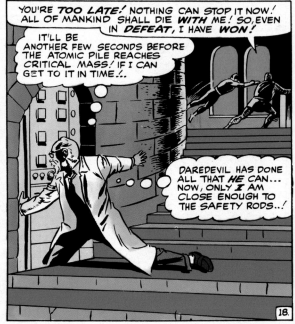

YOU'RE TOO LATE! NOTHING CAN STOP IT NOW! ALL OF MANKIND SHALL DIE WITH ME! SO, EVEN IN DEFEAT, I HAVE WON!

IT'LL BE ANOTHER FEW SECONDS BEFORE THE ATOMIC PILE REACHES CRITICAL MASS! IF I CAN GET TO IT IN TIME...!

DAREDEVIL HAS DONE ALL THAT HE CAN...NOW, ONLY I AM CLOSE ENOUGH TO THE SAFETY RODS...!

18.

I MUSTN'T BE TOO LATE!! I *MUSTN'T*!! TWO BILLION LIVES ARE AT STAKE!!

JUST ANOTHER SECOND...THAT'S ALL I *NEED*!!

IT'S *DONE*! THE RODS...ARE DISCONNECTED!! BUT...THE RADIATION.. SO INTENSE...SO AGONIZING...!

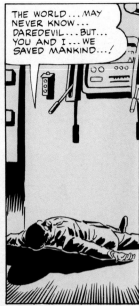

THE WORLD...MAY NEVER KNOW...DAREDEVIL...BUT...YOU AND I...WE SAVED MANKIND...!

WHILE, ON THE STAIRWAY OUTSIDE, DAREDEVIL'S SUPER-KEEN SENSES TELL HIM THAT THE DANGER IS PAST....!

SOMETHING INTERFERED WITH THE NUCLEAR PILE... THE WORLD'S *SAFE* AGAIN! SO I CAN REALLY CONCENTRATE ON THE JOB AT HAND!

WHY DO YOU CONTINUE TO *PURSUE* ME, YOU FOOL..?

BUT THEN, ATOP A HIGH, OUTSIDE PARAPET...

YOU CAN'T RUN ANY FURTHER, KLAUS! THIS IS THE END OF THE LINE!

SO! YOU WISH TO *HASTEN* YOUR ULTIMATE END! VERY WELL, I'LL BE HAPPY TO OBLIGE!

CAN YOU NOT SEE HOW *FUTILE* EVERYTHING IS? WE ARE ALL *DOOMED*... NO MATTER *WHAT*!

YOU'VE INTERFERED WITH MY PLANS FOR THE LAST TIME! UP HERE, ATOP *MY* CASTLE, I AM THE MASTER! KLAUS KRUGER CANNOT BE DEFEATED!!

KRUGER...STAY *BACK*! DON'T DO IT! YOU NEED A *DOCTOR*...A PSYCHIATRIST....IT MAY NOT BE HOPELESS!

YOU DARE SPEAK THUS TO THE MAN WHO HOLDS THE HUMAN RACE WITHIN HIS GRASP?!!

IT IS *YOU* WHO... ARHHHH! NO! NO!

STOP! I *WARN* YOU!! DON'T, KRUGER... *DON'T*..!

19.

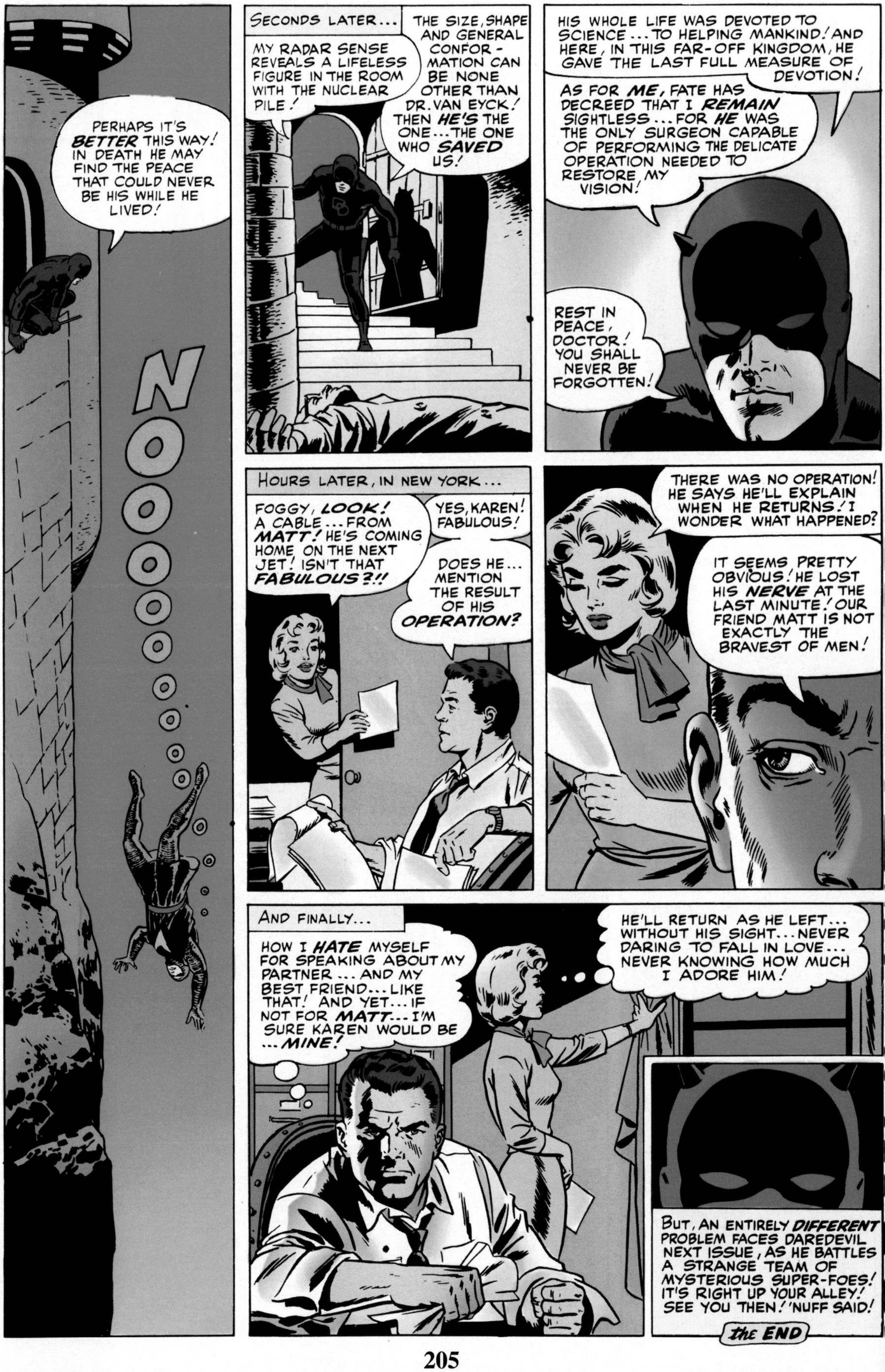
PERHAPS IT'S BETTER THIS WAY! IN DEATH HE MAY FIND THE PEACE THAT COULD NEVER BE HIS WHILE HE LIVED!
NOOOOOOOOOO
SECONDS LATER...
MY RADAR SENSE REVEALS A LIFELESS FIGURE IN THE ROOM WITH THE NUCLEAR PILE!
THE SIZE, SHAPE AND GENERAL CONFOR-MATION CAN BE NONE OTHER THAN DR. VAN EYCK! THEN HE'S THE ONE... THE ONE WHO SAVED US!
HIS WHOLE LIFE WAS DEVOTED TO SCIENCE... TO HELPING MANKIND! AND HERE, IN THIS FAR-OFF KINGDOM, HE GAVE THE LAST FULL MEASURE OF DEVOTION!
AS FOR ME, FATE HAS DECREED THAT I REMAIN SIGHTLESS... FOR HE WAS THE ONLY SURGEON CAPABLE OF PERFORMING THE DELICATE OPERATION NEEDED TO RESTORE MY VISION!
REST IN PEACE, DOCTOR! YOU SHALL NEVER BE FORGOTTEN!
HOURS LATER, IN NEW YORK...
FOGGY, LOOK! A CABLE... FROM MATT! HE'S COMING HOME ON THE NEXT JET! ISN'T THAT FABULOUS?!!
YES, KAREN! FABULOUS!
DOES HE... MENTION THE RESULT OF HIS OPERATION?
THERE WAS NO OPERATION! HE SAYS HE'LL EXPLAIN WHEN HE RETURNS! I WONDER WHAT HAPPENED?
IT SEEMS PRETTY OBVIOUS! HE LOST HIS NERVE AT THE LAST MINUTE! OUR FRIEND MATT IS NOT EXACTLY THE BRAVEST OF MEN!
AND FINALLY...
HOW I HATE MYSELF FOR SPEAKING ABOUT MY PARTNER... AND MY BEST FRIEND... LIKE THAT! AND YET... IF NOT FOR MATT... I'M SURE KAREN WOULD BE ...MINE!
HE'LL RETURN AS HE LEFT... WITHOUT HIS SIGHT... NEVER DARING TO FALL IN LOVE... NEVER KNOWING HOW MUCH I ADORE HIM!
BUT, AN ENTIRELY DIFFERENT PROBLEM FACES DAREDEVIL NEXT ISSUE, AS HE BATTLES A STRANGE TEAM OF MYSTERIOUS SUPER-FOES! IT'S RIGHT UP YOUR ALLEY! SEE YOU THEN! 'NUFF SAID!
the END

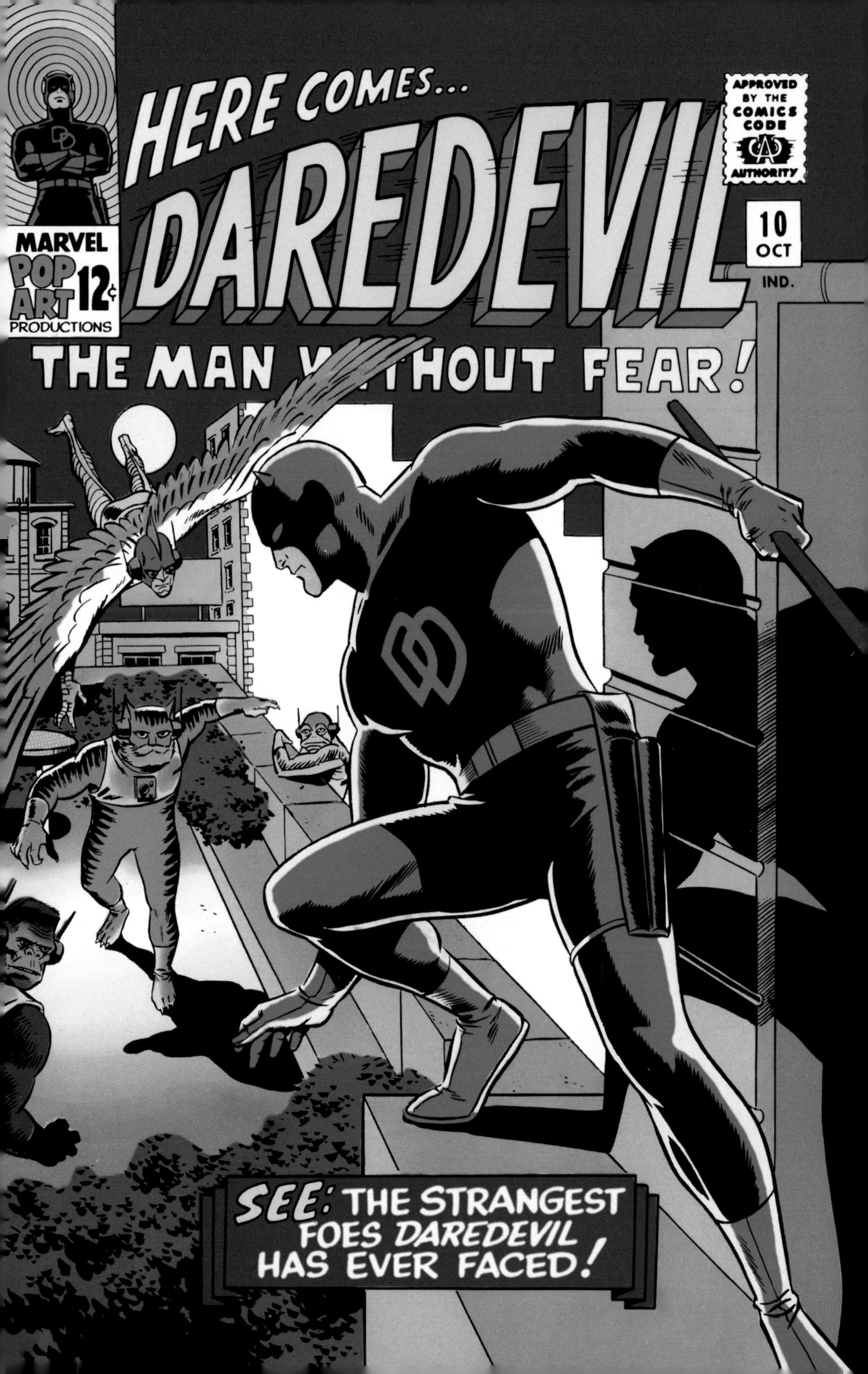
HERE COMES...
DAREDEVIL
THE MAN WITHOUT FEAR!
MARVEL POP ART PRODUCTIONS 12¢
APPROVED BY THE COMICS CODE AUTHORITY
10 OCT
IND.
SEE: THE STRANGEST FOES DAREDEVIL HAS EVER FACED!

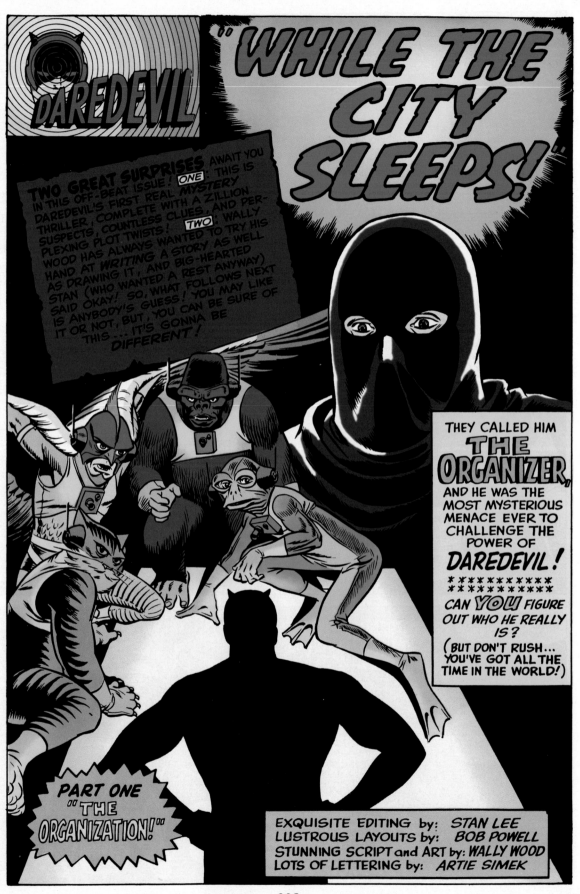

DAREDEVIL

"WHILE THE CITY SLEEPS!"

TWO GREAT SURPRISES AWAIT YOU IN THIS OFF-BEAT ISSUE! ONE: THIS IS DAREDEVIL'S FIRST REAL MYSTERY THRILLER, COMPLETE WITH A ZILLION SUSPECTS, COUNTLESS CLUES, AND PERPLEXING PLOT TWISTS! TWO: WALLY WOOD HAS ALWAYS WANTED TO TRY HIS HAND AT WRITING A STORY AS WELL AS DRAWING IT, AND BIG-HEARTED STAN (WHO WANTED A REST ANYWAY) SAID OKAY! SO, WHAT FOLLOWS NEXT IS ANYBODY'S GUESS! YOU MAY LIKE IT OR NOT, BUT, YOU CAN BE SURE OF THIS... IT'S GONNA BE DIFFERENT!

THEY CALLED HIM THE ORGANIZER, AND HE WAS THE MOST MYSTERIOUS MENACE EVER TO CHALLENGE THE POWER OF DAREDEVIL!
* * * * * * * * * *
* * * * * * * * * *
CAN YOU FIGURE OUT WHO HE REALLY IS?
(BUT DON'T RUSH... YOU'VE GOT ALL THE TIME IN THE WORLD!)

PART ONE "THE ORGANIZATION!"

EXQUISITE EDITING by: STAN LEE
LUSTROUS LAYOUTS by: BOB POWELL
STUNNING SCRIPT and ART by: WALLY WOOD
LOTS OF LETTERING by: ARTIE SIMEK

As DARKNESS SETTLES OVER THE EAST COAST...

A HELICOPTER! THERE'S SOMETHING FISHY GOING ON... I'D BETTER CALL THE WARDEN...

CAT MAN TO ORGANIZER... FEDERAL PRISON IN SIGHT... DO YOU READ ME? OVER...

HEY, MILT! TURN THE SPOTLIGHT ON THAT BIRD... HE'S UP TO SOMETHING!

THIS IS THE ORGANIZER... PROCEED WITH OPERATION BLACKOUT! OVER...

ROGER! AM RELEASING BLACKOUT BOMB NOW!

IT'S DROPPED SOME KIND OF GADGET BY PARACHUTE, WARDEN! *WARDEN?* WHY DON'T YOU *ANSWER?*

WHRRRRR

The "BOMB" DRIFTS DOWN INTO THE PRISON COURTYARD, EMITTING AN ELECTRONIC IMPULSE WHICH DISRUPTS EVERY CIRCUIT IN THE AREA...

R R R

HEY! THE LIGHTS! WHAT...?!

RRRRR

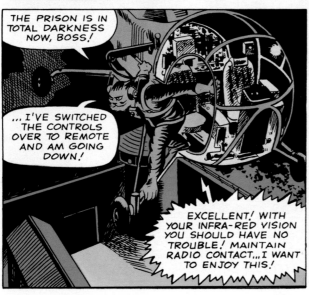

THE PRISON IS IN TOTAL DARKNESS NOW, BOSS!

... I'VE SWITCHED THE CONTROLS OVER TO REMOTE AND AM GOING DOWN!

EXCELLENT! WITH YOUR INFRA-RED VISION YOU SHOULD HAVE NO TROUBLE! MAINTAIN RADIO CONTACT... I WANT TO ENJOY THIS!

WHAT HAPPENED? CHECK THE FUSES!

SOME-BODY FIND A FLASH-LIGHT!

-! OOF!- I CAN'T SEE!

2

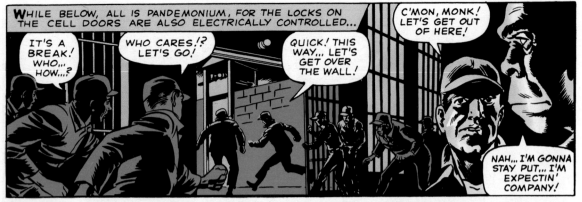

WHILE BELOW, ALL IS PANDEMONIUM, FOR THE LOCKS ON THE CELL DOORS ARE ALSO ELECTRICALLY CONTROLLED...

IT'S A BREAK! WHO...? HOW...?

WHO CARES!? LET'S GO!

QUICK! THIS WAY... LET'S GET OVER THE WALL!

C'MON, MONK! LET'S GET OUT OF HERE!

NAH... I'M GONNA STAY PUT... I'M EXPECTIN' COMPANY!

IN THE CONFUSION, THE UNCANNY "CAT-MAN" LOWERS HIMSELF INTO THE PRISON...

...GOT TO ADJUST MY "CAT EYES"... THERE! LIKE HIGH NOON!

STOP OR I'LL SHOOT!

WHO YOU TRYIN' TO KID?

CHICAGO, HERE I COME!

NO TIME TO WASTE... THIS IS IT! CELL BLOCK SEVEN...

NOW TO FIND MY MAN BEFORE THE 'BLACKOUT BOMB' RUNS OUT OF JUICE!

MONK KEEFER? COME WITH ME... THE ORGANIZER WANTS YOU!

YOU DON'T HAVE TO ASK ME TWICE... I BEEN GOIN' STIR-HAPPY WAITIN' FOR YOU!

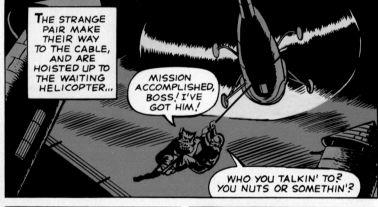

THE STRANGE PAIR MAKE THEIR WAY TO THE CABLE, AND ARE HOISTED UP TO THE WAITING HELICOPTER...

MISSION ACCOMPLISHED, BOSS! I'VE GOT HIM!

WHO YOU TALKIN' TO? YOU NUTS OR SOMETHIN'?

MINUTES LATER, ORDER IS RESTORED IN THE PRISON, AND A HEAD COUNT IS BEGUN...

...KEEFER? KEEFER'S MISSING!

HEAD FOR THE MAIN GATE!

2771

7614

DAILY SUN

FINAL

DARING PRISON BREAK

PUBLIC ENEMY ESCAPES

...l Using Remote-Control and Blackout Device From Prison

WARDEN REPORTS COMMENT

...APPARENTLY, THE WHOLE INCREDIBLE PLAN WAS PUT INTO EFFECT JUST TO GET THIS ONE MAN OUT OF PRISON...

3

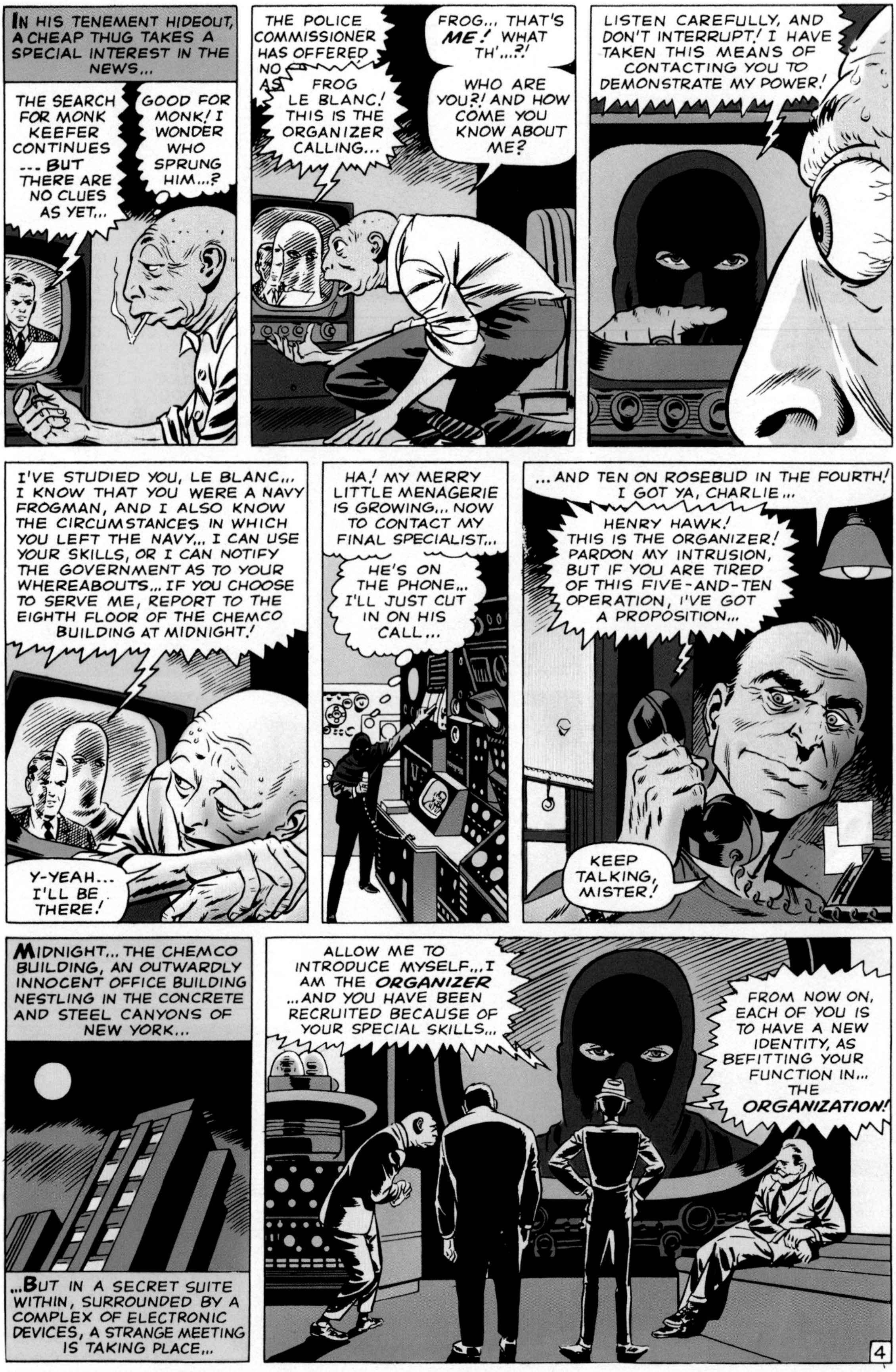
IN HIS TENEMENT HIDEOUT, A CHEAP THUG TAKES A SPECIAL INTEREST IN THE NEWS...
THE SEARCH FOR MONK KEEFER CONTINUES --- BUT THERE ARE NO CLUES AS YET...
GOOD FOR MONK! I WONDER WHO SPRUNG HIM...?
THE POLICE COMMISSIONER HAS OFFERED NO
FROG LE BLANC! THIS IS THE ORGANIZER CALLING...
FROG... THAT'S ME! WHAT TH'...?!
WHO ARE YOU?! AND HOW COME YOU KNOW ABOUT ME?
LISTEN CAREFULLY, AND DON'T INTERRUPT! I HAVE TAKEN THIS MEANS OF CONTACTING YOU TO DEMONSTRATE MY POWER!
I'VE STUDIED YOU, LE BLANC... I KNOW THAT YOU WERE A NAVY FROGMAN, AND I ALSO KNOW THE CIRCUMSTANCES IN WHICH YOU LEFT THE NAVY... I CAN USE YOUR SKILLS, OR I CAN NOTIFY THE GOVERNMENT AS TO YOUR WHEREABOUTS... IF YOU CHOOSE TO SERVE ME, REPORT TO THE EIGHTH FLOOR OF THE CHEMCO BUILDING AT MIDNIGHT!
Y-YEAH... I'LL BE THERE!
HA! MY MERRY LITTLE MENAGERIE IS GROWING... NOW TO CONTACT MY FINAL SPECIALIST...
HE'S ON THE PHONE... I'LL JUST CUT IN ON HIS CALL...
...AND TEN ON ROSEBUD IN THE FOURTH! I GOT YA, CHARLIE...
HENRY HAWK! THIS IS THE ORGANIZER! PARDON MY INTRUSION, BUT IF YOU ARE TIRED OF THIS FIVE-AND-TEN OPERATION, I'VE GOT A PROPOSITION...
KEEP TALKING, MISTER!
MIDNIGHT... THE CHEMCO BUILDING, AN OUTWARDLY INNOCENT OFFICE BUILDING NESTLING IN THE CONCRETE AND STEEL CANYONS OF NEW YORK...
...BUT IN A SECRET SUITE WITHIN, SURROUNDED BY A COMPLEX OF ELECTRONIC DEVICES, A STRANGE MEETING IS TAKING PLACE...
ALLOW ME TO INTRODUCE MYSELF... I AM THE ORGANIZER ...AND YOU HAVE BEEN RECRUITED BECAUSE OF YOUR SPECIAL SKILLS...
FROM NOW ON, EACH OF YOU IS TO HAVE A NEW IDENTITY, AS BEFITTING YOUR FUNCTION IN... THE ORGANIZATION!
4

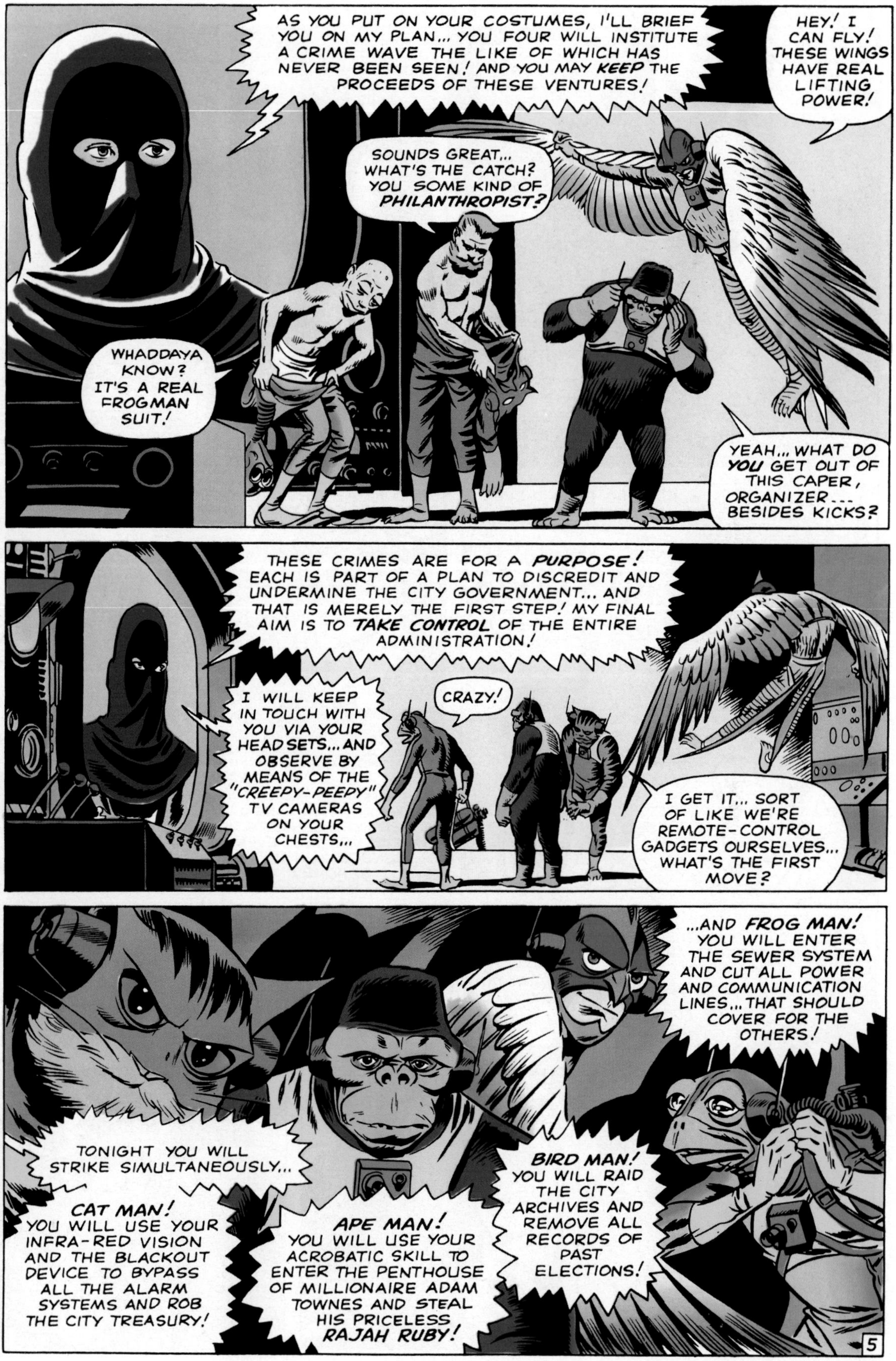
AS YOU PUT ON YOUR COSTUMES, I'LL BRIEF YOU ON MY PLAN... YOU FOUR WILL INSTITUTE A CRIME WAVE THE LIKE OF WHICH HAS NEVER BEEN SEEN! AND YOU MAY KEEP THE PROCEEDS OF THESE VENTURES!
HEY! I CAN FLY! THESE WINGS HAVE REAL LIFTING POWER!
SOUNDS GREAT... WHAT'S THE CATCH? YOU SOME KIND OF PHILANTHROPIST?
WHADDAYA KNOW? IT'S A REAL FROGMAN SUIT!
YEAH... WHAT DO YOU GET OUT OF THIS CAPER, ORGANIZER... BESIDES KICKS?
THESE CRIMES ARE FOR A PURPOSE! EACH IS PART OF A PLAN TO DISCREDIT AND UNDERMINE THE CITY GOVERNMENT... AND THAT IS MERELY THE FIRST STEP! MY FINAL AIM IS TO TAKE CONTROL OF THE ENTIRE ADMINISTRATION!
I WILL KEEP IN TOUCH WITH YOU VIA YOUR HEAD SETS... AND OBSERVE BY MEANS OF THE "CREEPY-PEEPY" TV CAMERAS ON YOUR CHESTS...
CRAZY!
I GET IT... SORT OF LIKE WE'RE REMOTE-CONTROL GADGETS OURSELVES... WHAT'S THE FIRST MOVE?
TONIGHT YOU WILL STRIKE SIMULTANEOUSLY...
CAT MAN! YOU WILL USE YOUR INFRA-RED VISION AND THE BLACKOUT DEVICE TO BYPASS ALL THE ALARM SYSTEMS AND ROB THE CITY TREASURY!
APE MAN! YOU WILL USE YOUR ACROBATIC SKILL TO ENTER THE PENTHOUSE OF MILLIONAIRE ADAM TOWNES AND STEAL HIS PRICELESS RAJAH RUBY!
BIRD MAN! YOU WILL RAID THE CITY ARCHIVES AND REMOVE ALL RECORDS OF PAST ELECTIONS!
...AND FROG MAN! YOU WILL ENTER THE SEWER SYSTEM AND CUT ALL POWER AND COMMUNICATION LINES... THAT SHOULD COVER FOR THE OTHERS!
5

HA! WHAT A CINCH! I CAN DO *ANYTHING* IN THIS OUTFIT!

THE *ORGANIZER* IS A FOOL TO LET US KEEP THIS LOOT!

WELL DONE, CAT MAN!

I GOT THE JEWEL, BOSS! IT WAS A CINCH!

GOOD! KEEP TO THE ROOF-TOPS, APE MAN!

ARE YOU GETTING THIS AERIAL VIEW ON YOUR TV, CHIEF?

YES,... VERY STRIKING... DID YOU GET THE RECORDS?

THE BOSS IS A REAL *WEIRDO*... BUT I'LL PLAY ALONG FOR THE LOOT!

MISSION ACCOMPLISHED, ORGANIZER!

EXCELLENT! THIS SHOULD DISCREDIT THE AUTHORITIES VERY NICELY!

IN CASE YOU WERE WONDERING IF WE'D EVER GET AROUND TO MATT MURDOCK, HERE HE IS, NEXT MORNING...

Daily Chronicle
FINAL!
CRIME WAVE HITS CITY!

LISTEN TO THIS, MATT...

..."IN THE WORST OUTBREAK OF LAWLESSNESS IN THE CITY'S HISTORY, THE POLICE STILL HAVE NO CLUES"...

DAREDEVIL WILL HAVE TO LOOK INTO THIS!

SOMEONE AT THE DOOR! IT'S *FOGGY!*

GOOD MORNING, YOU CHARMING PEOPLE! WHAT AN EXCELLENT MORNING IT IS!

FOGGY... WHAT IS IT? YOU'RE FRISKY AS A PUPPY!

FOGGY SEEMS MORE THAN *CHEERFUL*... HE'S RADIATING A SENSE OF *CONFIDENCE* I'VE NEVER SENSED IN HIM BEFORE!

YOU ARE LOOKING AT THE NEXT *D.A.* OF THIS CITY! THE REFORM PARTY HAS OFFERED *ME* THEIR NOMINATION!

OH, FOGGY! THAT'S *WONDERFUL!*

ER... THAT'S GREAT, FOGGY... BUT ARE YOU SURE... I MEAN, THEY COULD BE *USING* YOU...

WHAT DO YOU *KNOW* ABOUT THIS NEW THIRD PARTY?

ARE *YOU* SURE YOU AREN'T *JEALOUS*, MATT? HERE I GET A CHANCE TO DO SOMETHING ON MY OWN...

NO MATTER! I'VE MADE UP MY MIND, AND I'M GOING TO *ACCEPT*...

BY THE WAY, THERE'S GOING TO BE A *YACHT PARTY* IN MY HONOR THIS AFTERNOON... YOU MAY COME IF YOU LIKE!

OF COURSE, FOGGY... WOULDN'T MISS IT FOR THE WORLD...

6

LATER, AT THE YACHT BASIN...

WHAT A GALA AFFAIR, MATT! IT LOOKS LIKE THE WHOLE SOCIAL REGISTER IS HERE!

AND YET, BENEATH IT ALL, I SENSE SOMETHING WRONG... AN UNDERTONE OF MENACE!

MATT MURDOCK! I DON'T KNOW IF YOU REMEMBER ME... ABNER JONAS! I'M YOUR HOST FOR THIS JUNKET!

OF COURSE, MR. JONAS! WHO WOULDN'T REMEMBER THE REFORM PARTY'S CANDIDATE FOR MAYOR!

THERE YOU ARE, MATT... I'D LIKE YOU TO MEET OUR CANDIDATE FOR BOROUGH PRESIDENT, BERNARD HARRIS!

GLAD TO HAVE YOU ABOARD, MATT! GUESS YOU'RE PRETTY PROUD OF FOGGY, EH?

THEY'RE ALL PROMINENT, WEALTHY MEN... WHY DO I SENSE DANGER?

I DIDN'T CATCH YOUR NAME, SON... I'M MILTON MONROE, THE REFORM PARTY'S CANDIDATE FOR ASSEMBLYMAN... YOU MAY CALL ME MILT!

I'M NOT TOO GOOD AT NAMES! HOPE I CAN REMEMBER THEM ALL!

NAME'S MURDOCK, SIR, I'M FOGGY'S PARTNER!

FOGGY, I'VE GOT A SURPRISE FOR YOU... AN OLD FRIEND OF YOURS... DO YOU REMEMBER?

HE WOULDN'T REMEMBER LITTLE OL' ME, MR. JONAS... IT'S SO LONG AGO!

GEE, MR. JONAS... I THINK-- I MEAN I'D SURE LIKE TO... THAT IS, HEL-LO!

I'LL GIVE YOU A HINT... FILLMORE JUNIOR HIGH!

DEBORAH! IT'S DEBORAH HARRIS! HOW YOU'VE GROWN!

RIGHT THE FIRST TIME! I'VE NEVER FORGOTTEN YOU, FOGGY!

AHEM!

OH, KAREN... MEET MY OLD SCHOOL SWEETHEART--DEB AND I HAD A TERRIFIC CRUSH WHEN WE WERE KIDS...

♪ HOW SWEET ♪

♪ THANK YOU, DEAR! ♪

7

THAT EVENING, AS THE YACHT TURNS BACK TOWARD THE HARBOR.

WHY DID KAREN REACT THE WAY SHE DID? IS SHE IN LOVE WITH FOGGY?

FOGGY, DO YOU REMEMBER THE FIRST TIME WE MET? I DO...

AND WHY IS DEBORAH MAKING SUCH A BIG PLAY FOR FOGGY... IS THERE SOME ULTERIOR MOTIVE?

WHAT'S THAT?! MY RADAR HEARING HAS PICKED UP A RADIO MESSAGE! IT'S BEING TRANSMITTED FROM THIS YACHT!

ORGANIZER TO FROG MAN...THE TIME HAS COME FOR OUR NEXT MOVE...

THE YACHT IS IN YOUR AREA NOW, SO ANY TIME YOU'RE READY, FIRE AWAY!

THIS MEANS ONE OF THE MEMBERS OF THE REFORM PARTY ITSELF IS THE ORGANIZER!

AND HE'S NOW DIRECTING AN ATTACK ON ONE OF US!

OUT OF DARKNESS AND THE DEEP, IN ANSWER TO THE SIGNAL, A GROTESQUE FIGURE BREAKS THE SURFACE...

GATHER 'ROUND, FRIENDS... A TOAST TO FOGGY NELSON!

I CAN SENSE HIM MOVING TOWARD US IN THE WATER... BUT WHAT CAN I DO?!

THE BOOM! THIS SHOULD DO IT... NOW!!

OOPS! I TRIPPED!

LOOK OUT! HEADS UP!

BLAST IT! THAT SWINGING BOOM DEFLECTED MY SPEAR..!

BLANG!

SO FAR SO GOOD! NOW TO DROP OVERBOARD!

QUICKLY, MATT SHEDS HIS OUTER GARMENTS, AND GIVES CHASE AS... THE MAN WITHOUT FEAR!

DAREDEVIL!!

THERE HE IS -- I GUESS UNDERWATER MY "RADAR" BECOMES "SONAR"!

8

215

HEY, BOSS! I DIDN'T FIGURE ON PLAYING TAG WITH *DAREDEVIL!* WHAT'LL I DO? OVER...

I'M GAINING ON HIM-- THE ORGANIZER WON'T HELP HIM *NOW!*

THE MAN WITHOUT FEAR SWIFTLY CLOSES THE GAP, AND...

CALLING ORGANIZER-- COME IN-- COME--

GOT YOU, MY MURDEROUS LITTLE FRIEND!

HA! NOW I'VE GOT A LITTLE SURPRISE...

HE'S AS HARD TO HOLD AS A WET BAR OF SOAP!

...FOR YOU!

HAPPY CONCUSSION!

SSSS

...CAN'T GET OUT OF RANGE OF THE BLAST-- ->OHH!<--

BA- ROOM!

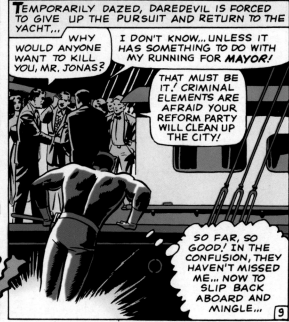

TEMPORARILY DAZED, DAREDEVIL IS FORCED TO GIVE UP THE PURSUIT AND RETURN TO THE YACHT...

WHY WOULD ANYONE WANT TO KILL YOU, MR. JONAS?

I DON'T KNOW... UNLESS IT HAS SOMETHING TO DO WITH MY RUNNING FOR *MAYOR!*

THAT MUST BE IT! CRIMINAL ELEMENTS ARE AFRAID YOUR REFORM PARTY WILL CLEAN UP THE CITY!

SO FAR, SO GOOD! IN THE CONFUSION, THEY HAVEN'T MISSED ME... NOW TO SLIP BACK ABOARD AND MINGLE...

9

PENT HOUSE

AIR LOCK CHAMBERS

MAIN CONTROL

EQUIPMENT ROOM

HELICOPTER HANGAR

ARSENAL

TRANSMITTER

LIVING QUARTERS

OFFICES

MAIN LOBBY

THE FROG MAN RETURNS TO THE HEADQUARTERS OF THE ORGANIZATION BY WAY OF AN UNDERGROUND WATER TUNNEL AND SHAFT! BENEATH THE FACADE OF THE CHEMCO BUILDING IS A VERITABLE FORTRESS, A NETWORK OF HIGHLY SOPHISTICATED ELECTRIC SYSTEMS AND COMMUNICATIONS...

FROGGY'S BACK! HOW DID IT GO? YOU'RE WAY BEHIND SCHEDULE...

YEAH-- WHAT HAPPENED? YOU LOOK BEAT!

I RAN INTO DAREDEVIL...

...HAD TO USE A GRENADE... IT NEARLY FINISHED ME, TOO!

LATER...

...YOU DID WELL, FROG! THE INTERFERENCE BY DAREDEVIL DIDN'T ALTER THE EFFECT OF AN ATTACK ON THE REFORM PARTY, AS LONG AS YOU WERE ABLE TO HANDLE HIM...

HOWEVER, IF HE CONTINUES TO PROVE TROUBLE- SOME, WE MAY HAVE TO FIND A **PERMANENT** SOLUTION FOR HIM!

WATER-FILLED ELEVATOR SHAFT

FILL

WATER LEVEL

FROG MAN

BEDROCK

WATER LOCK

TUNNEL TO WATERFRONT

...NOW WE MUST PRESS ON WITH MY PLAN! WE MUST GIVE THE ILLUSION OF AN ENDLESS ATTACK DIRECTED AGAINST THE REFORM PARTY! FIRST WE WILL ROB THEIR CAMPAIGN FUNDS,.. THAT WILL BE **YOUR** JOB, BIRD!

...NOW GO! AND DO NOT FAIL ME!

YOU MEAN **NOW**-- IN BROAD DAYLIGHT?

IF IT CAN BE **DONE**, HE'S THE ONE TO **DO** IT!

HOURS LATER, AT THE DOWNTOWN CAMPAIGN HEADQUARTERS OF THE REFORM PARTY...

GOT THE DOUGH ...LOOKS LIKE A CLEAN GET- AWAY.

STOP HIM--

HE...HE'S **FLYING OFF**... WITH THE PARTY'S MONEY!!

POLICE! CALL THE POLICE!

VOTE!

BUT, ON A NEARBY ROOFTOP...

I HAD A HUNCH THERE WOULD BE AN ATTEMPT LIKE THIS,.. GOOD THING I STAKED-OUT THE PLACE!

NOW TO FIND OUT IF I CAN COPE WITH A CROOK WHO CAN **FLY!**

10

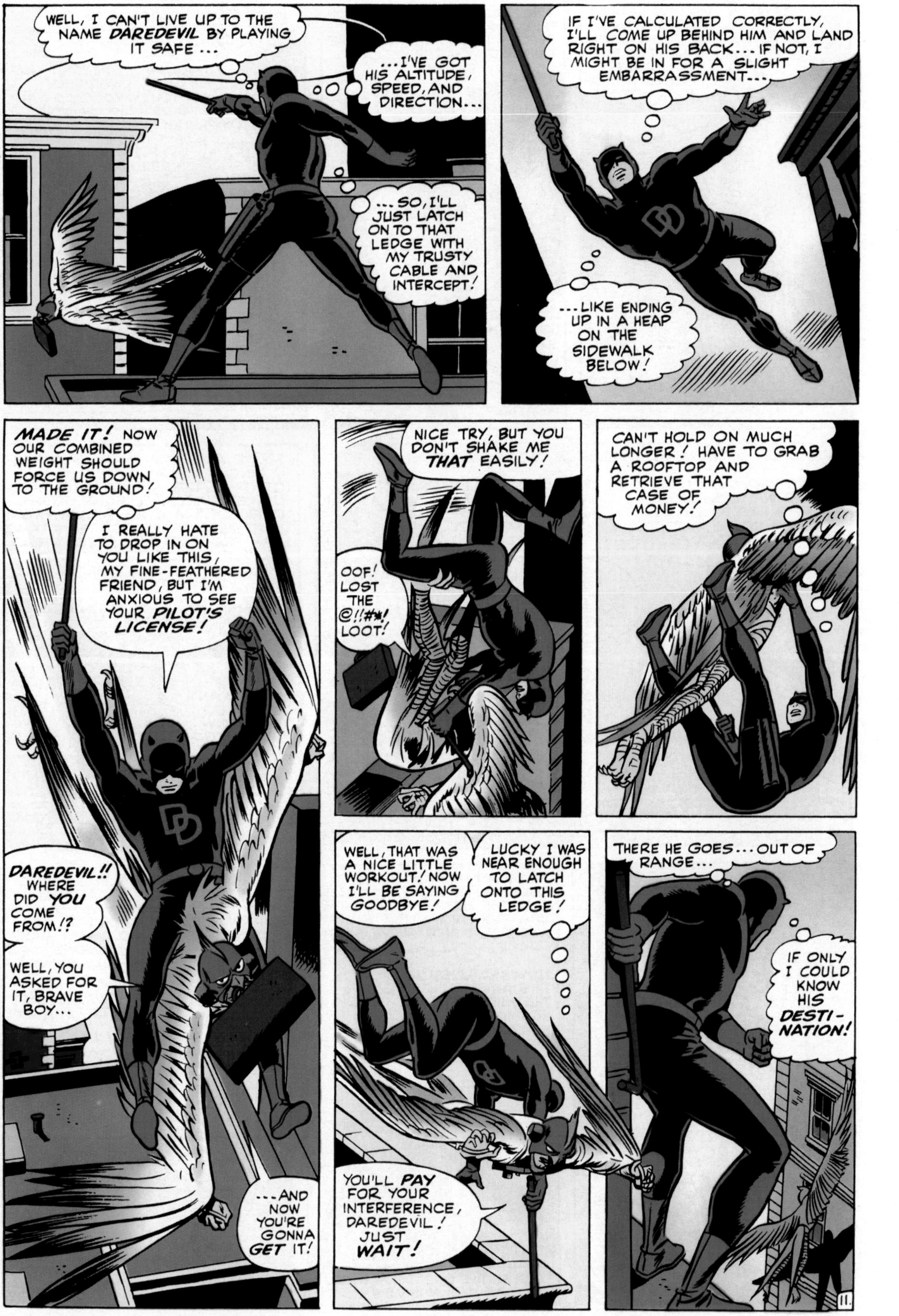

WELL, I CAN'T LIVE UP TO THE NAME DAREDEVIL BY PLAYING IT SAFE...
...I'VE GOT HIS ALTITUDE, SPEED, AND DIRECTION...
...SO, I'LL JUST LATCH ON TO THAT LEDGE WITH MY TRUSTY CABLE AND INTERCEPT!
IF I'VE CALCULATED CORRECTLY, I'LL COME UP BEHIND HIM AND LAND RIGHT ON HIS BACK... IF NOT, I MIGHT BE IN FOR A SLIGHT EMBARRASSMENT...
...LIKE ENDING UP IN A HEAP ON THE SIDEWALK BELOW!
MADE IT! NOW OUR COMBINED WEIGHT SHOULD FORCE US DOWN TO THE GROUND!
I REALLY HATE TO DROP IN ON YOU LIKE THIS, MY FINE-FEATHERED FRIEND, BUT I'M ANXIOUS TO SEE YOUR PILOT'S LICENSE!
DAREDEVIL!! WHERE DID YOU COME FROM!?
WELL, YOU ASKED FOR IT, BRAVE BOY...
...AND NOW YOU'RE GONNA GET IT!
NICE TRY, BUT YOU DON'T SHAKE ME THAT EASILY!
OOF! LOST THE @!!#*! LOOT!
CAN'T HOLD ON MUCH LONGER! HAVE TO GRAB A ROOFTOP AND RETRIEVE THAT CASE OF MONEY!
WELL, THAT WAS A NICE LITTLE WORKOUT! NOW I'LL BE SAYING GOODBYE!
LUCKY I WAS NEAR ENOUGH TO LATCH ONTO THIS LEDGE!
YOU'LL PAY FOR YOUR INTERFERENCE, DAREDEVIL! JUST WAIT!
THERE HE GOES... OUT OF RANGE...
IF ONLY I COULD KNOW HIS DESTI-NATION!
11.

THAT BIRD-MAN IS AN OPPONENT WORTH TAKING SERIOUSLY...

WELL, AT LEAST I SALVAGED THE CAMPAIGN FUNDS... NEVER LET IT BE SAID DAREDEVIL PARTED WITH A BUCK WITHOUT A STRUGGLE!

NOW, SINCE THE "ORGANIZER" OF THIS ZOO IS A MEMBER OF THE REFORM PARTY, WHY WOULD HE HAVE HIS MOB ROB HIS OWN FUNDS? ...

..AND HOW DOES FOGGY FIT IN? THEY CAN'T USE HIM FOR ANY DIRTY WORK...

I'D BETTER GET BACK TO THE OFFICE... FOGGY'S PROBABLY GETTING IMPATIENT...

BUT AS THE SIGHTLESS GLADIATOR RETURNS TO THE LAW FIRM OF NELSON AND MURDOCK, HE FINDS ...

OH, FOGGY... YOU'RE A DEAR, SWEET BOY TO CALL! AND YOU MUST COME TO MY PARTY ON FRIDAY!

I NEEDN'T HAVE WORRIED! FOGGY'S MIND IS ON OTHER THINGS...

IT'LL BE A PLEASURE, DEBORAH!

MEANWHILE, AT THE HEADQUARTERS OF THE ORGANIZATION...

I DON'T KNOW HOW, BUT HE WAS WAITING FOR ME! AS SOON AS I TOOK OFF WITH THE DOUGH, DAREDEVIL WAS ON MY BACK!

THAT DOES IT! BEFORE WE PROCEED WITH ANOTHER STEP, WE MUST ELIMINATE DAREDEVIL!

YEAH... HOW? HE DON'T ELIMINATE SO EASY...I STILL GOT LUMPS!

YOU GOT A PLAN, BOSS?

I HAVE A DOUBLE-PURPOSE SCHEME IN MIND... A PLAN THAT WILL CONTINUE THE "CRIME WAVE" AND CAUSE DAREDEVIL SOME SLIGHT DIFFICULTY WITH THE POLICE! WITH THAT MEDDLER OUT OF THE WAY, WE CAN PROCEED FULL SPEED AHEAD ON OUR MAJOR EFFORT...TO INFLUENCE THE OUTCOME OF THE ELECTION!

NOW, HERE'S WHAT I WANT YOU TO DO... TOMORROW YOU WILL GO INTO THE CHEMICAL EXCHANGE BANK IN CIVILIAN CLOTHES...

THE NEXT AFTERNOON, WE FIND THE MAN WITHOUT FEAR KEEPING THE VIGIL IN DOWNTOWN NEW YORK...

I'M GLAD FOGGY IS PREOCCUPIED WITH HIS POLITICAL CAREER AND THAT GIRL...

IT ENABLES ME TO PUT IN A DOUBLE SHIFT AS DAREDEVIL THESE DAYS!

I HAVE A FEELING I'LL NEED FREEDOM OF MOVEMENT NOW THAT THE ELECTION IS COMING UP...THE ORGANIZER MUST MAKE ANOTHER MOVE SOON...

NOW I'LL JUST CHECK THIS AREA...I CAN COVER THE WHOLE CITY IN NO TIME WITH MY SNOOPER-SCOPE...*

*A SENSITIVE DIRECTIONAL MICRO-PHONE, AS SHOWN IN D.D. #9...STAN.

THE USUAL MISCELLANEOUS BABEL OF SOUND COMES IN... AND THEN...!

BUT OFFICER.... I DIDN'T SEE THE SIGN!

STICK WITH ME, KID... WE'LL MAKE MILLIONS!

CALL THE POLICE! GET HELP! HURRY!

THERE'S SOMETHING! IT SEEMS TO BE IN THE NEXT BLOCK!

12.

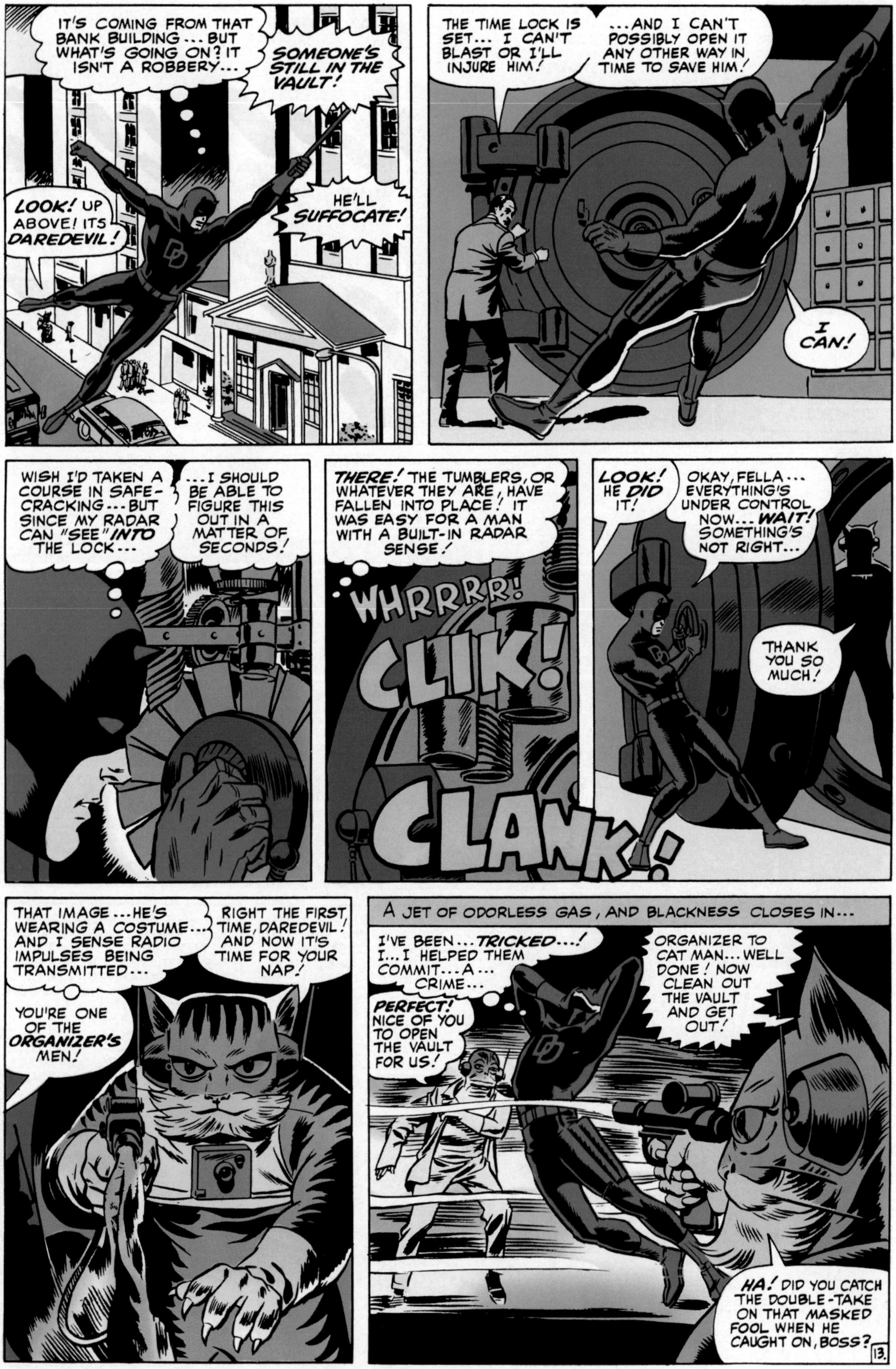
IT'S COMING FROM THAT BANK BUILDING... BUT WHAT'S GOING ON? IT ISN'T A ROBBERY...
SOMEONE'S STILL IN THE VAULT!
LOOK! UP ABOVE! ITS DAREDEVIL!
HE'LL SUFFOCATE!
THE TIME LOCK IS SET... I CAN'T BLAST OR I'LL INJURE HIM!
...AND I CAN'T POSSIBLY OPEN IT ANY OTHER WAY IN TIME TO SAVE HIM!
I CAN!
WISH I'D TAKEN A COURSE IN SAFE-CRACKING... BUT SINCE MY RADAR CAN "SEE" INTO THE LOCK...
...I SHOULD BE ABLE TO FIGURE THIS OUT IN A MATTER OF SECONDS!
THERE! THE TUMBLERS, OR WHATEVER THEY ARE, HAVE FALLEN INTO PLACE! IT WAS EASY FOR A MAN WITH A BUILT-IN RADAR SENSE!
WHRRRR!
CLIK!
CLANK!
LOOK! HE DID IT!
OKAY, FELLA... EVERYTHING'S UNDER CONTROL NOW... WAIT! SOMETHING'S NOT RIGHT...
THANK YOU SO MUCH!
THAT IMAGE... HE'S WEARING A COSTUME... AND I SENSE RADIO IMPULSES BEING TRANSMITTED...
RIGHT THE FIRST TIME, DAREDEVIL! AND NOW IT'S TIME FOR YOUR NAP!
YOU'RE ONE OF THE ORGANIZER'S MEN!
A JET OF ODORLESS GAS, AND BLACKNESS CLOSES IN...
I'VE BEEN... TRICKED...! I... I HELPED THEM COMMIT... A... CRIME...
ORGANIZER TO CAT MAN... WELL DONE! NOW CLEAN OUT THE VAULT AND GET OUT!
PERFECT! NICE OF YOU TO OPEN THE VAULT FOR US!
HA! DID YOU CATCH THE DOUBLE-TAKE ON THAT MASKED FOOL WHEN HE CAUGHT ON, BOSS?
13.

THIS IS INDEED GRATIFYING... MY MOST IRKSOME OPPONENT RENDERED HELPLESS BY A SIMPLE RUSE... BY THE TIME HE RECOVERS, HE'LL BE IN CUSTODY!

ORGANIZER TO BIRD MAN! PICK UP LOOT FROM CAT MAN! APE MAN... STAND BY WITH GETAWAY HELICOPTER!

HOW EASY IT IS FOR ME TO DEFEAT MY ENEMIES BY REMOTE CONTROL!

BUT THE ORGANIZER RECKONS WITHOUT THE REMARKABLE RECUPERATIVE POWERS OF HIS BLIND NEMESIS...

WHERE...? OH, NOW I REMEMBER! I'VE MUFFED IT AGAIN! SO FAR I'VE GOT A PERFECT SCORE!

EEEE...EEAWRRI

POLICE! I'VE GOT TO GET OUT OF HERE...

I'LL NEVER BE ABLE TO CONVINCE THEM THAT I WASN'T PART OF THAT PLOT... SO...

IT'S DARE-DEVIL!!

HE OPENED THAT VAULT... ROBBED THE BANK!!

I DON'T BELIEVE IT... DAREDEVIL BEING CHASED BY THE POLICE!

HALT! STOP OR WE'LL FIRE! OKAY, HARRY... TRY TO WING HIM!

POW!

POW!

HE'S TOO FAST... BUT WHY DID HE DO IT? WHAT MADE A GUY LIKE HIM TURN BAD?!!

...AND ALL EVIDENCE POINTS TO THE CONCLUSION THAT THE SENSATIONAL COSTUMED VIGILANTE HAS BECOME A CRIMINAL...

HA! PERFECT! THIS IS AS GOOD AS IF HE WERE CAPTURED!

DAILY NEWS

DAREDEVIL WANTED SUSPICION OF ROBBER

CITIZENS O ALARMED A IN CRIME

Police Attemp Apprehend Ma

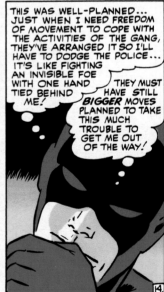

THIS WAS WELL-PLANNED... JUST WHEN I NEED FREEDOM OF MOVEMENT TO COPE WITH THE ACTIVITIES OF THE GANG, THEY'VE ARRANGED IT SO I'LL HAVE TO DODGE THE POLICE... IT'S LIKE FIGHTING AN INVISIBLE FOE WITH ONE HAND TIED BEHIND ME!

THEY MUST HAVE STILL BIGGER MOVES PLANNED TO TAKE THIS MUCH TROUBLE TO GET ME OUT OF THE WAY!

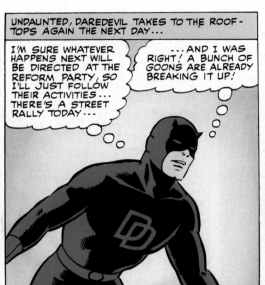

UNDAUNTED, DAREDEVIL TAKES TO THE ROOF-TOPS AGAIN THE NEXT DAY...

I'M SURE WHATEVER HAPPENS NEXT WILL BE DIRECTED AT THE REFORM PARTY, SO I'LL JUST FOLLOW THEIR ACTIVITIES... THERE'S A STREET RALLY TODAY...

...AND I WAS RIGHT! A BUNCH OF GOONS ARE ALREADY BREAKING IT UP!

WOW! WHAT A JUMBLE OF IMPRESSIONS I'M GETTING!

IT'LL BE HARD TO PICK OUT HOODS FROM PARTY WORKERS!

WE DON'T WANT REFORM MEETINGS HERE, SEE?

GET 'EM GUYS! WE GOT TO MOVE FAST!

HELP!

MIND IF I JOIN IN, BOYS? THIS GAME'S TOO ONE-SIDED!

IT'S DARE-DEVIL! THE BOSS SAID HE WOULDN'T DARE... UH!

POW!

VOTE THE HONEST TICKET

JUST AS I THOUGHT! THE FINE HAND OF THE ORGANIZER IS BEHIND THIS ATTACK!

DON'T HOLD BACK, MEN... I NEED THE EXERCISE!

IT'S NICE OF THEM TO KEEP ATTACKING ME... SAVING ME THE TROUBLE OF TRYING TO DISTINGUISH THEM!

WHAM!

IN QUICK ORDER, THE MASKED MARVEL TAKES CARE OF THE THUGS...

...AND REMEMBER, AS YOU LIE THERE, THAT POLITICS MAKES STRANGE BEDFELLOWS!

UH-OH! THE POLICE! TIME TO MAKE A STRATEGIC WITHDRAWAL!

IT'S HIM! DARE-DEVIL AGAIN!

CAN'T AFFORD TO HANG AROUND!

I'LL HAVE TO LET 'EM ALL GET AWAY!

POLICE

WHAT WAS DAREDEVIL UP TO THIS TIME?

BEAT IT... THE COPS!

MEANWHILE, AT THE LAW OFFICE, FOGGY IS ELATED...

KAREN, I'M BEGINNING TO BELIEVE I REALLY HAVE A CHANCE! THE LATEST POLL RESULTS SHOW THE PARTY IS GAINING LIKE CRAZY! YOU MAY BE LOOKING AT THE NEXT D.A.!

I HOPE SO, FOGGY!

BUT WHY DOES THE PROSPECT CHILL ME? IS IT BECAUSE OF HER... OF DEBORAH? AM I JEALOUS?

DO I REALLY CARE FOR FOGGY AFTER ALL?

15.

OH, BY THE WAY, KAREN...WOULD YOU LIKE TO ATTEND A PENTHOUSE PARTY TONIGHT? DEBBIE'S GIVING IT IN MY HONOR...I WISH YOU'D COME!

IMAGINE...ASKING *ME!* IS HE JUST BEING NICE? OR COULD HE BE TRYING TO MAKE *HER* JEALOUS?

OF COURSE, FOGGY...I'D LOVE TO!

I WONDER...IF *MATT* WILL BE THERE?

LATER, AT THE CHEMCO BUILDING, THE ORGANIZER HAS CALLED A COUNCIL OF WAR...

MEN, I'M PLEASED WITH OUR RESULTS SO FAR...

WE'VE SUCCEEDED VERY WELL IN THE FIRST PART OF OUR MASTER PLAN, IN MAKING PUBLIC SENTIMENT TURN TOWARD THE REFORM PARTY...NOW WE SHALL PROCEED TO PHASE TWO...TO TIGHTEN OUR CONTROL OF THE REFORM MOVEMENT BY GAINING POWER OVER INDIVIDUAL MEMBERS!

YEAH... HOW?

QUIET! HE'S ABOUT TO SPRING ANOTHER PLAN!

THAT NIGHT, AT THE HARRIS PENTHOUSE APARTMENT...

GOOD EVENING, FOGGY! DEBORAH TELLS ME YOU'VE MADE GREAT PROGRESS AS A CAMPAIGNER!

AND THAT ISN'T ALL, MR. JONAS... FOGGY HAS ALL KINDS OF HIDDEN TALENTS...

IS THAT SO? THANK YOU, DEB... EH, WOULD YOU LIKE TO DANCE?

NELSON! ARE YOU BLUSHING? THAT'S NO WAY FOR A POLITICIAN TO REACT!

JONAS, I'VE BEEN MEANING TO SPEAK TO YOU! I DON'T REALLY LIKE THE WAY THIS CAMPAIGN IS GOING...YOU'RE ATTEMPTING TO BENEFIT BY THE CRIME WAVE!

IN YOUR LAST SPEECH I FEEL YOU WENT TOO FAR, TRYING TO BLAME IT ON THE ADMINISTRATION!

TELL YOU WHAT, MONROE...YOU MAKE YOUR SPEECHES AND I'LL MAKE MINE!

IF THAT'S THE WAY YOU FEEL ABOUT IT, I'M AFRAID I'LL HAVE TO WITHDRAW FROM THE RACE! I WON'T RUN FOR OFFICE *YOUR* WAY!

MILTON, DON'T BE A FOOL! LET'S TALK THIS OVER LIKE REASONABLE MEN!

IF YOU PULL OUT NOW, IT'LL DESTROY THE WHOLE CAMPAIGN!

PLEASE, MILT... DON'T BE HASTY!

ORGANIZER TO ALL UNITS... ZERO HOUR! PREPARE TO MOVE IN ON MY CUE!

THERE THEY GO... I'M GLAD I WASN'T INVITED TO THAT BASH... MAKES IT EASIER TO GO INTO ACTION!

16.

THE CAT MAN MAKES HIS WAY INSIDE THE BUILDING AND WAITS...

TAKE YOUR POSITIONS... ARE YOU THERE, FROG MAN?

ROGER, CHIEF! I'M AT THE SWITCH!

...AND IN THE BASEMENT...

THIS CALLS FOR PERFECT TIMING... O.K.! GO!

AS THE BUILDING IS PLUNGED INTO DARKNESS, THE CATMAN ENTERS AND SINGLES OUT DEBORAH...

THE LIGHTS! WHAT HAPPENED?

NO! HELP! EEEEEE!

CHECK THE FUSES!

QUICK! PASS HER TO ME AND TAKE OFF!

HERE SHE IS! YOU KNOW WHAT TO DO NEXT!

HELP! SOMEONE PLEASE HELP ME!

THEY'RE TOO FAST... I WON'T HAVE TIME TO PREVENT THEM FROM CARRYING THE GIRL OFF... BUT MAYBE I CAN NAB THE CAT MAN!

AS THE BIRD MAN VANISHES INTO THE NIGHT WITH HIS HUMAN BURDEN, THE SIGHTLESS AVENGER STRIKES IN SILENCE!

A SAVAGE ENCOUNTER IN THE DARK ENSUES... INFRA-RED VISION PITTED AGAINST DAREDEVIL'S UNCANNY RADAR SENSE...

UH....! HE MUST BE ABLE TO SEE IN THE DARK, TOO!

OWW! I NEARLY BROKE MY HAND ON HIS COSTUME!

WITH ALL THE AGILITY OF A REAL CAT, THE COSTUMED THUG MANAGES TO EVADE HIS ATTACKER!

HE'S TRYING TO GET IN CLOSE... A TASTE OF MY CAT'S CLAWS SHOULD DISCOURAGE HIM...

HE NEARLY CAUGHT ME GOOD THAT TIME! I'VE GOT TO END THIS FAST!

17.

I'LL LET HIM THINK I'M BADLY **HURT**... LET HIM COME TO ME...

UHH! MY **ARM!** STAY BACK! DON'T COME CLOSER....!!

HA! THIS IS GOING TO BE A **PLEASURE!**

AND THEN...

ONE KARATE BLOW AND THE LIGHTS REALLY GO OUT FOR THE CAT MAN!

MOMENTS LATER, THE LIGHTS GO ON, AND...

WHAT **IS** IT? LOOKS LIKE SOMETHING OUT OF A NIGHT-MARE!

IT'S A MAN IN A CAT COSTUME... AND HE'S OUT COLD!

WHO KNOCKED HIM OUT? THERE WAS A REAL BATTLE!

WHAT WAS HE UP TO? AND WHO SCREAMED?

IT WAS DEBORAH! SHE'S GONE... SHE'S BEEN CAPTURED!

WELL, WE'VE GOT ONE OF THE GANG THAT DID IT! CALL THE POLICE! WE'LL GET HIM DOWN TO HEADQUARTERS AND MAKE HIM TALK!

I DON'T KNOW WHAT'S BEHIND THIS, BUT WE'LL FIND OUT ...AND GET HER BACK!

LATER, AT THE LAIR OF THE ORGANIZATION · · ·

YOU DID WELL THIS TIME! BUT WE HAVE A PROBLEM!

THE CAPTURE OF THE CAT MAN JEOPARDIZES OUR WHOLE OPERATION! HE MUST NOT TALK! **APE!** THIS WILL BE YOUR JOB...

JUST MY LUCK! WHAT DO I GOTTA DO... INVADE POLICE HEADQUARTERS?

BOSS... YOU DON'T MEAN TO... YOU WOULDN'T...

THE INTERROGATION BEGINS...

WE'VE IDENTIFIED YOU FROM OUR MUG BOOKS, HORGAN... MIGHT AS WELL COME CLEAN!

TELL US ALL ABOUT YOUR GANG, AND WHERE YOUR HIDEOUT IS...

WHAT'S IN IT FOR ME?

IF YOU **DON'T** TALK ...IT COULD BE A LIFETIME IN THE COOLER!

MAKE IT EASY ON YOURSELF! THIS IS A BAD RAP, HORGAN!

WELL, I'LL TELL YOU WHAT I KNOW...I'M A MEMBER OF A GANG CALLED "THE ORGANIZATION" ...THE HEAD MAN IS CALLED THE "ORGANIZER..."!

WHAT ABOUT THIS ORGANIZER? WHO IS HE AND WHAT'S HIS ANGLE?

I HATE TO DO THIS, CAT MAN, BUT ORDERS ARE ORDERS!

I DON'T KNOW... HONEST! NONE OF US HAS EVER SEEN HIM IN PERSON!

HE ONLY GETS IN TOUCH WITH US BY RADIO AND T.V. ---IT'S PRETTY WILD! HE AIN'T IN IT FOR DOUGH! HE ...

18.

225

BUT BEFORE THE APE MAN CAN ACT...

HEY! ...WHAT... YOU AGAIN!

A GRENADE! YOU GENTS REALLY PLAY FOR KEEPS!

I KNEW THEY'D TRY SOMETHING LIKE THIS! SO FAR I'VE MANAGED TO SECOND-GUESS THE ORGANIZER'S THINKING PRETTY WELL!

DAREDEVIL HURLS THE GRENADE HIGH INTO THE AIR, WHERE IT SPENDS ITS DESTRUCTIVE FORCE HARMLESSLY!

=WHEW= THAT WAS CLOSE!

WHROOM!

THE ORGANIZATION MUST BE PLENTY WORRIED TO TRY THAT!

HE'S MAKING A RUN FOR IT!

HOW CAN I GET HIM TO LEAD ME TO THEIR HIDEOUT? HE WON'T GO THERE IF HE KNOWS I'M FOLLOWING HIM!

WAIT FOR ME, APE! WE'RE NOT FINISHED!

APE TO ORGANIZER... WHAT'LL I DO NOW? I CAN'T SHAKE THAT HIGH-FLYIN' CREEP!

OVER ROOFTOPS, SWINGING FROM FIRE ESCAPES, THE CHASE CONTINUES ACROSS THE CITY...

MAYBE I CAN TAUNT HIM INTO FIGHTING ME...THEN I CAN LET HIM THINK HE'S DEFEATED ME SO HE'LL RETURN TO THEIR HEADQUARTERS...

CHICKENING OUT, APE? YOU ACTED PRETTY TOUGH LAST TIME WE MET! WHAT HAPPENED SINCE?

THIS IS THE ORGANIZER! YOU'D BETTER TURN AND FIGHT... GET RID OF THAT PEST FOR GOOD!

OKAY...THAT DOES IT! HE'S ASKING FOR IT! AND HE'S GONNA GET IT!

19.

226

He's on the ground again! Gonna make a fight of it... just as I hoped!

POST NO BILLS

KNOPF

I've got to make it look as though I'm really trying!

UNNG!

So far so good!

Now I'll give him a judo chop, just pulling it a little...

THOK!

Think you can hurt me with a little love tap like that, you fool? Try this for size!

WOW! I needn't have bothered taking it easy on him...

KRUMF!

Ape to boss... I took care of him... coming home... over!

Well, I succeeded in my plan to make him lead me to their H.Q.... one MORE success like that could retire me permanently from the masked crime-fighter business!

I think under that ape suit they've hidden a GORILLA!

Minutes later, on a ledge outside the Chemco building---

HA! Now that fool Nelson will do anything the boss wants...

Deborah! She ISN'T a prisoner! The abduction was a FAKE... now I know why she made a play for Foggy!

But, he's fallen for her... HARD! How can I tell him the truth? How many hard knocks can the poor fella take?

...if he thinks my safety depends on it, he'll stay in line!

I must rescue her, whether she likes it or not... for Foggy's sake!

It's Daredevil! And he's so busy spying on us, he hasn't seen me!

NOW that Wally got the writing out of his system, he left it for poor Stan to finish next issue! Can our leader do it? That's the real mystery! But, while you're waiting, see if you can find the clue we planted showing who the organizer is! It'll all come out in the wash next issue when Stan wraps it up! SEE YOU THEN!

20.

227

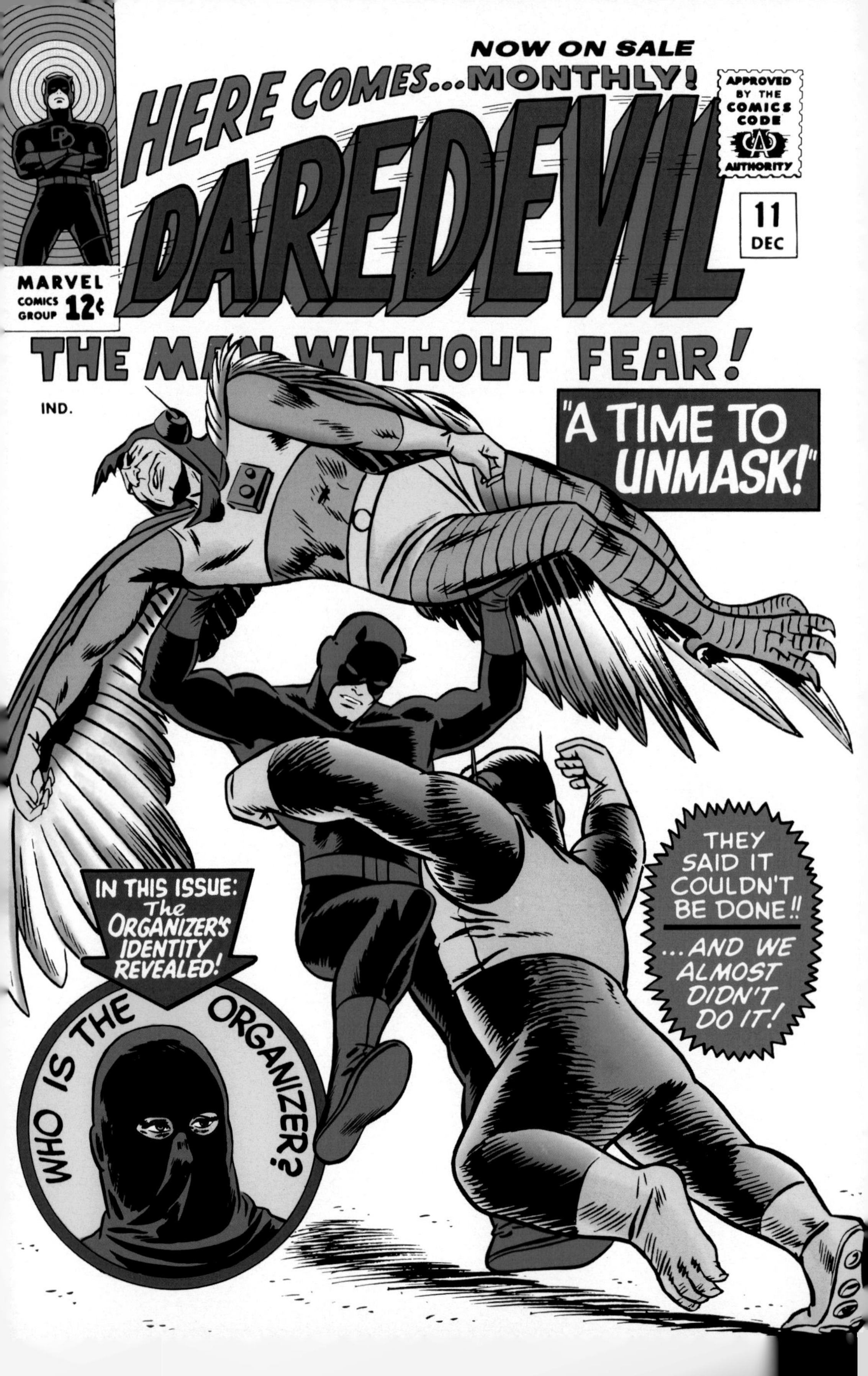
NOW ON SALE
HERE COMES...MONTHLY!
DAREDEVIL
THE MAN WITHOUT FEAR!
MARVEL COMICS GROUP 12¢
APPROVED BY THE COMICS CODE AUTHORITY
11
DEC
IND.
"A TIME TO UNMASK!"
IN THIS ISSUE: The ORGANIZER'S IDENTITY REVEALED!
WHO IS THE ORGANIZER?
THEY SAID IT COULDN'T BE DONE!!
...AND WE ALMOST DIDN'T DO IT!

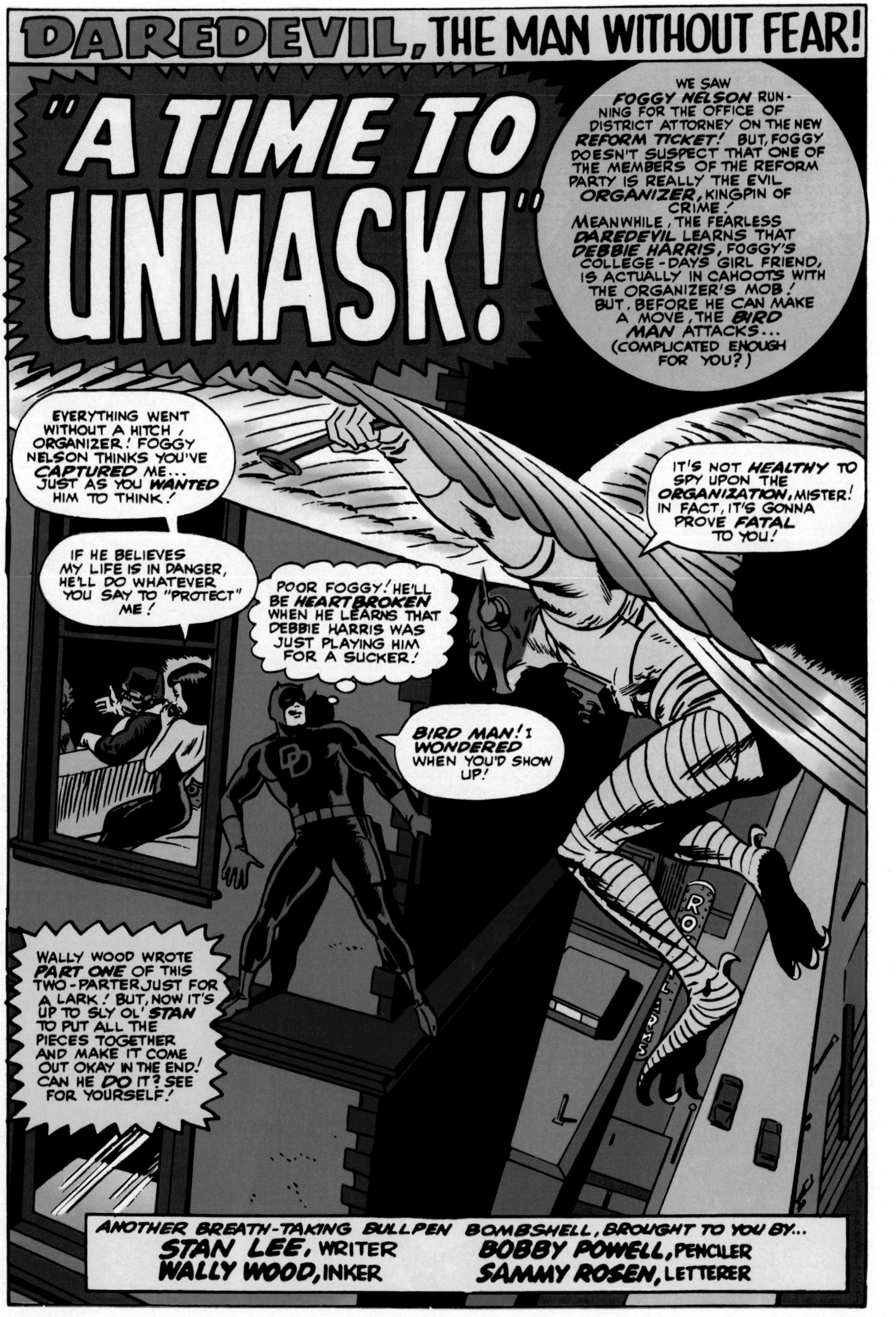
DAREDEVIL, THE MAN WITHOUT FEAR!
"A TIME TO UNMASK!"
WE SAW FOGGY NELSON RUNNING FOR THE OFFICE OF DISTRICT ATTORNEY ON THE NEW REFORM TICKET! BUT, FOGGY DOESN'T SUSPECT THAT ONE OF THE MEMBERS OF THE REFORM PARTY IS REALLY THE EVIL ORGANIZER, KINGPIN OF CRIME! MEANWHILE, THE FEARLESS DAREDEVIL LEARNS THAT DEBBIE HARRIS, FOGGY'S COLLEGE-DAYS GIRL FRIEND, IS ACTUALLY IN CAHOOTS WITH THE ORGANIZER'S MOB! BUT, BEFORE HE CAN MAKE A MOVE, THE BIRD MAN ATTACKS... (COMPLICATED ENOUGH FOR YOU?)
EVERYTHING WENT WITHOUT A HITCH, ORGANIZER! FOGGY NELSON THINKS YOU'VE CAPTURED ME... JUST AS YOU WANTED HIM TO THINK!
IF HE BELIEVES MY LIFE IS IN DANGER, HE'LL DO WHATEVER YOU SAY TO "PROTECT" ME!
POOR FOGGY! HE'LL BE HEARTBROKEN WHEN HE LEARNS THAT DEBBIE HARRIS WAS JUST PLAYING HIM FOR A SUCKER!
IT'S NOT HEALTHY TO SPY UPON THE ORGANIZATION, MISTER! IN FACT, IT'S GONNA PROVE FATAL TO YOU!
BIRD MAN! I WONDERED WHEN YOU'D SHOW UP!
WALLY WOOD WROTE PART ONE OF THIS TWO-PARTER JUST FOR A LARK! BUT, NOW IT'S UP TO SLY OL' STAN TO PUT ALL THE PIECES TOGETHER AND MAKE IT COME OUT OKAY IN THE END! CAN HE DO IT? SEE FOR YOURSELF!
ANOTHER BREATH-TAKING BULLPEN BOMBSHELL, BROUGHT TO YOU BY...
STAN LEE, WRITER
BOBBY POWELL, PENCILER
WALLY WOOD, INKER
SAMMY ROSEN, LETTERER

THE *LAST* TIME WE BATTLED, YOU GOT AWAY! *THIS* TIME YOU WON'T BE SO LUCKY!

FUNNY! I WAS JUST THINKING THE SAME THING ABOUT *YOU!*

I'VE GOT TO GET HIM AWAY FROM THE WINDOW, BEFORE THE *OTHERS* JUMP ME, TOO!

MY BEST BET IS TO DO WHAT HE'LL LEAST EXPECT... NAMELY, *THIS....!*

DID YOU LOSE YOUR *MARBLES?* WHAT GOOD'LL IT DO YOU TO PUSH YOURSELF OFF THAT LEDGE?? *I'M* THE ONLY ONE WITH WINGS HERE!

THAT SO? WELL, HERE'S WHERE YOU GET THEM *CLIPPED!*

MAYBE SO... BUT IT WON'T BE BY *YOU!* HAPPY LANDINGS, SMART GUY!

GOOD! JUST WHAT I *WANTED* HIM TO DO!

NOW, IF MY BUILT-IN *RADAR* DOESN'T FAIL ME...!

MADE IT! AM I GLAD THEY BUILT THESE OLD BUILDINGS WITH *LEDGES!*

THHIPP!

I HEAR HIS WINGS FLAPPING INTO THE WINDOW! HE'S SO SURE I'M DONE FOR, HE DIDN'T EVEN BOTHER TO LOOK BACK!

NOW, I'VE GOT TO GET UP TO THE *ORGANIZER'S* HEADQUARTERS BEFORE IT'S TOO LATE!

HEY, YOU! WHO'S GONNA PAY FOR THAT BROKEN WINDOW?

I'LL BE *GLAD* TO, FRIEND! CAN I PUT IT ON MY *DINERS CLUB* ACCOUNT?

2.

231

AND, JUST A FEW DOORS AWAY, WE FIND FEVERISH PREPARATIONS GOING ON...

YOU'RE A *FOOL*, BIRD MAN! YOU SHOULD HAVE MADE *SURE* DAREDEVIL WAS FINISHED!

STOP TALKING AND TIE ME UP! IN CASE HE *DOES* MANAGE TO RETURN HERE, I WANT MY ACT TO LOOK *CONVINCING* TO HIM!

C'MON, THAT'S GOOD ENOUGH! LET'S CUT OUT WHILE WE STILL *CAN!*

HE *COULDN'T* HAVE SURVIVED THAT FALL!

BUT SECONDS LATER, DESPITE THE BIRD MAN'S PREDICTION...

MISS *HARRIS!* ARE YOU ALL RIGHT?

OH, *DAREDEVIL!* THANK HEAVENS YOU'RE *HERE!* I'M SO *GLAD* TO SEE YOU!

I'LL *BET* YOU ARE, YOU LITTLE FRAUD!

I'LL HAVE YOU FREE IN A JIFFY! SORRY I CAN'T ESCORT YOU HOME!

DON'T WORRY! I'LL BE ALL RIGHT NOW!

GOOD! BECAUSE I'VE SOME THINGS TO DO..!

SUCH AS *FOLLOWING* YOU SO THAT YOU CAN LEAD ME TO THE *ORGANIZER* HIMSELF!

IT WON'T BE TOO HARD FOR ME TO SINGLE OUT HER DISTINCTIVE FOOTSTEPS! THE STREETS AREN'T TOO CROWDED AT THIS HOUR!

BUT, AFTER A FEW MINUTES OF SKILLFUL TRACKING...

TOO BAD! SHE SIMPLY RETURNED TO HER *OWN* APARTMENT! BUT, SHE'S *PHONING* THE ORGANIZER! I DON'T THINK DAREDEVIL SUSPECTS ANYTHING! VERY WELL, I'LL CONCENTRATE ON FOGGY, NELSON *AGAIN!*

THUS, A SHORT TIME LATER, AT THE LAW OFFICES OF NELSON AND MURDOCK...

DEBORAH! IT'S *YOU!* YOU'RE *SAFE!* HOW DID YOU ESCAPE FROM THE *ORGANIZER'S* MEN??

IT WAS *DAREDEVIL!* HE FOUND ME SOMEHOW, AND FREED ME! I COULDN'T WAIT TO FIND YOU... TO *SEE* YOU AGAIN!

I WAS WORRIED *SICK!* DIDN'T KNOW WHAT TO DO.. WHERE TO TURN!

OH, FOGGY, DARLING! THEN, YOU *DO* CARE! THAT MEANS I *AM* IMPORTANT TO YOU! I DIDN'T KNOW! I COULD ONLY *HOPE!*

DEBORAH! DEBBIE.. I NEVER KNEW YOU *FELT* THAT WAY! I.. I DON'T KNOW WHAT TO SAY!

POOR FOGGY! HE'S *PUTTY* IN THE HANDS OF A FEMALE LIKE HER! BUT, HOW CAN I TELL HIM THE *TRUTH* ABOUT DEBORAH! HE'S HAD *ENOUGH* DISAPPOINTMENTS ALREADY!

LOOK! ISN'T *THAT* DAREDEVIL? WHAT...?

NOTHING MORE I CAN DO *THERE!*

HE MUST HAVE FOLLOWED TO MAKE SURE I'D BE SAFE!

MY *MAIN* JOB IS STILL TO LEARN *WHICH* MEMBER OF THE REFORM PARTY IS REALLY THE *ORGANIZER!*

I HAVE A FEELING IT'S ONE OF THE *TOP BRASS!*

BUT.. *WHICH ONE??*

AS FOR *FOGGY,* HOW CAN I TELL HIM ABOUT DEBORAH? HE THINKS SHE *LOVES* HIM!

I HAVEN'T THE HEART TO GIVE HIM THE BAD NEWS! PERHAPS HE'LL SOON FIND OUT FOR HIMSELF!

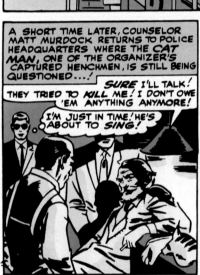

A SHORT TIME LATER, COUNSELOR MATT MURDOCK RETURNS TO POLICE HEADQUARTERS WHERE THE *CAT MAN,* ONE OF THE ORGANIZER'S CAPTURED HENCHMEN, IS STILL BEING QUESTIONED...!

SURE I'LL TALK! THEY TRIED TO *KILL* ME! I DON'T OWE 'EM ANYTHING ANYMORE!

I'M JUST IN TIME! HE'S ABOUT TO *SING!*

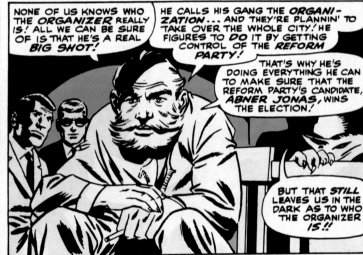

NONE OF US KNOWS WHO THE *ORGANIZER* REALLY IS! ALL WE CAN BE SURE OF IS THAT HE'S A REAL *BIG SHOT!*

HE CALLS HIS GANG THE *ORGANIZATION*... AND THEY'RE PLANNIN' TO TAKE OVER THE WHOLE CITY! HE FIGURES TO *DO* IT BY GETTING CONTROL OF THE *REFORM PARTY!*

THAT'S WHY HE'S DOING EVERYTHING HE CAN TO MAKE SURE THAT THE REFORM PARTY'S CANDIDATE, *ABNER JONAS,* WINS THE ELECTION!

BUT THAT *STILL* LEAVES US IN THE DARK AS TO WHO THE ORGANIZER *IS!!*

THOUGHTFULLY, MATT RETURNS TO HIS OFFICE, AND THEN...

EVEN IF I DON'T MENTION *DEBORAH,* I CAN STILL WARN HIM ABOUT THE *REFORM PARTY!*

FOGGY, PERHAPS YOU *SHOULDN'T* RUN FOR D.A. AS THE REFORM CANDIDATE!

WHAT'S WRONG, MATT? GETTING *JEALOUS?*

YOU'VE ALWAYS BEEN THE GLAMOR BOY OF OUR FIRM, WINNING ALL THE CASES FOR US! NOW, WHEN *I* GET A CHANCE FOR SOME *FAME,* YOU TRY TO TALK ME *OUT* OF IT!

THAT'S UNFAIR, AND YOU *KNOW* IT, MISTER! I JUST THINK THERE'S SOMETHING *FISHY* GOING ON IN THE PARTY, AND I DON'T WANT *YOU* GETTING HURT!

I CAN TAKE CARE OF *MYSELF!*

DON'T BE TOO *SURE* OF THAT!

I TELL YOU WHAT... ARE YOU GAME TO SET A *TRAP* AND *SEE* IF I'M RIGHT??

YOU *BET* I AM! I'LL *CALL* YOUR BLUFF THIS TIME, MATT!

OKAY, THEN! IT'S A *DEAL!*

THE NEXT DAY, MATT AND FOGGY HAVE A MEETING WITH THE REFORM PARTY'S THREE TOP CANDIDATES...

GENTLEMEN, MY PARTNER, MR. NELSON, HAS SOME *NEWS* FOR YOU!

HAVE YOU SEEN ANYTHING OF *DAREDEVIL?* I WANT TO THANK HIM FOR RESCUING MY DAUGHTER, *DEBORAH!*

COULD HARRIS *HIMSELF* HAVE ARRANGED THE PHONY CAPTURE OF HIS DAUGHTER?

AND WHAT ABOUT *JONAS?* HE HAS GREAT WEALTH AND INFLUENCE AT HIS COMMAND!

AND MONROE! HE WANTED TO *QUIT* THE PARTY RECENTLY! WAS THAT JUST AN *ACT?*

I CAN'T BELIEVE THAT MATT WOULD SUSPECT ANY OF *THESE* THREE MEN!

BERNARD HARRIS
CANDIDATE FOR BOROUGH PRES.

ABNER JONAS
CANDIDATE FOR MAYOR.

MILTON MONROE
CANDIDATE FOR ASSEMBLYMAN.

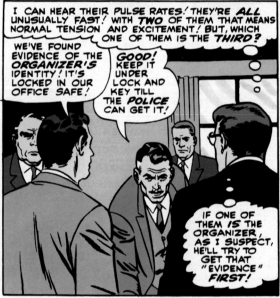

I CAN HEAR THEIR PULSE RATES! THEY'RE *ALL* UNUSUALLY FAST! WITH *TWO* OF THEM THAT MEANS NORMAL TENSION AND EXCITEMENT! BUT, WHICH ONE OF THEM IS THE *THIRD?*

WE'VE FOUND EVIDENCE OF THE *ORGANIZER'S* IDENTITY! IT'S LOCKED IN OUR OFFICE SAFE!

GOOD! KEEP IT UNDER LOCK AND KEY TILL THE *POLICE* CAN GET IT!

IF ONE OF THEM *IS* THE ORGANIZER, AS I SUSPECT, HE'LL TRY TO GET THAT "EVIDENCE" *FIRST!*

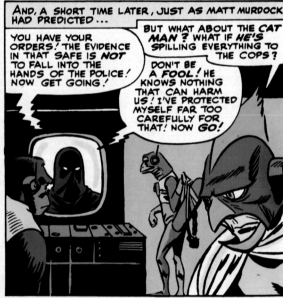

AND, A SHORT TIME LATER, JUST AS MATT MURDOCK HAD PREDICTED...

YOU HAVE YOUR *ORDERS!* THE EVIDENCE IN THAT SAFE IS *NOT* TO FALL INTO THE HANDS OF THE POLICE! NOW GET GOING!

BUT WHAT ABOUT THE *CAT MAN?* WHAT IF *HE'S* SPILLING EVERYTHING TO THE COPS?

DON'T BE A *FOOL!* HE KNOWS NOTHING THAT CAN HARM US! I'VE PROTECTED MYSELF FAR TOO CAREFULLY FOR THAT! NOW *GO!*

THEN, AS MATT AND FOGGY RETURN TO THE OFFICE WITH THEIR LOVELY SECRETARY, KAREN PAGE...

WELL, MATT... ARE YOU WILLING TO ADMIT YOUR SUSPICIONS WERE UNFOUNDED?

NOT QUITE *YET,* FOGGY!

KAREN'S HEART-BEAT IS UNUSUALLY RAPID! IF ONLY I COULD TELL WHETHER IT'S *FOGGY* OR *ME* WHO IS RESPONSIBLE?!

BUT, JUST THEN, THE SIGHTLESS ATTORNEY'S UN-CANNY NATURAL *RADAR INSTINCT* TAKES OVER...

THERE'S SOMEONE RANSACKING OUR OFFICE RIGHT *NOW!* JUST AS I EXPECTED!

THIS IS ALL THE PROOF I *NEEDED!* BUT I'VE GOT TO SCARE HIM AWAY BEFORE KAREN AND FOGGY BLUNDER IN AND GET *HURT!*

5.

THE EASIEST THING FOR A BLIND MAN TO DO IS TO PRETEND TO *FALL!*

UHHH! BLAST IT! HOW *CLUMSY* OF ME!

HE'S SURE TO HEAR *THIS* INSIDE!

OH... *MATT!*

THUD!

MATT! ARE YOU *ALL RIGHT??* HERE, LET ME HELP YOU UP!

I'M OKAY, *KAREN!* JUST GETTING CLUMSY IN MY OLD AGE, I GUESS!

I SHOULD HAVE KEPT MY EYE ON YOU, MATT! I *GUESS* I TAKE YOU SO MUCH FOR *GRANTED,* THAT I SOMETIMES FORGET YOU'RE... I MEAN... HERE, I'LL HELP YOU UP!

IT *WORKED!* I COULD HEAR HIM RACING OUT THE BACK DOOR!

OHH! *MATT! FOGGY!* COME *QUICK!*

THE PLACE IS A *SHAMBLES!* THEN... YOU WERE *RIGHT,* MATT! YOUR TRAP *WORKED! ONE* OF THEM WANTED THE "*EVIDENCE*" WE SAID WE HAD!

WHOEVER THE *ORGANIZER* IS, HE PROBABLY WANTED ME TO RUN FOR D.A., THINKING HE COULD *CONTROL* ME IF I GOT ELECTED! WHAT A *FOOL* I WAS!

DON'T TAKE IT TOO HARD, FELLA! NOW THAT WE'VE NARROWED DOWN THE SUSPECTS, MAY-BE WE CAN *CATCH* THE ONE WE WANT!

IT'LL TAKE *ALL DAY* TO PUT THE PLACE BACK IN ORDER!

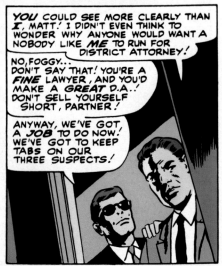

YOU COULD SEE MORE CLEARLY THAN *I,* MATT! I DIDN'T EVEN THINK TO WONDER WHY ANYONE WOULD WANT A NOBODY LIKE *ME* TO RUN FOR DISTRICT ATTORNEY!

NO, FOGGY... DON'T SAY THAT! YOU'RE A *FINE* LAWYER, AND YOU'D MAKE A *GREAT* D.A.! DON'T SELL YOURSELF SHORT, PARTNER!

ANYWAY, WE'VE GOT A *JOB* TO DO NOW! WE'VE GOT TO KEEP TABS ON OUR THREE SUSPECTS!

AND SO, A SHORT TIME LATER, MATT, FOGGY, AND KAREN EACH ATTEMPT TO KEEP ONE OF THE REFORM PARTY CANDIDATES UNDER SURVEILLANCE...

IS THAT *YOU,* MR. MONROE? I WANTED TO SPEAK....!

NOT *NOW,* MURDOCK! I'VE A HEAVY SCHEDULE! SORRY!

MR. JONAS, OUR OFFICE WAS BROKEN INTO LAST NIGHT, AND....!

WHY TELL *ME* ABOUT IT, NELSON? SEE THE *POLICE!* I'VE A *CAMPAIGN* TO TAKE CARE OF!

MR. HARRIS, I'VE BEEN WONDERING IF YOU'VE HEARD FROM YOUR *DAUGHTER* LATELY?

MY DAUGHTER? NO! I... I THINK SHE'S OUT OF TOWN! I'M NOT SURE! I HAVE TO RUSH NOW!

6.

THEN, AS MATT COMPARES NOTES WITH THE OTHERS...

ALL *THREE* OF THEM GOT AWAY FROM US, EH? BUT, THE ORGANIZER IS ONLY *ONE* MAN! WE'VE GOT TO NARROW THE SEARCH *SOMEHOW!*

I'LL HAVE TO CHECK WITH YOU LATER!

ALL THE OTHER LEADS HAVE FIZZLED OUT! THIS MEANS I'VE GOT TO DEPEND ON *DEBORAH HARRIS* TO LEAD ME TO THE ORGANIZER!

BUT, I CAN'T DO IT AS *MATT MURDOCK...!*

...NOT WHEN *DAREDEVIL* IS READY FOR ACTION!

MINUTES LATER, A SWASHBUCKLING SCARLET FIGURE APPEARS ON THE SKYLIGHT ABOVE DEBORAH HARRIS'S APARTMENT...

I CAN "SEE" HER MORE CLEARLY WITH MY *SENSES* THAN I EVER COULD WITH MY *EYES!*

SHE'S GOT HER TV SET ON... BUT, IT'S NO *ORDINARY* SHOW...IT'S A *CLOSED CIRCUIT* BROADCAST!

AND THE VOICE SHE'S LISTENING TO... IT'S THE VOICE OF THE *ORGANIZER!*

IT LOOKS AS THOUGH YOUR PLAN HAS *FAILED!*

NONSENSE! I *CANNOT* FAIL! YOU WILL *STILL* HELP ME TO SAVE THE DAY!

EVEN THOUGH THE POLLS INDICATE OUR PARTY HASN'T A CHANCE, WE SHALL SURPRISE THEM ALL!

IF THE PRESENT MAYOR WERE TO MEET WITH AN "ACCIDENT", THEN *OUR* CANDIDATE WOULD BE THE ONLY ONE LEFT TO VOTE FOR!.

NO! YOU CAN'T *MEAN* THAT!

I'VE HELPED YOU IN THE PAST, BECAUSE I THOUGHT I LOVED YOU! BUT YOU'VE GONE *TOO FAR!* YOU'RE *POWER MAD!*

TAKE WARNING! EVEN *YOU* CANNOT DEFY THE ORGANIZER WITHOUT *PAYING* FOR IT!

7.

HE BROKE THE CONNECTION! THAT MEANS MY LIFE IS IN DANGER, TOO! HE'LL... OH!–

DAREDEVIL! WHAT BRINGS YOU HERE ??

LET'S LEVEL WITH EACH OTHER, LADY! I KNOW OF YOUR TIE-IN WITH THE ORGANIZER!

I ALSO KNOW THAT HE DOESN'T LET ANYONE LEAVE HIS "ORGANIZATION"! BUT, I CAN PROTECT YOU...IF YOU'LL DO EXACTLY AS I TELL YOU!

I..I'M AFRAID I HAVEN'T ANY CHOICE!

GOOD! NOW CONTACT ONE OF THE ORGANIZER'S MEN, FAST... BEFORE HE BEATS YOU TO IT...!

AND SO, THE STAGE IS SET! MINUTES LATER, IN ANSWER TO DEBORAH HARRIS'S CALL, THE FROG MAN SILENTLY EMERGES FROM THE RIVER OUTSIDE THE MAYOR'S MANSION...

I DUNNO WHAT THE HURRY IS, BUT THE GAL SURE SOUNDED LIKE IT WAS AN EMERGENCY, SO I BETTER WORK FAST!

SHE SAID THE ORGANIZER DIDN'T WANT ME TO WASTE ANY TIME!

I'LL GET EVERYTHING SET, AND THEN...

HEY! WHAT'S THAT?

SMILE, SWEETIE! YOU'RE ON CANDID CAMERA!

DAREDEVIL!! I'VE BEEN WAITING FOR A CHANCE TO SHOW HOW I CAN BEAT YOU!

NO NEED TO WAIT! JUST WISH UPON A STAR, SON!

IF THIS IS WHAT YOU'VE BEEN WAITING FOR, I'VE GOT NEWS FOR YOU...

...IT WASN'T WORTH IT!

YOU'RE JUST LUCKY! I MUSTA TRIPPED! BUT WHEN I GET UP...!

YOU'LL HAVE THE GRAND-DADDY OF ALL HEADACHES! JUST HOLD THAT POSE....!

237

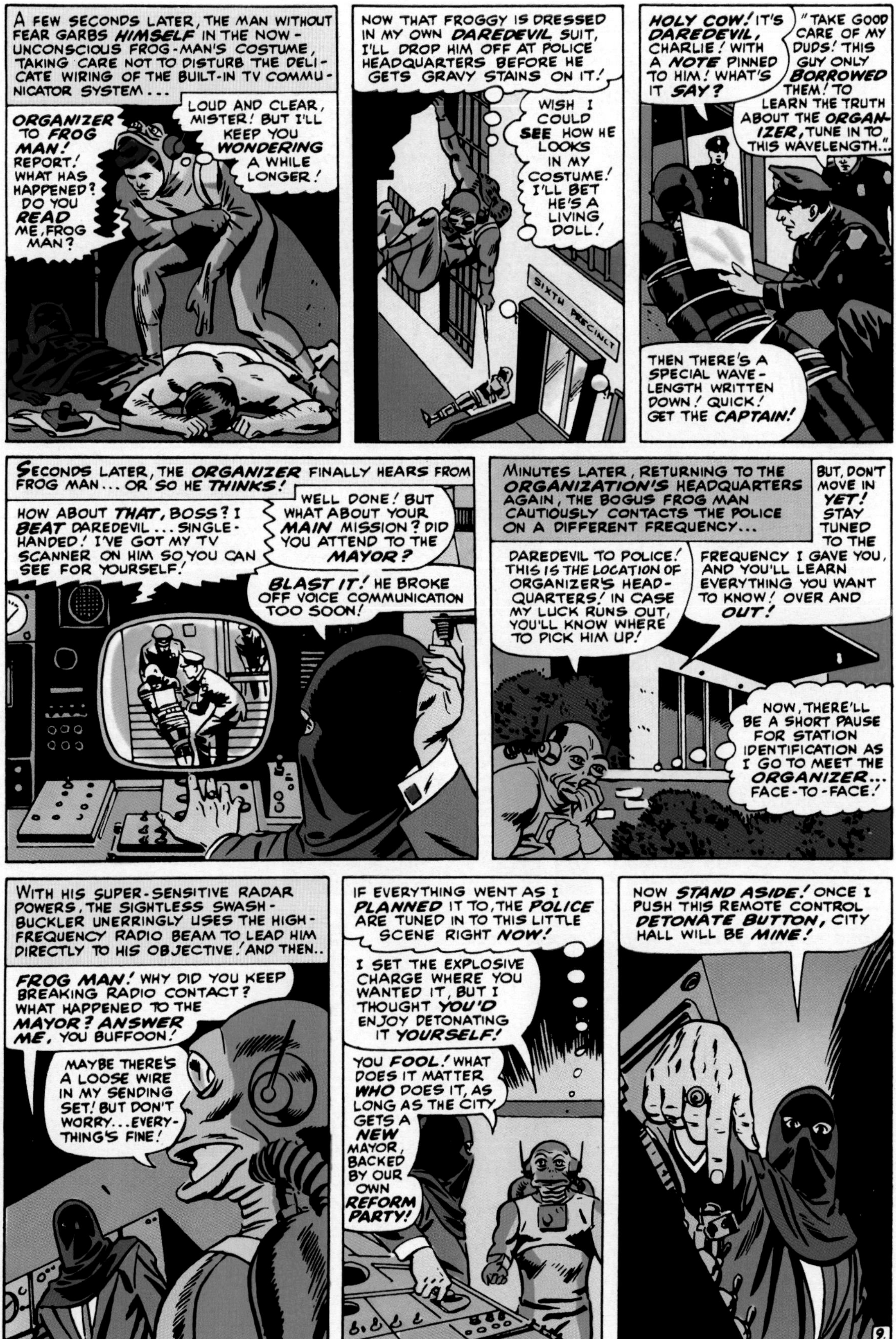
A FEW SECONDS LATER, THE MAN WITHOUT FEAR GARBS HIMSELF IN THE NOW-UNCONSCIOUS FROG-MAN'S COSTUME, TAKING CARE NOT TO DISTURB THE DELICATE WIRING OF THE BUILT-IN TV COMMUNICATOR SYSTEM...
ORGANIZER TO FROG MAN! REPORT! WHAT HAS HAPPENED? DO YOU READ ME, FROG MAN?
LOUD AND CLEAR, MISTER! BUT I'LL KEEP YOU WONDERING A WHILE LONGER!
NOW THAT FROGGY IS DRESSED IN MY OWN DAREDEVIL SUIT, I'LL DROP HIM OFF AT POLICE HEADQUARTERS BEFORE HE GETS GRAVY STAINS ON IT!
WISH I COULD SEE HOW HE LOOKS IN MY COSTUME! I'LL BET HE'S A LIVING DOLL!
SIXTH PRECINCT
HOLY COW! IT'S DAREDEVIL, CHARLIE! WITH A NOTE PINNED TO HIM! WHAT'S IT SAY?
"TAKE GOOD CARE OF MY DUDS! THIS GUY ONLY BORROWED THEM! TO LEARN THE TRUTH ABOUT THE ORGANIZER, TUNE IN TO THIS WAVELENGTH."
THEN THERE'S A SPECIAL WAVE-LENGTH WRITTEN DOWN! QUICK! GET THE CAPTAIN!
SECONDS LATER, THE ORGANIZER FINALLY HEARS FROM FROG MAN... OR SO HE THINKS!
HOW ABOUT THAT, BOSS? I BEAT DAREDEVIL... SINGLE-HANDED! I'VE GOT MY TV SCANNER ON HIM SO YOU CAN SEE FOR YOURSELF!
WELL DONE! BUT WHAT ABOUT YOUR MAIN MISSION? DID YOU ATTEND TO THE MAYOR?
BLAST IT! HE BROKE OFF VOICE COMMUNICATION TOO SOON!
MINUTES LATER, RETURNING TO THE ORGANIZATION'S HEADQUARTERS AGAIN, THE BOGUS FROG MAN CAUTIOUSLY CONTACTS THE POLICE ON A DIFFERENT FREQUENCY...
DAREDEVIL TO POLICE! THIS IS THE LOCATION OF ORGANIZER'S HEAD-QUARTERS! IN CASE MY LUCK RUNS OUT, YOU'LL KNOW WHERE TO PICK HIM UP!
BUT, DON'T MOVE IN YET! STAY TUNED TO THE FREQUENCY I GAVE YOU, AND YOU'LL LEARN EVERYTHING YOU WANT TO KNOW! OVER AND OUT!
NOW, THERE'LL BE A SHORT PAUSE FOR STATION IDENTIFICATION AS I GO TO MEET THE ORGANIZER... FACE-TO-FACE!
WITH HIS SUPER-SENSITIVE RADAR POWERS, THE SIGHTLESS SWASH-BUCKLER UNERRINGLY USES THE HIGH-FREQUENCY RADIO BEAM TO LEAD HIM DIRECTLY TO HIS OBJECTIVE! AND THEN..
FROG MAN! WHY DID YOU KEEP BREAKING RADIO CONTACT? WHAT HAPPENED TO THE MAYOR? ANSWER ME, YOU BUFFOON!
MAYBE THERE'S A LOOSE WIRE IN MY SENDING SET! BUT DON'T WORRY... EVERYTHING'S FINE!
IF EVERYTHING WENT AS I PLANNED IT TO, THE POLICE ARE TUNED IN TO THIS LITTLE SCENE RIGHT NOW!
I SET THE EXPLOSIVE CHARGE WHERE YOU WANTED IT, BUT I THOUGHT YOU'D ENJOY DETONATING IT YOURSELF!
YOU FOOL! WHAT DOES IT MATTER WHO DOES IT, AS LONG AS THE CITY GETS A NEW MAYOR, BACKED BY OUR OWN REFORM PARTY!
NOW STAND ASIDE! ONCE I PUSH THIS REMOTE CONTROL DETONATE BUTTON, CITY HALL WILL BE MINE!
9.

WHILE, IN A POLICE MONITORING LAB, ACROSS TOWN...

IT *WASN'T* A *HOAX!* WE'RE REALLY *GETTING* WHAT DARE-DEVIL PROMISED!

QUICK! CUT IN ON THE *REGULAR* CHANNELS! GIVE THIS THE WIDEST POSSIBLE EXPOSURE! THE *PEOPLE* HAVE THE RIGHT TO WITNESS THIS *LIVE!*

THE *ORGANIZER* DOESN'T REALIZE THAT HE'S *ON CAMERA* WHILE THE PHONY *FROG MAN* KEEPS HIS BUILT-IN LENS FACING HIM! THIS IS ONE FOR THE *BOOKS!*

NBS

WHAT *HAPPENED??* THE *DETONATE* LIGHT DIDN'T FLASH! THERE WAS NO EXPLOSION! YOU *BUNGLED* THE JOB!

UH UH! *YOU* BUNGLED IT, ORGANIZER! I *PLANNED* IT THIS WAY! I NEVER SET THE EXPLOSIVE CHARGE IN THE *FIRST* PLACE!

WHAT HAPPENED TO THE *REGULAR* SHOW? WHAT CAN *THIS* BE?

IT'S TOO *EARLY* FOR "AGENT OF SHIELD"!

THOSE SILLY *MYSTERIES* ALL SEEM THE SAME TO ME!

THEN, SUDDENLY, WHILE TALKING TO THE IMPOSTOR FROG MAN, THE ORGANIZER GLANCES AT HIS *OWN* TV SCREEN...

THIS VERY SCENE... IT'S BEING *TELEVISED!* THE WHOLE *CITY* IS TUNED IN TO US!

THIS VERY SCENE... IT'S BEING *TELEVISED!* THE WHOLE CITY IS TUNED IN TO US!

I WONDER IF OUR RATINGS WILL BEAT OUT *GUNSMOKE?*

IT'S *YOU!* YOU'VE *BETRAYED* ME! YOUR "TV" EYE IS OPERATING RIGHT *NOW!*

AND I DID *SO* WANT IT TO BE A *SURPRISE!*

GET HIM!

NOW, BOYS, WHY DON'T WE JUST *TALK* THIS OVER? TV CAN *USE* A NEW DEBATE SHOW!

YOUR TALKIN' DAYS ARE *OVER*, YOU DOUBLE-CROSSER!

THEY'RE *BOTH* RUSHING ME! I'VE GOT TO MOVE *FAST!*

THE ADVANTAGE IS MINE SO LONG AS THEY *STILL* DON'T REALIZE THEY'RE FIGHTING A MAN WHO CAN "READ" THEIR NEXT MOVES BY LISTENING TO THEIR PULSE AND HEARTBEAT!

THERE'S A *TRAP DOOR* UNDER ME! A SWITCH BEING THROWN! I'M *IN* FOR IT!

WOP!

THOK!

WHAT GOT *INTO* FROG MAN?? HE NEVER USEDTA BE ABLE TO FIGHT LIKE *THAT* BEFORE!

UNHHH! YOU'RE TELLIN' *ME!*

I WAS *RIGHT!* HERE I GO!

THAT'LL FINISH HIM OFF! NOW WE'VE GOT TO CLEAR *OUT* OF HERE!

10.

I DON'T KNOW WHAT GAVE HIM THE COURAGE TO *BETRAY* ME, BUT NO ONE *ELSE* WILL EVER DARE AFTER *THIS!*

MY *RADAR SENSE* TELLS ME EXACTLY HOW FAR THE DROP IS...

...AND MY *EXTRA-SWIFT REFLEXES* WILL ALLOW ME TO GO *LIMP* AT EXACTLY THE RIGHT SPLIT-SECOND!

SO, WITH LUCK... I'LL END UP WITH NOTHING MORE THAN A FEW BRUISES! BUT, *THEY* DON'T KNOW THAT!

FIRST *CAT MAN* GETS HIMSELF CAUGHT, AND NOW WE LOSE *FROG MAN!* SOME "ORGANIZATION" *THIS* IS!

DON'T WORRY! WE'LL ESCAPE, REORGANIZE, AND COME BACK *STRONGER* THAN EVER!

YEAH? THEN WE BETTER GET *STARTED!*

LOOK! THE COPS ARE STARTIN' TO SURROUND THE BLOCK!

LUCKY WE HAD THIS ESCAPE ROUTE PLANNED! *MOVE!*

WNRRRRRRR

AND, AS WHAT'S LEFT OF THE *ORGANIZATION* FADES INTO THE NIGHT...

I WOULDN'T WANT A STEADY DIET OF FALLS LIKE THAT!

BUT, AT LEAST THE *BELLS* ARE RINGING SOFTER NOW!

WOOOO! HOW CAN A FEW BRUISED MUSCLES AND BONES *ACHE* SO MUCH??

WELL, IT WAS *WORTH* IT! THE PUBLIC WILL *NEVER* VOTE FOR THE PHONY REFORM PARTY NOW!

AND, AT LAST I KNOW..BEYOND ANY DOUBT.. WHO THE *ORGANIZER* REALLY *IS!*

NOW, MY FIRST MOVE IS TO REACH MY *APARTMENT* ON THE DOUBLE! I'VE GOT AN EXTRA *DAREDEVIL* COSTUME WAITING FOR ME THERE! SOMEHOW, I JUST DON'T THINK I'M THE *FROG MAN* TYPE!

THEN, AFTER A HAIR-RAISING ROOF-TOP DASH ACROSS TOWN...

SO FAR, SO GOOD! NOW, IT'S TIME FOR D.D. TO MAKE LIKE A HERO BY WRAPPING THIS CASE UP IN A BLAZE OF GLORY!

11.

WE WANT TO ANNOUNCE THAT WE HAVE BEEN *DUPED!* THEREFORE WE ARE RESIGNING FROM THE REFORM PARTY *IMMEDIATELY!*

WHY ISN'T *MONROE* HERE? ONLY THE *ORGANIZER* HIMSELF WOULD NOT DARE TO SHOW UP!

ATTENTION, YOU *FOOLS!* THIS IS THE *ORGANIZER!* I AM ABOUT TO BROADCAST MY FINAL MESSAGE!

TOO BAD ABOUT *NELSON!* HE'D HAVE MADE A GOOD D.A.!

YEAH! IT'S TOO BAD ABOUT *ALL* OF THEM! THE *ORGANIZER* WAS JUST *USING* THEM!

LOOK! HE'S MANAGED TO CUT INTO THE NORMAL BROAD-CAST CHANNELS AGAIN!

THIS CITY HASN'T HEARD THE *LAST* OF ME! I'VE ONLY SUFFERED A MINOR SETBACK ...BUT I SHALL *RETURN!*

THIS *PROVES* IT! *MONROE* IS THE ONLY ONE OF US WHO ISN'T HERE! *HE'S* THE ORGANIZER!

I NEVER EVEN *SUSPECTED* HIM!

IT DOESN'T MATTER *WHO* IS ELECTED MAYOR! I'LL FIND *SOME* WAY TO GAIN CONTROL OF THE CITY! *NOTHING* CAN DEFEAT THE ORGANIZER! NO ONE CAN EVER CATCH ME!

HE MUST BE A *MADMAN!*

IF NOT FOR *DAREDEVIL* EXPOSING HIS PLAN, *ANYTHING* MIGHT HAVE HAPPENED!

WHY WOULD THE ORGANIZER HAVE TAKEN THE RISK OF MAKING THAT *BROADCAST*? IT DID HIM NO GOOD!

WHAT DO YOU *MEAN*, NELSON?

I JUST *THOUGHT* OF SOME-THING! WHAT IF THAT WAS A *PHONY*? HE COULD HAVE PUT THAT SPEECH ON *FILM*, AND SHOWN IT NOW, TO MAKE US THINK HE'S NOT ONE OF *US!*

THAT'S *RIDICULOUS*, NELSON! WITH IDEAS LIKE *THAT*, I'M GLAD YOU *WON'T* BE ELECTED D.A.!

IS THAT *SO*? HOW CAN YOU BE SO *SURE* I'M WRONG? WHAT IF SOMEONE SENT MONROE OUT OF TOWN, ON A FOOL'S ERRAND, JUST TO THROW SUSPICION ON HIM?

TAKE YOUR *HAND* OFF ME, YOU YOUNG PUP! DO YOU REALIZE WHO I *AM*?? I'LL *BREAK* YOU FOR THIS!

WHY SO *ANGRY*, JONAS? I'M NOT ACCUSING *YOU* OF ANYTHING!

NO? WELL, I'M ACCUSING *YOU!* YOU HAD THE MOST TO GAIN BY JOINING THE REFORM PARTY! YOU WERE A NOBODY...LIVING IN THE SHADOW OF MATT MURDOCK UNTIL THIS ELECTION!

IF *ANYBODY* HAS BEEN DECEIVING THE PUBLIC, I'M BETTING IT WAS *YOU!*

DON'T ANYBODY MAKE ANOTHER MOVE!

12.

THE *ORGANIZER* WANTS TO MAKE SURE NOBODY GETS TOO CLOSE TO HIM, SO WE'RE BRINGIN' *JONAS* TO HIM AS A *HOSTAGE!*

NO! YOU CAN'T *DO* THIS! *HELP ME,* SOMEBODY!

IF ANYONE *TRIES* ANYTHING, *YOU'LL* BE THE FIRST TO GET IT! YOU WOULDN'T WANT *THAT* TO HAPPEN, WOULD YOU?

WHY DOESN'T SOMEBODY *DO* SOMETHING??!

BUT, AT THAT VERY INSTANT, SOMEONE IS *ABOUT* TO "DO SOMETHING"...

FROM WHAT I HEAR INSIDE, I'M NOT A MINUTE TOO SOON!

THWIPP!

AND IF I'M *RIGHT* ABOUT WHO THE ORGANIZER REALLY *IS,* THEN I SHOULD BE ABLE TO WRAP THIS WHOLE CASE UP IN THE NEXT FEW MINUTES!

THAT'S IT! EVERYBODY STAY BACK AND NOBODY'LL GET HURT!

LET'S *GO,* JONAS!

I CAN SENSE THEIR POSITION IN FRONT OF ME AS CLEARLY AS THOUGH SOMEONE HAD DESCRIBED IT IN DETAIL!

JONAS... *DUCK!*

WHO *SAID* THAT?

LITTLE RED RIDING HOOD! WHO'D YOU *THINK* IT WAS?

GERONIMO!

THUD!

WHOP

WHOOOPFFF!

DAREDEVIL... ≡UHHH!≡

242

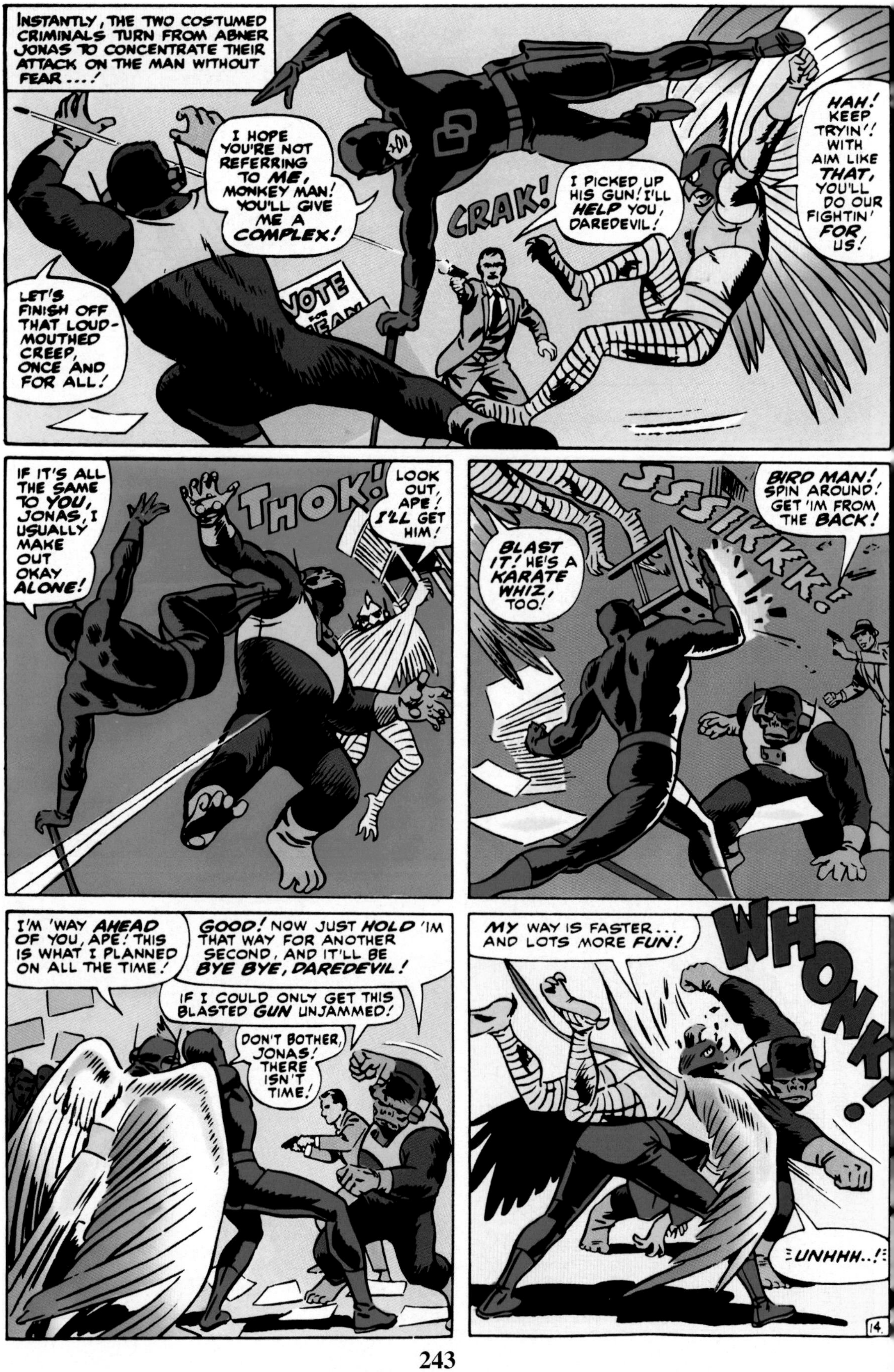
INSTANTLY, THE TWO COSTUMED CRIMINALS TURN FROM ABNER JONAS TO CONCENTRATE THEIR ATTACK ON THE MAN WITHOUT FEAR...!
I HOPE YOU'RE NOT REFERRING TO ME, MONKEY MAN! YOU'LL GIVE ME A COMPLEX!
HAH! KEEP TRYIN'! WITH AIM LIKE THAT, YOU'LL DO OUR FIGHTIN' FOR US!
I PICKED UP HIS GUN! I'LL HELP YOU, DAREDEVIL!
CRAK!
LET'S FINISH OFF THAT LOUD-MOUTHED CREEP, ONCE AND FOR ALL!
VOTE
IF IT'S ALL THE SAME TO YOU, JONAS, I USUALLY MAKE OUT OKAY ALONE!
THOK!
LOOK OUT, APE! I'LL GET HIM!
SSSIKKK!
BIRD MAN! SPIN AROUND! GET 'IM FROM THE BACK!
BLAST IT! HE'S A KARATE WHIZ, TOO!
I'M 'WAY AHEAD OF YOU, APE! THIS IS WHAT I PLANNED ON ALL THE TIME!
GOOD! NOW JUST HOLD 'IM THAT WAY FOR ANOTHER SECOND, AND IT'LL BE BYE BYE, DAREDEVIL!
IF I COULD ONLY GET THIS BLASTED GUN UNJAMMED!
DON'T BOTHER, JONAS! THERE ISN'T TIME!
MY WAY IS FASTER... AND LOTS MORE FUN!
WHONK!
UNHHH..!
14

THAT WAS VERY *UNFRIENDLY* OF YOU, MONKEY FACE! YOU SHOULD *DO* SOMETHING ABOUT THOSE SYMPTOMS OF *HOSTILITY* YOU SEEM TO BE SHOWING! PERHAPS A SYMPATHETIC PSYCHIATRIST..?

KEEP TALKIN', WISE GUY! ONCE I GET MY HANDS ON YOU, THE ONLY THING THAT *YOU'LL* BE ABLE TO USE WILL BE A *HOSPITAL*... ONLY IT'LL BE TOO *LATE* FOR THAT!

THUD!

HEY, JONAS! WHERE ARE *YOU* GOING??

TO GET THE *POLICE*, OF COURSE! SOMEONE'S GOT TO DO IT!

IF ONLY DARE-DEVIL CAN HOLD OUT A FEW MINUTES LONGER...!

EVEN DURING THE HEAT OF BATTLE, THE SHARP-EARED CRUSADER *HEARS* ABNER JONAS'S WORDS, AND THEN...

JONAS... *WAIT!*

STOP HIM, NELSON! THERE'S *DANGER*...

BUT, A SMASHING ROUND-HOUSE LEFT CUTS DAREDEVIL'S WARNING SHORT WITH THE SUDDEN IMPACT OF A RIFLE SHOT!

UHHHH!

BOK!

15.

244

I WAITED A *LONG TIME* FOR THIS, AND I'M GONNA MAKE THE NEXT FEW SECONDS *COUNT* NOW! YOU BETTER SAY YOUR *PRAYERS*, DAREDEVIL....'CAUSE THIS IS *IT!*

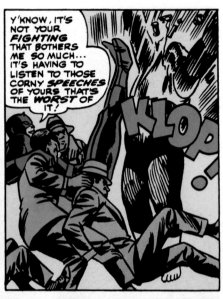

Y'KNOW, IT'S NOT YOUR *FIGHTING* THAT BOTHERS ME SO MUCH... IT'S HAVING TO LISTEN TO THOSE CORNY *SPEECHES* OF YOURS THAT'S THE *WORST* OF IT!

KLOP!

YOU WON'T BE ABLE TO GET RID OF *ME* AS EASY AS YOU DID WITH THAT BRAINLESS APE MAN....!

WHAT MAKES YOU THINK I WANT TO GET *RID* OF YOU? THE FLUTTERING OF YOUR LITTLE WINGS IS AS SOOTHING AS A LILTING LULLABY!

BUT, AFTER ALL, THERE *CAN* BE TOO *MUCH* OF A GOOD THING!

WHAP!

MPPPFFF...!

NOW DON'T YOU WORRY ABOUT A *THING*, PIN-FEATHERS! AFTER THIS, THEY'LL PUT YOU IN A NICE LITTLE *CAGE*, WHERE YOU'LL FEEL RIGHT AT *HOME!*

ONLY *DAREDEVIL* COULD FIGHT TWO KILLERS LIKE *THEM* AND MAKE IT LOOK EASY!

I'LL BET HE COULD RECITE *HAMLET* WHILE HE FIGHTS AND NEVER MISS A LINE!

ENOUGH! I..I *HAD* IT! I *GIVE UP!* I GIVE UP!

GEE, THAT'S REAL GINGER-PEACHY OF YOU! ALL THIS TIME I THOUGHT YOU WERE *WINNING!*

16

THEN, HEARING A SOFT SOUND BEHIND HIM, DAREDEVIL WHEELS ABOUT...

TENSE, ALERT, POISED, HE WAITS FOR THE APE MAN TO LAUNCH A NEW ATTACK...

BUT, AS DESPERATELY AS HIS ANTHROPOID FOE *WANTS* TO STRIKE ...

EVEN THOUGH THE SPIRIT IS WILLING... THE FLESH, BATTERED AND BEATEN BY DAREDEVIL'S POUNDING BLOWS...

...THE FLESH PROVES TO BE.. TOO WEAK!

IT APPEARS THE *ORGANIZATION* HAS JUST BEEN.. *DISBANDED!*

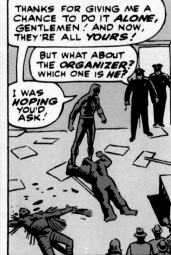

THANKS FOR GIVING ME A CHANCE TO DO IT *ALONE*, GENTLEMEN! AND NOW, THEY'RE ALL *YOURS!*

BUT WHAT ABOUT THE *ORGANIZER?* WHICH ONE IS *HE?*

I WAS *HOPING* YOU'D *ASK!*

AND, IF YOU'LL BE PATIENT A FEW MINUTES LONGER, I'LL BE RIGHT BACK... WITH THE *ANSWER!*

HEY, *WAIT..!*

LET HIM *GO!* HE KNOWS WHAT HE'S DOING!

I'VE GOT TO *CONCENTRATE...* TO SEPARATE THE THOUSANDS OF SOUNDS AND MENTAL IMAGES I'M RECEIVING ...UNTIL I FIND THE ONE I *SEEK!*

THEN, ONCE AWAY FROM THE OTHERS, THE CRIMSON CRIMEFIGHTER AGAIN PUTS HIS UNCANNY *RADAR SENSE* INTO PLAY...!

AND THERE IT *IS!* IN THE NEXT ROOM!

NOW FOR THE *MOMENT OF TRUTH!*

I DID AS YOU *SAID*, DAREDEVIL! JONAS WOULDN'T STOP, SO I *TACKLED* HIM! BUT, *WHY*? WHAT KIND OF *DANGER* WOULD HE HAVE BEEN IN IF HE RAN OUTSIDE?

NO DANGER! WHAT I STARTED TO SAY WAS... "THERE'S DANGER OF HIM *ESCAPING!*"

ESCAPING? WHAT DO YOU *MEAN?* WHAT WOULD *HE* HAVE TO ESCAPE FROM?

THE *LAW*, FOR ONE THING!

LET ME *UP!* I'LL *RUIN* YOU FOR THIS! I'M A WEALTHY MAN...I'LL *BREAK* YOU, NELSON!

YOU MIGHT AS WELL *DROP THE ACT* NOW, JONAS! OR, WOULD YOU FEEL MORE COMFORTABLE IF I ADDRESSED YOU BY YOUR *OTHER* NAME...IF I CALLED YOU *ORGANIZER?*

JONAS??! BUT...WHY WOULD THOSE TWO COSTUMED CROOKS TRY TO ABDUCT THEIR OWN *LEADER?*

THEY WERE *REALLY* TRYING TO HELP HIM *ESCAPE*...FOLLOWING HIS OWN *ORDERS!*

YOU'RE *MAD!* YOU HAVEN'T A SHRED OF *PROOF!*

THINK *NOT?* HOW ABOUT THIS *RING* FOR A STARTER!? YOU NEGLECTED TO TAKE IT *OFF* WHEN YOU APPEARED AS THE *ORGANIZER!**

*THAT'S THE CLUE WE ALERTED YOU TO LAST ISH..REMEMBER? -STAN.

BLAST IT! I FORGOT!

MY *RADAR SENSE* PICKED UP THE RING EARLIER...AND PICKED IT UP *AGAIN* WHEN I WAS NEAR JONAS!

WELL, THAT MAKES *ME* THE PRIZE CHUMP OF THE YEAR! HE SURE HAD *ME* FOOLED!

CHUMP *NOTHING!* *YOU* WERE THE FIRST TO SUSPECT THAT THE PICTURE OF THE ORGANIZER ON TV WAS A PHONY...TAPED IN ADVANCE TO THROW SUSPICION ON MONROE!

YOU'VE PROVEN YOU *DO* HAVE WHAT IT TAKES TO MAKE A FIGHTING D.A., MISTER!

THE NEXT MORNING...

I READ ALL ABOUT IT IN THE PAPER, FOGGY! YOU WERE A *HERO!* THEN, WHEN *DEBORAH HARRIS* POINTED THE FINGER AT HIM, JONAS *HAD* TO CONFESS! IT MUST HAVE BEEN SO *THRILLING!*

YES, KAREN...IT WAS REAL THRILLING!

WHY...WHAT'S *WRONG?* YOU SEEM SO..SO *DEPRESSED!*

I'M NO *HERO*, KAREN! I'M THE *GOAT!* DEBORAH HARRIS MADE A FOOL OF ME, AND JONAS HAD ME COMPLETELY BUFFALOED *TOO*...UNTIL THE END!

HE ONLY WANTED ME TO RUN FOR D.A. BECAUSE HE FELT HE COULD KEEP ME UNDER HIS THUMB AFTER THE ELECTION!

BUT, FOGGY...HE FOOLED *EVERYBODY!*

18.

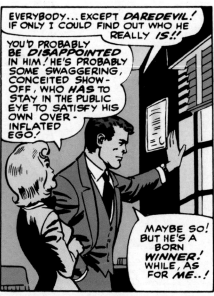

EVERYBODY...EXCEPT *DAREDEVIL!* IF ONLY I COULD FIND OUT WHO HE REALLY *IS!!*

YOU'D PROBABLY BE *DISAPPOINTED* IN HIM! HE'S PROBABLY SOME SWAGGERING, CONCEITED SHOW-OFF, WHO *HAS* TO STAY IN THE PUBLIC EYE TO SATISFY HIS OWN OVER-INFLATED EGO!

MAYBE SO! BUT HE'S A BORN *WINNER!* WHILE, AS FOR *ME..!*

YOU'RE JUST A BORN *GREAT GUY*...WHO DOESN'T KNOW HOW *NICE* HE REALLY IS!

IS THIS BECAUSE SHE FEELS *SORRY* FOR ME... OR DOES IT MEAN WHAT I *HOPE* IT DOES?

BUT, AT THAT VERY MOMENT, THE DOOR OPENS, AND...

KAREN AND FOGGY... *KISSING!* I MUSTN'T LET ON THAT I *KNOW* IT...!

KAREN.. FOGGY.. ARE YOU HERE?

OH! YES, MATT... WE WERE JUST... TALKING!

HER PULSE RATE HAS SPEEDED UP SINCE I WALKED IN! BUT, HOW CAN I TELL IF IT'S BECAUSE OF ANY *FEELING* FOR ME... OR JUST PLAIN EMBARRASSMENT?

WHEN IT COMES TO AFFAIRS OF THE HEART, I REALLY *AM* A BLIND MAN!

I SUP-POSE YOU'VE HEARD OF WHAT HAPPENED, MATT! IT LOOKS LIKE YOU WON'T BE HAVING A DISTRICT ATTORNEY FOR A PARTNER!

I WOULDN'T WORRY ABOUT IT, FOGGY!

ANYWAY, WE STILL HAVE A LAW PRACTICE TO TAKE CARE OF! WHAT'S THE FIRST CASE TO WORK ON TODAY, KAREN?

I..I'M AFRAID THERE *ISN'T* ANY, MATT! WE HAVEN'T HAD A SINGLE CLIENT!

IT'S *MY* FAULT.. FOR NEGLECTING OUR WORK DURING THE CAMPAIGN!

BR RING...

BUT, WHY DIDN'T *YOU* SPEND MORE TIME AT THE OFFICE, MATT?

SORRY, PARTNER, THAT'S *ONE* QUESTION I DON'T DARE ANSWER FOR YOU!

WHAT'S THAT? OH, MR. NESBITT... OUR LANDLORD! YES, I KNOW THE RENT IS OVERDUE! WELL, MR. NELSON AND MR. MURDOCK HAVE BEEN BUSY...YES...I'LL TELL THEM...!

NOT A CLIENT LEFT TO OUR NAME...AND NOW, THE *OFFICE RENT* IS OVERDUE!

THERE'S ONLY ONE THING TO DO! THEY'VE GOT TO MOVE TO A SMALLER, CHEAPER OFFICE...BUT THEY *CAN'T*, NOT SO LONG AS *I'M* PART OF THE FIRM!

Y'KNOW, I'VE BEEN WANTING TO TAKE A LEAVE OF ABSENCE FOR A LONG TIME... TO TRAVEL AND TAKE IT EASY! I THINK *THIS* WOULD BE A GOOD TIME TO *DO* IT!

YOU MEAN YOU WANT *OUT!* LIKE A RAT DESERTING A SINKING SHIP...IS *THAT* IT?

FOGGY! DON'T SAY THAT!

19.

CALL IT WHAT YOU LIKE, FOGGY! MY MIND'S MADE UP! I'M LEAVING!

OH, MATT! HOW WILL I BE ABLE TO BEAR IT WITHOUT YOU!?

HER HEARTBEAT HAS SPED UP AGAIN! IF I COULD ONLY TELL WHY!

OKAY, THEN ...GOOD-BYE.. AND GOOD RIDDANCE!

WHAT'S THE MATTER WITH ME? WHY AM I CARRYING ON THIS WAY? MATT IS MY BEST FRIEND... BUT, EVEN MORE THAN THAT... THIS IS MY CHANCE TO BE ALONE WITH KAREN AT LAST!

SURE, PARTNER... SURE! I UNDERSTAND!

BUT, WHAT WILL YOU DO, MATT? WHERE WILL YOU GO?

I'M SORRY, MATT! IF YOU REALLY WANT TO LEAVE, YOU'VE GOT EVERY RIGHT TO DO IT! FORGIVE MY OUTBURST... I'M JUST KINDA JITTERY THESE DAYS!

OH, I DON'T KNOW! I'VE ALWAYS WANTED TO TRAVEL ... VISIT OTHER COUNTRIES ... MEET NEW PEOPLE! I'VE SAVED UP A LITTLE MONEY, AND I MIGHT AS WELL SPEND SOME!

HOW MUCH MORE PROOF DO I NEED? HE DOESN'T LOVE ME! HE'S NEVER LOVED ME! HE COULDN'T LEAVE LIKE THIS IF HE DID!

OF COURSE, IF YOU SHOULD EVER NEED ME...

IF WE DO, WE'LL HOLLER!

IT WILL BE LIKE LEAVING A BIT OF MY HEART BEHIND TO BE LEAVING KAREN! NEVER TO HAVE REALLY SEEN HER FACE ... TO HAVE TOUCHED HER LIPS ... OR TOLD HER WHAT SHE MEANS TO ME!

MATT... MY DARLING... I'D HAVE WAITED FOR YOU FOREVER... IF ONLY YOU'D ASKED ME!

BUT, A GIRL CAN'T WASTE HER WHOLE LIFE, PINING OVER A HOPELESS LOVE! AT LAST I KNOW WHAT ANSWER I'LL GIVE IF FOGGY SHOULD PROPOSE AGAIN..!

KAREN, YOU'D BETTER HELP MATT CLEAR OUT HIS DESK...!

IT WON'T BE NECESSARY! THERE'S NOTHING I'LL BE NEEDING... EXCEPT YOUR GOOD WISHES!

OH, MATT... MATT! BEFORE YOU GO...!

YES, KAREN..?

I.. NEVER MIND! IT WASN'T... IMPORTANT!

GET IN TOUCH WHEN YOU RETURN, FELLA! YOU'LL ALWAYS KNOW WHERE TO FIND US!

I FEEL LIKE A HEEL! WHY AM I LETTING HIM GO? WHY DON'T I STOP HIM? BUT, I CAN'T! I MUST LEARN TO STAND ON MY OWN TWO FEET!

MATT! I JUST WANT YOU TO KNOW... I'M SORRY IT HAD TO END LIKE THIS...!

FORGET IT, FOGGY! THIS ISN'T THE END! IT'S A NEW BEGINNING! FOR ALL OF US!

NEXT ISH!

NEW ARTIST! NEW STORY LINE! NEW SURPRISE! BUT, THE SAME OLD ACTION, THRILLS, AND SUSPENSE! DON'T DARE MISS IT!

20.